Festivals, Tourism and Social C **FOR**
**REFERENCE ONLY**

**TOURISM AND CULTURAL CHANGE**
**Series Editors:** Professor Mike Robinson, *Centre for Tourism and Cultural Change, Leeds Metropolitan University, UK* and Dr Alison Phipps, *University of Glasgow, Scotland, UK*

Understanding tourism's relationships with culture(s) and vice versa, is of ever-increasing significance in a globalising world. This series will critically examine the dynamic inter-relationships between tourism and culture(s). Theoretical explorations, research-informed analyses, and detailed historical reviews from a variety of disciplinary perspectives are invited to consider such relationships.

**Other Books in the Series**
Irish Tourism: Image, Culture and Identity
    *Michael Cronin and Barbara O'Connor (eds)*
Tourism, Globalization and Cultural Change: An Island Community Perspective
    *Donald V.L. Macleod*
The Global Nomad: Backpacker Travel in Theory and Practice
    *Greg Richards and Julie Wilson (eds)*
Tourism and Intercultural Exchange: Why Tourism Matters
    *Gavin Jack and Alison Phipps*
Discourse, Communication and Tourism
    *Adam Jaworski and Annette Pritchard (eds)*
Histories of Tourism: Representation, Identity and Conflict
    *John K. Walton (ed.)*
Cultural Tourism in a Changing World: Politics, Participation and (Re)presentation
    *Melanie Smith and Mike Robinson (eds)*
Tourism in the Middle East: Continuity, Change and Transformation
    *Rami Farouk Daher (ed)*

**Other Books of Interest**
Natural Area Tourism: Ecology, Impacts and Management
    *D. Newsome, S.A. Moore and R. Dowling*
Progressing Tourism Research
    *Bill Faulkner, edited by Liz Fredline, Leo Jago and Chris Cooper*
Recreational Tourism: Demand and Impacts
    *Chris Ryan*
Shopping Tourism: Retailing and Leisure
    *Dallen Timothy*
Sport Tourism Development
    *Thomas Hinch and James Higham*
Sport Tourism: Interrelationships, Impact and Issues
    *Brent Ritchie and Daryl Adair (eds)*
Tourism Collaboration and Partnerships
    *Bill Bramwell and Bernard Lane (eds)*
Tourism and Development: Concepts and Issues
    *Richard Sharpley and David Telfer (eds)*

For more details of these or any other of our publications, please contact:
Channel View Publications, Frankfurt Lodge, Clevedon Hall,
Victoria Road, Clevedon, BS21 7HH, England
http://www.channelviewpublications.com

**TOURISM AND CULTURAL CHANGE 8**
*Series Editors*: Mike Robinson and Alison Phipps

# Festivals, Tourism and Social Change
## Remaking Worlds

Edited by
## David Picard and Mike Robinson

**CHANNEL VIEW PUBLICATIONS**
Clevedon • Buffalo • Toronto

**Library of Congress Cataloging in Publication Data**
Festivals, Tourism and Change: Remaking Worlds/Edited by David Picard and Mike Robinson.
Tourism and Cultural Change: 8
Includes bibliographical references and index.
1. Festivals. 2. Culture and tourism. I. Picard, David. II. Robinson, Mike. III. Series.
GT3930.F484 2006
394.26–dc22     2006011057

**British Library Cataloguing in Publication Data**
A catalogue entry for this book is available from the British Library.

ISBN 1-84541-048-3 / EAN 978-1-84541-048-3 (hbk)
ISBN 1-84541-047-5 / EAN 978-1-84541-047-6 (pbk)

**Channel View Publications**
An imprint of Multilingual Matters Ltd

*UK*: Frankfurt Lodge, Clevedon Hall, Victoria Road, Clevedon BS21 7HH.
*USA*: 2250 Military Road, Tonawanda, NY 14150, USA.
*Canada*: 5201 Dufferin Street, North York, Ontario, Canada M3H 5T8.

Typeset by Archetype-IT Ltd (http://www.archetype-it.com).
Printed and bound in Great Britain by the Cromwell Press.

# Contents

# Acknowledgements

We would like to extend a warm thank you to all of our contributors for their patience and good humour in putting this volume together. We firmly believe that all has been worth the wait.

Thanks go to Alison Phipps and to Philip Long for their advice and assistance along the way and to the various reviewers who have overseen the project and have offered their helpful and constructive advice.

Thanks also to all at Channel View Publications (particularly Sami!), for their professionalism and dedication.

Mike and David
*Centre for Tourism and Cultural Change*

# The Contributors

**Iride Azara**, University of Derby, Buxton, United Kingdom (i.e.azara@derby.ac.uk).

**Angela Burr**, London Metropolitan University, Institute for Culture, Tourism and Development, United Kingdom (a.burr@iconism.net).

**Elizabeth Carnegie**, Sheffield University, Management School, United Kingdom (e.carnegie@sheffield.ac.uk).

**Shirley Chappel**, University of South Australia, Australia (shirley.chappel@unisa.edu.au).

**David Crouch**, University of Derby, Buxton, United Kingdom (D.C.Crouch@derby.ac.uk).

**Kathryn Forrest**, ECOTEC, United Kingdom (KathFor78@hotmail.com).

**Oliver Haid**, University of Innsbruck, Institute for European Ethnology and Folklore Austria (Oliver.haid@uibk.ac.at).

**Howard L. Hughes**, Manchester Metropolitan University, Tourism Management, United Kingdom (H.Hughes@mmu.ac.uk).

**Gregory Loades**, University of South Australia, Australia.

**Scott McCabe**, Centre for Tourism and Cultural Change, Sheffield Hallam University, United Kingdom (s.mccabe@shu.ac.uk).

**Nicola E. MacLeod**, University of Greenwich, Business School, United Kingdom (n.e.macleod@gre.ac.uk).

**Sabine Marschall**, University of KwaZulu-Natal, South Africa (marschalls@ukzn.ac.za).

**Patricia Mathews-Salazar**, City University of New York, Anthropology–Social Science Department, USA (pmathews@bmcc.cuny.edu).

**Anka Misetic**, Institute of Social Sciences Ivo Pilar, Croatia (anka.misetic@pilar.hr).

**Nicola Palmer**, Centre for Tourism and Cultural Change, Sheffield Hallam University, United Kingdom (n.palmer@shu.ac.uk).

**David Picard**, Centre for Tourism and Cultural Change, Sheffield Hallam University, United Kingdom (d.picard@shu.ac.uk).

**Kirsty Robertson**, Queen's University, Canada (kirsty@mailodic.com).

**Mike Robinson**, Centre for Tourism and Cultural Change, Leeds Metropolitan University, United Kingdom (m.d.robinson@leedsmet.ac.uk).

**Ines Sabotic**, Institute of Social Sciences Ivo Pilar, Croatia (ines.sabotic@pilar.hr).

**Peter Schofield**, University of Salford, Management and Management Sciences Research Institute, United Kingdom (p.schofield@salford.ac.uk).

**Melanie Smith**, University of Greenwich, Business School, United Kingdom (melaniesmith2004@hotmail.com).

**Karen Thompson**, University of Strathclyde, Strathclyde Business School, United Kingdom (karen.thompson@strath.ac.uk).

Chapter 1

# Remaking Worlds: Festivals, Tourism and Change

David Picard and Mike Robinson

## Introduction

The observance of and participation in festivals, and what we may broadly term 'celebratory events', is an increasingly significant aspect of the contemporary tourist experience. Historically festivals, carnival processions and pageants have always provided points of meaningful connectivity and spectacle for visitors. Throughout the instances of European touring during the 18th and 19th centuries, the concentrated time-space frame of the festival helped to make visible the social life of 'foreign' townscapes and landscapes that while rich in historic and architectural significance, often lacked animation. Goethe, for instance, during his visit to Rome in 1788 reported on the vibrancy provided through the re-invigorated festivities of the 'Roman Carnival', loosely based on the early pagan festival of 'Saturnalia', an event that also attracted Stendhal, Casanova and Queen Christina of Sweden. Similarly, Thomas Gray and Byron, amongst other travelling literary notables, also observed the liveliness of the pre-Lent 'Carnevale' of Venice before it waned in its popularity during the 19th century. And Mark Twain, as ever the critical tourist, wistfully observed the romanticism of the Mardi Gras festival and how it succeeded in animating New Orleans in the last decade of the 19th century.

But independent of these well-documented encounters there has been a long tradition of communities using and devising festivals as opportunities for social and commercial exchange, the displaying of wealth, royal authority, and political/militaristic posturing, which frequently involved, and focused upon, travellers as naive and willing observers (Arnold,

1

2000). Abrahams (1982) speaks of festive celebrations as occasions for the community to 'boast' reflecting a common observation, in both historical and contemporary circumstances, that the various economic, social and political elements and materiality of festivals are geared to deliberate display. Handelman (1998: 41) uses the term 'events that present the lived in world' to encompass the variety of social situations and power relationships that are expressed through festivity. But it is the 'out of the ordinary' occasions of display, through ceremony, procession and the like, which provide focal points for consumption by an 'outside' audience. As Mark Twain (1923) pointed out with regard to the festivities and pageantry of the jubilee celebrations of Queen Victoria, the show and symbolism of such occasions mark them as a sight 'worth a long journey to see'.

It is not until relatively recently however that festivals have occupied significant status as part of organised domestic and international mass tourism, to the extent that we can clearly discern the phenomenon of 'festival tourism', even if it remains too elusive to quantify. The general pattern of tourism development in the developed world over the last 50 years or so intersects at numerous points with occasions of festivity, carnival and performance rituals across the world in general. Festivals, whether as 'traditional' moments of social celebration or as constructed and highly orchestrated events, have been absorbed into the expansive stock of 'products' that tourists desire.

Since the late 1960s, a steady increase in the number of newly created festivals in all continents has been noted (Arnold 2000; Chako and Schaffer, 1993; Getz, 1997). Some with long histories have been 'rediscovered', reinvigorated and reinvented while others have been *created*, often as a response to a myriad of social, political, demographic and economic realities. The explanation for the recent proliferation of festivals is complex, but in part relates to a response from communities seeking to re-assert their identities in the face of a feeling of cultural dislocation brought about by rapid structural change, social mobility and globalisation processes (De Bres & Davis, 2001; Quinn, 2003). Moreover, as Long *et al.* (2004) have suggested, for growing diasporic communities, festivals, carnivals and melas provide important moments of visibility and occasions of concentrated celebrations of identity beyond the confines of their 'host' communities. At the same time, the growth in the number of festivals also reflects the feeling of crisis in situations where recognised systems of symbolic continuity are challenged by the realities of new social, economic, and political environments. In this context, new webs of social relations seek to make themselves visible by adapting or reinventing forms of meaningful narration. International travel and tourism, as both a driver and an outcome of globalisation, have had, and continues to have, a significant role to play in the re-formulation of social relationships, providing new economies, audiences, communicative networks and structures for the processes of exchange as practised within a festival context.

In a world where there are few societies which that *not* open to tourism, festivals as markers of social and cultural life, intentionally or otherwise, increasingly share a set of relationships with tourists and the tourism sector. Tourism as a transitory phenomenon is bounded by and shares limited spatial and temporal realities (MacCannell, 1976). The tourist comes, and goes, with a bounded time and space frame. Festivals too are de facto limited in space and time – or 'time out of time' (Falassi, 1987). Both can be conceived of as a series of performances and rituals with attendant discourses that are contested, negotiated and re-negotiated and that generate their own social realities. And both can be viewed as liminal and playful practices, and both fundamentally, offer ways of exploring and securing being, belonging and meaning in the world.

Tourists encounter festivals in a number of ways. In some instances festivals, particularly large and spectacular events, become the key motivator for tourism and occupy a large part of the tourist time-space budget. In commercial terms, 'packages' are offered with the festival as the central attraction but increasingly tied to promoting the spatial setting. In such cases places become noted by the festivals they host. In other contexts, festivals merely form a part of, and are used to support, the overall 'cultural' offer of a destination. In this way the tourist may, or may not, encounter a festival. Further, beyond the strictures of the promoted place, tourists can stumble unexpectedly across smaller festivals as they engage in their more routine explorations of localities, or alternatively in the deliberate searching for the idea of otherness.

Over recent years the relationships between festivals and tourism have mainly been dealt with in a largely mechanistic and even deterministic way, and in general, have shied away from inductive observations. Borrowing in the main from the discipline and discourse of economics, dominant themes have related to the management and economic 'impact' of festivals. In this sense, festivals (often as a sub-set of 'events') are described and discussed as 'products' that can be 'purchased' and 'consumed' by festival visitors and participants. The web of social relations on which the festival organisation is based is mainly conceived of from a management perspective: how to involve volunteers; how to market and image festivals; how to deal with health and safety issues; how to 'produce' social coherence; how ultimately to make an 'economic impact' and generate 'profit'. While there is a certain social relevance, and indeed, an inevitability, regarding such approaches, it is important to recognise the capitalist, neo-liberal ideologies and contexts from which these emanate. Despite the dominance of such models in contemporary academic festival literature, human relations – the essence of any festival – cannot (nor should not) be reduced, nor confined, to a consequence of political action and to a utilitarian model of individual behaviour. Such approaches are more akin to a political programme seeking to mould social relations in terms of societal and economistic ideals rather than establishing an epistemology that aims to understand what is going on when people celebrate festivals.

Alongside managerial and economic literature on festivals, different anthropological and sociological schools have for a long time been implicated in studies of various a priori festive phenomena including cultural performance, ritual, sacrifice, celebration, pilgrimage, play and war. Approaches to these phenomena share the necessity of having to define a limited time and space frame in which a multitude of social interactions, aesthetic signs and narrative discourses can be observed. Within this however, defining festivals and their typology with any precision is problematic, and to an extent will always fall short of corresponding realities (Falassi, 1987). The interpretation of these observations often oscillates between two theoretical poles. One, based on Durkheim's idea of collective consciousness (Durkheim, 1976, 1992; Lukes, 1982) enacted through festive play and rhythm, and the other stressing the multivocality of ritual performance (Turner, 1982), and the polyphony of voices in power relationships manifested through the festival frame (Bakhtin, 1984). While these two broad approaches have much to offer the scholar of festival studies, and underscore many of the cases elaborated in this book and elsewhere, we should not be lured into some binary system of analysis. Attractive as the festival has been as a unifying and practical concept – or form – for examining human behaviour, it is nonetheless a contextualised concept, directed internally and externally by other social interactions, economic systems and communicative networks. Festivals, while containing worlds, also open out and spill over into 'outside' worlds and their multiple dimensions can only be understood by taking into consideration the different realities of these outside worlds.

The unearthing of festival morphology and meanings, together with its apparently expansive array of folkloric and carnivalesque variants, in both historical and contemporary contexts, has been undertaken and discussed from a variety of perspectives over the years (see for instance: Bakhtin, 1984; Bauman, 1992; Bruner, 1983; Cox, 1969; Danow, 1995; Falassi, 1987; Humphrey, 2001; Manning, 1983; Mesnil, 1974; Pieper, 1965; Turner, 1982, 1986). However, many studies of festivals, in both theoretical and empirical terms, are marked by tightly defined boundaries of their immediate social context, with an emphasis upon closed spaces, fixed times, indigenous social actors, internal regimes and symbolic contexts, and bounded rituals. Fewer studies have sought to position festivals in a context that is fluid, open to different scopes of (transnational) society and cultural vectors, and that resonates with the realities of ongoing change. Burke (1997), in a mainly historical analysis, points to the connections that tie the carnivals of the New World – North and South America – to Africa and the ways in which events such as the Rio Carnival can be viewed as having undergone an process of evolution that is, de facto, ongoing. What is useful in Burke's interpretation of carnival in South America, in which he draws upon and challenges the work of Da Matta (1978), is precisely that he places it in within a shifting frame of interactions between groups, traditions and practices that resonate with the various stages of development of European carnival, African religion and the rise of popular culture and commercialism. In this sense it becomes increasingly problematic to see the Rio Carnival, for instance, as solely a Brazilian phenomenon and an expression of a particular tradition.

At the same time, it is not a new idea to analyse forms of festivity in relation to, or as a symptom of, social life crisis. However, while most of the sociological and anthropological work has typically focused on cyclically or periodically returning forms of crisis (disease, possession, death, changing of the seasons, coming of age, etc.), little work has considered the appearance of festivals in relation to contexts or eras of rapid change. The principal focus and approach of this book lies in exploring the modalities underlying the relationships between an increasing number of 'newly' organised festivals which have appeared over the past 20 years or so worldwide, and the processes of rapid change that have recently affected most societies.

To operate this approach in the following chapters we have brought together a series of case studies that all in some way use tourism and touristic mobility as their central analyser. In these cases, tourism is synchronically related to three different types of social crisis and festivals can be broadly viewed as a form of response. In the first type, tourism development becomes a tangible expression of economic and spatial change and transition, often from agrarian to post-modern forms of economy. Here festivals are used to mobilise, negotiate and test new forms of discourse to make the new social reality meaningful. In the second type, tourism and tourists are used as a form of audience. As willing and usually naive observers seeking intercultural experience and translation, tourists are often mobilised and manipulated for the political and symbolic purposes of festival organisers and stakeholders. In this context, they can become an important social vector in the reformulation of ethnic, regional, diasporic, or national narratives and identities. In the third type of case, touristic mobility itself becomes the defining moment of festivity. Here, transnational events to which participants touristically travel become the symptom of the disappearance of former systems of social and symbolic boundaries and, at the same time, of the reinvention of new patterns of social existence.

## Remaking Worlds: Rupture and Re-enchantment

Of course, the observation of a link between festivals and complex, dynamic social contexts is not new or unique to the contemporary era. In different historic contexts, festivals, carnival and public 'play' have always been permitted, or have been politically used to mediate rapid change and to re-embed modified social realities in forms of symbolic continuity. Most major social crises, ruptures or revolutions in human history have been accompanied or closely followed by festive events or periods. The theatre plays, costume parties and pleasure gardens of the Renaissance, enacting and re-creating the idea of Eden, have been interpreted as nostalgic reactions to the 'disenchantment' of the world following the geographic discoveries of the 15th and 16th centuries (Délumeau, 2000). The idea of finding an earthly Eden embodied within the geographic imaginary of at least part of the European aristocratic class suddenly became obsolete and thus the world – abandoned and naked – needed to be re-clothed with signs and meaning. The dominant visions of the world needed to be adapted to the new geographical knowledge. At the same time, new forms of commercial exchange and geo-political organisation in Europe had to find a symbolic expression. Similarly, the scientific revolution and the European Enlightenment, and its 'discoveries' of laws and rules affecting (and effecting) the physical world, our perceptions of it, and with Darwin, the very nature and place of the human species within it, challenged the very conception of a God-given existence. The whole concept of society, of humankind and 'traditional' ways of thinking had to be re-thought and re-articulated with the new knowledge provided by the scientific approach. However, core beliefs, myths and discourses – religious and secular – often persisted and were promoted as part of the reaction of romanticism in late 18th/early 19th centuries and have, to varying extents, continued to be revealed in periodic 'rediscoveries' of the folkloric and re-enacted through festivals. In this sense the religious, albeit as an often challenged category, has continued and persisted despite its transformation in new semantic contexts.

Similarly throughout history, during times of significant political and militaristic revolution, festivals have been used to create a sort of mythical superstructure formulating/re-formulating the origins and compositions (cosmogony) of nation and empire, and, at the same time, providing and preserving social continuity and traditional structures of power through the use of codified symbols and rituals. In this sense, festivals would appear to act in the same way as social movements with their emphasis on the symbolic and their ritualisation of protest (Melucci, 1996) employed not only to articulate ideas but also to generate, structure, secure and highlight 'situations' and spaces in which central, meanings can be reproduced (Valeri, 1985). The idea of festivals and carnivals as forms of a social 'safety valve' (Gluckman, 1963), allowing the controlled release of social angst and dis-enchantment (usually within strongly hierarchical societies) is a powerful one. In Bataille's terms, festivals are ritualised transgressions of the taboo (Bataille, 1991, 1998), only ever temporary but occasions that permit societies to explore the realms of the excluded and the forbidden.

To what extent such interpretations represent festivals/carnivals as radical occasions, as true revolutionary moments of social transformation however, is debatable. As Eagleton points out: 'Carnival, after all, is a licensed affair in every sense, a permissible rupture of hegemony, a contained popular blow-off' (1981: 148). In this sense, what is apparently 'rupture of hegemony' is usually officially sanctioned rupture and thus ineffectual. Eco *et al.* (1984) also write of the limitations of festivals and their capacity to reinforce rather than transgress hegemonies, positioning, as he does, the modern mass festival as being bounded by limited spaces – limited by authority. Stallybrass and White (1986) also have made the point that feelings of freedom associated with festivity can be seen to be orchestrated moments of 'counter-sublimation' and hardly a real threat to political authority.

The idea of festivals as limited and 'permitted' transgressions, rather than time-fixed occurrences of whole-scale radicalism, emphasises the point that festivals exist and resonate within wider contexts and structures. It also reminds us that what once passed for occasions of real struggle, inversion and transgression as Bakhtin (1984) extolled, have since been socially and physically displaced and politically diluted. Partly, this reflects new political democratic and economic stabilities in the world (or at least the industrial and post-industrial world), and an apparent levelling of hierarchies. New spaces have also evolved to absorb social needs. Shields (1991) describes the adaptation of the theme of transgression in new spaces – theme parks, tourist resorts, fun-fairs and the like –, which provide opportunities for mis-behaviour and contravention that have thus relegated the importance of cyclical time periods of festivity. In this sense, contemporary festivals are bounded by the processes, patterns and actions of social change, rather than driving change, with festival practices and performances, as with other rituals, linked into changing realities of economy and local-global relations. Exposure is greater, communication instant and transnational, and commercial and material imperatives hold considerable weight, audiences are more diverse and extremes of social behaviour are attenuated by the desire for goals of festive stability in politically correct ordered social settings. This is not to argue that the carnivalesque is completely negated, or that the significance of transgression has been lost, merely that the effects of festivals as direct agents of social political change have to a large extent waned – at least in parts of the Western world. In Humphrey's (2001) discussion of the politics of carnival in medieval England, he suggests that festivity and the fact that it was 'permitted' and controlled did not amount to any significant challenge to the ruling elite. In his words (2001: 33); 'showing off your bottom in public, while admittedly fun, doesn't tend to free people from the shackles of whatever economic system binds them'. In such a way, we may suggest that the modern festival, still centred on the idea of ritualised yet controlled transgression, remains a relatively weak form for significant social transformation.

All of this, however, does not entail that festivals have somehow lost their significance, nor their meaning for participants. Far from it. Whatever the realities and limits, festivals provide arenas for possibilities and this would seem to be a mark of their persistence and pervasiveness, indicating the (potentially universal) human desire to re-enchant the world in, or shortly after, situations of societal life crisis caused by changes in the political, economic, demographic, scientific or natural environments. Turner (1988) refers to these possibilities as the 'indicative mood' of a festival or performance representing the states of desire and hypothesis amongst audience and participants, which he contrasts with what he terms the 'subjunctive mood' as representing the actual and the real.

In the contemporary context, societies face a type of crisis often implicitly referred to by the term 'globalisation'. Flows of people, capital, information and the increasing adoption of liberal economies and models of exchange have led, all over the world, to situations of increased individual mobility, demographic change and new work and life rhythms. In this context, former social nodes as expressed through social-symbolic systems such as kinship, social group, place, nation, religion or history have either disappeared, or at least have been transformed and have gathered different meanings. The psychological difficulties expressed in relation to this crisis are articulated in particular through feelings of 'insecurity', 'senselessness' and 'placelessness'. Festivals seem an important part of the response that acts to reproduce and reinstall normative social order amongst people, organisations, objects and ideas (Handleman, 1998). As a period of concentrated reflection relating to substantive questions of identity and direction, festivals would seem to offer moments of stasis in a highly mobile world.

While festivals and their 'righting' functions are directed to the participating social groups, they can have an external profiling role at the same time. As societies position themselves within the transnational fabric of globalisation they find themselves locked within an agenda of apparent competitivity as newly established social categories such as countries, cities or communities jostle to establish/re-establish profile and power. Hughes (1999), focusing upon the responses of the urban centres of Europe to the 'ontological uncertainties' of the global economy (Giddens, 1990), locates the festival (in this case the Edinburgh Hogmanay Festival) as a strategic event designed and managed to symbolically re-position cities in the face of deindustrialisation, and concomitant social realignment. In this sense there is clearly a parallel with the culturally constructed and politically intentioned displays of power that are World Fairs and Expos (Benedict, 1983; Coutancier & Barthe, 1995) and mega events such as the Olympics (Roche, 2000).

## Theorising Festival Practice

Festivity is used here in a sociological/anthropological sense as an analytical category to define and delimit sets of festive practice observed in human society. Academics from various disciplinary backgrounds have observed such sets of festive practice in very different geographical and historical contexts. Through the variety of these particular social and socio-symbolic contexts, a set of formal aspects or characteristics seems to emerge across these disciplinary perspectives. These are outlined below. While it remains problematic to then explain the processes underlying the necessarily cross-cultural communality or universal nature of these aspects, nevertheless, their examination provides a useful grounding for understanding festivals and the relationships they share with tourism.

### Forms of life crisis

Festivity seems to accompany various forms of 'life crisis'. The concept of life crisis is used here in a very broad sense to include all types of cycli-

cally returning or unexpected events that interrupt, challenge or terminate
particular micro- or macro-sociological spaces, temporalities or identities. In this sense, on the micro level, often very short and transitional life
crises are provoked by situations of social interaction, or by the individual trespassing of spatial and temporal limits or boundaries. These short,
'everyday' life crises can be distinguished from more collective life crises
and result from individual deviation from the norms that define everyday
life identities and roles, such as, for instance, someone dying, coming of
age, falling in love, being ill, being jobless, etc. Such crises challenge, in a
more or less dramatic way, the ways in which an individual conceives and
perceives his or her being in the world, but also how he or she is perceived
by others.

Another form of collective life crisis is constituted by the cyclical turn
of environmental conditions, most prominently those of seasonal change
and associated cycles of agricultural production. In a broader sense, the
birth, coming of age and death of family or group members, and even
ritualised forms of war and conflict, can also be included here. A further
form of life crisis, particular relevant to this book, concerns extraordinary
and unexpected alterations of the social, economic, ecological or political
environment, often leading to fundamental and lasting changes in the
way that life is organised and conceived. These types of life crisis can be
provoked by epidemics, natural catastrophes, famine, war and invasion,
large-scale immigration, economic crisis, technological, geographic,
medical and scientific revolutions.

There is, of course, no direct cause and effect relationship at work here,
but such moments of life crises, while not necessarily initiating festivity,
as events of significance and shared meaning, can be recognised, marked
and celebrated.

## Moments of social concentration and connectivity

All types of festivity seem to involve some form of social concentration
and connectivity. In its most simple form, this occurs at the individual level
when at least two individuals meet and exchange a form of interaction. At
the macro level, this occurs when one or several 'groups' of individuals
meet in a single time-space frame. 'Group' is seen here in a necessarily
broad sense including, on one hand, highly structured social entities based
on established kinship, friendship or professional networks. On the other
hand, it includes much loser social entities, often without a strong internal
structure, based on a form of shared reference to, for instance, common
interests, problems, feelings of belonging, residence, ethnicity, race, social
status, etc. The meeting of members of such 'groups', whatever their

motivation or criteria to define 'group inclusion', is a necessary formal principle of any form of festivity. Of course this does beg the question as to what number constitutes group size within a festival context? Clearly, it is difficult to answer this with any meaningful precision, suffice to say that would appear to be necessary for there to be a critical mass available to play out the various roles within a festival so that it may accord with an ascribed form.

## Liminality

Festivals utilise, create and transform social spaces. While certain spaces can be specially recognised and reserved for periodic festivity, it is more usual for general spaces to be transformed by festive acts in which they are imbued with 'the meaning and the power of the occasion' (Abrahams, 1987: 178) Thus, streets normally used as thoroughfares for public and vehicular access during the course of daily working hours may be cordoned off and 'reserved' for festive performances. Previous spatial functionalities become hidden and forgotten, signs become meaningless, directions reverse, boundaries cease to bound and the mundane is decorated and disguised and overtaken by different rituals and practices. The festive practices of eating and drinking, usually contained within restaurants and bars, spill over onto the streets and notions of private behaviour are similarly made public in defiance, it would seem, of usual social conventions, though controls, if relaxed, are still usually in force (Turner, 1987). The temporary re-alignment, and in some cases reversal, of space and its uses is part of what Turner (1988) sees as liminality, moments (time) and places (space) of ambiguity where daily realities are suspended. The festival participant and the tourist share this liminal condition not only as something that is merely transitional and marginal as van Gennep (1960) has posited, but also as a time and space that is genuinely creative and desired; indeed, as a state that is increasingly cultivated by societies.

## Ritualised transgressions

Perhaps one of the best-known features of festivity relates to the idea of transgression of the boundaries and taboos that define social and symbolic everyday life spaces. Festivals constitute spaces organised by alternate norms of behaviour, often linked to forms of exaltation and the satisfaction of various erotic desires. This includes a larger permeability of social boundaries, carnivalesque inversions of social roles, permitted sexual intercourse, the right to meet and dance, the excessive and abusive consumption of food, alcohol and drugs. Rabelaisian misrule and inversions of social mores in the medieval period, as examined by Bakhtin (1984) and

Humphrey (2001), portray festivities as acts of transgression signifying the symbolic destruction of officialdom. However, the concept of transgression has itself undergone something of a transformation as society's organisational categories of morality and aesthetics have themselves become elongated. In much of the Western world, no longer does society have to wait for any designated moment of festival to invert and violate social, moral and legal rules and codes. Any city in the United Kingdom on a Friday night is awash with festive, carnivalesque transgressions and challenges to normative behaviour. But then normative behaviour itself has been re-defined and, arguably, the body of society engaged in transgressions has grown. Nonetheless, festivals as socially sanctioned (and generally policed) occasions, can be said to still provide opportunity for organised and symbolic transgression. In particular, they provide a kind of official or semi-official permission for outsiders (tourists) to share in transgressive behaviour which increasingly, as the tourist comes under an ethical spotlight for his/her behaviour within the environments of others, offers some moral shelter.

**Performance, symbolic recreation and the enactment of tradition**

Following on closely from above, all types of festivity seem to include forms of staged and non-staged performances and enactments, through which individuals and groups can discursively manifest their visions of the world and create meaningful frameworks of their being together. Performances are public and private expressions of ritual serving different groups with differing meanings allowing people to project 'images of themselves and their worlds to their audiences' (Palmer & Jankowiak, 1996: 226). These performances and the symbols they mobilise can express a unified collective consciousness or set of identities and they have the power to transport and communicate, and also contest systems of apparent common sense. Festivals are, in a sense, constructed around particular performances and rituals that facilitate the diffusion of 'truths' to new audiences of inheriting generations, and increasingly interested observers/outsiders. Through performances, traditions as practices informed by rules and rituals of a symbolic nature can be maintained, and histories, whatever their accuracy, can be told and re-told with the regularity of festivity so instilling their values into social life (Hobsbawm, 1983a). Within the festival-tourism relationship, the status and integrity of performance has pre-occupied researchers for many years. The tourist, commonly portrayed as seeking authenticity, frequently locates the festival as an episodic exposé of tradition; a real insight into behaviour stripped of its social and political frameworks. But within the festival the tourist also seeks an enjoyable experience through performance, akin to Aristotlean mimesis; as a way of gaining knowledge and pleasure through performance.

### Ostentation, sacrifice and exchange

All types of festivity seem to include forms of exchange between various participants. These can include, on a micro-sociological level, the exchange of smiles, words or hand-shakes. On a larger level, these can include the distribution, destruction or exchange of often very expensive gifts or sacrifices including free or subsidised food, drinks and drugs, the permission to satisfy various erotic desires, the killing of animals, sponsorship, free concerts, the suffering or execution of individuals, the pardon and amnesty of criminal records. Festivals are increasingly used as occasions for the generation of economic benefit both for local community participants and for professional organising agencies that may operate transnationally. National and international tourism has been influential in shaping both form and function of festivals as globalising commercial models of exchange have gained primacy over ritual symbolic and aesthetic aspects as common community practices of festivity have attained alternate value in the face of new audiences. These economic aspects related to collective exaltation, satisfaction of desires and happiness closely relate to the political aspects underlying festivity.

### Politics, political economy and power

Festivals provide important occasions for the overt exhibition of political power in particular demonstrated by the practices of spectacle, play and gifting. Through conspicuous displays of wealth, the giving away of produce, and the deliberate loosening of social boundaries, ruling elites would be able to express their dominance over their own populations and various class territories, and also amongst their political rivals (van Konigsbruggen, 1997). Contemporary festivals imply and manifest various forms of political relations of authority between the participants or particular networks of participants (though generally these will simply be ignored by most participants). In particular, these concern the official and informal economies of gifts, official recognition and spiritual power. As a consequence of what Mauss (1973) defines as the 'principle of reciprocity', the donor of gifts can usually expect a return: reaffirmation of a position of authority, peace and friendly relationships, medium- and long-term economic and social benefits, etc. Political and spiritual stakeholders and other doorkeepers of heaven can transform individual conditions by 'granting' people symbolic promotions, purifications and social passages.

At the same time, the political relations embodied in these different forms of exchange can be subtly or violently contested and resisted by organisers, participants and visitors.

## Cultural creativity and change

Despite the role of festivals as instances to *reproduce* power and order, they are also points of direct connection with social and political change. In this sense, festivals form privileged arenas of cultural creativity whereby communities can innovate as a means of coping with moments of social crisis, the introduction of new models of political economy and as a way of innovating new markers of being and meaning. Creativity in this sense relates to an ability to generate symbolic adaptations and alternatives to existing states, but also a process to initiate change that could modify existing states. Some commentators have observed that 'major' political revolts and revolutions have started out of festival contexts, such as when workers have refused to go back to work (Guss, 2000).

It should be noted that in differentiating the formal characteristics of festivity as outlined above this is not meant to imply that each of them can be observed in a separate or independent way, rather, that they normally appear simultaneously and are interconnected with one another. Then again, this is not to suggest that these elements are co-ordinated by a form of unified or totalising collective consciousness or any other form of collective metaphysical clod transcending individualism and linking them into a mechanic social system or deterministic web of social relations. We do not want to deny the influence and importance of Durkheimian approaches to the study of festivity, yet we believe that the idea of a collective consciousness mobilised, enacted and reproduced through the festival space and its diverse festive practices does not account for, on one hand, the complexity of social relations and networks mobilised in and through festivals and, on the other, the polysemy of individual and collective festive experience, performativity and understanding.

On another level, we do not believe that festivals are the *only*, or the predominant, spaces to manifest and reproduce political power. This is not to deny that festivals, through the mobilisation of diverse discourses, performances, sacrifices and exchanges, imply an important political dimension, which certainly often does work towards the poetic naturalisation of social and political power, authority and domination. But this political dimension, which works at different levels at the same time, is, we believe, only one formal aspect among others. Finally, we do not want to overemphasise another important formal aspect, which can, a priori, be observed in all types of festivals: the perceived eroticism by festival participants linked to the transgression of social, temporal and spatial taboos. This is, we believe, another central, but not *the* only aspect defining festivity.

## Festivals, Signs and International Tourism

In the contemporary context, identity patterns mobilised to re-define social boundaries and new modes of existence seem to be increasingly based on globally interchangeable formats. Individuals and collectives worldwide appear to adopt similar types of identity patterns, usually based on criteria of national, religious, ethnic and local 'culture'. Adapting Baudrillard's approach of the consumption society and projecting it at a global ethnoscape (Appadurai, 2003), 'culture' is thus mobilised as a concept to produce signs to differentiate one social entity from the other (Baudrillard, 1998) and make them globally visible. In this context, 'culture' itself becomes a social discourse based on a set of, more or less, arbitrary signs to define the self and the other (Featherstone, 1990), and each such defined entity becomes part of a global system linking spaces and people through internationalised forms of production, exchange and consumption.

International tourism, along with the global media, international conventions and multinational business, plays a key role in the global development of this seemingly post-modern economy of signs and spaces (Lash & Urry, 1994). To build tourism 'products', operators and agents naturally use the categories, terminology and language of the paying tourists. They 'package' destinations by translating selected spaces, stories and social practices in touristic terms and categories. In analogy to classical ethnographic work, they translate and make visible the 'culture' of the other in terms that tourists, and in a more partic- ular sense, the tourists of the developed, largely Western world, can understand (Said, 1978; Tambiah, 1990; Clifford, 1997). Consequently, according to Lanfant (1995), international tourism can be defined as a total social phenomenon involving a complex web of global and tran- snational political, economic and social instances. Lanfant emphasises in particular, the importance of legal frameworks elaborated by inter- national organisations including the World Bank and UNESCO, which can act to institutionalise the terminology and categories used by, among others, tourists, as a common global format to communicate and exchange. Neo-Marxist authors (see, for instance, Aisner & Plüss, 1983; Nash, 1976) have hence claimed that international tourism operates neo-colonial polities by imposing its own categories and agendas upon non-Western countries. For Wallerstein (1990), questions related to the very idea of 'culture' as a format to think of human society or, of how to fill this format with content, become the very 'battle ground' of modernity.

The largely pessimistic conclusions both of neo-Marxist and post-modern theory have been challenged by various ethnographic works focusing on appropriation and transformation processes in non-European societies. Michel Picard (1998), for instance, in his case study of Bali shows how 'cultural traditions' adapted for touristic purposes in the beginning of the 20th century become naturalised as essential values that the Balinese associate with their society and its relation with the world outside. Analogue observations of invention and magnification of 'local cultural traditions' in the eye of tourism have also been made in a number of other places (see, for instance, Doumenge, 1984; Guss, 2000; Hobsbawn & Ranger, 1992). In this sense, 'culture' in whatever configuration becomes a signifier for relationships with the 'world outside'. At the same time, as has been shown through our own research in La Reunion, in the Indian Ocean, culture is integrated and semantically adapted to existing communication systems (Picard, 2004). In the post-plantation society context of La Reunion, for instance, the introduction and rapid popularisation of the concept of 'culture' in everyday life discourse, through material objects, art craft, oral traditions, music, landscape, etc., was successful because it became socially recognised as a form of 'modernity' (Picard, 2003). In this sense, communication systems related to social appearance and mobility that probably grew out of the plantation society, largely managed to metamorphose into a new social and semantic context.

From this point, the study of 'culture' and the various 'cultural' resources mobilised during festivals visited by, and adapted/translated for, tourists, involves a number of epistemological and conceptual dilemmas (Bruner, 1994, 2001; Kirshenblatt-Gimblett, 1998). We can easily observe the multitude of signs and discourses performed during a festival. We can record the multiple voices of, and comments by, various participants in the festival, yet, all this tells us very little about how festively performed signs and discourses relate to, or are embedded in, social realities beyond the festival time and space. The analytical frame becomes even more heterogeneous when taking into consideration touristic participation in 'other' people's festivals. The researcher always risks being trapped in simplistic dichotomies, most prominently the opposition between 'locals' and 'tourists' underlying much of the tourism 'impact' literature (Lanfant & Graburn, 1992).

## Tourists, the Festival Experience and Transnational Connections

The metaphor of escape, aptly reflected in the phrase 'getting away from it all' has often been used to summarise the re-creative and rejuvenative aspects of tourism (Enzensberger, 1996). This metaphor implies a certain analogy to the festival experience, as participants find themselves in a different space and time. Both the tourist and the festival goer are engaged in transformative events where the notion of re-enchantment does not only refer to the process of structural repair or return to a communal feeling of primordial delight, but also to the individual's (re)introduction to a magical time where all things appear possible. This would seem to elevate the idea of a festival to a state beyond where it can merely be referred to as a 'product' to be consumed by tourists. Tourists have been defined as transitional, transnational and transcultural 'consumers' in terms of material objects or services and also by the multiplicity of 'commodity-signs' exchanged in the tourist space (Urry, 2002). But, while frequently thwarted in their attempts to *deeply* penetrate 'other worlds' (Robinson *et al.*, 2004), tourists nonetheless seek to effectively make sense of the experiences they have. The tourist encounters background as well as foreground experiences, and is defined by the action of travelling towards festivals, often with incomplete knowledge. This raises fundamental conceptual, but also political, issues related to the production, interpretation, ownership and remuneration of those 'products' (Hobsbawm, 1983b; Mosse, 1971).

Festivals provide moments of spectacle. Rapidly shifting collages of colour, the beautiful juxtaposed against the ugly, three-dimensional performances of the wild, the strange and the taboo are presented to the eye. The festival is constructed around both the production and consumption of spectacle, not simply as a collection of images but as essential social relationships mediated by images (Debord, 1995). Debord clearly recognised the role of spectacle as commodity and thus the power of commodity in its colonisation of social life to a point where 'the world we see is the world of the commodity' (2000: 29). But while the observation that we exist within a 'society of spectacle' may hold some truth, to see spectacle simply as some form of false consciousness, or as sham and banal is to overlook both the act of creating the spectacular and the role it can play as a form of human resistance to attempts to reduce culture and its consumption to a subordinate of economic aesthetic production. The creation of the spectacular within a festival is an important process of social expression, instrumental in marking and celebrating identity and collective consciousness. The gaudy, the bright and the bizarre are deliberate and concentrated displays of social renewal and/or the maintenance of social and political order. Cantwell (1993) uses the term 'ethnomimisis' to identify a process of imitation by which cultures express themselves. Festivals provide tourists the opportunity to view their hosts in their moments of play and in the state of social renewal. Indeed, as MacCannell (1992: 233) suggests: 'Tourists are absolutely promiscuous when it comes to festival versus carnival, official versus unofficial drama. They seem to have a natural capacity to seize the spectacle that is essential to both forms as the aspect of both that was made especially for them.'

Of course tourism itself has been conceived of as an occularcentric activity (MacCannell, 1976; Urry, 2002) and in this sense festivals possess an integral capacity to transfix the tourist eye. Yet the spectacular is more than purely a visual experience impinging as it does on all of the senses and drawing upon a diverse set of emotions. Fireworks, costumed parades, various forms of eating and drinking, games and ritual and staged performances are essential communicative forms that represent culture through exhibition and bodily expression. The widely promulgated notion of tourism as essentially a visual activity has privileged the eye at the expense of the rest of the senses. During festivals all of the senses are played with and manipulated to a greater or lesser extent, yet this dominance of the idea that the tourist merely observes has permeated much of the extant literature on festivals and tourism.

Today, more than ever, festivals of whatever complexion and duration, are strongly woven into the various trajectories and textures of international tourism. While the inter-relationships between festivity and tourism are far from inevitable, the two phenomena appear to be increasingly entwined as the tourism extends its influence. Festivals, as time specific moments, have now been added to the long list of 'destinations' available for tourists. Relationships between the two can be taken to be structured around both the organisational system of international tourism, and the behaviour of individual tourists. Operating various transnational flows and forms of exchanges in almost any place of the world, tourists and tourism organisations economically, demographically and symbolically participate (temporarily) in so-called 'host-societies', replete with their social practices and 'traditions'. As a result, touristic places become heterogeneous transnational spaces characterised by a multitude of actors, images, ideologies and aesthetic models.

From this point, the very term of 'host society', which appears both in academic and social discourse, becomes obsolete. Instead, we observe human beings and the various relations between them, breaking down the systems of oppositions between an 'us' and a 'them', which allows a more fruitful analysis between objectively changing realities of contemporary society, on one hand, and, the adoption and adaptation of different layers of subjectivity and discourse, on the other. Indeed, tourism is a visible expression of globalisation, subject to different forms of discourse and symbolic negotiation. Breaking down meta-narratives of tourism to the level of individual encounter and experience allows us to address aspects of connectivity between tourism and festivals.

However, in the face of such perspectives, tourism facilitates a type of transnational connectivity whereby tourists actively participate in mediating formulations of the 'other'. Tourists are frequently cast in the role of passive observers, part of the audience, distanced from the stage and the performers, and largely unaware of deeper meanings and contexts of particular festival performances. Though, as Turner and Turner (1978) point out, tourists at the time of 'being' somewhere else are effectively free, engaged in practices in places and times through their own volition, they are nevertheless not immune from the sensory draw, the emotional curiosities and human insights that a festival can exert, to the point where the tourist becomes absorbed into the event and its drama and is, by extension unwittingly caught up in the symbolic struggles of others. In the context of the symbolic and social reconfigurations played out through festivals, what then is the role of the tourist?

In much of the tourist studies literature, the 'tourist' is frequently attributed the role of being an external force capable of exerting particular 'impacts' upon social situations and thus 'causing' change. On one level, the simplicity of this approach is appealing; change becomes a clearly defined product rather than a complex process. However, on another level, this view fails to acknowledge the heterogeneity of tourism spaces and the dialectic processes that take place between tourism institutions, tourists and settings (de Weerdt, 1987). Given that festivals are de facto 'public' celebrations designed to extend into an audience, new social as well as symbolic relationships are created, and tourists are not seen as separate but as elements of the social systems of host societies, or rather of enlarged transnational social systems (Robinson *et al.*, 2004). Change is enacted via the micro politics of hospitality (Dietler, 2001) as tourists and other strangers share in the space and materialities of certain festival rites. Falassi (1987: 4) identifies a number of rites that to a greater or lesser degree combine within a festival: rites of purification, rites of passage (after van Gennep, 1960), rites of reversal, rites of conspicuous display, rites of conspicuous consumption, rites of exchange, rites of competition, ritual dramas and rites of devalorisation. At surface level and within the notion of tourist 'impacts', obvious relationships can accrue in a direct and economic way as money goods and services are exchanged. But, at various points during a festival and to varying extents, tourists are able to enact these rites along with the hosts in sense of notional equality. Actors and audiences can get mixed up; the audience becomes part of the stage (Bakhtin, 1984). Each opportunity for participation marks an opportunity for contact, engagement, dialogue, conflict and meaning. As part of this, tourists may operate the privilege to observe only, or are appropriated by the host community for various symbolic and political purposes. In many instances the tourist 'becomes' part of, and is changed through, the festival. Change is thus conceived as a complex reflexive process, and focused at the level of the individual caught up in largely transnational processes (Hannerz, 1996).

However, we can also witness the concept of change as operating at the structural level as festivals have become locked into the wider connectivity and transformation of space, aesthetics, geo-politics and socio-political relations, which are both in, and of, the realities of tourism. Boissevain (1992) suggests that in a European context, the recent growth in public festivals and celebrations has been stimulated by the rise of secularism, the increase in diasporic populations, together with increasing democratisation, general mobility and tourism. It is thus useful to think of festivals not as with fixed supporters, audiences and spaces but as evolving in unison with the changing socio-economic conditions of production (Williams, 1980), consumption (Featherstone, 1990) and political landscapes (Cohen, 1993). In the past 30 years or so, the shifting vectors of globalisation have created new relations between the local and global, the religious and secular, that constantly challenge traditional notions of place, identity, the sacred and the just milieu. In this context, the festival needs to be linked to the wider sociological, economic and political context of change, as a site to adapt, reconstruct and re-enact meaningful narrations of the collective being in the – globally enlarged – world. Tourists are a part of this world, which should find a form of articulation in the festival.

This leads us back to the question of the meanings of festivals in the contemporary worlds. Durkheimian notions of festivals as somehow systemically 'rooted' in societies (Caillois, 2001) have been challenged in the face of 'rootlessness' in an inter-connected and fast moving world. Authors often coming from a neo-Marxist perspective approached the social phenomenon of the festival through its implicit political economies and the reproduction and naturalisation, but also contestation, processes of power implicit to the mobilisation of aesthetic signs and performance (Cherubini 1986; Hobsbawm, 1983a; Mosse, 1971; Schwimmer, 1986; Turner, 1995). At the same time, the work of Goffman (1959) has been highly influential with its emphasis on social life as a stage and its focus on social relations and interaction processes. However, significant works on festival tourism influenced by Goffman seem to be kept prisoner of the conceptual dichotomy between front and back stage. For instance, works by MacCannell (1973), Boissevain (1996) and Kirshenblatt-Gimblett (1998) often seem to reduce the festival space to a binomial event, with 'inauthentic', 'artificial' or 'de-contextualised' on-stage spectacles performed for touristic audiences and the 'real' things happening behind the stage or elsewhere. Yet, the constant emphasis on the opposition between insider 'folk', on one hand and outsider 'fake', on the other, prevents these authors from analysing festivals and festival tourism through their complex, heterogeneous and dynamic political, economic and social webs. In this sense, Goffman's frameworks and their later adaptations in the tourism field often seem to lack analytical sharpness amongst the complex layering of social reality. For the researcher it becomes critical not only to understand the festival as a *particular* and located event, but also as a dis-located event capable of reproduction, relative to, and subject to, wider social changes in audiences and political agendas.

## Cases and Contexts

In this book, we have selected a number of case studies that analyse different types of festivals in relation to social contexts of change. The cases focus upon studies of tourism and forms of mobility, not as having unilateral 'impacts' upon festivals, but as part of the symbolic and social spaces of the festival and the social contexts out of which the festival has emerged. The following chapters offer innovative and challenging observations, which are able to set a new light on current debates in the wider field of tourism and cultural change.

Iride Azara and David Crouch (Chapter 2) analyse *La Cavalcata Sarda*, an annual festival in Sardinia, Italy, and uncover complex social spaces and political structures that manifest themselves through the event. The festival, which for more than a hundred years, has been mobilising folklore groups, horse riders and visitors from different parts of the island, now attracts international tourists. The festival is analysed through different re-signification processes that have been taking place since its invention as a folkloric spectacle for the King of Italy more than a hundred years ago. From being a symbol for the colonial power of the King, through to the development of mass tourism in the 1960s and 1970s, and with the increasing touristic emphasis on 'cultural products' in the 1990s, the festival seems to have gained a new status and role as a place to enact forms of local belonging, pride and beauty. Hence, the festival appears to have initiated a revalorisation process of forms of material culture and folklore, which have become locally accepted metaphors of Sardinia's participation in the contemporary world.

David Picard (Chapter 3) explores different sets of cultural performance observed during the preparations and celebrations of the abolition of slavery festivities in a fishing village in the French island of La Reunion, in the Indian Ocean. This festival 'appears' in the mid-1990s, in a context characterised by rapid structural and demographic change inside the island and new geo-politic and economic relations with its wider environments. Rapid coastal tourism development and the reformulation of agricultural lands into aestheticised 'landscape' are among the most visible manifestations of this change. Picard suggests that various participants use the festival to create, formulate and test metaphoric spaces (in particular the 'past'), which allows people to express feelings of nostalgia and angst, and to make sense of the uncertain realities and modalities of the new type of economy and society.

Patricia Mathews-Salazar (Chapter 4) looks at the *Pachamama* Queens, or Mother-Earth festival, in the province of Tucuman, Argentina, which, though originally invented for tourism, has become an important transnational arena to recapture, formulate and celebrate forms of pan-American Indianity. The author describes the festival as a complex and socially heterogeneous event, where various exchanges take place, where social roles (gender, age, etc.) are reaffirmed, and where ethnic identities are formulated and playfully tested. The author emphasises the role of the 'past' in the building of these identities suggesting that the Indians have learnt about 'their' past to a large extent from outsiders and tourists. At the same time, the enactment of forms of this past becomes an element of social pride and a space for often very subtle political contestation.

Angela Burr (Chapter 5) discusses the political and social underpinnings of the creation and the later transformations of Notting Hill Carnival in London, United Kingdom. While originally staged to remember and celebrate social emancipation protests by Afro-Caribbeans in London in the early 1970s, the carnival has transformed into a large-scale festival during the 1980s and 1990s. Burr focuses in particular on different organisation cultures, which are brought forward or symbolically mobilised to defend and contest the ownership and spatial control of the event. In this context, the metaphor and symbolic act of freely walking in the street, symbol of the historic abolition of slavery, is regularly used by the organisers to protest against the administration culture and security concerns of city authorities and police forces.

Scott McCabe (Chapter 6) examines the Ashbourne 'football' game, which is an annual festival in the town of Ashbourne in England. The festival was revitalised by inhabitants of the town in the 1980s, in a context characterised by rural exodus and new types of urban populations moving to the countryside and reinventing countryside styles of life. Through various and multi-layered forms of participation, festive performance and discourse, this festival constitutes an occasion for different villagers, old ones and the newly arrived as well as for expatriates, to generate collective experiences and revive memories and feelings of belonging linked to the place of collective residence or, at least, reference. At the same time, it – implicitly or explicitly – allows the reaffirmation and re-establishment of social values and identities (local hospitality and friendliness, male toughness, role of patrons, etc.).

Anka Misetic and Ines Sabotic (Chapter 7) look at the 'Days of Radunica', a street festival in the Croatian town of Split. This festival has been revitalised in the post-war context of the 1990s characterised by rapid economic and political change and national identity crisis. After the Yugoslavian civil war, the Croatians looked to re-invent themselves as an independent geographical and political entity. By organising a street festival, the inhabitants of Radunica, a quarter of the Croatian town of Split, created a space to formulate meaningful metaphors of their being in the world. Misetic and Sabotic stress that, by bringing together and relating folkloric elements (including food, language, cloth and play) from different historic periods, the festival allows the formulation of a collective history. In the interplay between external touristic audiences and different local actors, this formulation manages to poetically embed feelings of collective belonging in a form of societal rationale. At the same time, it is re-arranged and re-interpreted by various festival participants including the external tourism audiences in terms of their own symbolic systems.

Melanie Smith and Kathryn Forrest (Chapter 8) analyse the processes of touristification of festivals in mainly urban settings, particularly in the London borough of Greenwich, in the United Kingdom. Here festivals have been devised relatively recently to animate local communities and address issues of 'belonging' within the contexts of economic decline and considerable ethnic diversity. The idea of utilising festivals as a tool for local economic regeneration and social cohesion is problematised against the raising of the profile of the festivals through tourism. While tourism can be an important part of the regenerative element of the festivals, it can also impact upon and alienate the very communities the festivals were designed for.

Sabine Marschall (Chapter 9) examines the National Women's Art

Festival in Durban, South Africa. In the context of rapid political change and national identity crisis related to the end of the apartheid system, this festival becomes a platform to test new formulations and symbolic expressions of the nation. The festival aims in particular to bring together various formerly separated social entities and modes of artistic expression. At the same time, however, through the very selection of the type of festive performances (theatre, arts, dance and poetry), the festival traditionally organised by Afrikaner communities, transforms its established categories, formats and dramaturgy into the new political and social context. It imposes itself upon its very different participants. By doing so, it allows the collective enactment of a metaphoric rainbow style story, with different colours (standing for 'ethnic groups'), which provides a rationale to the idea of 'nation'.

Karen Thompson, Peter Schofield, Nicola Palmer and Gulnara Bakieva (Chapter 10) analyse the festival of Manas Epos in Kyrgyzstan, which in the politically difficult context of the post-Soviet nation-state crisis provides a meta-narrative of and for the 'nation'. In this context, marked by the risk of inter-ethnic disputes and economic emergency, the performances, costumes and food mobilised during the Manas epos celebrations partly manage to embed the complex social realities of Kyrgyzstan in a system of symbolic continuity. The nation is symbolically built upon a corpus of primordial tribes and historic heroes, which become identifiable figures and metaphors for the struggles and often contradictory existences of the nation itself. The authors describe the subtle intervention of UNESCO in the artistic production of the event and the role international tourism plays as a global audience to legitimise the story.

Shirley Chappel and Gregory Loades (Chapter 11) analyse the recent creation of 'camp oven' and bushmen festivals in Australia. For Chappel and Loades, these new festivals can be related to debates on national Australian identity; the subject of major political controversies in Australia during the 1980s and 1990s. The authors describe how the demographic reorganisation of the country related to Southern European and Asian immigration since the 1960s, and rural decline led to challenge the then dominant conception of Australian national identity based on romanticised Anglo-Celtic 'bushmen' stories. In this context, the performing of cooking competitions, folkloric dances and bushmen dress during the camp oven festival is seen as a reaction to the debate about a multicultural Australia and as a way to defend or re-adapt traditional bushmen legends. In this case international tourism becomes an audience, taking part directly through this festival, or via the mediation of films, in the battle for national identity.

Oliver Haid (Chapter 12) focuses upon Christmas festivity, and in particular the role of Christmas markets as sites of exchange and transformation in the German-speaking area of the South Tyrol, Italy. Haid introduces his approach by a helpful historic analysis on the transformation of Christmas and Christmas markets, which he suggests can be read as a metaphor for changing family models and national institutionalisation processes in Germany since the 19th century and the emergence of the consumption society during the 20th century. In this latest context, Christmas markets have shifted away from being prime providers of children's toys and have become spaces for more or less organised mass tourism. In the South Tyrolean context, the consumer oriented marketing and outlets of many of the Christmas market stalls, adapted in particular for Italian tourists, is at the heart of major controversies amongst stakeholders of the German-speaking minority regarding the 'authenticity' of the market.

Nicola MacLeod (Chapter 13) analyses the problem of 'placelessness' by focusing in particular on city festivals in the United Kingdom. According to the author, the problem of 'placelessness' is a result of the divorce between festival and 'local community'. Through tourism marketing and the adaptation of festivals according to international standards and formats, MacLeod claims that festivals are transformed into largely meaningless tourist spectacles. The author relates the 'lack of authenticity' of many festivals to the dislocation of people from their original spatial identities. In this context, according to MacLeod, globalisation and massive migration can lead to the dissolution of the category of place as a very generator of feelings of belonging.

Howard Hughes (Chapter 14) follows the transformation of gay and lesbian festivals, which originated from protest movements in the late 1960s and have become largely transnational party spaces. The author approaches the complex and changing political and symbolic underpinnings of the festivals by focusing in particular on contested festival spaces and official themes of gay festivals in Manchester, United Kingdom. By promoting gay festivals and gay space as urban spectacles for tourists, Hughes claims, city authorities contribute to the 'de-gaying' and loss of ownership of gay festivals and space by local gay communities. The festival space becomes the scene for a largely transnational crowd to meet and party.

Elizabeth Carnegie and Melanie Smith (Chapter 15) examine the transnationality of the festive form of the South Asian Mela and the ways in which it faces the challenges of its different cultural setting of Edinburgh, Scotland. Underlying the case of the Edinburgh Mela is an ongoing process (struggle) of adaptation and accommodation, as conflicts are acted out within and without the festival's organisation. In a city which has long demonstrated the strong connection between tourism and festivals, the Mela faces pressures to conform to being a part of an emergent multi-cultural tourism product, while at the same time provide an outlet for expressions of Scottishness. In addition the form, content and spaces of the Edinburgh Mela are continually being shaped by what younger Asian audiences want to see.

Kirsty Robertson (Chapter 16) analyses one of the first large-scale 'anti-globalisation' demonstrations, in Quebec, Canada, in 2001, as a touristic and carnivalesque happening bringing together under the theme of anti-capitalism, a transnational crowd of mainly young people from countries of the Northern hemisphere. Robertson describes the creation of festive *communitas* through collective moments and symbols, the invention of a festive inversion of Quebec's established geography and the collective – mainly symbolic and often satirised – battle against the police. The author describes her own use of photography as a means to capture the moments and experiences of the event and transform them into tear gas free souvenirs. Robertson questions whether the 'anti-globalisation' movement is any more than a Western middle-class fan culture and a metaphoric way to make sense of the battles and con-tradictions of contemporary social contexts and conditions in Western countries.

What all these cases do, to a greater or lesser extent, is to locate festivals within the much wider and constantly changing socio-economic and political contexts that they always operate and respond to – contexts that are historical and modern at the same time. Tourism is bound closely together with such contexts; feeding and challenging festivals with audiences that are increasingly transient and transnational, and with extended numbers of stakeholders and socio-political interests. The presence of tourists at the periphery of festivity, and also at its centre, interrogates notions of ritual and tradition, shapes new spaces and creates and renews relation-ships between participants and observers, and between a festival and the conditions of its operation. We cannot dismiss tourists simply as value neutral and crass consumers of spectacle, nor tourism as some inevitable commercial force. It is no longer appropriate to view festivals as somehow disjointed and 'framed' instances outside of social, economic and political realities. Indeed, as Guss (2000) has pointed out, it is the porosity of festival boundaries that makes them fascinating and worthy of study. Festivals draw our attention as participants, tourists and scholars precisely because they provide moments of time and space to reflect upon our being in the world and questions of collective meaning and belonging. Tourism and festivals alike, assist us, adapting the sentiments of Zygmunt Bauman (2001: 149), 'gain control over the conditions under which we struggle with the challenges of life' and allow us to make, re-make and experience the world. The fact that their boundaries are fluid merely mirrors the fluidity of our own lives and the seemingly constant need to keep in touch with continuity while engaging with change.

## References

Abrahams, R.D. (1982) The language of festivals: Celebrating the economy. In V. Turner (ed.) *Celebration: Studies in Festivity and Ritual* (pp.160–77). Washington DC: Smithsonian Institution Press.

Abrahams, R.D. (1987) An American vocabulary of celebrations. In A. Falassi (ed.) *Time out of Time: Essays on the Festival* (pp. 173–83). Albuquerque: University of New Mexico Press.

Aisner, P. and Plüss, C. (1983) *La ruée vers le soleil*. Paris: L'Harmattan.

Appadurai, A. (2003) Disjuncture and difference in the global cultural economy. In *Modernity at Large*. Minneapolis and London: University of Minnesota Press.

Arnold, N. (2000) Festival tourism: Recognizing the challenges – linking multiple pathways between global villages of the new century. In B. Faulkner, G. Moscardo and E. Laws (eds.) *Tourism in the 21st Century – Lessons from Experience*. London and New York: Continuum.

Bakthin, M. (1984) *Rabelais and His World* (Hélène Iswolsky trans.). Bloomington: Indiana University Press.

Bataille, G. (1991) *Eroticism* (M. Dalwood, trans.). San Francisco: City Lights.

Bataille, G. (1998) *The Accursed Share: Volume 1 – Consumption* (Robert Hurley, trans.). New York: Zone Books.

Baudrillard, J. (1998) *The Consumer Society: Myths and Structures*. London, Sage.

Bauman, R. (ed.) (1992) *Folklore, Cultural Performances, and Popular Entertainments*, Oxford: Oxford University Press.

Bauman, Z. (2001) *Seeking Safety in an Insecure World*. Polity Press, Cambridge.

Benedict, B. (1983) *The Anthropology of World's Fairs: San Francisco's Panama Pacific International Exposition of 1915*. London: Scolar Press.

Boissevain, J. (ed.) (1992) *Revitalizing European Rituals*. London: Routledge.

Boissevain, J. (1996) Ritual, tourism and cultural commoditization in Malta: Culture by the Pound. In T. Selwyn (ed.) *The Tourist Image. Myths and Myth Making in Tourism* (pp. 105–120). Chichester: John Wiley and Sons.

Bruner, E. (ed.) (1983) *Text, Play, and Story: The Construction and Reconstruction of Self and Society*. Washington DC: The American Ethnological Society.

Bruner, E.M. (1994) Abraham Lincoln as authentic reproduction: A critique of postmodernism. *American Anthropologist*, 96 (2), 397–415.

Bruner, E.M. (2001) The Maasai and the Lion King: Authenticity, nationalism, and globalization in African tourism. *American Ethnologist*, 28 (4), 881–908.

Burke, P. (1997) *Varieties of Cultural History*. Ithaca, New York: Cornell University Press.

Caillois, R. (2001) The sacred as transgression: Theory of the festival. In R. Caillois (French edn 1939) *Man and the Sacred* (pp. 97–127). Urbana: University of Illinois Press.

Cantwell, R. (1993) *Ethnomimesis: Folklore and the Representation of Culture.* Chapel Hill and London: University of North Carolina Press.

Chako, H.E. and Schaffer, J.D. (1993) The evolution of a restival: Creole Christmas in New Orleans. *Tourism Management* 14 (6) 475–82.

Cherubini, B. (1996) Les mises en scène du monde agricole: Foire, fêtes, identités locales. In B. Cherubini (ed.) *Le Monde Rural à La Réunion* (pp.61–84). Paris: L'Harmattan.

Clifford, J. (1997) *Routes: Travel and Translation in the Late Twentieth Century.* Cambridge and London: Harvard University Press.

Cohen, A. (1993) *Masquerade Politics: Explorations in the Structure of Urban Cultural Movements.* Berkeley and Los Angeles: University of California Press.

Coutancier, B. and Barthe, C. (1995) Au jardin d'acclimatation: Représentations de l'autre (1877–1890). In P. Blanchard, S. Blanchoin, N. Bancel and G. Boëtsch (eds) *L'Autre et Nous – Scènes et Types* (pp.144–51). Paris: Syro.

Cox, H. (1969) *The Feast of Fools: A Theological Essay on Festivity and Fantasy.* Cambridge MA: Harvard University Press.

Da Matta, R. (1978) *Carnivals, Rogues and Heroes: An Interpretation of the Brazilian Dilemma.* Notre Dame Ind: University of Notre Dame Press.

Danow, D.K. (1995) *The Spirit of Carnival: Magical Realism and the Grotesque.* Lexington: University Press of Kentucky.

Debord, G. (1973) *The Society of the Spectacle.* New York: Zone Books.

De Bres, K. and Davis, J. (2001) Celebrating group and place identity: A case study of a new regional festival. *Tourism Geographies* 3 (3), 326–37.

Délumeau, J. (2000) *History of Paradise.* Urbana : Univeristy of Illinois.

de Weerdt, J. (1987), Espace rural et tourisme en France – Orientations de la recherche. *Problems of Tourism* 2 (36), 83–93.

Dietler, M. (2001) Theorizing the feast: Rituals of consumption, commensal politics and power in African contexts. In M. Dietler and B. Hayden (eds) *Feasts. Archaeological and Ethnographic Perspectives on Food, Politics and Power* (65–114). Washington DC: Smithonian.

Doumenge, J.P. (1984) Enjeu géopolitique et intérêt scientifique des espaces insulaires. In *Nature et Hommes dans les îles Tropicales* (Vol.3, pp. 1–6). Talence: CEGET-CRET.

Durkheim, E. (1976) *The Elementary Forms of the Religious Life.* London: George Allen & Unwin.

Durkheim, E. (1992) *Les Règles de la Méthode Sociologique* (6th edn). Paris : PUF.

Eagleton, T. (1981) *Walter Benjamin or, Towards a Revolutionary Criticism.* London: New Left Books.

Eco, U., Ivanov, V.V. and Rector, M. (1984) *Carnival!.* The Hague: Mouton.

Enzensberger, H.M. (1996) A theory of tourism (with an Introduction by G. Gemunden), *New German Critique* 68, 113–35.

Falassi, A. (ed.) (1987) *Time out of Time: Essays on the Festival.* Albuquerque: University of New Mexico Press.

Featherstone, M. (1990) Global culture: An introduction. In M. Featherstone (ed.) *Global Culture* (pp. 1–14). London: Sage.

Getz, D. (1997) *Event Management and Event Tourism.* New York: Cognizant Communications.

Giddens, A. (1990) *The Consequences of Modernity.* Cambridge: Polity Press.

Gluckman, M. (1963) *Order and Rebellion in Tribal Africa.* New York: The Free Press.

Goffman, E. (1959) *The Presentation of Self in Everyday Life.* New York: Doubleday.

Guss, D.M. (2000) *The Festive State – Race, Ethnicity, and Nationalism as Cultural Performance.* Los Angeles: University of California.

Handelman, D. (1998) *Models and Mirrors: Towards an Anthropology of Public Events.* Oxford: Berghahn Books.

Hannerz, U. (1996) *Transnational Connections: Culture, People, Places.* London: Routledge.

Hobsbawm, E. (1983a) Mass-producing traditions: Europe, 1870–1914. In E. Hobsbawm and T. Ranger (eds) *The Invention of Tradition* (pp. 263–308). Cambridge: Cambridge University Press.

Hobsbawm, E. (1983b) Introduction: Inventing traditions. In E. Hobsbawm and T. Ranger (eds) *The Invention of Tradition* (pp. 1–14). Cambridge: Cambridge University Press.

Hobsbawn, E. and Ranger, T. (eds) (1983) *The Invention of Tradition.* Cambridge: Cambridge University Press.

Hughes, C.G. (1999) Urban revitalisation: The use of festive time strategies. *Leisure Studies* 18 (2), 119–35.

Humphrey, C. (2001) *The Politics of Carnival: Festive Misrule in Medieval England.* Manchester: Manchester University Press.

Kirshenblatt-Gimblett, B. (1998) *Destination Culture: Tourism, Museums, and Heritage.* Berkeley, Los Angeles and London: University of California Press.

Lanfant, M-F. (1995) International tourism, internationalization and the challenge to identity. In M-F. Lanfant, J.B. Allock and E. Bruner (eds) *International Tourism: Identity and Change* (pp.24–43). London: Sage.

Lanfant M-F. and Graburn, N. (1992) International tourism reconsidered: The principle of the alternative. In V.L. Smith and W.R. Eadington (eds) *Tourism Alternatives. Potentials and Problems in the Development of Tourism* (pp. 88–112). Chichester: John Wiley & Sons.

Lash, S. and Urry J. (1994) *Economies of Signs and Space.* London: Sage.

Long, P., Robinson, M. and Picard, D. (2004) Festivals and tourism: Links and developments. In P. Long and M. Robinson (eds) *Festivals and Tourism: Marketing, Management and Evaluation* (pp. 1–14). Sunderland: Business Education Publishers.

Lukes, S. (ed.) (1982) *Emile Durkheim, The Rules of the Sociological Method* (W.D. Halls, trans.). London: Free Press.

MacCannell, D. (1973) Staged authenticity: Arrangements of social space in tourist settings. *American Journal of Sociology* 79 (3), 589–603.

MacCannell, D. (1976) *The Tourist. A New Theory of the Leisure Class.* New York: Schocken.

MacCannell, D. (1992) *Empty Meeting Grounds: The Tourist Papers.* London: Routledge.

Manning, F.E. (ed.) (1983) *The Celebration of Society: Perspectives on Contemporary Cultural Performance.* Bowling Green: Bowling Green State University Popular Press.

Mauss, M. (1973) *Sociologie et Anthropologie.* Paris: PUF.

Melucci, A. (1996) *Challenging Codes: Collective Action in the Information Age.* Cambridge: Cambridge University Press.

Mesnil, M. (1974) The masked festival: Disguise or affirmation? *Culture* 3 (2), 11–29.

Mosse, G.L. (1971) Caesarism, circuses and monuments. *Journal of Contemporary History* 6 (4), 167–82.

Palmer, G.B. and Jankowiak, W.R. (1996) Performance and imagination: Toward an anthropology of the spectacular and the mundane. *Cultural Anthropology* 11 (2), 225–58.

Picard, M. (1998) *Bali: Cultural Tourism and Touristic Culture*. New York : Archipelago Press.

Picard, D. (2003) Being 'traditional' in order to be 'modern' – tourism and postmodernity in La Réunion (in German). In T. Gohlis, C. Hennig, D. Richter and H. Spode (eds) *Voyage – Studies on Travel and Tourism* (Vol. 6, pp. 109–26). Köln: Du Mont Buchverlag.

Picard, D. (2004) International tourism and cultural transformation: Variations of the creole garden in La Réunion, Indian Ocean. In P. Tsartas and J.K. Steen Jacobsen (eds) *Understanding Tourism – Theoretical Advances. Proceedings of the Interim Symposium of the Research Committee on International Tourism (RC 50) of the International Sociological Association (ISA), 14–16 May 2004* (pp. 503–22). Mytilini, Greece: University of the Aegean.

Pieper, J. (1965) *In Tune with the World: A Theory of Festivity*. New York: Harcourt.

Quinn, B (2003) Shaping tourism places: Agency and interconnection in festival settings. In M. Cronin and B. O'Connor (eds) *Irish Tourism: Image, Culture and Identity* (pp. 61–80). Clevedon: Channel View Publications.

Robinson, M., Long, P. and Picard, D (2004) Festival tourism – producing, translating and consuming expressions of culture(s). *Event Management* 8 (3), 187–90.

Robinson, M., Picard, D., Schneider, I., Haid, O. (eds) (2004) *Conference Proceedings of Journeys of Expression III: Tourism and Festivals as Transnational Practice*. Innsbruck, Austria, 5–7 May 2004. Sheffield: Centre for Tourism and Cultural Change.

Roche, M. (2000) *Mega-events: Olympics and Expos in the Growth of Global Culture*. London: Routledge.

Said, E. (1978) *Orientalism*. London : Routledge & Kegan Paul.

Schwimmer, E. (1986) La construction oolitique de l'objet esthétique. *Anthropologie et Sociétés*, 10 (3), 1–10.

Shields, R. (1991) *Places on the Margin: Alternative Geographies of Modernity*. London: Routledge/Chapman Hall.

Stallybrass, P. and White, A. (1986) *The Politics and Poetics of Transgression*. Ithaca, NY: Cornell University Press.

Tambiah, S.J. (1990) Rationality, relativism, and the translation and commensurability of cultures. In *Magic, Science, Religion, and the Scope of Rationality* (pp. 111–39). Cambridge: Cambridge University Press.

Turner, V. (ed.) (1982) *Celebration: Studies in Festivity and Ritual*. Washington DC: Smithsonian Institution Press.

Turner, V. (1988) *The Anthropology of Performance*. New York: PAJ Publications.

Turner, V. (1995) *The Ritual Process: Structure and Anti-Structure*. New Brunswick, NJ: Aldine Transactions.

Turner, V. and Turner, E. (1978) *Image and Pilgrimage in Christian Culture*. New York: Columbia University Press.

Twain, M. (1923) Queen Victoria's jubilee. In *The Complete Works of Mark Twain* (*Vol. 20: Europe and Elsewhere*) (pp.193–210). New York: Harper.

Urry, J. (2002) *The Tourist Gaze* (2nd edn). London: Sage.

Van Gennep, A. (1960) *The Rites of Passage* (M.B. Vizedom and G.L. Caffee, trans.). London: Routledge and Paul. (Original publication 1909.)

Van Koningsbruggen, P. (1997) *Trinidad Carnival: A Quest for National Identity*. London: Macmillan Education Ltd.

Valeri, V. (1985) *Kingship and Sacrifice: Ritual and Society in Ancient Hawaii*. Chicago : University of Chicago Press.

Wallerstein, I. (1990) Culture as the ideological battleground of the modern world-system. In M. Featherstone (ed.) *Global Culture* (pp. 31–55). London: Sage.

Williams, R. (1980) *Problems in Materialism and Culture*. London: Verso.

Chapter 2

# La Cavalcata Sarda: Performing Identities in a Contemporary Sardinian Festival

Iride Azara and David Crouch

> *It was too lost in the sea to play an important role, too far from the enriching contacts that linked Sicily, for example, with Italy and Africa. Mountainous, excessively divided, a prison of its poverty, it was a self-contained world with its own language, custom, archaic economy and pervasive pastoralism in some regions; remaining as Rome must have found it, long ago.*
> (Braudel, 1986: 150)

## Introduction

*La Cavalcata Sarda* is an annual festival held every third Sunday of May in Sassari, a northern town in Sardinia, Italy. Also locally known as 'the festival of the beauty and youth', this is a folkloristic parade of many representative villages of the island, who from early morning to late evening gather together to celebrate their communal identity through the exhibition of traditional, colourful and very diverse dresses, jewellery, local products and through the performance of traditional dances and songs. It is a unique event among other similar but local and religious performances (such as the *Redentore* and *St Efisio*) and is a lay celebration on a regional scale, attracting participants from all the four provinces of the island. The following study focuses on this particular festival aiming to understand how politics of representations mix with performances of identity and combinations of ideologies in what Hobsbawn and Ranger (1983) have termed a 'recent invented tradition'. Indeed, in historical terms this event is relatively modern, its conception being in 1899. Since its creation it has obtained tinctures and combined traditional ritualistic elements and cultural symbols peculiar to the island's cultural heritage, which have become extremely popular with contemporary tourism forms, but which have not been traditionally popular with locals.

Indeed, for many years young Sardinians preferred going to the beach and avoiding the towns and villages crowded with tourists whenever this, or other similar festivals, were being held. The younger generations, described by Magliocco (2001), which grew up under the influences of mass consumption were very keen to leave behind all the signs of backwardness traditionally linked to Sardinian 'culture'. This study closely explores this event, which the youthful generation would have normally discarded because of its association with this traditional image of Sardinia. Through connecting with performers, locals and tourists this chapter seeks to re-evaluate this position and argues against claims of 'inauthenticity' of so called 'folkloric festivals' brought about by authors such as Magliocco. Furthermore, the findings presented here argue that newly invented and 'touristified' festivals remain expressions of community participation and identity operating within different social and spatial scopes. On one hand, a 'romantic' imagery of Sardinia created in the 19th century still drives the island's identity in its relation to the Italian mainland. On the other hand, this festival is a space in which different internal dynamics and oppositions come to life by the performance of distinctive narratives and values.

This festival appears to be part of a broader social phenomenon of the contemporary world. Indeed, according to Manning (1983: 4), 'new celebrations are being created and older ones revived on a scale that is surely unmatched in human history'. This phenomenon seems to be particularly evident in Europe, and possibly the result of the socio-cultural and economic transformations that took place in industrialised countries after the Second World War (Boissevain, 1992). Decay in religious influences, increased industrialisation, media explosion, changes in work-leisure times and patterns, the increase in mass-tourism, together with an increased pressure towards democratisation and more regional autonomy, are all factors which seem to have contributed to the revival, revitalisation and even recent creation of a variety of different events, rituals, festivals, celebrations and performances. Festivals in particular have long been the object of scrutiny of many anthropological, sociological and folkloristic studies. Although a reductionist viewpoint, it appears that they are 'rites' enacted to mark special social or individual transitions (Van Gennep, 1960), to reinforce a collective view of society and to strengthen social cohesion. Additionally, they act as a form of symbolic response or counter-action to the experiences of rapid socio-cultural change (Worsley, 1957). Consequently, whenever the normal social order is perceived to be threatened, it is possible to see an intensification of ritualistic activity. As vehicles of communication of shared meanings, values and ideologies (Falassi, 1987), they then become loci of interpretation and dialectics and subsequently open to manipulation.

This chapter begins with a brief overview of the historical context from which this festival originates and examines the ways a particular imagery of Sardinian culture is being currently adopted and used for tourism purposes. Based on data gathered through participant observation, the chapter then discusses the festival's characteristics and the ways its meanings and values are constantly produced and re-interpreted through performative enactments. With regard to the sample of findings here presented, the principle adopted was to assure confidentiality of respondents. Hence participants are generically identified according to the broad categories of performers, locals and tourists. Nevertheless, public exponents due to the public position they hold are generally named in the text. For this thanks are due to the President of the Azienda Autonoma di soggiorno e turismo, Sassari (AASST), Mr Arcadu, for his kind help and useful comments.

## Historical Context

In order to understand the reasons that originally brought this festival to life I believe it is necessary to explore the island's historical, political and cultural dynamics of the past two centuries, which I will argue have contributed to the creation and maintenance of a specific representation of Sardinian culture. I will argue that this particular representation is the result of the influence tourism is having on the island and that it is indeed tourism that is enabling this kind of knowledge to continue existing.

Sardinia has always been a 'middle-earth', a land subjected to various and different colonisations and even today, due to its geographical isolation from the mainland, the island still retains in some respect the status of an Italian 'colony', relying, as it does, political and cultural ties to from the mainland (Magliocco, 2001). Particularly on the last aspect, if its geographical isolation on one hand has allowed some sort of 'cultural conservatism', on the other side it has led to what Magliocco (2001: 171) defines as 'a set of interlocking and complementary colonialist representations', created firstly by travellers and colonizers and later by Italian mainlanders. Starting significantly from the mid-19th century and up to the 20th century, numerous and different literary representations have been produced, oscillating between discourses on an extremely wild, rough or barbarian island inhabited by a savage people in need of taming and control such as those expounded by Honoré de Balzac and Gustave Jourdan (Mazzette 2002), and the land of a fierce, proud but welcoming population, holder of most ancient and most authentic traditions as portrayed by Filippo Vivanet (Mazzette, 2002). During a long period, colonisers, and in general Europeans travellers, have helped constructing the discourse of the 'Other', describing Sardinia as different, savage, primitive, untouched by civilisation, inferior but also as a living fossil; intriguing, exotic. According to Magliocco, the romantic representation of the island seems to stretch up to the 21st century and is being gradually adopted and used by cultural intermediaries with the purpose of stimulating tourism, feeding in what Duncan (1993) calls 'a burgeoning travel industry'.

Within this context, *La Cavalcata Sarda* has played a role in diffusing and institutionalising these competing images on an international, national and local level since the late 19th century. Indeed, the festival came to life in 1899, when a horse parade was organised in honour of the King of Italy (former King of Sardinia and Piedmont), Umberto I and his family. On that occasion, 3000 men and women were called to Sassari, the capital of the homonymous province, from the surrounding villages and asked to parade. In the intentions of the organisers there was both the will to welcome the authority and to display the power, pride and richness of the King's former colony through the staging of a very impressive celebration (Demartis, 2000). The event had an astonishing resonance outside Sardinia. Not only did it have regional and national newspaper coverage but it was also filmed by the Lumière brothers commissioned by the King.

From the perspective of the local villagers, this event had major significance as the local rural populations were quite reluctant to show themselves on such a big display (Demartis, 2000). Subsequently, the parade was organised on a rather sporadic base, in conjunction with a royal visit or to honour important regional representatives. This was mainly due to the vast organisational costs involved and to the enormous difficulties of moving large numbers of people and animals using a poor road system. It was only in 1951, when the Italian national Rotary Club decided to hold its congress in Sardinia that the local Rotarians arranged to revive the event for tourism purposes. In that occasion for the first-time participants from the province of Nuoro paraded together with the representative groups of the province of Sassari. The following year, given the enormous success with tourists, participants and locals, the invitation to participate at the parade was extended to the representatives of the other two provinces of Cagliari and Oristano, who willingly decided to take part, attracted primarily by the promises of the rising tourism industry.

Indeed according to Odermatt (1996) since the 1950s, Sardinia's regional government has willingly adopted tourism development schemes in order to stimulate economic and social development and to 'fill the gap' existing within the rest of the Italian peninsula. In four decades the island has undergone an extensive and impressive development relying heavily on tourism incomes and nowadays it is trying to use its peculiar and distinctive local features to attract new segments of the tourist market. Since then, *La Cavalcata Sarda* has become an international tourism venue, promoted worldwide and enacted each year in Sassari for the participation and pleasure of the ever increasing internal and external audiences and performers. New features have been added to the original formula and nowadays the festival features three climactic moments: the actual costumed parade in the morning where tourists and visitors can admire the dresses, listen to local songs and taste different local products; a horse race at the local hippodrome in the early afternoon, where highly skilled riders compete amongst each other; and finally a display of idiosyncratic songs and dances in the main squares of the town until late evening. The main attraction of the day is still the parade of the morning attracting the majority of holidaymakers from all over Sardinia, whereas the two other events seem to be reserved for a local and regional audience. Originally created as a 'gift' to the authorities (to symbolise an alliance between the Sardinians, their culture and the King, but also as a tribute to legitimate the power-apparatus of that time), the meaning of this festival has shifted and transformed with the passing of time, becoming a tourist exhibition during the large dominance of mass-tourism (1970/mid-1980s); consequently being rediscovered and reutilised in a different way.

As Mazzette (2002) stresses, contemporary tourism forms are changing, differentiating in typologies and offers and making possible for consumers to appreciate different types of tourism at different levels. Sardinia too has seen an increase in alternative forms of tourism such as cultural and nature based. Stimulated by the increasing competition from the neighbouring countries, by changes in consumer demand and needs, local, provincial and regional governmental bodies are all pushing towards the preservation and valorisation of all those cultural forms (such as costumes, songs, dances), which have or have not yet totally disappeared in Sardinia due to the short lapse of time. In a sense then, the very same Sardinian past and 'culture' that for two centuries has been the 'romanticised' symbol of backwardness and primitivism, has been gradually transformed since the rise of mass-tourism into a symbolic entity used for the purposes of consumption, preserved or even created *ex-novo* if it does not exist.

## *La Cavalcata Sarda:* Ethnographic Accounts

The data hereby presented has been gathered through participant obser-vation of the 53rd and 54th anniversary of this festival, through informal interviews and the analysis of published secondary data. Engaging in eth-nographic study has allowed the researchers to gain valuable knowledge and significant insights into the dynamics of this festival. Therefore, the information hereby presented is divided in two main sections: firstly focusing on a description of the events as they happen in sequence during the festival; the chapter then continues with the analysis of how the festival is re-presented by the regional agencies and how the national-regional imagery is perpetuated by official discourse. Finally, it illustrates how competing local-regional imageries intersect the official one, examining the manner in which performers and regional/local visitors challenge, respond and re-interpret those meanings.

### The parade

The parade starts at 9 o'clock in the morning and ends at around 2 o'clock in the afternoon, stretching along the main streets of the town centre. There is neither a fixed number of villages nor performers chosen to participate. In observing the event in 2002, 75 villages (out of 300, which originally applied to participate) were selected and 70 the following year for a total of approximately 3000 performers. The selection criteria seem to favour those groups which are traditionally considered the 'most rep-resentative' of their own region, over the less notorious ones, although in both 2002 and 2003, the local and regional media noted and praised the presence of new groups, which 'long lost their traditional heritage', re-discovering it and presenting it to the audience for 'the first time' (Meloni, 2002). The groups that have been granted participation generally gather in the elementary school of Piazza S. Giuseppe before dawn. Many (espe-cially those coming from the farthest province of Cagliari) have to travel all night to be there on time to get dressed and get ready to parade. This is an exhausting trip, which often starts as early as 2 am. Marco (one of the performers from Cagliari) comments: Often we do sleep only a couple hours, as you are so excited and there are so many things to do. You do have to make sure everything is ready for the parade.

A delegation of Sassari city council members usually opens the parade being followed by delegations from the provinces of Cagliari, Oristano, Nuoro and finally Sassari. Each folkloristic group participating counts elders, youngsters and children among its members. It is the children who usually open each individual procession carrying a banner with the name of the village they represent and the name of the folkloristic group they belong to. They are followed by men and women, who line in couples or singularly, in two parallel rows offering to the public and to the authorities fruits, sweets, wines and other products representative of their own area. They alternate between groups on horses and groups who perform traditional dances and songs. Villages distinguish themselves not only in terms of the dances and products they present but also, most importantly, in the types of costumes they portray. Each group displays at least two dresses: one for ceremonies and the daily one, although it's not uncommon to see wedding dresses and mourning dresses. According to Meloni (2001) almost all folkloristic groups are becoming more and more involved in the process of researching, re-discovering and claiming back their own heritage and dresses. These, in particular, have now become symbolic to each community. Indeed, only few original costumes now survive as the majority of them have disappeared during the first half of the 20th century. Increasing pressures for human development and more availability of cheap and more modern clothes have forced communities to renounce to the traditional dress. Nevertheless, the endurance of the manufacturing techniques is allowing the re-production and survival of these types of clothing, which come to be displayed together with the few originals in this and in similar events. The pride and the care participants put into the preservation and protection of their dresses are well expressed in the words of Giovanna from Oristano: 'I inherited this dress from my grandmother and it is my duty to preserve it and to pass it on to my kids as pristine as I can.'

Both in 2002 and 2003, this event was visited by approximately 50,000 tourists and regional/local visitors. Usually, the majority of the spectators gather from early in the morning along the route to gain a good spot. Nevertheless, a small group of viewers (generally local and regional politicians, members of the various tourist and commerce agencies, international tourists on special package tours and media) enjoy the parade from special stages erected in the main squares. There, designated speakers provide a comment of the exhibition in Italian, French and English. During the whole event, traffic in the town centre comes to a standstill and no commercial activity takes place. Only a few restaurants and bars remain open to cater for external tourists and local visitors. It is interesting to note that since 2003, the town council of Sassari has designated a small square to host a small number of stands, each of one selling 'typical' food and beverages. This has soon become a meeting point both for local residents, visitors and performers, who gather there to relax after the parade. Additionally, visitors can also explore the small markets and the exhibition stalls, which provide them with additional information on other touristic events of the island and trinkets/souvenirs.

### The horse race

After a pause of two hours for lunch, participants and spectators gather in the near hippodrome, where a horse race takes place. Here, only those villages perform that hold traditional thoroughbred stables for the purposes of racing (approximately 12). Each stable firm competes against each other in a series of risky acrobatics until late in the afternoon. Although gaining popularity with external tourists from Italy and the European continent, this second event of the day seems generally reserved to a local and regional audience: mostly families with children, young men and women and elderly couples. In 2002 the expectant crowd outnumbered 10,000. Unlike the parade, this is a more familiar space, where spectators relax on the stands, chatting, drinking and taking pictures of the most skilful horse riders, whilst a speaker introduces each of the stables and describes the specific acrobatics of the riders. This event also represents a unique possibility for the villages participating to showcase their horses and to compete against each other. One performer explains: 'This event allows tourists to witness the abilities and skills of our riders and the beauty of our horses; it is a fun occasion where we meet friends (from competing stables) and we get to prove who's the best rider.' Although relatively popular, this event seems to suffer from organisational and financial constraints. Indeed it was organised in 2002 but it did not take place in the following years due to these specific problems.

### The Party

The final event, the party, starts at around 8 p.m. and continues until approximately 11 p.m. This is also reserved for a local audience, although some regional visitors and external tourists decide to remain in town for the conclusion of the festivities. Started as an addition to complement the main event of the morning, this has become through the years another important occasion for the performers to showcase their own cultural differences, expressed through such forms as different dresses, songs and dances. Indeed in line with the horse race, this event is enacted in a joyful but competitive spirit as not all the groups remain in town until late at night. The few villages that remain are generally among the most illustrious in terms of their historical significance and folkloristic activity. As it is a less formalised space, spectators are free to approach and meet the performers: asking questions, talking to them or walking around the main square, chatting and generally enjoying the ambience. This is particularly welcomed, as one performer explains: 'People want to learn a bit more about our specific traditions and history [ . . . ] we don't have enough time to talk or to spend time with them [tourists/visitors] during the parade, but here they can ask about anything: about our costumes, our jewellery, our songs.'

## National-Regional Imagery

*La Cavalcata Sarda* is planned and managed by the Azienda Zutonoma di soggiorno e turismo, Sassari (AASST) in cooperation with different regional tourism agencies. At a both national and regional level it is promoted through newspapers, websites and brochures and it is broadcasted live on local television. Part of the tourist schemes to reshape the island's traditional image as a 'mass tourism' destination (Arcadu, 2001), this festival plays a pivotal role in enacting a new, albeit romantic, imagery of Sardinia and hence in innovating the island's identity for outsiders.

According to the official brochure the aim of the event is to give tourists 'an insight into the deep past of a mysterious and fascinating island'; the possibility of experiencing 'a living celebration of the island's folklore and to have an enjoyable time listening to the numerous and different songs and watching traditional dances' (AASST, 2003). Visitors are reminded of the possibility to gaze at a 'unique' and 'ancient' Sardinian custom of 'welcoming illustrious and noble guests with a parade of men and beautiful women on horseback, wearing their most beautiful and colourful dresses', because it is 'in memory of this tradition, that every year on the last Sunday of May La Cavalcata is enacted'. Similar discourses are maintained by the media, which nostalgically stress the 'uniqueness' of this festival in terms of its origins, its content and the way it is enacted. Posters offer visual images of young couples, families with children, all wearing their different traditional costumes; of fiery and proud horse-riders on the back of their finely dressed horses, conveying the message that this is an event worth seeing. This is the imagery which the political elite and certain sectors of the middle class seek to identify with and to promote to the external audiences. Accordingly, Mr Arcadu, the organiser of the whole festival perceives it as 'a powerful celebration of our distinctive culture' (2001). In order to maintain this representation everything is carefully designed to make a 'distinctive pitch' (Coleman and Crang, 2002), to underline and reinforce the authenticity and the credibility of the event (hence the continuous reminiscences of its historical and noble origins).

Such functionalist approaches seem to be common to many festivals and rituals originally created during the 19th-century romantic nationalism stream (Hobsbawn & Ranger, 1983). Geared to display national attributes and symbolic meanings, to legitimise power and historical grandeur, these events appear strongly disciplined relying on repetition to create the perception of immutability and continuity with the past. Although expression of regional identities, this recently invented festival is similarly constructed, being designed as a highly controlled performance (Edensor, 2001), as an 'incorporating ritual' (Connerton, 1989), which tries to justify certain values and meanings 'by linking back to a suitable historical past [ . . . ] by borrowing and using ancient rituals and symbols and strictly adhering to them' (Hobsbawn & Ranger, 1983: 2). Furthermore, the progressive mediatisation of this festival and the increased presence of tourists have contributed to enhance the need for a controlled performance, transforming *La Cavalcata Sarda* into a spectacular event for – to a large extent – visual consumption (Edensor, 2001). Nostalgically on display are then all the folkloric aspects of Sardinian culture, which may be easily understood and consumed by the spectators and which are inevitably embedded in the romantic imagery. Magliocco (2001: 176) believes this to be a common characteristic of many contemporary Sardinian festivals, as 'the projection of immutability is part of a mechanism by which the island has been transformed into a magic mirror in which tourists can see reflected an image of their own past' (Magliocco, 2002: 174). The presence of tourists as spectators she adds 'clearly marks the transformation of a communal rite onto a consumer product', throwing doubts into the authenticity of what is presented.

Nevertheless, the argument of 'inauthenticity' and commodification, although very intriguing, does not take into account the potential that the revival, re-construction or even the invention of festivals holds in terms of replenishing traditions, re-negotiating communal identity and strengthening group solidarity (Wood, 1998). Furthermore, as festivals are naturally arenas where symbolic knowledge is continuously created and recreated, challenged and opposed in dynamic ways, where the message communicated may vary, from the one sent by the organisers to the one conveyed by the performers and the one actually interpreted by the spectators (Kaeppler, 1983). How performers, locals and tourists interpret and respond to the official imagery of this festival will be discussed in the next section.

## Local-Regional Imagery

According to both Mazzette (2002) and Magliocco (2001), the increase in new forms of the often called 'alternative tourism' is quite a recent phenomenon in Sardinia. As far back as 20 years ago, Sardinia was a popular tourist destination mainly for its beaches and its sea. Traditions, customs and heritage were seen as complementary part of the tourist experience, but not attractive enough to be the focus of an entire holiday. Within the new context, the linking of this festival to the regional tourism policies and schemes has allowed the government to lay claims on it and to use it as a medium to attract new segments of the tourist market. Furthermore by rooting this festival into the different regional cultures, the government has sought to involve different communities in the project and to stimulate the process of rejuvenation of many of those localised cultures, which would have otherwise disappeared. Indeed, folkloristic groups have enthusiastically embraced the possibility of re-discovering 'their' own traditions and their preservation and conservation for future generations. Additionally, the promise of new tourist incomes and new economic development is further contributing to attract villages to *La Cavalcata Sarda* for the potential exposure it guarantees.

Nevertheless, if the socio-economic motives for hosting this event are commonly accepted and are driving the participation of an ever increasing number of villages, there seems to be a divergence in the interpretation of the romantic imagery promoted by the organisers and in the way performers approach and use the spaces of this festival. For the groups of performers interviewed in 2002 and 2003, *La Cavalcata Sarda* is primarily an annual celebration of their own identity rather than a festival/tribute of 'a proud and fiery population to illustrious guests' (AASST, 2003). Indeed, it appears that the majority of them not only are unaware of the romantic imagery portrayed, but also when made aware, consider it insignificant for the existence and enactment of this event. Furthermore, this festival is for them both a social occasion to celebrate the whole communal yet distinctive Sardinian identity (through the display of costumes, songs, dances, etc.) and a 'sacred space and time', which naturally breaks and opposes the mundanity of everyday life. Admittedly, this is an event that is awaited with hope and excitement by all the performers. It is a *festa*, during which, in a 'suspended time and space' (Falassi, 1987), they engage in a series of rites, each of which finds its expression through different modalities and in the different spaces of the festival. According to the morphological categories provided by Falassi (1987), throughout the day performers engage in rites of valorisation; rites of conspicuous display (of their distinctive icons of identity); rites of exchange (of symbolic gifts with the audience and among the organisers); rites of consumption and rites of competition. Rather than merely a formalised and spectacular ritual,

*La Cavalcata Sarda* is for them a moulding space in which distinctions are created, identities re-appropriated and narratives contested.

To some extent diverging from the performers' position, the indigenous population of Sassari experience *La Cavalcata Sarda* as 'a yearly invasion of their own social and cultural space' as many locals interviewed admitted. Not only do they discard the romantic imagery portrayed as lacking any emotional connotation, but they reject this festival altogether, preferring to go away from the town or to engage in free or matching other activities. They perceive this event as an exogenous social occasion, which is not specifically embedded in their culture and historical memory. Along these lines of reasoning, both performers and regional, national or international visitors are regarded as outsiders, who for one day occupy physically and symbolically their own social space. 'La Cavalcata doesn't represent anything for us', says Mauro (a local from Sassari). 'As there is no reason to stay here', he continues, 'it's better to go to the beach than stay with the rest of the Sardinian people or with the herds of tourists'.

As for the majority of the international and national audience, *La Cavalcata Sarda* is an important folkloristic event, which allows them to briefly reconnect with the past, providing at the same time easily consumable and entertaining elements (MacCannell, 1989). By attending this festival, tourists have a taste of that 'exotic' Sardinian peasant life without any of its negative connotations. For regional visitors instead, this event represents the opportunity of reconnecting with their own past, to resist and re-negotiate a communal identity which for a long time has been source of shame or denial (Magliocco, 2001).

## Conclusion

The aim of this chapter was to examine different layers of meaning, engagement and participation observed during *La Cavalcata Sarda*, an annual Sardinian folkloric festival. The overview of the historical context from which this festival originates has highlighted the existence of a particular romantic imagery of the island, which, created in the 19th century, is still in use and is driving the projection of Sardinia's identity in its relation to outsiders as a place loaded with fear, danger and, simultaneously, a natural beauty. Additionally, it has been argued that newly invented traditions enacted through this festival, rather than being merely commodified and spectacular events geared to tourist consumption are instead loci of dialectics where distinctive narratives and ideologies come to be expressed through performative enactments. Finally, from the analysis of the intersecting imageries of this festival, it becomes clear that *La Cavalcata Sarda* is a powerful symbol, which far from producing a unifying narrative, mobilises the different imageries and meanings, being able to communicate different things to different people.

## References

Arcadu (2001) Personal communications with Mr Arcadu, President of the Provincial Tourism Board of Sassari, Sardinia.

AASST (2003) *La Cavalcata Sarda*. Official guide.

Boissevain, J. (1992) Introduction. In J. Boissevain (ed.) *Revitalizing European Rituals* (pp. 1–19). London: Routledge.

Braudel, F. (1986) *The Mediterranean and the Mediterranean World in the Age of Phillip II* (Vol. 1). Glasgow: Fontana Press.

Coleman, S. and Crang, M. (2002) Grounded tourists, travelling theory. In S. Coleman and M. Crang (eds) *Tourism. Between Place and Performance* (pp. 1–17). New York: Berghahn Books.

Connerton, P. (1989) *How Societies Remember*. London: Cambridge University Press.

Demartis, G.M. (2000) *La Cavalcata Sarda. I costumi, l'orgoglio di un popolo*. Piedimonte Matese: Imago Media Editrice.

Duncan, J. (1993) Sites of representation: Place and time and the discourse of the 'Other'. In J. Duncan and D. Ley (eds) *Place, Culture, Representation* (pp. 39–56). London: Routledge.

Edensor, T. (2001) Performing tourism, staging tourism. (Re)producing tourist space and practice. In *Tourist Studies* (Vol. I (I)) (pp. 59–81). London: Sage Publications.

Falassi, A. (1987) *Time out of Time: Essays on the Festival*. Albuquerque: University of New Mexico.

Hobsbawn, E. and Ranger, T. (eds) (1983) *The Invention of Tradition*. Cambridge: Cambridge University Press.

Kaeppler, A. (1983) Dance in Tonga: The communication of social values through an artistic medium. *Journal for the Anthropological Study of Human Movement* 2 (3), 122–28.

MacCannell, D. (1989) *The Tourist: A New Theory of the Leisure Class*. New York: Schoken Books.

Magliocco, S. (2001) Coordinates of power and performance. Festivals as sites of (re)presentation and reclamation in Sardinia. In *Ethnologies* 23 (1), 167–88.

Manning, F.E. (1983) Cosmos and chaos: Celebrating the modern world. In F.E. Manning (ed.) *The Celebration of Society: Perspectives on Contemporary Cultural Performances* (pp. 3–30). Bowling Green, OH: Bowling Green University Press.

Mazzette, A. (2002) *Modelli di turismo in Sardegna, tra sviluppo locale e processi di globalizzazione*. Milano: FrancoAngeli.

Meloni, A. (2001) La prima festa laica dell'isola. In *La Nuova Sardegna*, inserto speciale 'La Cavalcata Sarda', 19 May 2001, p. III.

Odermatt, P. (1996) A case of neglect? The politics of (re)presentation: A Sardinian case. In J. Boissevain (ed.) *Coping with Tourists, European Reactions to Mass Tourism* (pp.112–42). New York: Berghahn Books.

Van Gennep, A. (1960) *The Rites of Passage*. London: Routledge and Kegan Paul Ltd.

Wood, R. (1998) Tourist ethnicity: A brief itinerary. *Ethnic and Racial Studies* 21, 218–41.

Worsley, P. (1968) *The Trumpet Shall Sound: A Study of 'Cargo' Cults in Melanesia.* London: Mackibbon & Kee.

## Chapter 3

# Gardening the Past and Being in the World: A Popular Celebration of the Abolition of Slavery in La Réunion

David Picard

## Introduction

La Réunion is a tropical island in the Indian Ocean that saw, over the past 30 years, a steady transition from a plantation economy to a so-called post-modern society. At the end of the 1990s, the key economic sectors of the island had shifted from sugar cane plantation and production towards public and service sector activities including tourism. A rapid urbanisation process and the emergence of new forms of social and geographic organisation accompanied this economic transformation. In this context, spatial and demographic structures related to the agricultural functions of the former sugar cane industry were challenged by the increasing importance of coastal urban centres and a new attitude towards natural landscapes. This new attitude is manifested in particular through shifting values attached to the sandy littoral of the west coast, the volcanic calderas of the south and southeast and the mountainous interior of the island. For the most part of marginal economic and symbolic value within the former plantation economy, these spaces partly transformed into high-priced residential areas and touristic places of recreation and escape. In this sense, the system of values attached to the land seemed to have shifted from an initially agricultural and colonial logic to an aesthetic and spiritual one. In this new context, economic wealth became less a product of cultivating the land for its agricultural surplus, than for gardening it for its aesthetic and symbolic 'fruits'.

This shift can be understood within the wider theoretical framework of international tourism. Lanfant (1980) suggests approaching international tourism as a complex, multilayered transnational social phenomenon involving not only the spatial movement of tourists or the capitalist expansion of tour operators but also, and in particular, the institutional conditions allowing tourists, touristic models of space, culture and society, and tourism related capital to move. According to Lanfant, these conditions are set by international policy frameworks and, in particular, by the idea to mobilise tourism as an economic and social development tool. Within the context of this transnationalised system of production and exchange, landscapes,[1] together with other symbolic-aesthetic forms or formats including folklore, art, heritage, material culture, ethnicity and history seemed to have became vehicles to renegotiate and manifest La Réunion's and the Réunions' 'being in' the world[2] (Picard, 2003). The object of widespread public discussion and dialectisation in the local newspapers and television since the late 1980s (Idelson, 1999), these new signifying frameworks – usually brought in from outside – provided new narratives and metaphors of the island's and the islanders' regional and local self-identities.

At the same time, since the mid-1990s, the structural changes of economic and social life on the island, and the symbolic reformulations and challenges these implied, were accompanied by a sharp increase in the number of publicly celebrated local-folkloristic, ethnic or sport festivals (Cherubini, 1996a). Almost all villages and urban quarters of the island started to initiate or revitalise public festivals, often themed around former pastoral activities, products or plants: Chou-Chou Festival in Hell-Bourg, Curcuma Festival in Plaine-des-Grègues, Lentil Festival and Wine Festival in Cilaos, Mango Festival in Saint-Paul, Pineapple Festival in Saint-Denis, Milk and Goyavier Festival in Plaine-des-Palmistes, Agaves Festival in Entre-Deux, Coffee Festival in Saint-Louis, Palm Festival in Saint-Philippe, Orchid Festival in Tampon, Garlic Festival in Petite-Ile, Green Honey Festival in Plaine-des-Cafres, Bichiques Festival in Bras-Panon. Also, a large number of commonly so-called 'ethnic' festivals were created or were made visible in the public space of the island, discursively emphasising for various reasons either the 'cultural distinctiveness' of particular 'communities' (usually defined by combinations of religious, phenotype and origin criteria – cf. Labache, 1996) or the cultural creolisation of La Réunion's population. Moreover, almost at the same time, an important number of sport festivals appeared or were re-profiled to become regional or international events focusing usually on so-called 'outdoor' or 'natural spac' activities.

The idea of this chapter is to approach this recent festival boom – observed in La Réunion, but also elsewhere in the world[3] – in relation to the structural and symbolic life crisis that appeared in the island in the last decades of the 20th century. 'Life crisis' is understood here in the sense originally given by van Gennep (1960), with the idea that particular types of festivity or 'passage rites' are being organised in situations of rupture, transition or alienation. While such 'passage rites' seem to appear in more or less organised and cyclically recurring ways in all forms of social life and existence (Turner, 1969), this chapter will focus on longer-lasting 'cycles of festivity' accompanying or following shortly after contexts of wider economic and social change. Such cycles of 'festive re-enchantment' have been observed in various historical contexts characterised by social and cognitive rupture and revolution; contexts in which common sense failed to provide symbolic continuity and metaphors to make sense of everyday life relationships. In such contexts, festivity is thought of as a complex phenomenon of social concentration enabling individuals and social actors, at different social and symbolic levels, to test, adapt and recreate forms and narratives adding sense to their being in the world (see Chapter 1).

This approach is adopted through a case study of a particular festival in La Réunion, the Abolition of Slavery Day celebrated in the village of L'Hermitage-les-bains on the island's west coast. Like many other contemporary festivals in the island, this festival, held each 20th of December, appeared during the mid-1990s and has since then politically and socially been institutionalised as a major popular festival. The aim of this approach is to gather data on the different aesthetic and discursive productions and performances of the festival and to analyse them in relation to the wider structural changes that recently occurred in the village and in the island as a whole. L'Hermitage-les-bains is a former fishing village that was recently surrounded by new middle-class residential areas and a major international seaside resort. The case of L'Hermitage-les-bains hence provides a manageable research frame for this study, which is part of a more important ethnographic work on tourism and social transformations on the island's west coast involving a long-term observation and residence from 1997 to 2001.

Gardening the past, the term used in the title of this chapter, makes a reference to the staging of a flower and agricultural garden as the spatial and thematic frame of the event. Gardening as a way to cultivate, embody and perform a vision of the world by selections and spatial arrangements of flowers, artefacts and plants, can be understood as a highly metaphoric cultural practice, which has transformed in various other fields of social life. I have suggested earlier that many social and also academic understandings of the world are underpinned by the ontology of gardening.[4]

The chapter is organised in three parts, the first introducing to the ethno-historic, demographic, economic and geopolitical environments affecting everyday life in La Réunion and L'Hermitage-les-bains, the second presenting a selection of relevant primary data in form of observation transcripts made before and during the festival (focusing on the festival organisation, spaces and performances), and the third articulating this selection of observed festival performances and narratives with the contexts of change affecting the protagonists and central stakeholders in this festival.

## Historising the Contemporary Context of Change in La Réunion

La Réunion is situated in the south of the Indian Ocean, at around 1000 km in the east of Madagascar and 200 km in the southwest of Mauritius. Initially colonised in the 17th century to become a supply harbour of the French East India Company, the island has transformed into an important coffee and sugar plantation colony during the 19th century and gained the status of a French overseas *département* (DOM) in 1946.

Since its first colonisation in the 17th century, the island's demographic, economic and political conditions and realities have largely been dependent on external forces. These were related in particular to imperialist geopolitical and commercial strategies by Western European countries and, more recently, by the US and the Soviet Union. While colonial powers including Portugal, the Netherlands, France and the United Kingdom were primarily aiming to dominate the commercial trade routes between Europe and India and China during the 17th and 18th centuries, the militaristic and geopolitical control of the Indian Ocean was considered a key to 'world domination' during the 19th and 20th centuries (Guebourg, 1999). During the cold war of the 1960s and 1970s, this had led to a competition between the Western and Eastern blocs aiming to control strategically important territories in the Indian Ocean.

In this context, La Réunion gained geo-strategic importance for the French authorities that had since then shown rather little interest in the island's fate. Facing the resistance and struggle for decolonisation by the Reunion Communist Party, the French government, through its local representatives, applied a firm and often violent policy prohibiting the public expression of symbols of political, cultural or geographical independence or resistance, including public performances of folklore, music and Creole language. At the same time, it developed a hearts and minds strategy put into practice through the distribution of milk and food, the introduction of a generalised education and health system and, later, from the 1980s, the implementation of the French social welfare state. In the absence of a pertinent economic redevelopment policy, a large part of the former agricultural population was consequently 'absorbed' in the public sector or lived off social welfare. As a result, at the end of the 1980s, La Réunion's economy was heavily subsidised. About half of the island's gross internal product consisted of money transfers in form of European and French structural funds, public sector wages, social welfare, economic subsidies and public spending.

Beside these geo-strategic considerations, the island's destiny was and still is largely dependent on external technological innovations in the transport, communication and agriculture sectors. This is exemplified for instance through the consequences that had the opening of the Suez Canal in 1869. In this context, the island suddenly lost most of its logistic utility as a harbour on the European East India route. The island's political and economic marginalisation was further amplified by falling world market prices for raw sugar at the end of the 19th century, a consequence of the innovation of new sugar production procedures based on sugar beet planted in the northern hemisphere. While many of the island's elites were able to leave and look for new opportunities in other French colonies or the French mainland (Palmas, 1996), a large proletariat remained and struggled to survive.

The local cold war opposing La Réunion's Communist Party, local republican parties, and national French authorities vanished approximately at the same time as the global communist system, during the late 1980s. In this context, the falling of the Berlin Wall in 1989 – again an external event – seemed to have created the condition for a new economic era basing the island's wealth on tourism and the tourism related mobilisation of natural landscapes, folklore and other 'cultural resources'. During the cold war, the development of a tourism sector was heavily contested, in particular as a result of successful polemics by La Réunion's Communist Party that formulated tourism as a form of Western imperialism and hegemony (Serviable, 1983). As a consequence, most of the tourism master plans elaborated during the 1950s and early 1960s were never put into practice. The only major tourism developments were realised in the island's capital city Saint-Denis and on the sandy west coast around Saint-Gilles – usually privately without a larger spatial concept, often illegally without a construction permit.

Yet, the election of the leader of the island's Communist Party and enigmatic figure of the decolonisation struggle, Paul Verges, as the president of the regional assembly, seemed to represent a turning point in the public and political consideration of tourism, not anymore seen as a form of imperialism, but as an opportunity to get out of economic decay, high unemployment, and the island's financial (and symbolic) dependence on Europe and the French mainland. Under the direction of the Regional Tourist Board (CTR), newly created in 1989, the number of external tourists had increased from less than 100,000 in 1990 to almost 500,000 in 2000. At the end of the 1990s, the large majority of the island's hotel beds were concentrated on the island's west coast. While Réunion's bourgeois and aristocratic milieux had been adapting European models of spa, health and leisure practice since the early 19th century, their seasonal settlements usually remained sporadic and largely self-contained. A significant and dramatic change in the demographic and urban configuration of the west coast hence only occurred during the 1960s, with the emergence of a local middle class adopting Western seaside-related leisure fashions and creating new residential areas along the sea shore. This process was further amplified by, and was partly related to, the arrival of a large number of migrants from the *métropole* (French mainland) who settled on the island during the 1960s, 1970s, 1980s and 1990s.

As a result of these relatively recent demographic and spatial transformations, the three principal agricultural settlements situated in this area, since then officially called 'first', 'second' and 'third' village, became urban pockets within new middle-class residential areas and international seaside resorts (Maestri, 1998). From an economic perspective, the alteration of the littoral space is witnessed in particular by a sharp increase in property prices, which have risen by up to 3000% between 1980 and 2002. This increase in property prices seems to translate a more important underlying process: the widespread reformulation of the symbolic systems underpinning the island's geography. Former patterns of spatial and social organisation, historically linked to a large extent to the economic functions of the sugar cane industry (Benoist, 1983; Bonniol, 1988; Defos du Rau, 1960; Eve, 1992; Fuma, 1994)[5] were clearly shifting (Benoist & Bonniol 1994; Ottino, 1999). In the plantation culture system, the structure of social relations and geographic space could usually be related to values of agricultural productiveness and to land ownership. In this context, L'Hermitage-les-bains, the 'second village' situated on the sandy, salty and arid beaches of the west coast, unsuitable for the plantation of sugar cane, had been attributed a marginal symbolic place and role. Yet, in the new context, the spatial reality of this village, close to the beach and sea, became one of the most cherished dreams of middle-class Réunions and French mainland immigrants.

## Celebrating the Abolition of Slavery in L'Hermitage-les-Bains

It has been stated earlier that the recent structural changes in the island were accompanied, since the 1990s, by the appearance of new types of festivity typically focusing on local-folkloristic, ethnic or sportive themes. It has been suggested to analyse this phenomenon in analogy to the concept of 'passage rite', a form of festivity accompanying a context of collective life crisis. To operate this approach, this study will focus on observations made before and during the Abolition of Slavery Day celebrated in the village of L'Hermitage-les-bains. This section will present a body of empirical data gathered during the festival and its preparation.

### Preparations

In December 1999, I was invited by Mrs Carlson,[6] secretary of the L'Hermitage Village Committee I knew through the City Council of St Paul, to participate in a preparatory meeting for the *fête kaf* (*kaf* being the Creole term for persons of African descent, *fête* being French for 'festival'). The Village Committee was an umbrella group that united other associations in the area and had organised the festival celebrations in the two previous years. A dozen people, men and women, were present introducing themselves as members and volunteers of various sports and cultural associations of the quarter. During this first meeting, different administrative problems as well as the organisation and logistics of the festival were discussed. Mrs Carlson explained that the *Belle Jeunesse* dance group wished to perform a dance depicting the abolition of slavery, which they had spent several months preparing. The culminating point of the festival was meant to be a procession through the coastal area, the central element of which was to be a group of 'chained slaves' and a 'white master'. Mrs Carlson's husband, Albert, who was the only *Métropolitan* (name given to Frenchman from the France mainland) in this meeting, was asked to play the role of the master. He declined, saying that he shouldn't have to take the role simply because he is *Zoreil* (alternative name for *Métropolitan*). 'Why not Fred, he's white as well?', he proposed. Fred, a red-haired man of clear skin colour, originally from the village, looked estranged. The response of the others came promptly: 'Fred doesn't have to, because he's Creole.' Daniel, father-in-law of Mrs Carlson's daughter Emilie, took over the discussion and established the preparation schedule. He suggested the construction of three straw huts and a podium, and a bar where sandwiches, cakes and alcohol would be sold. Musical groups were needed as well and Daniel's son, François, affirmed he would take the lead. Who will do what, who has a lorry, who will bring straw for the huts, and where will it be cut? In several minutes time all seemed to be settled. A second meeting was set for the next Saturday 18 December, at the home of Mrs Carlson's brother Claude.

### The men construct straw huts

On the day of the meeting, I arrived at around 9.30 a.m. A Peugeot 406 was parked at the entrance. Daniel and another man were unloading straw gathered at the house of a denizen of the *hauts* (name given to the mountainous inner region of the island). Several trips were necessary. Around 10.30 a.m. other men arrived, and we began to construct the huts. Pierre and Daniel showed us what to do. Pierre, another brother of Mrs Carlson, told us that he had been familiar with straw huts as a child. He explained how to put up the wire so as to be able to attach the straw. We worked in groups of two or three. Bamboo and aloe branches were attached to wire to create two metre by two metre squares. The straw was sewn on top, not too densely because 'it's just decoration', as Daniel put it, and at the end of two hour's work we had six panels completed. Claude, Mrs Carlson's brother, sent one of his sons to bring us cold beers, which went down nicely. Some people drank Coca-Cola. A short time before, as we were working, Claude and his wife arrived, observing and commenting on the construction. 'But they didn't have wire back then', he said with a hidden smile in his eyes. 'Anyway, you should build with concrete, it's stronger', he added and smiled cheerfully about his joke. Around midday two Creole women from the quarter, both with *Métropolitan* husbands, arrived. One of the men commented on the work and the beer we were drinking: 'The dodo [name of an extinct bird and the local beer] didn't exist then.' Then, later on, to one of Mrs Carlson's brothers: 'So they're having a festival for you Monday.' The brother responded that he had a pointed nose and therefore wasn't *Kaf* but *Indian*. Everyone laughed. The men set a meeting for the next evening to build the podium. The next day, they agreed, they would pick up pallets and support frames from a building site run by the Carlson brothers' construction company.

### Setting up the festival space

The festival took place on a Monday. Early in the morning the entrance to the car park, normally used by visitors to the beach, was closed off with a red and white banner and the set-up of the festival space began. The space was marked off by the road, the bowls field, the community centre and the boundary between the car park and the backshore undergrowth. The space was converted by means of the implantation of various structures and the planting of a choice of vegetation. Two straw panels respectively formed, in all, three huts installed in the corners of the festival grounds. A fourth hut, constructed of palm leaves, housed the *boutik karner*, where the Bowls Club sold sodas, beer, rum and sandwiches. 'Karner was the name of an old Chinese man who owned a shop in the village', Pierre explained. A sign announced the price of drinks, written first in French by one of the organisers, then rewritten in Creole by Mrs Carlson's (*Métropolitan*) husband. The rum bottles were placed under the bar.

The entire festival ground was decorated with flowers and plants taken from participants' gardens. Cut banana trees, sugar cane, palm leaves, flowering plants, agaves and corn stalks were 'replanted' (they no longer had roots) and watered. Palm, coconut palm, and *vacoa* leaves were tied to the podium and the bar. 'We used to work in the cane fields', Pierre explained to his children and outside visitors that were passing by. Daniel dug a hole in front of the podium to create a *boucan*, an open fire for cooking in a suspended pot. Three trunks served as benches. A *tramail* (a string for capuchin fishing), was hung between wooden sticks, placed in the ground at the festival entrance. 'We put the *tramail* there because in our quarter, there are fishermen', Daniel said.

While the men conceptualised and constructed the material space of the festival, the women of *Belle Jeunesse* met to prepare their contributions to the festival. Partly aided by their daughters and granddaughters, they made cakes and contributed 'old-time' household items: an iron, a coffee grinder, two corn grinders and a *gregue* (coffee pot), which they placed on a small chest of drawers in front of and inside the straw huts. Mrs Carlson told a woman that she used one of the carbon irons until the 1980s and that her 'unfortunate' (meaning 'poor') mother hadn't had the means to purchase a coffee grinder. A platter with fruits that, according to one woman, 'we no longer know' was set in front of the hut to the left of the podium, where the women sold their cake. A gas stove was installed behind the podium, under the roof of the community centre, and a *cari volaille* (a dish consisting of rice and chicken) was cooked at midday. Behind the podium, in the shade of a large tree, was placed the sound equipment and the compere's post. Two large speakers were put on the podium. The space behind and on the podium was arranged by two young men, nephews of Mrs Carlson, belonging to the 'Maloya Tradition- nel' association.

### Dressing-up

By the end of the morning, at around 11 a.m., the festival space had been set up. Mrs Carlson asked the children to leave the grounds. She, her husband, Pierre, Daniel, Fred, and other helpers then went home. A quarter of an hour later, they reappeared, costumed in 'old-time' clothes. Mrs Carlson was in a floral dress and has a scarf around her head. Pierre and Fred had put on suits, 'good' shoes, and hats. Daniel wore torn trousers and a shirt with red flowers. Daniel and Mrs Carlson sat down beside the *boucan*. A fire was lit beneath the cauldron. Daniel peeled bananas and manioc for cooking. This proved amusing to the other men who had gathered around the *boutik karner* to talk and drink rum. Actually, it is not usual in La Réunion to cook bananas, and this was thus a very individual contribution that Daniel, from Martinique, brought to the festival. When I asked if I could film them cooking, Mrs Carlson requested me to wait for her to take off her sandals and dispose of a little bottle of gas used to light the fire. 'Because they didn't have those back then', she explained and both Mrs Carlson and Daniel started laughing.

### Inspection of the festival space

From 11.30 a.m., women with children, adolescents and men arrived in small groups to look around the grounds and then to assemble, the women with the other women who were selling cake and the men with the other men who continued to drink rum at the *boutik*. They joked about, wishing to all people of African phenotype a 'Happy festival, *Kaf*! Today's our day.' This banter continued all day. Tourists with cameras and people visiting the beach passed through, some stopped a moment to look or talk, and then left. The children and teenagers were found mostly near the cake stand or on or behind the podium. Some of them jumped about and danced to the music. A little before noon, Mrs Carlson asked them to get off of the podium. Daniel came up and took the microphone to welcome everyone. The public was invited to visit the grounds, eat, drink and watch the performances. It was midday and quite hot. The space was deserted little by little. Most people went back to their homes, at a couple of hundred metres from the festival ground, to eat and rest.

### Getting the party started

People only began to come back around 2.30 p.m. This time there were far more people. Elderly men and women surrounded by children and adults, groups of teenagers, men and women, and Métropolitan families all came to look at the straw huts, to talk. Mrs Carlson invited her daughter and grandchildren to a hut to explain the old ways of life and showed how to use the various household objects. 'Even in full sunlight, the air stays cool under the straw,' she said, 'it's better adapted to the tropical climate than houses made of concrete'. Another women explained where to find and how to eat the 'forgotten' fruits she was displaying on a platter.

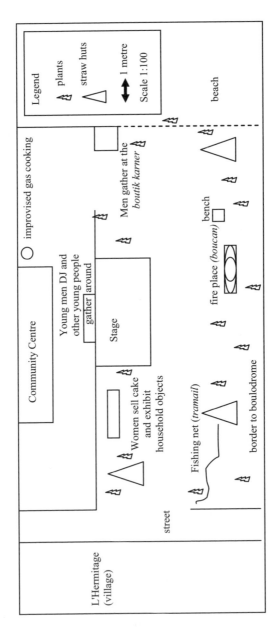

**Figure 3.1** Map of festival space

Pierre joined in explaining that the planters of the quarter grinded their corn at the home of one of the few men in the area who owned a corn grinder. 'And the pestle serves to crush chilli peppers and to make *rougail* [a spicy sauce]. Sometimes, to punish a child, my parents made me stand outside in the sun with a pestle on my head', he added. For others, the visual encounter with the agave plants triggered memories of working on the *moulin kader*, a mill which transformed the stalks of this species of aloe for the fabrication of rope. The fruits, today rare or little-known, lead to conversations about a common childhood, of the 'freedom' of strolls through land not yet developed, where everyone knew when and where the harvest took place. All the stories associated with these objects and fruits brought back pieces of memories, and were told with nostalgia, with laughter, and, sometimes, with eyes on the verge of tears.

The festival focuses upon a central stage or podium (see Figure 3.1). The podium, as a central space, separates the festival space along two axes. The first passed between the front of the stage and the backstage, which was appropriated by young adults grouped around the sound system and the DJ. The other opposed the area to the left of the podium, occupied by the women and children, to that on the right, where the men gathered. In front of the podium, family clusters were grouped around several elderly people, seated comfortably in chairs someone had brought in. Several tourists, easily recognised by their clothes, their cameras and the whiteness (or redness) of their skin, mixed with the crowd. They watched, photographed and filmed the performances that followed. These visitors did not go unnoticed, as is later proved by a proud remark made by Mrs Carlson: 'They filmed it, so they liked it, didn't they?'

The performances on the podium began with children dancing to the song 'Ibiza', followed by three teenage girls in tank tops and black trousers who had choreographed a dance accompanied by *ragga* music. Next were three girls in *pareos* who danced a *maloya*. The tension gradually rose. The last two acts were sexually very provocative, the female body stirred, men whistled, the public got enthusiastic and applauded. Next, about 10 people, joined by some of the festival supporters, got on the podium to sing and dance bits of *maloya*. The crowd, now quite large, around 200 people, looked on and applauded. At the end of this musical act, the women of the *Belle Jeunesse* group prepared themselves for their dance on the abolition of slavery. The act involved the public's participation and culminated in a collective dance.

The festival came to a sudden end when it was learnt that a resident of the quarter had just died. Daniel made the announcement, apologised and thanked everyone. The festival audiences dispersed rapidly. The festival grounds had to be quickly deconstructed: 'You can't have a festival when someone's just died', Mrs Carlson told me.

## The 'Abolition Dance' performed by the Belle Jeunesse group

Using a small video-camera, I filmed the 'Abolition Dance' performed by the *Belle Jeunesse* group, which proved helpful later to transcribe the observations with more detail. The act had a multipartite structure. It was begun by seven women lying on the ground, barefoot, in dresses and straw hats. One of them 'woke up', looked about, got on her knees, and touched the others, who then 'woke up' as well. The women joined hands, then rose their arms to the sky. This opening lasted about two minutes and ended as it began: women stretched out along the ground.

Next, a group of five women in dresses, cloth in hair and barefoot, 'worked' the manioc then walked, 'with difficulty', towards the centre of the stage. They then made movements representing the cutting of sugar cane, and after that joined the other women still on the ground. After this, two 'bourgeois' women entered, wearing light dresses and 'good' shoes and holding Chinese parasols, and went towards the women grouped on the ground. One said 'Look how dirty you are!' then shouted at them: 'Come, you must work!' The women on the ground cried: 'pity!' One of the 'bourgeois' women closed her parasol and used it to hit one of the women on the ground. The audience cheered. The two 'bourgeois' women then left. The other women took care of their 'wounded' companion. Another woman appeared, barefoot, wearing a dress and straw hat, and went towards the women stretched on the ground. She said in Creole: 'We all live in this miserable state, we get up in the morning, rain or shine, because we must work . . . The day will come when we can teach others how much pain the whip causes. Come then, you must rise . . . ' A *maloya* song was plaid and she started dancing and, one by one, touched the shoulders of the other women, who then stood up. The scene terminated in a collective dance and the frenetic applause of the audience.

In the following scene, a woman stirred a cauldron. Others 'worked the earth' and 'drank rum'. One of them went towards the centre stage and said (in Creole): 'So many years of painful stories, one never forgets the whip.' She called the others, who then gathered around her. One woman said, 'I'm tired. My back hurts.' The first woman asked: 'Children of the islands, where are our roots?' The other women responded: ' . . . close your eyes!' They started clapping their hands to the rhythm of another *maloya* song and formed two lines. They chanted 'ah-ah-ah-ah-ah' and raised their arms towards the sky. They then lowered their arms and dispersed, going off to imitate household tasks again. This 'work' scene ended in the 'death from fatigue' of one of the women. While she lay on the ground, the others were dancing around her, screaming and crying, and then carried her off stage. They cried: 'alive, alive, alive . . . ' A woman on the podium started reading a poem (in French) about the *marron* (escaped slave) Anchaing, the heroism of his actions, the liberty he found in the *hauts* (mountainous interior) of the island. The last sentence of the poem is: 'I am free!', which the other women, still below the podium, repeated 'free, free . . . ' Then, at the podium, Mrs Carlson started reading another text (in French): 'The Secretary of State, Victor Schoelcher, presided over the commission that wrote the declaration of emancipation of all slaves on French territory, on 7 April 1848. It wasn't until eight months later when Sarda Garriga, Commissioner of State, announced the abolition of slavery on the island.' The women cried now even stronger: 'free, free . . . ' while clapping their hands.

Accompanied by a *maloya* song, they began to dance and invited the public, especially the men and women of the quarter, to join them. At the end of this song, women dressed in black spandex, dresses or T-shirts, wearing masks of coloured feathers, assembled in front of the podium. Imitating the flight of birds with their arms, they began to dance. The crowd applauded. Other women, now in brightly coloured floral dresses, got on stage and invited the audience to dance. Most men and women first hesitated, finally many joined into a collective dance.

## Narratives, Metaphors and Being in the World

The aim of this section is to produce interpretative elements helping to understand the relationship between narratives and metaphors mobilised during the festival and the contexts of wider structural change affecting the village and its inhabitants.

### Social and social-symbolic discontinuities

The festival organisers are linked by different types of relations, which are characterised by social and symbolic discontinuities based on residence, kinship, gender and age group categories.

On a social level, all organisers were born in or had been living in L'Hermitage-les-bains for a long time. They were linked by different social networks and tight kinship relations around Mrs Carlson (cf. Figure 3.2): her husband Albert, her brother and neighbour Pierre, her brother Claude (living 50 m away from her house), her daughter Emilie, her nephew François, Daniel father of François, Fred (all living in the same street). During the festival, these relationship networks were further developed;

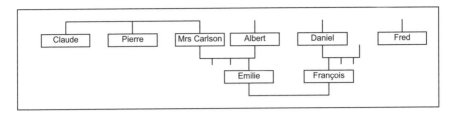

**Figure 3.2** Kinship relations between the organisation team

indeed, the wider family of Mrs Carlson and other neighbours formed a large proportion of the festival audience. The distribution of tasks and spaces within the festival mirrors two further systems of social discontinuity based on gender and age. Accordingly, a major part of the older women who were selling cake, exhibited household tools and performed the abolition dances usually met three evenings a week to do gymnastics and to choreograph dances (the *Belle Jeunesse* association). The older men who were selling and drinking sodas and rum usually met every evening around 5 o'clock to play bowls (the Lagoon Bowls Club). The teenagers and young adults, both male and female, who organised the music entertainment and performed dances, usually met several times a week to make music (the *Maloya Traditionnel* association). Some of the older men involved in the festival regularly met each other at the *Kap Zamo* association, which regroups farmers growing vegetables in the 'gardens' beside Bruniquel Road, close to the quarter. They also formed a team, which was regularly going to fish capuchin in the lagoon. Each of these social entities became responsible for a number of tasks in the festival (Table 3.1).

Yet, this festival did not concern solely the network of festival organisers and other inhabitants living in the village, but also involved a concerted effort to address an outside public. By voluntarily staging the festival in the contact zone between the village and the public space of the highly frequented beach and seafront, the festival organisers manifested efforts to tie in their village in the broader social-symbolic frameworks of La Réunion. This strategy was equally manifested through the sending out of press releases by Mrs Carlson, aiming for recognition of the village in the public spheres of the island. Other more intimate or family celebrations (sports club, baptisms, marriages, bereavements, etc.) were usually organised on a small place within the village, its private space. At the same time, as a result of this public strategy, residence in the village revealed itself as a significant category to define social identities within the festival, opposing villagers to non-villagers.

**Table 3.1** Gender and age group related festive roles and activities

|  | *More than 25 years old* | *Less than 25 years old* | *All ages* |
|---|---|---|---|
| Women | – dance choreography on *maloya* rhythm<br>– Decoration of the festival space with household articles<br>– Cake selling | – Dance choreography on disco rhythm | – Baking cake |
| Men | – Construction of the festival space<br>– 'Plantation' of plants<br>– Beer, soda and rum selling | – Sonorisation of the festival space<br>– Disc-jockey | – Preparing straw huts and the podium |
| Women and men | – Conceptualisation and organisation of the festival | – Music group (*maloya*)<br>– Mixed dance performance | – Cooking and eating in the improvised kitchen with gas cooker behind the podium<br>– Collective dance |

## Memory, objects and the symbolic world of the past

The selection of plants, objects and performances within the festival ground allowed individual memories of the past to be triggered, especially for the older participants. The encounters with these objects or practices often initiated the narrating and poetic reconstruction of childhood experiences and different life phases. This is witnessed in particular through stories told around household objects like the coffee pot or sweetcorn grinder that played a central symbolic role in the establishment of social relations within the village. In the context of the Creole house, the reception of visitors played – and still plays – a fundamental role. The usual hospitality rite involves the offering of a cup of coffee served either in a room in the front of the house, visible from the street (for 'official' visitors) or in the backyard (for more familiar visitors and friends) (Watin, 1991; Ghasarian, 1988). The sweetcorn grinder used to produce maize flour and animal food, constituted another important household object enabling its owner to establish neighbourhood relationships and exchanges. From this perspective, both the coffee pot and the grinder were objects of value not always accessible to all agricultural households of times passed, symbols of participation in social life, objects of desire and fear, objects ritually given at the event of a wedding. During the festival, older participants rediscovered these objects together with experiences, tastes and smells from their childhood. They remembered moments of their past, talked about fragments of souvenirs and shared these souvenirs with the younger generation and the non-Réunion audience. The festival thus became a space of individual reflectivity on and reconstruction of life histories.

At the same time, it also allowed resignification of the past as a narrated space. Initially, a collection of individual memories, the 'past' was festively transformed into a more structured narration contextualised within the contemporary social world. Furthermore, the symbolic values attached to the 'past' seemed to shift. This is illustrated in particular through the example of Mrs Carlson's discourse on the straw hut, which, according to her, was 'better than modern constructions to protect against the heat'. Until the 1960s, straw huts were the principal form of housing for the island's agricultural population. They then quickly disappeared with the introduction of new materials, most notably sheet metal and concrete. Vegetable building materials such as straw and wood were consequently experiencing a heavy depreciation amongst a large part of La Réunion's population, considered then as symbols of misery and economic poverty (Niollet, 1999). In the late 1990s, except for some very marginal cases, there were no more people living in straw huts in La Réunion. In this sense, the empirical history of the straw hut did not have an effect on the contemporary world anymore. This seemed to have constituted the condition to give it a new signification, no longer a symbol of poverty and exclusion, but of collective identity. In this sense, Mrs Carlson's discursive idealisation of the straw hut together with other festive performances linked to the past can be understood as narratives resituating the past as a symbol of participation and being in the contemporary world. From this point, the ability to display one's past through performances and objects seems to become a necessary condition of social participation in the contemporary world.

### Origin and phenotype as cultural performance

The celebration of the abolition of slavery is often the object of public debate in La Réunion and regularly engenders political controversy. The content and linguistic form of its title shifts between *fet kaf* (Creole), or *fête kaf* (French and Creole), as well as The Festival of 20 December, The Liberation Festival or The Réunion Freedom Festival. Among the participants in the quarter, very minute differences of opinion were expressed concerning the title. Everyone seemed to agree on *fet kaf*.

However, a relation between phenotype and origin criteria of festival organisers and the roles they were attributed to perform in the festival systematically appeared through the observation data. This is illustrated by five examples.

(1)   Provoked by the sentence: 'So they're having a festival for you Monday', one of Mrs Carlson's brothers responded by pointing to his 'Indian' nose – to say that he isn't '*Kaf*' (of African descent).

(2)   In another context, at home, Mrs Carlson explained that 'the festival commemorates the abolition of the enslavement of black people'. 'But there were Indian slaves, and even white ones', replied her husband, who had been listening in.

(3)   The joke of wishing persons of African phenotype a 'happy *fet kaf*' (or 'happy *fet, Kaf*') furthermore reaffirmed humorously the symbolic relation made between 'Black' phenotype and slavery.

(4)   For the scene in which several slaves were to be led by a master, the choice of actor to play the master fell, as though it were the natural thing to do, on Mrs Carlson's *Métropolitan* husband. He defended himself by instead suggesting Fred, a 'white Creole'. This proposition was turned down because, according to the other participants in this meeting: 'Fred is Creole'. In this sense, the role of the master is positively attributed to individuals from the French mainland.

(5)   This observation is confirmed by the choice of actors for the roles in the abolition dance performance. Two *Métropolitan* women who live close to the quarter played the 'bourgeois ladies'.

These examples indicate that the dramaturgic slave-master opposition performed in the festival is used in a metaphorical way to contextually make sense of the social and political relationship between La Réunion and the French mainland ('*la métropole*'). The choice about who is performing which festive role seems to depend on geographical origin criteria. Subjects from the French mainland (called *Z'oreils*) are asked to play the master roles whereas subjects from La Réunion are exempted. This even is the case where the subjects from La Réunion manifestly have ancestors from the French mainland witnessed through phenotype criteria such as clear skin. At the same time, the decision on who should or should not play the role of the slaves appear to based on a set of phenotype criteria. Subjects with a 'black skin' and an 'African nose' are attributed the festive slave role. At the same time, 'black skin' and an 'Indian nose' seem to allow negotiation or to refusal of the attribution of this festive slave role. These inductions are based only on a few observations, yet they give some indications on social-symbolic models or social scripts upon which the

**Table 3.2** Origin and festive role (same phenotype: 'white skin')

| Origin | Festive role |
|---|---|
| France mainland ('Metropolitan') | Master (because 'Metropolitan') |
| La Réunion ('Creole') | Non-master (because 'Creole' = non-'Metropolitan') |

**Table 3.3** Phenotype and festive role (same origin: La Réunion)

| Phenotype | Festive role |
|---|---|
| 'Black skin' + 'African nose' | Slave (because 'black skin' + 'African nose') |
| 'Black skin' + 'Indian nose' | Non-slave (because 'Indian' = 'non African nose') |

festive performances appear to be based on (cf. Tables 3.2 and 3.3). This is not to say that society and social interrelations, in festive time or other, in La Réunion are fixed by stable collective models, but that the observation of various festive performances seems to show the existence of collective systems of representation linking phenotype, origin and social role (cf. also Labache, 1996).

**Narratives of the past as metaphors of contemporary social contexts and issues**

The festival involved very different types of participants, who engaged in different types of performances and social interrelations. In such a complex and multileveled context, a large number of social relationships and subjectivities could have been observed. For instance, the disco-style dance performances by groups of children and young girls using particular styles of clothing and music seems an important aspect of the festival enabling the younger generation to introduce and communicate new age and gender related elements in the social space of the village. Many more, equally interesting and important aspects – maybe less spectacular or hidden to the ethnographic eye – have certainly been ignored by my observations. In this context, it is a choice to rather focus on a small number of particular subjectivities and perspectives of individual festival participants. In what follows, I wish to concentrate in particular on the dramaturgy of the 'Abolition Dance' performed by the *Belle Jeunesse* dance group choreographed by Mrs Carlson. Here again, the analysis will necessarily be reduced to an analysis of the underlying narratives and symbols mobilised by this dance rather than of the manifold meanings different performers and spectators of this dance may have attached to it.

The dramaturgy of the 'Abolition Dance' was structured by different time and space frames situating the story and its heroes in historic time and concrete places of the island. In the first act of the dance, two synchronic worlds of the past – a 'slavery world' and a 'maroons world' – were enacted within a common historic time-space frame ('before 1848'). Both worlds were situated in the island, although spatially opposed with the 'slavery world' on the island's coasts and the 'maroons world' in the mountainous interior. This opposition was overcome by the narrative figure of the maroons who fled the plantations on the coast to find freedom in the inner sanctums of the island.

When comparing the narratives mobilised by discourses on recent social change by the villagers and by the first act of this stage performance, a striking analogy appears. Both are based on the fundamental opposition between freedom and non-freedom and the heroic act of transgressing the boundary between these two conditions. In this sense, they appear as variations of a same theme. Consequently, it can be said that this dance performance is not focusing primarily on wild nature, freed slaves or individual freedom, but functions as a narrative allowing people to articulate and make sense in a metaphorical way of the recent changes the village has recently seen. Through its spatiality, plot and heroes, the story seems able to encapsulate and manifest the festival organisers' feelings of nostalgia and loss of spaces of freedom. The mountainous inside, where most of the festival organisers have physically never been, can thus be seen as a narrative space of escape rather than a geographic reality, eventually allowing articulation and making sense of feelings of loss, of not being able anymore to 'go freely through the fields to pick fruits'. In this sense, the narratives of the past enacted through the dance performance, but also the staging of the 'traditional garden' can be seen as metaphors of current issues marking the social world of the village (or at least of Mrs Carlson's vision of the village).

This admittedly far-reaching interpretation is supported by the analysis of the second and third acts of the 'Abolition Dance'. Here, the performances implicitly oppose a world of the past to a world of the present. These performed worlds are linked by the act of abolition, by a French administrator, initiating a world of colour, light and social inclusion (symbolised by floral and brightly coloured 'pretty' dresses and the final collective dance). The emphasis made by the narrative on the French administrator and the introduction of legal and juridical institutions to stop slavery can again be interpreted as a metaphorical strategy to make

**Table 3.4** Time-space frame and attributes of the performed worlds

| Performed worlds | Attributed space | Attributed time | Attributed qualities | |
|---|---|---|---|---|
| 1. Slavery world | West coast | Before 1848 | 'Domination' | } Chaos', |
| 2. Maroons world | Mountains | Before 1848 | 'Freedom' | } 'poverty' |
| 3. Contemporary world | Whole island | After 1848 | 'Legality', 'order', 'wealth' | |

sense of contemporary contexts. Social-economic and political relations in the contemporary post-plantation context are based to a large extent on persisting paternalistic networks and informal economies (or in other terms: on discrimination, clienteles and corruption). In the particular context of L'Hermitage-les-bains, but also elsewhere in La Réunion, this has led to a very common belief that a few people have gained a lot of money by speculating on land property, by manipulating spatial development plans and by corrupting political decision-making processes. In this sense, the heroic role of transgressing the boundary between freedom and non-freedom, attributed to the maroons in the first act of the dance, is now quite explicitly attributed to the legal and juridical authority of the French governmental institutions. This might be interpreted as a way for Mrs Carlson to metaphorically communicate her trust in the role and integrity of contemporary governmental authorities and, corollary, her mistrust in regional politics and forms of authority. The various attributes of the worlds being performed here are summarised in Table 3.4.

## Conclusion

The aim of this chapter was to analyse the relation between contexts of rapid social, economic and political change, and the emergence of forms of public festivity. The study focused in particular on the inhabitants of L'Hermitage-les-bains, formerly a marginalised fishing village that has recently become integrated to or, at least, surrounded by newly constructed middle class residential areas and international tourism resorts. The observation and study of a festival in this village, themed around the abolition of slavery, allowed the gathering of relevant data and hopefully the production of some answers.

From a methodological point of view, the study shows that the festival can be observed as a delimited time-space frame of social concentration enabling various actors to meet and express differentiated visions of and beings in the world. Despite the multiplicity of individuals that met in, and the different layers of sociality of, this concentrated time-space frame, a number of social and symbolic continuities could be observed. In this sense, through its underlying social organisation, the festival manifested different social spaces for festival organisers and participants to perform, re-produce, and re-signify age-, gender-, phenotype- and kinship-related identities. Accordingly, women and men, insiders and outsiders, young and old respectively, played socially differentiated roles, accomplished socially differentiated tasks and were attributed socially differentiated spaces. Consequently, it can be said that the social pattern underpinning the organisation of the festival was largely independent from its symbolic contents, the abolition of slavery. The only social division and underlying symbolic discrimination relevant to the abolition theme concerned the attribution of roles in the festive performances. A widely accepted consensus seemed to exist here that slaves shall be played by actors of 'African' phenotype (based on nose, hair and skin colour criteria) whereas masters shall played by actors of 'Metropolitan' origin. This 'system' of both phenotype and origin criteria was exemplified through two marginal cases. In the first, a Réunion man with an 'Indian' nose, but 'African' hair and skin colour refused to play a slave role. In the second, a Réunion man with 'white' skin colour was exempted from playing a master role.

Beyond the social organisation underlying the festival, seen on a larger social scale, the festive enactments could be seen as a coercive effort of at least some of the festival organisers to articulate their being in the world with the wider social environment of the island. Accordingly, some of the on-stage performances, but also discourses around various objects formulated temporal and spatial frames, which through their underlying narratives linked the abolition theme to current issues and problems marking the social and social-symbolic context of the village. In particular the narratives of the past embodied in objects and danced performances seemed to have become detached from the actual past. For instance, the 'Abolition Dance' performed during this event seemed not primarily concerned with the empiric history of slavery or its abolition, but rather appeared as a way to make sense of, or to give answers to, contemporary contexts. In this sense, the abolition of slavery seemed to allow the mobilisation of narratives that, in a metaphorical way, encapsulated nostalgic feelings related to more recent change and mistrust in local political leaders. From this point, this festival was not, as it appeared, about remembering a far away violent past or anything like this, but offered a stage and a set of familiar aesthetic objects and narrative elements and formats through which various organisers and participants were enabled to create and perform meaningful expressions of their contemporary social existence and being in the world.

The adoption and narrative adaptation of the 'past' as a format to formulate the being in the world is not an observation limited to the contemporary La Réunion case. Researchers of various strands have observed similar processes of mobilising the past as a symbolic resource to generate and articulate elements of social inclusion and being in the world in a large range of other contemporary contexts (Appadurai, 1981; Hobsbawn & Ranger, 1983; Featherstone, 1990; Dirks, 1990; Kirshenblatt-Gimblett, 1998). Although, as this chapter has shown, the symbolic contents individuals and groups create within this format are socially contextualised, it needs to be asked which processes generate and which types of authority legitimate its apparent global hegemony. It further needs to be asked which alternative forms or formats have been observed or are possible to escape from the process of packaging the world in standardised ethno-historic boxes and easy-to-consume (non-)cultures.[7] I believe a more systematic study of international tourism and its various transnational instances of power and exchange may open the problem to new answers and theoretical perspectives.

## Notes

1. It should be mentioned here that the idea of romantic landscapes already appears in La Réunion in the 19th century, when aristocratic and bourgeois milieux introduce and locally adapt European bath, tourism and leisure fashions. Moreover, in the 1960s and 1970s, romantic landscapes and local folklore, based mainly on European models, are mobilised during the decolonisation struggles lead by La Réunion's Communist Party. Yet, in both cases, the idea and model of landscape or local folklore remain largely within the demographically marginal social spheres of the 19th century bourgeois milieu or the – equally bourgeois – 1960s and 1970s independence movements (Lilette, 1999).

2. The study of 'being in the world' ('*das Dasein*'), as perceived and experienced directly by human beings, in Heidegger (1962) terms as a phenomenological concept, is approached here as a form of socially embedded subjectivity making meaningful the individual being through its relations to other beings, things, time and space. This approach is believed to allow to articulate individual action and reflexivity with empirically observed collective models of behaviour, world vision and sensibility.

3. The observation of an increase in the number of public festivities following a momentum of social change is not specific to the La Réunion case. Similar observations have been made in a variety of other geographical and sociohistoric contexts indicating a more systemic nature of the relation between festivity and change (cf. Chapter 1, this volume).

4. This relates in particular to understandings of the ontological roots of the notions of 'cultivation' as a metaphor of humanising 'nature' and of 'cultures' as a system of knowledge of 'nature' (Picard, 2001).

5. From a broader anthropology perspective, the structural links between economic production, social organisation and symbolic superstructures are far from being verified. History in La Réunion did not *start* with the colonization of the island in the 17th century; various demographic inputs from Europe, Madagascar, India, China and Africa did bring in their specific cultural patterns which, according to a more dynamic anthropological perspective, 'creolised' through selection, resemanticisation and recomposition processes of different kinship, symbolic, communication and economic systems (cf. Cherubini, 1996b). However, for this study, the question of *how* the symbolic systems expressed through the festival have historically and demographically been created is not of a primary interest.

6. All names of festival participants have been changed to protect their anonymity.

7. With reference to Augé's idea of 'non-places' (Augé, 1992) and the post-colonial critique of ethnographic 'pigeonholes' used to make sense of and translate the Other in terms of mainly European models and categories of society (Albers and James, 1988; Clifford, 1988; Fabian, 1983; Geertz, 1973). Far from being contested, these pigeonholes continue to be widely used to structure the chapters of contemporary tourism guide books and travel catalogues. This seems to indicate the role tourism plays alongside with mass media and other transnational institutions to globally proliferate these categories of thinking and organising the social.

## References

Albers, P.C. and James, W.R. (1988) Travel photography: A methodological approach. *Annals of Tourism Research* 15, 134–58.

Appadurai, A. (1981) The past as a scarce resource. *Man* 16, 201–19.

Augé, M. (1992) *Non Lieux*. Paris: Seuil.

Benoist, J. (1983) *Un développement ambigu. Structure et changement de la société réunionnaise*. Saint-Denis: FRDOI.

Benoist, J. and Bonniol, J.-L. (1994) *Un ordre étagé mis à bas*. Aix-en-Provence: Laboratoire d'écologie humaine et d'anthropologie.

Bonniol, J.-L. (1988) Couleur et identité. Le miroir des appartenances dans la genèse de populations créoles. Unpublished PhD thesis. Aix-en-Provence: Université de Provence.

Clifford, J. (1988) *The Predicament of Culture: Twentieth Century Ethnography, Literature and Art*. Cambridge, MA: Harvard University Press.

Cherubini, B. (1996a) Les mises en scène du monde agricole: foire, fêtes, identités locales. In B. Cherubini (ed.) *Le Monde Rural à La Réunion* (pp. 61–84). Paris: L'Harmattan.

Cherubini, B. (1996b) La construction symbolique des identités dans le monde créole: Exemples réunionnais. In B. Cherubini (ed.) *De la tradition à la postmodernité. Ecrits en hommage à Jean Poirier* (pp. 267–77). Paris: PUF.

Defos du Rau, J. (1960) L'île de la Réunion. Etude de géographie humaine. Unpublished PhD thesis. Bordeaux: Université de Bordeaux.

Dirks, N. (1990) History as a sign of the modern. *Public Culture* 2 (2), 25–32.

Eve, P. (1992) *Ile à peur – la peur redoutée ou récupérée des origines à nos jours*. Saint-André: Océan éditions.

Fabian, J. (1983) *Time and the Other: How Anthropology Makes its Object*. New York: Columbia University Press.

Featherstone, M. (ed.) (1990) *Global Culture*. London: Sage.

Fuma, S. (1994) *Histoire d'un peuple: La Réunion (1848–1900)*. Saint-Denis: Université de la Réunion/CNH.

Geertz, C. (1973) *The Interpretation of Cultures*. New York: Basic Books.

Ghasarian, C. (1988) Salazie: Espace social quotidien d'un village des hauts de La Réunion. In C. Ghasarian and J.-P. Cambefort (eds) *Roles & Enjeux* (pp. 1–37). Saint-Denis: University of La Réunion Press.

Guebourg, J.-L. (1999) *Petites Îles et Archipels de L'océan Indien*. Paris: Karthala.

Heidegger, M. (1962) *Being and Time*. New York: Harper & Row.

Hobsbawm, E. and Ranger, T. (eds) (1983) *The Invention of Tradition*. Cambridge: Cambridge University Press.

Idelson, B. (1999) La presse quotidienne régionale (P.Q.R.), acteur social local. Analyse d'un discours de presse: le cas du 'Quotidien de La Réunion' (1976–1997). Unpublished PhD thesis. Saint-Denis: Université de La Réunion.

Kirshenblatt-Gimblett, B. (1998) *Destination Culture: Tourism, Museums, and Heritage*. Berkeley: University of California Press.

Labache, L. (1996) La question de l'ethnicité à la Réunion. Vers un 'melting-pot? Unpublished PhD thesis. Paris: EHESS.

Lanfant, M.-F. (1980) Tourism in the process of internationalisation. *International Social Sciences Journal* 17 (1), 14–43.

Lilette, V. (1999) Le mythe du marronnage. Symbole de 'résistance' à l'île de la Réunion. Unpublished MA dissertation. Saint-Denis: Université de La Réunion.

Maestri, E. (1998) *Groupe Bourbon – 1948–1998*. Saint-Denis: Gaphica.

Niollet, L. (1999) *L'habitation en Bois-sous-tôle*. Hell-Bourg: Ecomuséé Salazie.

Ottino, P. (1999) Quelques réflexions sur les milieux créoles réunnais. In B. Cherubini (ed.) *La Recherche Anthropologique à La Réunion* (pp. 65–95). Paris: L'Harmattan.

Palmas, J. de (1996) La Sakay. Une réponse au surpeuplement de La Réunion. Unpublished MA dissertation. Saint-Denis: Université de La Réunion.

Picard, D. (2001) *Les nouveaux jardins sacrés: Une approche anthropologique du tourisme international à la Réunion*. PhD Anthropology Dissertation, directed by B. Cherubini. Saint-Denis: Department of Anthropology, University of La Réunion.

Picard, D. (2003) Being 'traditional' in order to be 'modern' – tourism and post-modernity in La Réunion (in German). In T. Gohlis, C. Hennig, D. Richter, H. Spode (eds) *Voyage – Studies on Travel and Tourism* (Vol. 6) (pp. 109–26). Köln, Germany: Dumont.

Serviable, M. (1983) *Le Tourisme aux Mascareignes-Seychelles*. Saint-Denis: Réunion University Press.

Turner, V. (1969) *The Ritual Process*. Chicago: Aldine.

van Gennep, A. (1960) *The Rites of Passage*. London: Routledge & Kegan Paul. (French edn 1906.)

Watin, M. (1991) Habiter: Approche Anthropologique de l'espace domestique à La Réunion. Unpublished PhD thesis. Saint-Denis: Université de La Réunion.

## Chapter 4

# Becoming All Indian: Gauchos, Pachamama Queens and Tourists in the Remaking of an Andean Festival

Patricia Mathews-Salazar

## Introduction

Throughout the Andes, people make offerings to the *Pachamama* or 'mother earth', the source of fertility and reproduction of life. These rites centre on the idea that all human beings are connected to the soil. As it is explained by most Andean residents: 'If we eat from the Earth, we live from the Earth, and it is the Earth that will take us away.' In the northwest town of Amaicha del Valle, rites for the *Pachamama* have acquired new dimensions. They have become the defining markers of 'Indianness'. They are also evidence of the efforts made by current residents to stress transnational connections with other indigenous groups throughout the Americas. Why are these residents so interested in making this celebration an Indian ritual of such unprecedented dimensions at the margins of the Andes?

This chapter examines the evolution of a festival originally created for tourist purposes in one of the few Indian communities in the Argentine northwest. It describes the changes that have taken place to transform it into an economic and social asset for those who participate in the performance of these pre-hispanic rituals. The current *Pachamama* festival in Amaicha del Valle has opened grounds for gender and ethnic solidarity throughout the Andes, making Indian identity a transnational element. Revitalisation of Indian identity is a phenomenon not new to many groups throughout the Americas. In recent decades, with the intensification of media communications and information systems, members of indigenous communities have taken new initiatives to recapture their Indian identity and made it a marker of cultural pride and political contestation. By reasserting their Indianness, indigenous groups throughout the continent hope to obtain recognition of both their autonomy as beholders of a prehispanic ancestry and their equality as citizens.

This chapter is mainly an ethnographic account based on two periods of fieldwork conducted in Amaicha del Valle in 1992–1994 and in 1999.

## The Nation and the Region

Different from other parts of Latin America, Argentina is a country where the majority of the population is of European descent. According to official statistics, groups identified as 'Indian' made up for less than 2% of the national population, a big contrast with the figures in neighbouring nations of Bolivia and Perú, where population identified as 'Indian' was at least 20 times higher (Hernández, 1992; Stavenhagen, 1996). Lack of population of Indian descent in Argentina is mostly due to the strong policies of eradication of this population since before Independence. One area where small concentrations of Indians inhabit today is the northwest region, where the Pampas meet the Andes. The people here who claim an Indian ancestry are descendants of many groups including Diaguitas, Quechuas and Aymaras, who are known in Argentina as '*Collas*', maybe in reference to the Collasuyu, one of the four regions of the Inca state that covered that area before Spanish arrival.

In recent years, Indian identity has been articulated mostly in terms of a 'culturalist' rhetoric devoid of any political or socio-economic agenda. But as Tambiah has argued, 'even the most purely culturalist demands open arenas that will be reformulated by locals and will lead to a rising awareness of the imminent connection of cultural rights with economic and political marginality' (Tambiah *et al.*, 1988). Beneath the apparent culturalist discourses and practices of people who claim an Indian identity, there are concrete political and economic demands, which have been obscured in recent past by state efforts to both homogenise and repress its population by ignoring ethnic diversity of subordinate groups.

In Argentina, Indians are absent from the national imaginary and they only appeared in the imagined landscape of the interior of the country as reminiscent of a remote past. Indian identity has historically been associated with 'provincialism' and 'backwardness'. The northern province of Tucumán (see Figure 4.1) is part of the interior. It is, however, also a province of much national symbolism: Tucumán is known as the 'Cradle of Independence', the site where one of the last battles against Spanish colonialism was won, the battle of Tucumán still commemorated every 24

**Figure 4.1** Map of Argentina – location of Tucumán

September. In this peripheral region of the country, with strong nationalistic symbols, Indians have gained a distinctive status. At the turn of the 21st century, at a time of intense globalisation and neo-liberal policies designed to modernise Argentine society, people opt for asserting an Indian identity. Local residents of these communities are demanding access to the benefits of modernity without giving up their status as Indians. Or more precisely, they seek access *through* this status. Indian groups are demanding more control over their cultural and economic resources. They want to raise awareness and pride of their ancestry without sacrificing their access to water, electricity, phone lines and access to media.

## The Local Setting: Amaicha

Amaicha del Valle is located in the south central area of the Calchaquí Valley in the mountain region of the province of Tucumán. There are approximately 5000 residents of which some 3500 are indigenous – descendants of the Calchaquíes, part of the larger ethnic Diaguita language group which disappeared in the 18th century. The region had been subdued by the Incas for just a few decades before Spanish invasion in the 15th century. Today, everybody speaks Spanish with a series of words that are borrowed from Quechua and others that may have roots in the extinct Diaguita language.

From a culturalist perspective, Amaicheños use three elements to assert their Indian ancestry. One is an identification with the land. Amaicheños hold to some 90,000 hectares of land and the common ancestry to the Calchaquí Indians and their leader, *cacique* Chapurfe. In 1716, a royal decree from the Spanish Crown granted them legal recognition as an Indian community with rights to these communal holdings.

A second element is the collective memory of the community's efforts to survive and protect their resources from powerful outsiders. Key to the community's survival – according to this popular history – was their ancestors' skill as negotiators. After the Spanish conquest, they peacefully accepted subordination to the Spanish Crown and to the Catholic religion. By complying with their conquerors, they received a more benevolent treatment than other ethnic groups such as the neighbouring Quilmes, who were warriors and chose to fight against the Spanish and were then defeated, killed and finally dispersed in exile to Buenos Aires. Both Quilmes people and Amaicheños today use their history to reassert their identity together as survivors of Spanish colonisation. Whereas Quilmes residents have transformed the archaeological remains into a sacred fortress, visited daily by hundreds of national and international tourists,

Amaicheños have made their *Cédula Real* – their communal title – the most important document that asserts their identity as Indians today. In 1920, a group of Amaicheños led by their *cacique* Juan Pablo Pastrana, walked over 1000 miles to the capital of Buenos Aires, to have these land boundaries legitimised and their communal rights protected from neighbouring landlords with desires of expansion. The recognition obtained by the Argentine government is remembered as another milestone that confirms their reputation as 'good negotiators' with foreign authorities.

A third element that reasserts their Indian ancestry is expressed through an aesthetic that has transformed the cultural landscape of Amaicha. In 1993, the provincial government funded a project of restoration of the main plaza in town. The traditional square of Spanish style was replaced by a series of winding paths surrounded by *'pircas'*, or fences made of river rocks following the style of Inca terraces common to the region; statues of saints and national heroes were replaced by *'apachetas,'* small mounds of offerings, and other sites of pre-hispanic beliefs. Following those changes, new houses built by local residents are trying to preserve this pre-hispanic style by using indigenous materials such as adobe.

These three elements are associated with Inca and pre-Inca presence in that region. They are used to reaffirm Amaicheño authority as natives of that area through various public displays performed periodically. An obvious example of these demonstrations of ethnic pride focuses on the rituals to the earth mother. The rest of this paper will focus on the development of a festival that is inspired by these fertility rituals to promote tourism.

## From Household Rituals to Regional *Feria*: An Ethnography of the *Pachamama* Rites

Rituals to honour the *Pachamama* or 'mother earth' take place all year round but particularly during the month of August, before the sowing season. August is the coldest month of the winter season in the southern Andes. At this time, people feel more vulnerable to illness because of the strong winds and sudden weather changes that are said to affect people's health. August then, is regarded as a 'tricky month' – mischievous and a little evil – so people need to be on good terms with nature to keep healthy and have their crops and livestock protected. Families follow some cleansing rituals by burning medicinal plants, wood and other items, in order to scare evil spirits, who are said to wander more frequently at this time of the year. People drink a special kind of *mate* tea, made of the male variety of a plant called *'ruda'*, which gives good luck. On the eve of 1

August, families and neighbours get ready to honour *Pachamama*. The host or hostess calls for the gathering. 'Neighbours, families, compadres, get together: come tonight and keep me company, I must give food to the Pachamama' (personal interview).

Families prepare a meal and start cooking at midnight. Food made of guts must boil all night long; everything goes inside the cooking pot. When the meal is ready, they set a plate aside for the main guest. The host makes a hole in the ground. If the soil comes out nicely, it means that it will be a good year. If it doesn't, the year won't be so productive. Before anyone starts eating, the host gives the first plate for the *Pachamama*. All the food that was left aside is now poured onto the ground together with other offerings such as coca leaves, ear parts of the recently marked animals, and drinks. A pitcher of '*chicha*' or corn beer and a jar of wine circulate regularly among the guests, who must throw a little bit on the ground to pay their offerings while saying:

> Here I am *Pachamama*, your day has finally come. We are here to venerate you. Thank you for what you gave us this past year, for the harvest that I may have, for my cattle, for my children. I bring you here 50 *damajuanas* [special large containers] of wine, ten pitchers of chichi [corn beer], here is the food I have prepared in your name. This is product of what I received this past year from you. I hope that next year I continue to have more, so in this way I can give you even more.

Several people claim they have seen the *Pachamama* in person. They describe her as an old shepherdess pasturing guanacos in the highland plateaux. The personification of the *Pachamama* is a distinctive element in the Argentine northwest and it is much less common in other areas of the Andes.

Reports from the 1920s and 1930s already showed interest in building roads that provided easier access to those towns regarded as desirable summer resorts and as retreat areas for people with respiratory problems such as asthma. The Secretary of Tourism of the Province used to provide free transportation then, in order to assist tourists from the capital city and surrounding areas in attending this festival. Government authorities from the northern provinces of Tucumán, Salta, Catamarca, and Santiago del Estero attended this first celebration and later they sponsored similar festivals in their own provinces.

In 1947, the populist regime of Juan Domingo Perón assigned national status to a series of 'traditional' celebrations in the rural northwest. The main purpose of this measure was to sponsor tourism and to integrate the rural workers into national politics. Although the traditional rites for *Pachamama* had taken place in August and February, after 1947, the celebration for the *Pachamama* was scheduled to coincide with carnival, the time of summer vacation that attracts large number of urban tourists from the city capital of San Miguel de Tucumán. The first planning committee of the *Pachamama* Festival was integrated by provincial authorities, some urban intellectuals who spent summer months in Amaicha and a few male members of the elite from the local community.

The timing of the festival is fundamental to explain these transformations. A celebration that is juxtaposed to carnival in the southern hemisphere combines the middle of summer, with vacation time, harvest and time of excess and permissible disorder characteristic of most carnival celebrations around the world. The senior residents find themselves more reluctant to accept this time as a symbol of their town and community identity. Because they lived most of their lives during a time when Creole identity paralleled being 'civilised' and patriotic, most of them reject the new notions of Indianness outside this public event. Newer generations, on the other hand, have openly embraced it. Today there are associations of teenagers and young Amaicheños who choose to return to their community and become active promoters of this Indian identity in Amaicha and outside.

Although both media reporters and Amaicheños are aware of its origins, they continue to describe this festival as an 'authentic' celebration of their Indian heritage. The references used, however, are related to Inca religion, rather than merely Diaguita. Although the Incas subdued the Diaguitas in the late 14th century, their presence in this area was rather brief and it was replaced by the Spanish within six decades of their arrival.

*La Gaceta*, the daily newspaper in the province wrote:

> Pachamama comes from the Quechua words 'pacha,' that means 'earth' and 'mama' that means 'mother'. Pachamama is the wife of 'pachakámac; her sons are 'inti,' the sun, and a male deity, and 'killa,' the moon and a female deity. In Quechua cosmology these are the four organizing principles of nature based on water, earth, sun, and moon. Cusiyá, cusiyá! This was the ancestral Inca expression that the Calchaquí nations used to invoke when they requested protection from the mother earth. Pachamama is the only authentic celebration and one of the last rituals of Argentine folklore! (*La Gaceta*, 27 February, 1949: 10)

Forty-five years later, the newspaper continued to describe this festival as an ancestral celebration:

Residents of the Calchaquí Valley leave aside their daily activities for three days, they dress up and cross the colourful mountains, valleys, and ravines to arrive, as soon as possible, to this humble and small place that becomes a giant in February when one of the last rituals of Argentine folklore is celebrated. (*La Gaceta*, 27 February 1949)

The events scheduled range from entirely nationalist Creole performances, such as the opening with the singing of the national anthem, or the Gaucho parade, followed by the performances of the *Chayeras* or *Copleras*, singers and dancers of indigenous tunes, and ending in a '*baile*,' the dance of massive dimensions that closes the event each evening.

Through time, Amaicheños have taken a more active participation in the planning of the celebration. The planning committee is now composed mostly of Amaicheños from the villa or centre, and a growing number of residents from the surroundings of the community.

## The *Pachamama* Queen and the Sunday Parade

The central figure of the celebration is the *Pachamama*. The organising committee of the Fiesta searches for the oldest woman in the community to be elected '*Pachamama* Queen of the Year'. The first *Pachamama* was elected in 1949. Indigenous women, and particularly senior women, are seen as incarnations of tradition and as symbols of wisdom, life, fertility and reproduction. The elected *Pachamama* will be escorted by a series of characters associated with the mountains and with carnival and by the Gauchos who circle the plaza in their horses and salute her during the Sunday Parade.

The programme of events lasts from three to five days. Several performances – from local and regional music to various forms of current urban music – have been added to the programme. Amaicha is radically transformed during this annual event. In addition to the flow of summer tourists, the *Pachamama* festival attracts hundreds of people of all ages who arrive from different parts of the region and country, artisans, merchants and migrants who return during this time.

The Sunday Parade marks the climax of the festival. At 9.00 a.m. the '*bombo*', a large drum, is the sound that invites people to gather in the plaza. The '*ramada*', the main stage, has been especially built for this three-day event coming to an end. It will serve as the place where authorities and other guests will sit to attend the parade, surrounding the *Pachamama* Queen. As soon as people gather, men from the local Gaucho Association prepare themselves to ride their horses around the square. Gauchos dressed in traditional clothes carry the Argentine flag and the image of the

**Figure 4.2** *Pachamama* Sunday Parade

Virgin of Mercy, the patroness of the province. Once announced they circle the plaza on their horses, moving the flag and bowing to the authorities.

The Queen is carried in a type of chariot called '*aipa*', which is pulled by a donkey and decorated with local plants and flowers. She is holding a basket containing the products of the harvest. Two carnevalesque characters accompany her: the '*Llactay*' protector of the livestock, and the '*Pukllay*', a goblin who salutes the audience while mocking other characters in the parade. Following them is the '*Ñusta*' or '*Alhajita*', a young teenager, who is symbol of the new crops and of the reproduction of Amaicheño people.

As the *Pachamama* approaches the stage, people in the audience wave her and try to reach her chariot. The basil leaves she carries in a basket, together with peaches, apples and other recently harvested fruit, are tokens of good luck and people will try to reach a few of those leaves to take home.

Local authorities, Gauchos and other guests stand up to welcome the *Pachamama* and her retinue. After being taken up to the stage, the *Pachamama* Queen will be introduced by name, age, place of residence and number of offspring. Behind hers, other chariots and floats continue to parade. Each of them has been prepared by a local institution in town: the school, the cooperative, the bank, the municipality, etc. All of them will yield to salute the *Pachamama*.

The Fiesta provides Amaicha women with an opportunity to occupy the centre stage. In addition to the *Pachamama*, other women perform as *Copleras*. They sing and dance music that combines pre-hispanic rhythms and instruments with traditional or *Criollo* ones. In recent years, these *Copleras* have 'become more Indian' in their costumes and in their music. Moreover, they have stepped outside the stage to continue singing in the streets. Some women gather groups of people in the square and prepare an '*apacheta*', or tell about the uses of indigenous herbs as remedies and amulets. *Copleras* thus, take the initiative in diffusing music, dance, local history and various indigenous beliefs and practices.

In the past, Gauchos were in charge of framing every public ceremony in town. More recently, however, these efforts have been subverted by the apparently chaotic expressions of Indianness outside the traditional scenarios. And *Copleras* have extended their performances beyond the Fiesta. They now perform at other public events in Amaicha and in other parts of the Valley and the country.

These performances serve diverging purposes of maintaining and contesting the social order of which they are part. On one hand, *Pachamama* and *Copleras* are sponsored by the state apparatus. On the other hand, the spontaneous additions and reformulations of their performances are new creations that use the state project but ultimately challenge it by subordinating national loyalties to an Indian affiliation of transnational dimension.

## Conclusions

The expansion of the performances of *Copleras* during this touristic celebration has crucial effects in the reformulation of Indian identity as the main marker of residents of Amaicha. Although at time of the celebration originated Amaicheños have recalled their Indian ancestry, in most contexts they described themselves as Creoles, the bearers of a regional / national identity, whose archetype, the northern Gaucho (a variation of the Gaucho of the Pampas in the South) is an expression of regional pride and patriotism linked to the soil but also to a mixed Spanish ancestry that is markedly Catholic and male.

Since its implementation by outsiders, the *Pachamama* has been reappropriated first by the local elite of Amaicha, and more recently, the committee has included non elite residents, particularly women not bound by many of the lifestyle rules of the local elite. More than the *Pachamama* Queen herself, the *Copleras* and their off-script performances, are slowly transforming this festival into a transnational Andean event. Although it continues to attract a large number of urban tourists from the region and nation and abroad, there is an increasing percentage of migrants who return during this time to join the celebratory events.

The current *Pachamama* celebration challenges gender, ethnic, and social hierarchies of power during the festival, while the *Copleras* stress the importance of embracing Indianness as the main symbol of local identity in Amaicha. In this way, *Copleras* constitute a dynamic and almost subversive strategy to place not only Indian identity but also women's public performances, and more specifically non-elite women's performances, as important expression of Amaicheño identity. Rather than being subordinated to regional and national, male and Catholic affiliations, *Copleras* are providing local and transnational, female and more inclusive alternatives. In the last few years, the annual conference of 'Women in the Calchaquí Valley' is scheduled a week before the *Pachamama* Festival in Amaicha. This event is used to strengthen bonds among women of Calchaquí descent and other residents of the Valley. Thus, through ethnic solidarity, in the process of affirming Indian culture, the women set grounds for discussions on gender, race and other forms of social inequality.

Although ethnic identities are fluid and malleable, they can still be connected to socio-economic processes and concerns from the people who embrace them. I have tried not to separate cultural from economic phenomena, mainly to be fair to the subjects of this study who experience them as inseparable. As Hall and Gilroy have argued, manifestations of Indianness may also be the modality in which class is 'lived' (Gilroy, 1987; Hall, 1992). In various parts of Latin America, Indians see themselves as different from Whites and therefore, Indians are also different from wealthy. In this way, indigenous groups in this region demand both, a recognition of equality as citizens, but also of difference as Indians (Cervone, 1996: 52).

Amaicheños have learned about their Indian past to a large extent from outsiders. For decades, they coexisted with urban intellectuals who enamoured of their town settled in comfortable summer resorts. At the same time, like their fellow Calchaquí neighbours, Amaicheños joined thousands of rural migrants to the sugar plantations since the end of the 19th century. The effects of Peronism in the 1940s, the Dirty War in the 1970s, and the neo-liberal policies implemented throughout the country during the 1990s have caused new forms of expression of their situation. However, while neo-liberalism has created new forms of exclusion and

inequality and new forms of state control, it has also set new alternatives for collective action, operating within the discourses and practices
once proposed – or imposed by elites, state agents and urban intellectuals
(Ong, 1999).

Indian identity in Amaicha is not a mask, or a cosmetic feature that
is only used for economic gain, as some scholars may argue (Cervone,
1998; Hernández, 1992, 1993). It is not just part of some 'strategies' used
by local residents to, borrowing from García Canclini (1992, 1995), to
enter and leave modernity'. Although one dimension of Indian identity
as commodity that can be exploited for economic gain may have been
enhanced by aspects of globalisation and post-cold war identity politics,
other dimensions are part of this cultural resource. Indian identity is also
a site of social and political struggle, where local residents who have
inherited the fear and distrust of the past repression feel that they can
safely use the channels given by state and elites and explore new forms
of solidarity. Their strategies of struggle are slowly broadening the spaces
that young people will use to challenge the official projects in new and
radical ways.

With the influence of Indian movements in the Americas, Indian identity
has become a means of cultural, economic and cultural reaffirmation and
political empowerment of the less privileged within the community.
*Copleras* have continued to establish alliances with other women and men
of Indian ancestry in the Valley, across the region and throughout the
continent. In this way Amaicheños try to reconcile the ambiguous cultural
affiliations available to them at the margins of both the Andes and Buenos
Aires.

## References

Cervone, E. (1996) Los Desafíos de la Etnicidad: Las Luchas del Movimiento
    Indígena en la Modernidad. *Journal of Latin American Anthropology* 4 (1), 46–73.
García Canclini, N. (1992) *Culturas Híbridas. Estrategias para entrar y salir de la Mod-
    ernidad*. Buenos Aires: Sudamericana.
García Canclini, N. (1995) *Hybrid Cultures. Strategies for Entering and Leaving
    Modernity*. Minneapolis: University of Minnesota Press.
Gilroy, P. (1987) *There ain't No Black in the Union Jack: The Cultural Politics of Race and
    Nation*. London: Hutchinson.
Hall, S. (1992) The new ethnicities. In J. Donald and A. Rattansi (eds) *Race, Culture
    and Difference*. New York: Sage Publications.
Hernández, I. (1992) *Los Indios de Argentina*. Madrid, Spain: Editorial Mapfre.
Hernández, I. (1993) *La Identidad Enmascarada. Los Mapuche de los Toldos*. Buenos
    Aires, Argentina: Eudeba.
Ong, A. (1999) *Flexible Citizenship. The Cultural Logics of Transnationality*. Durham,
    NC: Duke University Press.

Stavenhagen, R. (1996) Indigenous rights: Some conceptual problems. In E. Jelin and E. Hershberg (eds) *Constructing Democracy: Human Rights, Citizenship and Society in Latin America*. Boulder, CO: Westview Press.
Tambiah, S., Guidieri, R. and Pellizzi (eds) (1988) *Ethnicities and Nations: Processes of Inter-Ethnic relations in Latin America, South East Asia and the Pacific*. Houston: Texas University Press.

## Chapter 5

# The 'Freedom of the Slaves to Walk the Streets': Celebration, Spontaneity and Revelry versus Logistics at the Notting Hill Carnival

Angela Burr

## Introduction

The London Notting Hill Carnival, frequently referred to as the 'biggest street party in Europe', is held over the August Bank Holiday weekend. The present-day street Carnival started in the mid-1960s. Although Notting Hill is now a wealthy residential area, 40 years ago it was run down. Initially (Cohen, 1993) it was a small-scale, grassroots, localised, voluntary, multicultural event with its roots in local social deprivation and social protest. This area had a large Afro-Caribbean community and by the early 1970s it had become a mainly Afro-Caribbean- and black-led event. However, by the year 2000 it had grown enormously and changed radically, becoming a multicultural mega-event, attracting around a million visitors in 2000 and somewhat less, in subsequent years.

'Carnival', as Carnivalists refer to the event (a usage that will be followed here), has in recent years become a source of controversy and attracted a great deal of criticism and media interest and publicity. The event has been beset by problems, or, at least, it has been seen as such by the media who have conveyed to the public a negative image of it. The statutory stake-holder organisations that provide the event with support services and /or financial help have also been highly critical. For example, the Greater London Authority (GLA) which is the strategic government of London, the Royal Boroughs of Kensington and Chelsea (RKBC) and Westminster City Council (WCC), which are the local District Councils, the Arts

Council, the government arts funding body and the London Metropolitan Police. These problems include crowd congestion and organisational and procession chaos, an alleged increase in crime and violence, including two murders in 2000, health and safety hazards caused by vast quantities of litter, large-scale urinating in the street and deafening noise produced by steel bands and static sound systems. In fact, the Carnival has been described as 'a logistic nightmare'.

Many of the Carnival's problems have been laid at the feet of those responsible for its planning and management, which has come in for heavy criticism and become a source of controversy and political intrigue. At the centre of this is the Notting Hill Carnival Trust (or 'Trust'); the Afro-Caribbean-led voluntary organisation and charity that grew out of the original organisation and management and which managed the Carnival and linked cultural events until 2002. Because of the event's alleged problems, conflict between the Trust Chief Executive and some of the Trustees in 2001–2 which led to the Trust's implosion and dissolution, as well as pressure from some of the statutory stakeholders who wanted to see major changes in Carnival management and organisation, the planning and management of the event has, since early 2002, been undergoing restructuring. This chapter aims to contribute to the ongoing debate as to the form that the Carnival's planning and management should take and it offers suggestions for its improvement and the event's future.

Carnival focuses around participation, celebration, spontaneity, revelry and bacchanal and, as such, fits in with Nurse's (1999: 664) definition of a Carnival. This analysis, in particular, aims to shed light on the dilemma posed by small bacchanalian Carnivals which become mega-events in major western cities, namely how to retain their spontaneity and bacchanalian core whilst at the same time provide the logistics needed for very large numbers of visitors and fulfil the requirements of local statutory regulating bodies (e.g. transport, communications, service provision, public safety and health and safety).

## Conceptual Framework

Much is written in the tourism field about the cultural and organisational content of carnivals, festivals and events, along with practical issues and logistics relating to the planning, and management of such occasions (see for instance: Bowdin *et al.*, 2001; Bramwell, 1997; Getz, 1990; 1997; McDonnell *et al.*, 1999; Shone and Parry, 2004; Sonder, 2004). However, little has been written on how these planning, management and logistic issues are connected to and embedded in cultural constructions of reality together with accompanying issues of ideology, identity, the agendas of participant organisations and political and social discourse. Such issues need to be taken into account, as they have a profound effect on, and play a major role in, determining the form of the planning, management and content of an event, particularly through their structuring of the decision-making processes. They shape the choice and success of new structures and the way problems are constructed, articulated, handled and resolved, as will be seen from this study of the Notting Hill Carnival. This chapter examines the connections that link carnival content, planning, management and logistics to the ideologies and the agendas of Carnivalists and the Trust, and the main service-providing statutory stakeholders who have been critical of Carnival management (such as the RBKC, the GLA and the Metropolitan Police) within the context of the social and political discourse which they are articulated, and the ways in which they centre on the concepts of freedom, ownership and control.

## Carnival Planning and Management

Up until 2002 the Notting Hill Carnival was managed and planned by the Trust, with the assistance of local statutory stakeholders and still with a very much grassroots, voluntary-based approach. This can be characterised by its individualistic, face-to-face, ad hoc, fluid nature but with a strong sense of group solidarity. The organisation contained limited role specialisation and ostensibly had not grown to match the Carnival as the mega-event it had become. This is particularly reflected in the structure of the Trust. Representatives of the five disciplines or 'arts arenas', as they are now called, which make up Carnival (masquerade, steel bands, static sound systems, soca and calypso) sat on the Trust Board. But, in practice, Carnival was essentially a 'one woman' band. Until more recent conflicts, its day-to-day affairs were run by the Chief Executive, a dynamic Trinidadian-born lady who was the driving force behind Carnival for nearly 10 years. She relied mainly on volunteers, including close members of her family, which led some to refer to Carnival as a 'family business'. She was in charge of getting Carnival on the street. She would fundraise, liaise with each Carnival organisation and negotiate with local statutory stakeholders for funding and service provision, such as toilets, licensing, litter collection, the use of parks and roads, etc.

As a response to the murders at the 2000 Carnival, there was a realisation of the need to radically rethink the event's organisation. Under the auspices of the GLA, a Review Committee was set up which included the Chief Executive and a range of statutory stakeholders. This committee had the effect of bringing the statutory stakeholders together, particularly the GLA, RBKC and WCC and the London Arts Board. The Carnival had always been chronically under-funded for a variety of reasons and the Trust had come to rely on local statutory stakeholders for a range of service provision and funding. Seeing in the internal conflict within the Trust a chance to push through and introduce changes that they thought were needed, the statutory stakeholders used their financial clout and withdrew their funding. Carnivalists, unable to get the event on the road without their help, were forced to negotiate with them and agree to introduce changes.

## Constructions of Reality, Ideologies and Agendas Amongst Carnivalists

Carnivalist stakeholders and those statutory service providing stakeholders have diametrically opposed perspectives, ideologies, rationales and agendas, both individual and group, which have played a major role in structuring new management negotiations. However, both groups share a common modality that centres on the concepts of ownership and control, i.e. who owns and controls Carnival as an institution, and who owns and/or controls the streets of Notting Hill over the Bank Holiday weekend. Carnival politics are thus essentially about who owns and controls the event. Competition over ownership and control of Carnival is shaped by each organisation's ideology and agenda and provides a major vehicle through which the latter are articulated.

This competition has been exacerbated by not having an overall director in charge with real power and the loosely structured nature of the alliance between stakeholders down the years, which has often made decision-making difficult and not infrequently led to conflict, particularly between the Trust and some of the statutory stakeholders. The Trust and RBKC, in particular have a history of intermittent conflict. Added to which the GLA, WCC and RBKC have been embroiled in a range of disagreements since 2001 about the content, management and control of the event.

## Ideological Perspectives of Carnivalists and the Carnival Management

Most Carnivalists no longer live in Notting Hill and Carnival has moved on and lost much of its social protest role as Afro-Caribbeans now have other channels for airing their views. Nevertheless, Carnival ideology is still rooted in, and reflects, its original grassroots, loosely structured and tightly knit social organisation. Viewing Carnival from the perspective of Carnival participants, until management changes, Carnivalists claimed ownership of the event and viewed its organisation, management and planning as *their* domain. They were proud of the large numbers who attend Carnival, but in viewing the Bank Holiday event as *theirs* and as a creative performance art, they tended to disassociate and separate themselves from visitors and tourists. They resented and rejected its image as the 'biggest street party in Europe' and 'party in the park image' and poured scorn on the small handful of visitors who caused trouble and gave the Carnival a bad name. Many conveyed the impression that visitors and tourists are irrelevant, and were not a part of their approach when planning the event.

Until 2002, whilst they accepted other ethnic groups as participants, Carnivalists viewed the event as essentially an Afro-Caribbean event and maintained that it should be run by Carnivalists. Rank and file Carnivalists, along with Carnival management, have always accommodated a wide range of diverse and often conflicting perspectives, as would be expected in such an ad hoc grouping, while still sharing a similar core ideology and ethos. Their attitude to ownership and control is rooted in the ethos of the Trinidad Carnival. During slavery in Trinidad, the slaves had not been allowed to walk on the pavements. After the liberation of the slaves in 1834, the Carnival, which had previously been a white and coloured event, was appropriated by the slaves and the notion of the right of the slaves to walk the streets that had become a symbol of their new found freedom, was incorporated in, and became a rationale for, the Trinidad Carnival and a vehicle for social protest.

These beliefs were gradually incorporated into Carnivalist core ideology in the 1970s as Afro-Caribbeans suffering racial harassment and living in deprived circumstances in London during this time could easily identify with the rights of slaves and with the freedom of slaves from slavery. The phrase 'freedom of the slaves to walk the streets' is a phrase Carnivalists actually use themselves to express their perspective. It structures their whole outlook on Carnival and their attitudes to outsiders. From their perspective they have the right to take over the streets and do as they choose in Notting Hill over the Bank Holiday. Any attempt to stop them doing so they view as denying them their freedom and black people their rights.

Carnivalists attach great value to celebration and spontaneity. The term bacchanal is used frequently by Carnivalists. One senior Carnivalist commented: 'It [the Carnival] shouldn't be organised or regulated, it is bacchanal.' Another commented: 'How can the Carnival be organised or have vehicle licensing [referring to a major source of conflict between the Trust and RBKC prior to Carnival 2001], 'People just turn up. We don't know until a few days before who or what is going to be in the procession.' Yet, another commented: 'We don't want it to be a party in the park. It shouldn't be regulated or organised, it's bacchanal.'

As a consequence of their ideology, many Carnivalists feel they don't have to conform to rules and regulations. Community resistance, including resistance to change, is built into the Carnivalist's agenda. Any perceived attempt to encroach on their patch and control Carnival by statutory stakeholders is seen as preventing the 'slaves' from freely walking the streets and denying them the right to celebrate and be spontaneous. It is viewed as a further sign of racism and cultural domination by the wider society and attracts immediate antagonism, resistance and rejection. This commitment to individualism and spontaneity has arguably hindered the development within the Carnivalist movement to introduce the kind of role specialisation, management, planning, financial and logistical organisation needed, and has also deterred an outward looking approach where management ideas or personnel with the right kind of qualifications could be brought in from 'outside'. It also partly accounts for Carnivalist's willingness to allow other organisations to provide services.

Conflict within the Trust is not unique. Confrontation and conflict from the 1970s has been endemic amongst Carnivalists which has been partly fostered by Carnivalists' individualism. This is reflected in, and fuelled by, fierce competition between arts arenas and individuals, which has been fostered by a range of competitions held during Carnival which all Carnivalists want to win or at least do well in. Competition has been accentuated by the overall lack of resources available to the Trust. This internal conflict has exposed Carnivalists to encroaching external organisations.

## Statutory Stakeholder Perspectives

The ideologies of the Carnival's statutory stakeholders can be seen to be diametrically opposed to the Carnivalists and Carnival management. Like all bureaucracies they are legal-rational organisations governed by and implementing local and national laws, rules and regulations and view Carnival and its planning and management from a similar bureaucratic perspective. Critically, they also adopt the perspectives of being an outsider to, and an external observer of, the event.

### Royal Borough of Kensington and Chelsea (RBKC) Council

The RBKC Council covers an extremely wealthy area of London. The Council has a political arm, the elected Council as well as a bureaucratic administration of officers which implements its directives. The steady growth in regulation for festivals and events, particularly via the European

Union and in the fields of health and safety, has manifested itself in relation to the Carnival. As statutory providers of basic services, the RBKC has taken a necessary controlling role with regard to the running of the event. Basic provision for the health and safety of all involved with the Carnival is a priority. This involves registering street traders and food stalls, and the licensing of relevant vehicles through the Road Traffic Act and the general monitoring and enforcement of such activities.

The RBKC as with other local authorities is well aware that in an increasingly litigious society they will be held responsible and prosecuted if any disasters occur due to negligence in the performance of their duties. Given that the 2000 Carnival has been marked by crowd congestion, procession chaos and an increase in crime and violence, it was inevitable that RBKC officials should become anxious and attempt to control the situation. Risk assessment to prevent accidents and disasters has become extremely important in Britain in recent years and pervades the whole Council strategy. It has helped in shaping the Council's attitude to Carnival since much of its involvement and service provision focuses around public safety. Council health and safety officers generally place great value on risk assessment studies since if they have carried out a risk assessment analysis of a particular issue and followed the correct procedures, if there is an accident or disaster then prosecution is unlikely.

The Council has been accused of not wanting the Carnival in its Borough, though there is little overt evidence to support this view. But the political agenda of the elected Council, which feeds into the administration, is certainly influenced by the wealth and voting power of its residents, particularly those that resent Carnival. Wishing to play up to the electorate and be seen to be doing something about Carnival's problems, may have been a motivating factor in leading the RBKC to play a major role in spearheading an attempt by statutory stakeholders to take control of Carnival.

Given the positive value placed by Carnivalists on ownership and freedom and the RBKC's (and this holds for the other statutory stakeholders too) diametrically opposed mandate on the need for regulation, it is almost inevitable that intermittently over the years both parties should have come into conflict. Such clashes point to the essence of Carnival, which goes beyond race or ethnicity and relates to the concept of freedom – however momentary – in this case exercised on the streets of Notting Hill, part of a wealthy London Borough.

In 2001 vehicle licensing became a contentious issue precisely because it provided the Trust and RBKC with an opportunity to articulate their different perspectives and attitudes to freedom and control. The Council demanded, using the Road Traffic Act to support its actions, that the Trust provides the names and addresses of all vehicles taking part in Carnival to prevent crowd congestion and terrorist bombings. In general, Carnivalists viewed this suspiciously and resented having to provide their names and addresses. Some designated it as a sign of racism and a further attempt by RBKC to control them and it was rejected. This induced some Council officials to portray the response of the Trust bloody mindedness, and as an unwillingness to do their job properly and incompetence. As one official put it: 'They think they don't have to conform to any rules.' Without an overall director or co-ordinator to deal with the situation, it was inevitable that the situation should get out of hand and it ended up as a public slanging match aired in the media. Such conflictual attitudes are emblematic of the changes felt in many festivals as traditional modalities of chaos and disorder have given way to the need for regulation, particularly when tourists have become involved.

## The London Metropolitan Police

During the Carnival of 2001 there were over 10,000 police on duty. The heavy policing of Carnival in recent years has been viewed by Carnivalists as an infringement of public freedom. Indeed, Carnival has been described by some Carnivalists as a 'Police Carnival'. One Carnivalist even concluded from an analysis of the history of policing the event, that the police had a full-time press officer and that it had manipulated the media coverage of Carnival over the years as a tool for controlling Carnivalists. Because of the high cost of policing the Carnival (about £4 million in 2001) and the poor publicity that heavy policing attracts, the police announced that they would like to decrease their involvement in Carnival and hand over their crowd control work, which takes up a large proportion of their manpower, to stewards.

Over the years, the Carnival has had, given the large numbers attending, a low level of crime and violence and is no more likely to generate lawlessness than the average football match. Arguably, as an ethnic event, it is also less likely to be attractive to terrorists than the latter. However, the very need for a highly visible police presence to uphold law and order does contrast obviously with some of the more laissez-faire attitudes of the Carnivalists and an ideology of disorder.

## The Greater London Authority (GLA)

The GLA as the strategic government body of London has an attitude toward the Carnival that is also rooted in the culture of regulation and control though more indirectly. When the GLA was established in 1999, it involved itself in London-wide activities and issues, one of which was

Carnival. The murders at the Carnival 2000, which led to a media outcry, provided a pretext for it to become involved with the event. According to a GLA official, in the aftermath of the problems incurred in 2000, the Carnival Committee approached the Mayor asking his help to carry out a survey of the management and funding of the Carnival. Pressure from black workers, including Lee Jasper, the GLA Adviser on race relations, himself a former Carnivalist, also contributed to the GLA becoming involved in Carnival. 'When I became adviser, I wanted to see what we could do to support Carnival', he stated in a lecture he gave on the GLA's involvement in Carnival at the 2003 'On Route, World Carnival Conference' in London. He also made a range of other emphatic and supportive comments relating to the strategic role of the GLA in the Carnival: not as a funding organisation, nor as direct regulators. The GLA's aim, Lee Jasper said:

> Is to raise the level of debate, it seeks to ensure that the first class administration in Carnival is equal to the level of the arts. We need an administration to match, that's where we are weak . . . Carnivalists are lions run by donkeys. . . . The GLA's aim is to take this art form and turn it into the major artistic institution in the country.

The GLA has used a wide range of mechanisms to extend its sphere of influence. One was to be proactive in helping solve Carnival's problems. For example, it employed the Intelligent Space Company to carry out a spatial modelling survey of the 2001 Carnival to find solutions to problems such as crowd congestion. The GLA also commissioned a study of stewarding problems and the feasibility of a stewarding training scheme. To solve some of Carnival's financial problems and to develop Carnival's economic potential it commissioned an Economic Impact Study (GLA EIS) of the Carnival through the London Development Agency, which also included a brief to examine Carnival's management structure. The latter found that in 2002, the Notting Hill Carnival generated approximately £93 million and supported the equivalent of 3000 full-time jobs (GLA, 2004). The GLA used the studies that it commissioned to provide support for any changes that it wanted to introduce in Carnival planning and management.

The GLA, as with the other stakeholders, have all become drawn ever further into the running of the Carnival, as regulators, strategists and critically, as funders.

## Inter-relations between Statutory Stakeholders

The statutory stakeholders, each with different organisational agendas that shape their interactions with each other, have also generated conflicts amongst themselves regarding how the Carnival should be managed, what the content of Carnival should be, the route taken by the Carnival procession and how the event should develop.

The GLA's expansionism and involvement in London-wide activities and issues, not infrequently has brought it into conflict with local Councils, who viewed this expansionism as an attempt to encroach on their patch and interfere with, and take over, their power and responsibilities. Carnival provided an arena for the GLA and RBKC and WWC to articulate their agendas and play out their conflicts of interest.

The GLA Review Committee soon became a forum for articulating, within a legal rationalist discourse, each organisation's agenda and political priorities. It soon became a hotbed of intrigue and conflict on both an organisational and the individual level. This conflict has been played out between at various meetings between the GLA and the local Councils, with the RBKC in particular, competing for influence and control of Carnival. Indeed, relationships by the summer of 2003 between the GLA and RBKC had become extremely negative and confrontational. The procession route, which is viewed as a major cause of the Carnival's problems, particularly crowd congestion, has become a major focus of attention and source of controversy, providing statutory stakeholders with a major vehicle for articulating and acting out their competing positions.

The elected 'New Labour' GLA, is headed by Ken Livingstone, a noted socialist, while both WWC and RBKC are well established Conservative Boroughs. Reflecting the GLA's political agenda, one of the suggestions it aired in its initial Review Committee Report, was that the procession should end in Hyde Park, a Royal Park and a high-class area. This was rejected by the Royal Park authorities and the local Councils partly on health and safety grounds. No doubt, too a reason was that they did not want the park ruined and the area covered in litter. Nevertheless, the GLA remained committed to its point of view. As a compromise, but sticking to its leftist principles, it suggested the following year that it should go across the wealthy Bayswater Road, part of WCC's catchment area. A suggestion quickly rejected by the latter who until then had delegated most of its Carnival responsibilities to RBKC. After this incident the WCC took a more proactive part in Carnival discussion relating to planning and management.

The GLA's use of research and the latter's suggestions were frequently viewed with suspicion by some of the other statutory organisations. 'Where did they get the numbers from' was one comment, referring to Intelligent Spaces' estimation that the optimum carrying capacity at Carnival should be 750,000. A comment was made that the number was drawn out of the air to support the GLA's political agenda. The GLA's reasons for commissioning an economic survey of Carnival were also questioned.

In 2004, the GLA published its long awaited Strategic Review of the Notting Hill Carnival having being scheduled for December 2001 (GLA, 2004). The Review Group was chaired by Lee Jasper. The Report recognised the economic and cultural value of the Carnival but while recognising that the event has 'World Carnival' Status, it pointed out that it lacked the infrastructure and resources commensurate with this label. It further recognised that the perception of the Carnival is dominated more by the associated crime figures than by the economic and socio-cultural benefits it generates.

Critically the Review recognised that lack of structure and representation were contributing to the essential tension between regulation and spontaneity. It stated:

> The history of the Notting Hill Carnival and the reason for its existence are firmly rooted in the ideals of freedom, unity and community empowerment. And yet so much of the language and debate about the Carnival has been centred on how the event should be 'contained'. Until the establishment of a new community-based Carnival organising body in 2003 [London Notting Hill Carnival Ltd.], the majority of the carnival arts community were neither democratically represented within the Carnival management structure, nor legally entitled to influence it. (GLA, 2004: 9)

## Spontaneity and Revelry versus Logistics

With regard to the Carnival's planning and management, concern has been over whether this occasion of celebration and spontaneity is gradually being transformed into a corporate event. Attempts to rationalise and focus upon an urban mega-event for logistical, safety and financial reasons have raised concerns about the sanitisation of the Carnival, loss of its grassroots spontaneousness and its loss of meaning. It is important that the Notting Hill Carnival should retain its celebratory bacchanal core, not only because it is highly valued by the Afro-Caribbean community, but also because it is epitomises Carnival and provides London with such a unique event able to attract tourists. However, in attempting this bacchanalian core clashes have become inevitable between the Carnivalists and those stakeholders who have a duty to service and manage the event in line with the relevant legislation.

What is evident from Notting Hill is that the ideologies and agendas of Carnivalists and service-providing statutory stakeholders need to be addressed, confronted and taken into account and allowed for, particularly if conflict between them is be avoided. Each organisation needs to have greater insight and be more aware of their own agendas and the effect these may have on the other participant organisations. Carnivalists need to be flexible and realistic about the responsibilities and restrictions placed on statutory stakeholders by their organisations, and need to take account of the regulations, responsibilities and legal obligations, they are bound to enact.

Good communication is essential. Part of the problem has been that until 2002 most rank-and-file Carnivalists had little personal communication with statutory stakeholders and most negotiations took place through the Chief Executive. Management changes have enabled Carnivalists to have greater face-to-face contact with statutory stakeholders and thus gain a more realistic and greater understanding of the perspective of and demands placed on the statutory stakeholders. It has made them more aware and accepting of the need for the detailed logistic planning that takes place behind the scenes in Carnival which they used to just take for granted.

This has been enhanced by (and as such should be encouraged and financed) increased numbers of Carnivalists, particularly managers of member organisations, going to management and health and safety lectures and courses. This has pulled them further into the planning and management community enhanced their knowledge of the bureaucratic perspective, approach, discourse and agenda and has helped them develop a more open perspective towards the logistics required.

Statutory stakeholders are generally very knowledgeable about the Carnivalist 'freedom of the slaves to walk the streets' ideology. But rather than dismiss Carnival chaos and disorganisation and expect Carnivalists to renounce their ideology and conform to their rules and regulations, it is argued that there should be a greater tolerance of Carnivalist history and the inherent spontaneous nature of the event. Indeed, although Carnivalist's behaviour may appear disorderly and chaotic, there is usually a rational reason for much of it. As is the case with the big and most famous steel bands arriving late and joining the procession in the late evening, a source of much annoyance to the Councils and the Police, who for logistic reasons, want to finish the procession early. The band leaders have to do so as that is the time when their followers, who come to Carnival to see them, turn up.

Statutory stakeholders need to take into account and work within Carnivalist ideologies and the agendas of the masquerade clubs, steel bands and static sound systems, rather than try to change them radically and rationalise them, which would stifle the event's creativity. This is beginning to occur. Whilst it is *more* difficult to plan the logistic framework of a disorganised and chaotic mega-event, it is possible to do so. A view that appears to be beginning to be taken on board by at least one RBKC official who described his view of Carnival as 'disorderly order'. This view is also recognised by the police who have moved to a more facilitating role, rather than over-policing.

This Strategic Review (GLA, 2004, p.12) recommended that 'legal, finance, management, public safety, business and marketing experience and skills must be present on the board of any Carnival organising body [recommendation 18d].' This seems to emphasise the view of the associated statutory bodies of the need to rationalise and professionalise. Indeed, training in the above areas is also a recommendation of the report. While this can be viewed as a moving away from what some Carnivalists would like, it does have the ring of inevitability about it. Certainly Carnival needs professional specialist officers, especially if the very negative image of it created by the media is to be improved. This would include a full-time media officer to develop long-term relationships with the media and a full-time permanent Road Director to oversee and organise the procession.

## Conclusion

This study has shown that Carnival is essentially about control. Who controls and manages Carnival is a fundamental issue since it will influence the form that the event will take. There is a clear need for a balance to be struck between sound management and professionalism to minimise the pitfalls that the Carnival suffered in 2002 and between maintaining it as a public occasion open to tourists as well as the local community, and losing the essential creativity and spontaneity that has hallmarked the event and which ultimately provides it with meaning.

Critically, though not unusually, funding is a key issue for the Carnival. To retain some degree of balance, Carnivalists need to achieve some financial independence and find alternative sources of income. Many mega-events gain vast incomes from major sponsorship and yet in the past the Carnival has only been able to obtain short-term major sponsorship, partly because of its negative image, partly because of underdeveloped business skills, a lack of professional specialisation, internal Trust politics and a lack of enthusiasm by big business to become major sponsors of black events. In 2002 it obtained none at all. The suggestions that have been made for making the Carnival more economic, and indeed better realising its economic potential, could well threaten the event's spontaneity, creativity and performance arts.

In fact, carnivals and festivals are frequently used by urban and national governments to attract tourists to a city and enhance its economy. Caribana in Toronto, Canada, has been used as an example of such by the GLA who have indicated that by similarly turning the Notting Hill Carnival into a tourist attraction this will encourage even larger numbers of visitors to attend. If Carnival became a London-wide event, most tourists would want to see the Carnival procession and there would be even greater numbers of tourists in the locale of Notting Hill and this could lead to problems of crowd congestion. Increases in numbers with attendant controls (increased policing, stewarding, crowd control, etc.) could restrict the spontaneity and free flow of the Carnival procession through the narrow streets of Notting Hill. It would turn a participatory bacchanalian event into little more than a highly controlled spectacle.

These core tensions between large-scale public and smaller-scale private, between creativity and good management, between the staged and the meaningful, are common to many festivals across the world, particularly in urban settings. Tourism is bound up in these tensions. Whilst it may be desirable for tourists to freely engage in the spontaneity and revelry which mark out the Carnival, operational, management and control issues can play a role in creating a more subdued and, to some, a less meaningful experience for all participants. Carnivalist and statutory stakeholder ideologies, when opposed, are likely to come into conflict regularly in all such mega-events. In 2003, one of the Trinidad Carnival Associations sued the National Commission, the government agency in overall charge of the Carnival, ostensibly over a funding issue, but in effect it related to who was seen to 'control' the event. It appears from this study that the constructions of reality, ideologies and historically informed agendas of Carnival stakeholders need to be understood reflexively as part of the process of achieving a bridge between the values, traditions and practices that make Carnival what it is and, the rapidly shifting audiences of the event and an increasing number of stakeholders.

## References

Bowdin, G. *et al.* (2001) *Events Management.* Oxford: Butterworth-Heinemann.

Bramwell, B. (1997) Strategic planning before and after a mega-event. *Tourism Management* 18 (3), 167–76.

Cohen, A. (1993) *Masquerade Politics, Explorations in the Structure of Urban Cultural Movements.* Oxford: Berg.

Getz, D. (1990) *Festivals, Special Events and Tourism.* Reinhold: Van Nostrand.

Getz, D. (1997) *Event Management and Event Tourism.* Reinhold: Van Nostrand.

GLA (2004) *Notting Hill Carnival: A Strategic Review*. London: GLA.

McDonnell, I. *et al.* (1999) *Festival and Special Event Management*. Chichester: John Wiley & Sons.

Nurse, K. (1999) Globalization and Trinidad Carnival: Diaspora, hybridity and identity in global culture. *Cultural Studies* 13 (4), 661–90.

Shone, A. and Parry, B. (2004) *Successful Event Management*. London: Thomson Learning.

Sonder, M. (2004) *Event Entertainment and Production*. Chichester: John Wiley & Sons.

*Chapter 6*

# The Making of Community Identity through Historic Festive Practice: The Case of Ashbourne Royal Shrovetide Football

Scott McCabe

> *Nowadays we are always on the move. Many of us change places – moving homes or travelling to and from places which are not our homes.*
> Bauman (1998)

## Introduction

This chapter addresses the idea that the condition of post-modernity has impacted upon the local meanings of festivals and events. It is often assumed that in developed societies these 'conditions', including the omniscient gaze of the media as well as touristic consumption, have led to loss of a feeling of community identity. Yet this chapter seeks to present an example of an historic event that demonstrates the very real ways in which communities can retain a sense of belonging and identity despite forces of social change. It seeks to understand how the processes of event organisation, the attitude of locals and their sense of ownership and community belonging, work to maintain an historic event in its traditional form despite increasing attention from the media, tourists and the process of population change in the locality. By 'traditional form', it is not intended to mean some absolute stasis. Rather, the argument is that the formal structures of an event provide pivots around which incongruent social transformations cohere. Thus, it may be possible to explain how communities can both 'move with the times' yet retain a sense of their distinctiveness and thus, a strong community identity. As such, it is proposed that events and cultural festivals can work to promote and increase a sense of community identity that can counteract the largely negatively constructed impacts of global mobility and media attention. This chapter focuses on the Royal Shrovetide Football Game in Ashbourne, Derbyshire in the heart of the UK Midlands region.

Ashbourne is a small market town that is known locally as the 'gateway to Dovedale' (a local beauty spot). It lies in a valley on the southernmost tip of the Peak District National Park, the first National Park to be designated in the UK in 1949 (Glyptis, 1991), and the second most-visited National Park in the world with between 22 and 26 million visitors each year (McCabe & Stokoe, 2004). Hence it receives much trade from the tourism industry as it lies only 2 miles south of Dovedale, a local beauty spot made famous in 1655 by the publication of Isaak Walton's *The Compleat Angler* and now owned and managed by the National Trust. The town also provides the focus for tourism in the southern part of the Peak District as it provides a good range of shopping facilities, both amenity and leisure shopping, and since it lies outside the planning control of the National Park, it has become the focus for people moving into the area who may not be able to afford the premiums on houses within the Park itself. Therefore the town has recently seen many structural changes including the move from more traditional industries to modern service-based economies including tourism. (For example, the cattle market in the centre of the town has recently been closed and developed for housing. Also the secondary school was previously split in two sites, one of which has closed and developed for housing, the other being expanded to accommodate a rise in student intakes.)

The Royal Ashbourne Shrovetide Football Game is an historic mass participation game played each year on Shrove Tuesday and Ash Wednesday throughout the centre of the town. There is evidence to suggest that these forms of games were once commonplace in England, but they were all halted during the Victorian move to factory production systems, urbanisation of the workforce and the move to 'rational recreation' forms of leisure activity (Clarke & Critcher, 1985). It is often mentioned in news reports of the game that these forms of leisure illuminate the origins of conventional football and rugby games today, but there is no firm evidence that these games are based upon the early mass participation events. There are virtually no rules, no boundaries to the play, no limits on who can play, and how the play proceeds during the game, and so to an outsider the game more resembles a riot, havoc wrecked upon an unsuspecting, quaint, rather up-market Georgian town. As such, the game provides an interesting case study not only in the sense that it is an anomaly, a remnant of a distant era, almost totally out of context of the modern world, but exactly *because* of such anomalousness. The interesting analysis lies in understanding how the game manages to overcome the pressures exacted upon it by modernity, but also in understanding the community identity politics, why the townspeople manage and strive to ensure that it continues against all the pressures. The chapter begins by outlining how community identity is shifting in response to forces of modernity before going on to describe the historical context of the game, and finally on to analyse how the certain conditions work to maintain community identity and sense of place.

## Community Identity and 'Sense of Place'

There is little doubt that post-modern societies are distinguished by the amount, pace and rate of mobility (Urry, 2002b). Lash and Urry argue that the 'post-organised capitalist order' (1994: 12) is characterised by being information-saturated, service-rich, communications-laden, making relationships between people and places more ephemeral. For Giddens (1990), as societies move towards post-modernity, the conventional relations between 'space and time' become more abstract and emptied of meaning. Such theories in the context of the political economy have profound impacts upon social structures of local communities leading to changes in community identities (Morley: 2001; Urry: 2002a). Morley argues that through post-modern accounts, ideas of home and homeland have become unsettled. The mass media infused landscapes in which we all now exist are characterised by a range of cultural anxieties that arise from this 'destabilising flux' (Morley, 2001: 426). The relationships between the strange and the familiar have become problematic, the processes of physical and virtual migration in contemporary societies through actual travel and mass media representations, bring alterity into the quotidian world and vice versa (Baumann, 1998; Morley, 2001). Featherstone puts this argument succinctly, that it is 'often assumed that we live in localities where the flows of information and images have obliterated the sense of collective memory and tradition in the locality to the extent that there is "no sense of place"' (Featherstone, 1990). However, these meta-theoretical global debates on the conditions of post-modernity can be contrasted with the perspective of everyday reality, those processes by which ordinary people conceive their sense of community identity, and how these conceptions work to achieve and maintain a feeling of belonging, or inclusion within a community.

Interesting recent theoretical work has contrasted the largely pessimistic, global political economy position, especially in terms of the significance of local narratives, festivals and events in the making of cultural (regional or local) identities. In a recent article, Bird (2002) discusses how local narratives about places are interconnected with the creation, and more specifically the maintenance of, cultural identity constructions. She asks 'how does this construction of place [through cultural narratives] contribute to a sense of cultural identity?' (2002: 521). In focusing not on the multiplicity of narratives about place but rather, a drawing together of different 'stories', or legends, about Minnesota into a broader set of arguments describing how a sense of place is achieved through the narratives, Bird suggests that situated social actors use stories to make sense of their lives within their cultural settings. From this perspective, leisure is meaningful for people in their constructions and presentations of self (e.g. Kelly, 1983; Rojek, 1995). Place is both a physical and socially constructed reality and therefore has meaning to ordinary people intrinsically (Lefebvre, 1991, see also Harvey, 1993). In the context of narratives, Bird argues that:

Through our tales about place, we mark out spatial boundaries, which may extend over a whole town or just over a particular space – a bridge, a hill, a lake. The tale confirms that this piece of space actually means something, and it may also tell us who belongs in that space and who does not. (2002: 523).

In the case of the High Bridge at Stillwater, Minnesota, Bird identifies how folklore and legends are disseminated throughout the area and from generation to generation through the popular telling of stories in the community. Bird concludes that probably most people in the community do not believe these ancient tales, yet members of the community continue to 're-create and re-create' (Bird, 2002: 542) these folks tales of the past as they relate to *their* sense of belonging to the place. In this way, 'home' is created as a symbolic association between actual physical places, and stories connected with the past and the people of those places.

Some cultural theorists question the true extent of mobility in local cultures at all. Morley (2001) discusses transformations in the idea of 'home' both as the physical space of the home and also the symbolic ideas of *Heimat* the 'spaces of belonging' (2001: 425), or a sense of identity in different geographical scales. In the current social theory of 'hypermobility' (Morley, 2001: 428), new understandings about the idea of 'home' need to be developed. Morley argues that in Britain at least, there is much evidence that contradicts the argument that society is highly mobile, citing that; 'the majority of people in the U.K still live within one hour's journey time of their relatives and within 5 miles of where they were born' (2001: 429). Class is a key issue in discussing mobility, since economic capital is necessary to enable mobile cultures. But specifically in response to changing cultural norms and values in post-modern societies, Morley misses the chance to celebrate the obverse of the coin – the occasions through which communities join together, locals, outsiders, migrants and tourists participating in an event, celebrating tradition and community in an inclusive, changing, but not commodified, sense of excitement, thrill and good fun. There are a number of case studies on festivals and events proposing that such events contribute greatly in locating community identity through acts of celebration and communality (De Bres & Davis, 2001; Hubbard & Lilley, 2000; Seaton, 1997). In recent work, I have argued that in relation to touristic experience, there is a blurring of the conventional theories distinguishing touristic reality from everyday life, the qualities of, and interactions within, places of 'abroad' and the domestic space (McCabe, 2002). Here in this chapter the focus is on the community, and the methods through which communities can retain a sense of collective identity notwithstanding the forces of post-modernity. These themes can be explored in the context of the Ashbourne Royal Shrovetide Football Game, to which this discussion now turns.

## The Heritage and Characteristics of the Ashbourne Royal Shrovetide Football Game

The analysis that follows rests upon a number of sources of data. Firstly, the author undertook a period of secondary, largely historical data collection. The main sources of information here are historical texts and past issues of the *Ashbourne News Telegraph* (ANT), a weekly newspaper that produces a special edition each year on the game. This data was collected over a period between 2001 and 2004. This was backed up by two periods of ethnographic, participant observation research in 2002 and 2004. Informal interviews were conducted as the researcher followed the game, recording events with a camera and making field notes, which were subsequently transcribed. Follow-up interviews were also conducted in 2004.

Porter (1992) argues that the history of these mass football games goes back a thousand years, possibly brought over to England by the French, but first recorded in around 1175. Robertson (1967), however, traces their history as a means for recreation back to Homer's descriptions of handball games at the time of the destruction of Troy. Firm evidence of the existence of these games in the UK though dates back to an attempt to stop a Shrove Tuesday game in Chester 1533 (Robertson, 1967). Recent news reports suggest that Henry VIII had a pair of football boots commissioned for his wardrobe in 1526. 'They were ordered so that the King could take part in a

football match on Shrove Tuesday, the one day of the year when the game
was traditionally played' (Chaudhary, 2004). This form of street game was
characterised even then by its brutality and lack of rules. However there
remain few places where the tradition continues to this day (similar mass
football games are held in Workington, Sedgefield in County Durham,
Kirkwall in Orkney, Alnwyck in Northumberland, with a small number
of related games held in Devon). Porter points to the many striking simi-
larities between the Ashbourne game and that played in the Kirkwall 'Ba
Game' in Orkney, described in rich historical detail by Robertson (1967), as
evidence of the once-widespread popularity of these games. The fact that
only a handful of games survive in modern times is substantially due to
the havoc, destruction and inconvenience that these games wrecked upon
the local people and the ruling classes. Porter (1992: 254) cites Llewellyn
Jewitt's 1821 'Derbyshire Ballads', published in *The Reliquary* in 1867: 'The
game has been played from time immemorial until "put down" by the
strong arm of the law – not without much unpleasantness and strenuous
opposition – a few years ago.' This 'putting down' was effected partially
through the implementation of part of the Highways Act, but there were
other local difficulties in Ashbourne's history recorded by Porter, including
the sad death of a young man in the river at the Clifton goal, and drunkenness accompanied by fighting which marred the game for many years in
the late 19th century.

The Ashbourne game is played annually on Shrove Tuesday and Ash
Wednesday supposedly to provide fun and amusement prior to the
austerity of Lent that follows. The game focuses around two teams. There
are no strict guidelines as to who can join in and on which team one
should play, there are no distinguishing colours or dress. Although the
game has changed considerably form its beginnings, including how the
teams are organised, the current system is that anyone born north of the
river Henmore (which runs through the centre of Ashbourne) is on the
'Up'ards' team, and anyone born south of the river is on the 'Down'ards'
team. Robertson (1967) argues that the game was usually played between
men from two local parishes, and in ancient times, the town was split by
the river into two discrete communities. The ball is 'turned up' (hurled
into the baying crowd) from a podium erected in the main shopping car
park in the town centre. The custom is that a dignitary not from the town
turns the ball up on the Tuesday, but on the Wednesday it is done by a local
person of standing. The goals are 3 miles apart, roughly 1.5 miles equidis-
tant from the town centre on the site of two old mills (Clifton and Sturston).
The goals are now the mill wheels and are positioned in the river to make
scoring that little bit more difficult. A goal is scored when a player strikes

the ball on the mill wheel three times. The ball may be kicked, carried or thrown, but generally proceeds in a series of 'hugs' and remains invisible to the spectator. The game starts at 2 o'clock in the afternoon, when a specially prepared ball – larger than a football, made of tough leather and filled with cork that weighs around 4 lbs – is thrown into the 'hug', waiting below the podium. The balls used for the Shrovetide games are made by Ashbourne man John Harrison. Local artists Stuart Avery and Tim Baker paint the balls. Balls are usually painted in a design relevant to the person turning up the ball. The balls are a work of art and take a few weeks to paint. If the ball is goaled, then it will become the possession of the person who has scored it. If the ball remains un-goaled, then it is returned to the person who turned it up to keep. In 2002, Tuesday's game was won by the Up'ards when Kirk Maskell goaled the ball at 9.20 p.m. The ball for Wednesday's game was turned up by the Mayor of Ashbourne, Tony Millward. That game was a draw, as no one had scored by 10 p.m., which meant he took the ball home with him. In 2003 there were three goals scored, one on the Tuesday for the Up'ards, and one goal for each team on the Wednesday. In 2003, the game once again received Royal patronage as the Prince of Wales turned up the ball on the Wednesday, similarly to 1928 when the then Prince of Wales (later Duke of Windsor) first gave the game Royal approval. In 2004, neither team managed to score a goal so the balls became the property of the people who *turned* them up.

Perhaps, this rather perfunctory definition of the game does no justice to the sense of excitement and thrill that pervades the atmosphere of the town during these two days each year. Figure 6.1 shows the play in the river Henmore. Despite often freezing temperatures, the play will remain for much of the day in the water. In order to provide testimony to the enduring and rich tradition of this game, perhaps this description of the game taken from the reference work, *The History and Topography of Ashbourn and the Valley of the Dove* (Author: 1839 unknown) and quoting from Glover (*History and Gazetteer of the County of Derby*, Vol. 1: 310), may provide more sense of the colour of the game:

The game commences in the market-place, where the partisans of each parish are assembled, and, about noon a large ball is tossed up in the midst of them. This is seized upon by some of the strongest and most active men of each party. The rest of the players immediately close in upon them, and a solid mass is formed. It then becomes the object of each party to impel the course of the crowd towards their particular goal. The struggle to obtain the ball, which is carried in the arms of those who have possessed themselves of it, is then violent, and the motion of this human tide heaving to and fro, without the least regard to consequences is tre-

**Figure 6.1** Hunting for the ball in the local river

mendous. Broken shins, broken heads, torn coats, and lost hats, are among the minor accidents of this fearful contest, and it frequently happens that persons fall in consequence of the intensity of the pressure, fainting and bleeding beneath the feet of the surrounding mob . . . the crown is encouraged by respectable persons attached to each party, and who take a surprising interest in the result of the day's sport. (Author unknown, 1839 59. Edition used, published in 1978)

Although this short description goes no way towards a full elaboration of the nuances of the game, it provides a useful context to some of the themes that appear to interact within the local community that enables them to continue holding this traditional event, maintain a sense of their identity in the face of forces of societal change outlined earlier.

## Creating and Maintining Community Identity

### 'Tradition' as glue binding the community

The whole premise for continuation of the game is that it is rooted in tradition, something that is largely unique to Ashbourne and handed down in much the same format from generation to generation. Analysis of the local newspaper coverage of the event, together with interview data, reveals a discourse of the town's tradition as being the driving force for continuance of the game. 'Its a traditional game unique to the town although there are variations of it but its played in the modern world and that causes terrible upsets and difficulties for the committee' (interview with John Harrison – maker of the Shrovetide balls).

The local people have enjoyed a reputation for hospitality and friendliness for many centuries, Ashbourne having a good reputation for its markets and fairs (cf. Author unknown, 1839: 57–8. Edition used, published in 1978). This reputation extends to the present day, when the yearly influx of tourists making their way to the Peak District National Park or visiting the town during the Shrovetide Football Game, is mostly welcomed by the local people. One of the reasons that the game has survived must in part be because of the good-natured behaviour of the local Ashbourne people, borne out by one of the many songs about the Ashbourne game, performed by a comedian (a Mr Fawcett) in the Ashbourne Theatre in 1821:

> I'll sing you a song of a neat little place
> top full of good humour and beauty and grace;
> where coaches are rolling by day and by night
> and playing at football the people delight.
> Where health and good humour does always abound
> And hospitality's cup flows freely around
> Where friendship and harmony are to be found
> In the neat little town of Ashbourne . . . '

(Quoted in Porter, 1992: 185)

The game attracts much media attention both locally but also internationally, the game featured for example on the 'Visit Britain' website on a section peculiar English pastimes, but the majority of visitors are local people returning to visit for the week (what I refer to as 'ex-pat' Ashburnians), bringing with them friends and visitors from within the immediate vicinity. In an interview in the ANT souvenir edition 2002, Mr John Gadsby (Chair of the Shrovetide Committee for 17 years) is quoted as saying in relation to the increasing worldwide media coverage received by the game (one Japanese film crew having hired a helicopter in 2002 to film the event):

> Its nice for Ashbourne to be on the front pages, but it is really our own private game. We have to keep the right balance. Enough publicity to satisfy curiosity and little enough so it goes unnoticed by the general population of the country. It is a private game really, though theoretically anyone can play. (ANT, 2002: 18).

Despite the changing nature of the game, the duration of the game has recently been shortened and the continuation rules (when a ball has been scored) altered, there is a strong sense that media portrayals and coverage in the souvenir issue dwells on the heritage and tradition of the game. Headlines including emotive language such as: 'Ashbourne must preserve its "beautiful game"' and 'Culture changes – but the passion remains' coupled with numerous interviews and reportage devoted to the challenges of staging the present game, its role in the town's heritage, and the use of narratives of games in the past all work to solidify a sense of the link between the event now, its role in providing a sense of the uniqueness of the place, and a strong focus on the history of the town.

The use of photographs from the late 19th and early 20th centuries, the board containing the roll of honour (the names of ball throwers and scorers from the late 19th century onwards placed in the Green Man Hotel – the central meeting point for the event), the traditional timing and sequence of events during the two days on which the game is played, all serve to strengthen community identity through continuity. Knowledge of the sequence of events, the particular language and terminology of the game, the meeting times, obtaining tickets for the Shrovetide lunch, knowledge of the Shrovetide song, carrying aloft the person turning up the ball through the streets at a particular time are an essential part of the ritualistic incorporation of traditional rites of the game into the modern event and works to distinguish those who know and practice the traditions from those who do not.

In Figure 6.2, we see the members of the organising committee receiving the new scorer's board in its new position in the Green Man Hotel in the centre of the town, which also acts as the conventional meeting point for the committee and the traditional venue in which the Shrovetide luncheon is held. This photograph comes from the souvenir edition of the ANT in

**Figure 6.2** The organising committee receiving the new scorer's board

2000. The roll of honour provides a reference point for local people to connect memories of events past, goals scored, and also to relate their current practice to an enduring and mythical tradition. It is included in full in every year's special edition of ANT. Family names that are distinct to the local area are represented in abundance and this in itself endows the members of the modern game with a sense of ownership in terms of their involvement in the game (Mr C. Purdy, my own great, great grandfather – a champion penny-farthing cyclist – turned up the ball in 1892). Through the act of recognition of those who have both turned up the ball – itself a great honour – and scored with it, a focus is provided for the attentions of the younger generation. Interest is stimulated and maintained; there is a constant reminder on display of the importance of the game to the townspeople. The link between historical events and the modern game is vital in the continuing popularity and community participation in the game, and therefore it is argued, a deep sense of community identity. In the ANT edition of Wednesday 25 February 2004, an article 'Youngsters are taught the rules of the game' describes how two previous goals scorers have made visits to local schools to 'talk to pupils about the traditional game' (ANT, 2004b). The purpose of these visits was to encourage young people of the town to take an interest in the game, participate properly in the game, to respect the town's tradition. As the interview with John Harrison revealed, 'people move into the town and don't understand the heritage of the game'. As the town succumbs to the forces of post-modern social mobility, the game becomes at once more threatened but also more protected. Young people are 'taught' the heritage; positive role models promote the game and participation in the town's unique sport in school but also in the wider community. Nothing from the research suggested that social change is viewed as negative or undesired, but as something that just happens naturally, the main problem identified was that the 'rules' had to be respected. However, considering that the entire game is constructed as being without 'rules' or limits, it seemed incongruous that this discourse of obeying the 'rules' should emerge.

## The significance of the 'rules' and roles

It was discovered during the research that knowledge of the rules works to establish a person's legitimate participation in the event, it authorises credence and empowers 'locals' to talk to other local people in an informed and warranted manner. Although it is the lack of formal rules that makes the game unique and such an attraction to outsiders, there are subtle and distinct rules both that are drawn from the Shrovetide Committee as a means to control the event, and also within the unwritten procedures of engagement in the game itself. To be considered a 'local', one must not only appreciate the rules of engagement, but also understand the significance of hierarchy within the teams. The hierarchical organisation of the teams means that people have specific rules to follow and roles to play.

In Figure 6.3, it is not possible to distinguish members of each team; however, the players know who their team is.

Each team is comprised of a core of larger, heavy men who play in the 'hug' (the mêlée at the centre of the ball – most akin to a Rugby Scrum and identified on Figure 6.3 by the people at the centre of the steam cloud on the upper right of centre) and faster-paced 'runner' whose role is to run with the ball should it break free from the 'pack' (in Figure 6.3 we can note that a number of 'runners' are hanging on the boarding around Partners stationary store). Those who are established members of the team (people who have played the game since they were children) and

**Figure 6.3** Crowds at the game

have never missed, nor would ever miss a single match, can expect to be central players, and may expect also to be scorers of the ball someday. Scoring of the ball is also subject to unwritten rules. A senior member of the team will be responsible for the drawing of straws to decide on who should be allowed to score the ball should the occasion arise that the team becomes in the position of scoring. Informal interviews with local people reveal that such 'fixing' is having a negative impact upon the way they see the game. For example, Cate (not real name) argues that this fixing has 'taken the essence out of the game'. The rules of the game, both unwritten and articulated more formally by the Shrovetide Committee (which has been in existence since 1892 and is essentially responsible for the game), make clear the legitimate knowledge required to enable people to position themselves as part of the community and through either playing the game or by being a spectator. The Shrovetide Committee now produce a leaflet that is distributed throughout the town during the event. It lists areas which should be avoided by players and spectators (all private property, churchyards, cemeteries, hospitals and grounds, memorial gardens), identifies times and rules pertaining to scoring. This leaflet uses emotive language to try to instil a sense of the tradition and also respect for the rules. For example, under the heading: 'Respect for people and property: Although this is a tough and sometimes rough game, the players respect other people's property. If our game is to continue in the years to come, you must help by ensuring that you keep away from no-play areas and avoid causing damage' and further on: 'Pressure in a modern age: It is a tradition which could so easily be lost in the name of "progress". It is "progress" which has led to the loss of buildings, habitats, wildlife, ancient pastimes and much of the fabric of the countryside. The pressure on us in Ashbourne to conform to the dictates of ever increasing European and national legislation is a very real and insidious threat. We have a responsibility to take care of our game so that our children's children continue to enjoy the unique pleasure of playing Shrovetide football in the streets of Ashbourne.'

Of course all this rhetoric is aimed not at the players but the spectators who also play a vital function. Spectators participate not only in supporting the players, but also in adding to the general thrill of getting embroiled in the play should the ball become 'loose'. Spectatorship is an intrinsic part of establishing the community. There are clear roles for women and men in the play of the game and spectatorship. Women 'follow' the 'ball', by following the men, their men, and by taking their children to watch thereby inculcating a sense of identity as an Ashburnian. There are also women players, however, but for the majority theirs is a peculiar role, responsible for telling stories of events past, providing sustenance whilst the men are playing (I observed a large number of women carrying water bottles for their sons and husbands to take refreshment), and all spectators, men and women, working to provide a legitimate narrative of the events of the day, in what can often be a very confusing and contested game. Talking to people during the event, it was noticed that people ask each other what has happened, where the ball is now, has it been goaled all the time. Following the ball also serves an important function. Not only do people meet their friends and relatives whilst in the act of spectatorship, they shore up their identity as members of the community. In reality there are long periods of lack of movement in the play, this allows men and women a chance to catch up with talk and also allows the men to take turns to rest in between the action. Social relationships are re-established and renewed, as people mingle and chat and meet up with old friends, supporters of teams and particular players can discuss tactics and make arrangements for meeting later in the evening, or the month or the year. The game provides a vital link in the yearly social cycle of the town, and many people I spoke to during the two days argued that the only reason they come out at Shrovetide is to meet up with old friends (not to play or follow the game) thereby reinforcing social ties and friendships.

## The effects of patronage in the game and on local arts

The impact and effect of patronage by the establishment is not lost on the local people and organisers of the game. This is effected through the selection of influential persons to turn up the ball (such as members of the Royal family in 1928 and 2003). In 2004 the ball was turned up by Sir Richard Fiztherbert, a member of the local landed aristocracy whose family have been feudal rulers of a nearby country estate for hundreds of years. In the ANT edition of Thursday 26 February 2004, the speech given by Sir Richard at the Shrovetide lunch was described. He recounted how his uncle, the last Lord of Tissington, turned up the ball in 1980 and according to the article, Sir Richard had researched his uncles speech for the occasion: 'Sir John had referred to the "yobbish footballers" of the day, commenting that they could well take a few tips on their behaviour from Ashbourne's game of mass football, a tradition which Sir Richard stressed, must be preserved locally.' Therefore the interaction between welcoming important, influential members of the establishment into the game whilst retaining a distinct working-class feel to the membership of the Shrovetide Committee and certainly the playing of the game, is an important factor in the games' enduring ability to survive pressures of modernity. Such patronage lends credibility and status to the game and has the effect of negating the opposition to the game. Opposition comes, not only from newcomers into the town, some of whom do not support the yearly rampage through the streets and gardens, causing much damage to personal property. But also, opposition comes from some locals and businesses. Local people are fully aware that they tread a fine line between having a free hand in the town during these two days of festival and being responsible for their own actions. There is much celebration in the towns numerous public houses during these two days, in no small part due to the timing of the event, which often means that the weather is bitterly cold. This timing (weekdays in February/March) also has the effect of making the game less accessible to masses of tourists. There is much evidence that suggests that the game is difficult to justify in such circumstances as the interviews conducted with committee member and ball-maker, John Harrison shows. He recounted that each year there are growing claims made for compensation for damage to property, and the work of the committee is focused upon trying to get insurance cover for the games, establishing a limit to the responsibility of the committee for damage in individual circumstances and liaise with the public services on issues of order and culpability. This aspect of the game has presented a perennial problem. Therefore the event needs patronage not only in the old-world sense from the nobility, but also in the modern sense in terms of co-operation from the police and the local authorities, from the schools (half-term holidays are rearranged in that part of Derbyshire to coincide with the event), from local businesses, from the highways authority, and most of all from the people who come to visit and take part.

The most likely explanation for the ability of the Ashbourne game to continue to survive into the present day must surely be due to patronage of the ruling classes. There has always been a substantial prosperous ruling class in and around Ashbourne, and the relationship between the ruling class and the working classes appears to have been good and harmonious (according to the *Ashbourne and the Valley of the Dove* reference work, the town was prosperous and substantial in size (equal to Nottingham, Litchfield and Derby – now all much more developed) from the 17th century right up until the early 19th century. Porter later describes how the authorities attempted to suppress the game at Ashbourne during the period 1860–91, mainly due to disturbances caused by drunkenness and fighting, but also he argues due to a lack of interest by the community in continuing the game. However, the game became legitimated thereafter partially through patronage, and Porter notes that players were cheered on by 'respectable' supporters (1992: 74). This patronage has made a related contribution to the development of community arts and crafts. It has already been mentioned that the balls are made and painted by local artisans and artists who have learnt their trade over many years, the skills and techniques being passed down through the generations. Figure 6.4 shows Tim Baker, one of the artists who paint the balls. However local painters and ball-makers are not the only people for whom the football game provides artistic inspiration. Local people have found that the game and the community identity it engenders provides a platform for them to create artistic expression through writing and photography as well as in terms of the physical arts and crafts associated with the game such as the ball-making and painting. An example comes from the ANT (10/3/94) with the publication of a local builder's short story on Shrovetide football.

I argue here that the fact the event has such an effect upon the local people, that it garners creative expression, that local people find support and patronage confirms the strength of feeling locally about the game. The game continues and succeeds in retaining its sense of originality in postmodernity through complicated interactions between the historic and the modern, the rules and the roles of individuals involved and the continued

**Figure 6.4** Local artist and ball painter, Tim Baker

support of the establishment, and so, a strong sense of community identity is made possible and maintained through this event.

## Concluding Remarks

This chapter has sought to describe how an historic sporting event can contribute to a continuing sense of community identity in the face of pressures of change associated with the condition of post-modernity. It was argued that given the peculiar characteristics of the game, its lawlessness and a seeming lack of rules and limits, being played in the streets of a popular tourist town, suggest that special conditions must apply to enable the game to survive. People who play the game are responsible for organising it, those who argue for its discontinuation are not only outsiders but also frustrated local people, whose land or gardens have been trampled and spoiled, whose daily lives are affected by the mayhem that surrounds the town for more than a week. There is continual negotiation and renegotiation within the community. There are inevitable tensions that arise out of the modernisation process as people move into the town to live and media interest grows, such as increases in insurance claims for damages, the growing and shifting sense of community that comes from the town being one of the principal gateways into the Peak District National Park, yet all of the issues seem to have little consequence for the people of the town for whom the game plays an integral part of their sense of belonging.

In the case of Ashbourne's football game, a sense of place is made not through legend or recreation of events, but in a determined effort to continue the event as a means to provide a symbolic system of continuity to the past. Thus, authenticity is not the key issue here, rather a sense of belonging, the ability to tell stories about the events of previous years both in the build up to the Shrove Tuesday and Ash Wednesday games, and in telling stories after the game, help to establish a community knowledge that is often passed down from generation to generation. Being a member of the community extends as far as one can tell and relate stories about the games, personal experiences and knowledge of events past, as the physical taking-part in the games is such a hit and miss affair. With up to 10,000 people taking part at any given time, the establishment of community sense of place, is made more through sheer fun and excitement and thrill, and through the physical proximity of people playing the game, knowledge of the routes and channels around and through the town (the town is little changed in the centre from Georgian times, and there is a warren of hidden yards, alleys and channels that connect and divide houses, roads and places of work). Without the ability to name key places where key events took place, members are established as outsiders. Yet to be cast as an outsider is not a negative in the case of the Ashbourne events.

The game is played in the full knowledge that people have for centuries visited the event and the town and will continue to do so for centuries to come. Outsiders have a limited impact on the game due to the unwritten but well-defined rules of the game. But also because so many people, Ashbourne's diaspora, return to visit during this event. There is a continual flux in the society, and this is an accepted feature of the social life of the town during the event. Outsiders are largely welcomed, people who settle in the town are often made to feel part of the established community, and they are expected to participate (though in approved ways). Perhaps interlopers contribute much towards the game's continuance in a circular fashion, their interest providing greater impetus to continue the traditional form, which in turn is an attraction and helps sustain interest from the local population. The traditional form of the game: its unruly characteristics, the timing of the event and the characteristics of development of rules and roles by its people together create a strong and sustained sense of community identity. The data discussed illustrate the connectedness of local media reportage to the making of community identity and the forceful processes by which 'locals' are made distinct from 'outsiders'. I argue that far from being a threat to a sense of community, in the case of the Ashbourne Royal Shrovetide Football Game, outsiders provide local people with one more explicit demonstration of what makes Ashbourne people unique. Outsiders appear to be welcomed rather than tolerated, included rather than excluded, yet cannot be classed as 'local' unless they participate in the spirit of the game or the physical playing of the game, and accept its formal structures. These traditional forms connect locals, diasporas and outsiders despite whatever discontinuities in social life occur beyond the game. Participation is the key to this strong community identity, participation in the game, spectatorship, the organisation, and participating in the ideal of a heritage event, connecting community to individuals in a real, inclusive fashion.

**Note**
1.   Although it is clear that Glover referred to the Derby game and not specifically the Ashbourne game, which he clearly states is a more recent phenomenon, the games in each town were played in much the same way, and continue as such in Ashbourne.

**References**
ANT (incorporating *The Derbyshire Advertiser and the Uttoxeter News*) (2002) *Ashbourne Royal Shrovetide Football Souvenir* (special edition) 14 February 2002.
ANT (incorporating *The Derbyshire Advertiser and the Uttoxeter News*) (2004) 24 February 2004.
ANT (incorporating *The Derbyshire Advertiser and the Uttoxeter News*) (2004) *Ashbourne Royal Shrovetide Football Souvenir* (special edition) 25 February 2004.
Author unknown (1839; facsimile edition made 1978 used) *The History and Topography of Ashbourn and the Valley of the Dove*. Buxton: Moorland Publishing.
Bauman, Z. (1998) *Globalization: The Human Consequences* Cambridge: Polity.
Bird, S.E. (2002) 'It makes sense to us': Cultural identity in local legends of place. *Journal of Contemporary Ethnography* 31 (5), 519–47.
Chaudhary, V. (2004) Who's the fat bloke in the number eight shirt? *The Guardian* 18 February 2004.
Clarke, J and Critcher, C. (1985) *The Devil Makes Work: Leisure in Capitalist Britain*. London: MacMillan.

De Bres, K. and Davis. J. (2001) Celebrating group and place identity: A case study of a new regional festival. *Tourism Geographies* 3 (1), 326–37.

Featherstone, M. (ed.) (1990) *Global Culture: Nationalism, Globalisation and Modernity*. London: Sage.

Giddens, A. (1990) *The Consequences of Modernity*. Cambridge: Polity.

Glyptis, S. (1991) *Countryside Recreation*. Harlow, Essex: Longman in association with the ILAM.

Harvey, D. (1993) From space to place and back again: Reflections on the condition of postmodernity. In J. Bird, B. Curtis, T. Putnam, G. Robertson and L. Tickner (eds) *Mapping the Futures: Local Cultures, Global Change* (pp. 3–29). New York: Routledge.

Hubbard, P. and Lilley, K. (2000) Selling the past: Heritage tourism and place identity in Stratford-upon-Avon. *Tourism Geography* 85 (3), 221–32.

Kelly, J.R. (1983) *Leisure, Identities and Interactions*. London: George Allen and Unwin.

Lash, S. and Urry, J. (1994) *Economies of Signs and Space*. London: Sage.

Lefebvre, H. (1991) *The Production of Space*. (Donald Nicholson-Smith, trans.). Oxford: Blackwell.

McCabe, S. (2002) The tourist experience and everyday life. In G.M.S Dann (ed.) *The Tourist as a Metaphor of the Social World*. Wallingford, CAB International.

McCabe, S. and Stokoe, E.H. (2004) Place and identity in tourist's accounts. *Annals of Tourism Research* 31 (3), 601–22.

Morley, D. (2001) Belongings: Place, space and identity in a mediated world. *European Journal of Cultural Studies* 4 (4), 425–48.

Porter, L. (1992) *Ashbourne Royal Shrovetide Football: The Official History*. Ashbourne: AE Press.

Robertson, J. (1967) *'Uppies and Doonies': The Story of the Kirkwall Ba' Game*. Aberdeen: Aberdeen University Press.

Rojek, C. (1995) *Decentring Leisure: Rethinking Leisure Theory*. London: Routledge.

Seaton, A. (1997) Unobtrusive observational measures as a qualitative extension of visitor surveys at festivals and events: Mass observation revisited. *Tourism Management* 35 (4), 25–30.

Urry, J. (2002a) *The Tourist Gaze* (2nd edn). London: Sage.

Urry, J. (2002b) Mobility and proximity. *Sociology* 36 (2), 255–74.

*Chapter 7*

# 'Days of Radunica': A Street Festival in the Croatian Town of Split

Anka Misetic and Ines Sabotic

## Introduction

Street festivals and their social life are characteristic of many Mediterranean towns. In this chapter we are particularly interested in the street festival 'Days of Radunica', one of the largest and most notable public festivities organized in the Croatian town of Split. 'Days of Radunica' was first held in 1994, only three years after Croatia achieved its independence. The festival has been held at the end of June every year since its inception and forms part of a wider context of political and societal transformation in Croatia. During the 1990s, Croatian society had been affected by changes that were common to the majority of European ex-socialist countries following the adoption of democratic processes in the political systems and a shift to Western European-style market economies. Such a shift has raised important questions regarding social and cultural identities, and how society functions in a new civic culture. As Cifri (1995) points out, one result of these changes has been the deconstruction of the existing system of values and the need to replace it with a new structure. It is in this context that we wish to observe and understand the 'Days of Radunica' festival, since it originates from a time when new social elites, values and identity models were in the process of being legitimised. It is important to note that this festival is not a 'revived tradition' of the numerous rituals that were extinguished or repressed during the period of socialism. Unlike other town rituals dating from the pre-communist time that have been revived and almost authentically re-instated by Church initiatives and with the help of government and media support, 'Days of Radunica' is a product of civil society and expresses the desires and ideologies of residents of the urban quarter of Radunica.

Originally, Radunica was the name of a main street of the quarter of Lu ac (which used to be on the outskirts of Split in the past), but it is now often used to refer to this whole quarter – an intersection of one main street and several smaller alleyways, all built in the same medieval urban style. It is an area with a long, urban tradition that influenced the way of living, as well as the types of sociability pervading the town. From a sociological perspective, 'Days of Radunica' therefore represents a fascinating example of an 'invented ritual' using 'tradition' as one of its major reference points. The approach of this social event allows us to analyse the processes underlying the contemporary phenomena of 're-traditionalisation' and 'horizontal societal stratification', which appear to be linked to the shaping of new communities or groups calling for 'their place' in the emergent public spheres.

## On Split and its Festivities

Split is the second largest town in Croatia and a centre of the Dalmatian region. Situated on the Adriatic coast, it has a 1700-year-old history. This is witnessed in the form of the old historical core, constituted by an antique palace of rectangular shape with high walls surrounding it, built by the Roman emperor Diocletian (around 295–305 AD) who, after his abdication, spent the last years of his life there. Over the centuries, a medieval town was built within the walls of this palace, which has today become a huge pedestrian zone (30,000 m$^2$) with narrow alleyways and small squares. History is 'written' all over the walls of the old Split, with its monumental limestone buildings dating back to the Roman times, its refinements of the Venetian Renaissance, traces of different European architectural styles and epochs, and modern infrastructure.

Split's *place memory* (*lieux de mémoire*) is to a significant extent defined by the historic antagonism between the Roman Diocletian and the first Christian Archbishop Doimus (*Duje*). By choosing this place for his summer villa and, later, his principal residence, the Roman emperor gave Split a touch of exclusivity. His contemporary, Doimus, the first Archbishop who lived in Salona, an ancient town in the close proximity of the Palace, introduced Christianity to the town. Doimus was later executed by the order of Diocletioan. The death of the Archbishop was understood as a martyr's death and became a symbolic reference point, first for the town's identity, and then for national identity. This was accentuated some time later when the Christian Church officially recognised the Archbishop as a saint. Shortly after Christianity became an officially recognised religion in the Empire, Salona developed as an ecclesiastical centre. In the beginning of the 7th century, the invasions of Avars and Slavs forced the inhabitants of Salona to take refuge in Split. At the same time, the Church found a peaceful shelter in Split as well as a new centre for its activities and Dio- cletian's mausoleum was turned into St Doimus Cathedral.

Under mostly Byzantine administration until the 10th century, Split was integrated in the Croatian Kingdom (which became the Hungarian-Croatian Kingdom) in 1102. This position benefited Split in both economic and socio-political terms. The Palace was transformed into a medieval town, its urban territory spreading out north, east and west of the Palace walls. The eastern outskirts of the town – named Lučac – where the street Radunica is located, were inhabited mostly by craftsman and farm labourers who built churches for their own needs (for example, the church of St Peter). During the medieval period this quarter was characterised as a town quarter (*urbs*) as opposed to the outskirts (*burgus*) (Novak, 1978), but still it retained essentially rural characteristics. The government adminis- tration keeps on changing through the turbulent town history.

The medieval 'free commune' was replaced by the Venetian admin- istration (1420–1797), then by the Austrians at the beginning of 19th century (1797–1806), followed by the French (1806–13), and then, again, the Austrians, under the Hapsburgs (1813–67) and then the Austrian-Hungarian Empire (1867–1918). As a consequence of these differing periods of political administration, Split has absorbed different traditions and cultures. Economic development, however, did not always follow, par- ticularly during Austrian-Hungarian rule when Dalmatia was effectively cut off from Austria. Although the Croats from Croatia and Dalmatia are of the same nation, administrative differences as well as economic under- development disabled a possible fruitful cooperation. While the most of Europe had reached full industrial development, Split retained an essen- tially rural character (in 1910, 6000 of its 21,500 inhabitants were farm labourers) and remained under-developed (Novak, 1978).

Throughout the 18th and 19th centuries, public festivities in Split bore the characteristics of religious ceremonies. For example in the 18th century, during the Day of St Doimus, one of the most celebrated festivities in Split, all the citizens – Venetian administrators, soldiers, noblemen, fraternities, etc. – took part in the celebrations and gathered around and stood behind the statue of the saint – a collective symbol that united the community – sending it off on the way to the church. Central parts of this celebration were the procession and the mass. On that special day everybody wore his or her finest clothes, the town was decorated, the coast was lit up with torches, thick wax-candles and lanterns, and musketeers fired from *mascolo* swivel guns. The town municipality also provided financial aid for the oils and candle wax for the altars of St Doimus and St Anastasia, and for monastery charities. On the day of celebration there were also numerous folk feasts and games: singing contests, folk dances, regattas,[1] *giostras*,[2] fist fighting, tossing the stone (from the shoulder), walking races, and different games of strength and skill, with the town municipality donating prizes for the contestants. Fireworks were also organised (financed by the Archbishop) to entertain the crowds.

On the Day of St Doimus, according to certain local rules, the government granted an amnesty to prisoners and outcasts (Božić-Bižančić, 1982). Public areas, such as streets, town squares and yards, played an important role because they were 'open' to everybody, enabling the whole community to meet. This bears comparison with the traditional role of town squares and streets in the ancient, medieval Mediterranean towns where, during similar occasions, those public areas turned into large open-air stages allowing viewers to also become, at the same time, active participants. We can see that religious festivities were not only a moment of spiritual renewal, but also of social renewal as well, as these venues of urban sociability were approachable to all and provided an opportunity for the whole community to meet in one place..

At the beginning of 20th century, as part of the general processes of modernisation and secularisation, such forms of religious festivities were steadily pushed aside and allowed to disappear as an expression of social life – a tendency that is less visible in the segments of society that experience a rather slow time-frame for industrial development and modernisation. In the case of Croatia, the secularization of society is directly linked to the country's historical and political context. In the political systems of the 20th century, the First Yugoslavia (1918–41) replaced traditional Mediterranean and Middle-European references with those of the Yugoslavs and the Balkans. At the same time, the Independent State of Croatia (NDH) (1914–45) and the socialist Yugoslavia (1945–90) selectively tried to erase the idea of 'national' history and Christian traditions. As a result, folk festivities with a religious character were transformed into secular, almost exclusively, political celebrations (Rihtman-Auguštin, 1990, 1992).

From the 1970s, the town of Split kept on being developed, revived and reinvigorated with the arrival of new residents from the rural hinterland and the islands to work in the town. But, as opposed to other parts of the town where huge skyscrapers were built and where the street ceased to be a gathering point for the people, the urban quarter of 'Radunica' retained its medieval appearance and qualities of being gentle and human. It is no longer in the outskirts, as it used to be during the Middle Ages, but has become a part of the inner town, fully belonging to the historical core of Split in its appearance and characteristics. In the early 1990s, the quarter entered a new period of development and the 'Days of Radunica' festival partly revived a long and fascinating history based on Christianity and the sociability found in other Mediterranean towns; a history almost extinguished during the period of socialism.

## As if it Were the Celebration of St Peter's Day

The 'Days of Radunica' festival is held during the last week of June since it officially refers to the celebration of St Peter. The setting of the town-quarter itself today forms part of the parish of St Dominics but there are still very strong historical links between Radunica and its former patron saint – St Peter – whose church was demolished during the Second World War and was not restored on the site. Besides St Peter's Day, there are other religious celebrations in June: the Day of St Anthony (13 June) whose chapel also used to be in the locality of Lučac, and the Day of St John (24 June). Still, 'Days of Radunica' excels all of the aforementioned church holidays. One of the reasons for this festivity not to institutionalise with any particular saint lies in the fact that today in Radunica there are no preserved churches or parishes of those saints. There are no official organisers of such ritual celebrations of cult figures, no mass and no procession. The only thing that is preserved is a collective memory of the former 'divine patrons' that used to be part of everyday life in the past (through sacraments and religious ceremonies) and who today are recalled only on a symbolic level, such as they were experienced and remembered by the common people.

In this 'intimate' relationship between patron saints and the people, there is no interference from the 'official Church', therefore this ritual only partially falls under the category of a 'cult figure/patron saint'. Thematically, this festivity is a 'combination' of a cult figure ritual and a 'situation' ritual with accentuated elements of play. Although the saints are no longer the main characters around whom the scenario of the celebration unfolds (as it is the case in the St Doimus Day celebration), their presence plays an important part in maintaining continuity with the past. This continuity of existence is an important foundation for every community so that it presents itself to its members and other people as a social formation resistant to time; as a community that exists and endures, affirming its own importance and value.

The perception of this street festival as a *new town* ritual is confirmed through the structure of the participants/organisers and the previously mentioned manifestation of the detachment of civil society and citizens as active participants liberated from the dual tutorship of government and the Church. A group of citizens that are mutually identified through their belonging to the same locality, regardless of social, educational and other status differences and thus ignoring the characteristics that stratify them 'vertically', come together united by their identity bonds. Double detachment (from the government and the Church) is expressed in the following ways.

Firstly, this detachment is seen through the autonomous activity of organisers who appear as, at least, to be an equal partner to the government. From the official authorities the organisers expect (possible) sponsorship and (absolute) non-interference with festival protocols. As a result of that, there are no usual 'addresses of welcome' or 'self-promotion' of those who attend the celebration to 'perform their official duties'. To be a *member of Radunica* becomes a characteristic beyond competition, therefore to be a *member of the government* loses its general meaning and strength of legitimacy. Even when they make an appearance in the celebration, the town mayors (different politicians exchange this role) are just guests (citizens) and communication with them does not follow standard protocol.[3] Furthermore, members of authorities are often received with slight irony. This is best reflected in the centerfold article of the *Days of Radunica Bulletin* from 1997, entitled: 'Superiors change – Radunica stays!'

Secondly, the detachment of the civilian sphere from the Church (although allies during the period of socialism) is a process inseparable from modern democracy. In this case, it is almost 'over-stressed' since we are now witnessing a celebration of saints (the formal motive) without the participation of the Church. Should we stay faithful to this partition of active participants/organisers, it is notable that elementary schools (falling within the category of 'public institutions'), actively participate in this festivity in several ways such as: greeting with the headmaster, holding a small reception party at the school and a special programme organised by the pupils, etc. As the *Days of Radunica Bulletin* (1997) reads: 'School is in the festivity, festivity is in school. The best liaison officers are the school choirs, their fan-supporters and their teacher with a guitar, full of love and patience.' Various cultural associations, traditional folk-choirs, musicians and other 'associations of citizens' are also engaged in this celebration together with elementary schools.

Therefore, in distinction from the traditional public festivities where the government authorities and the Church are the chief organisers and the saints are the central figures, this is a festivity in which the citizens play all the central roles. The people of Radunica have thus become the organisers as well as the motive for this gathering, the administration (clerical as well as secular) has been rejected and only the saints remain as a symbolic liaison between the generations of the past, present and future.

## The 'Traditions' of the Festival

The fact that this town ritual is a representation of the already familiar case of inventing new rituals by use of traditional elements (Hobsbawm & Ranger, 1983) is emphasised by the organisers in their own 'festivity analysis': ' . . . it gave to its hometown Split . . . certain new-old mood for the St Peter's Day' (*Days of Radunica Bulletin*, 1996). Apart from the use of traditional heritage in forming a new street festival, this new 'festivity' wanted to establish itself and 'become' a tradition since its success and continuance depend directly on it. Thus, the realisation of this goal is dependent on successfully combining old (traditional) and new (modern) elements. The proportions of these elements in this ritual event can be considered through several dimensions.

### Name

So-called 'language retraditionalisation' preceded, and possibly even initiated, the organisation of the 'Days of Radunica'. Since the Second World War the name of the street where the festival is located was *Trumbićeva*,[4] but in 1992 the street was given back its old name *Radunica*, which probably originates from the water-springs that used to exist in this locality, one of which still functions.

### Media

Depending on the financial support from sponsors, a special bulletin is printed on the occasion of the 'Days of Radunica' festival. In distinction from the regular reports of this event in the press, the *Days of Radunica Bulletin* is at the same time a part of the ritual and its product. Thanks to this bulletin there is a written account of these street festivals, which helps in reconstructing the development of the event, providing information on the organisers, participants and a general profile of the ritual. This bulletin acts as both an invitation and an identification card for the festival and its participants. It is also a reminder of the history of this part of the town drawing upon preserved historical documents and often being scripted by some of the older citizens of the community.

## Language

The practices of the festival act to're-traditionalise' language and this is demonstrated in several ways. Speeches and public addresses are conducted in dialect and this is also mirrored in written form used in the *Days of Radunica Bulletin*. There are 'evenings of poetry', held since 1996, to promote 'fair speeches', where Split poets recite poetry in the Dalmatian dialect of Chakavian. Dialect in this sense is used as one of the strongest identity points of festivity, together with instances of word play and humour.

## Scene

The location of the event ensures a traditional scenography. The typical medieval entanglement of narrow streets with serried houses made of stone (albeit with some modern interventions) provide a backdrop that generally appears as pre-modern. One intervention that was made in the area (and that was probably induced by the mobilising force of the 'Days of Radunica' emphasising the 'authenticity' of the street festival) was that the asphalt road surface was removed and replaced by traditional limestone blocks. In addition, 'modern' streetlights were replaced by the traditional lanterns *(ferali)*. These interventions in the scenery (which, at the same time is inseparable from the real, everyday environment) have provided an authentic, traditional ambiance in spite of certain modern-day additions such as electric lights in different colours, streamers and banners.

## Clothing

The most noticeable garment, which is also a symbol of this festivity is a modern T-shirt (sewn up according to general modern standards) with the printed name of the festival written in local dialect so binding the modern with the traditional. Apart from the performers (musicians, singers, etc.) and 'official hostesses', nobody wears traditional clothes. Still, one of the 'accessories' notably worn is a traditional hat that used to be worn by local farm labourers.

## Food and Drink

In line with many festivities traditionally prepared food and drinks are specially chosen and recommended for this occasion. These include fish, wine and traditional sweet desserts such as *'fritule'*[5] and *'kroštule'*.[6] However, it is also possible to find sandwiches, hamburgers, Coca-Cola, beer and other similar products of the modern age.

## Dramatization of the Performance

The daily schedule of events is well established revealing the structure of the celebrations. The opening ceremony includes jumping over a bonfire on the eve of St John's holiday, in line with traditional and characteristic celebrations. During the following days (the festivity ends on the first Saturday following St John's Day – thus the number of days differs each year) various competitive games with prizes are organised for the participants. These are usually traditional games such as card games, various sport contests, and games of strength and skill. These games hold an important place in the scenario of the 'Days of Radunica'. The ones that especially stand out are the 'children's marathon' (a modern version of a traditional race along the waterfront) and a 'card tournament' in *briškula* and *trešeta*[7] whose winners receive a (material) prize and also an enhanced reputation in the community. Sports successes are fully covered in the *Days of Radunica Bulletin*.

The importance that is given to sport surpasses the active participation in it. The *Days of Radunica Bulletin* gives considerable coverage to sports, mostly via articles that remind readers of the famous native sportsmen of Radunica. This reporting also upholds the idea of the special value of being a member of the community and strengthens social identity. For example, in 1999, famous sportsmen of Radunica were given two full pages of text in the Bulletin. In the same issue there is a typology of children's games that classifies a list of traditional games 'combining' several different criteria (time, place, gender). The article lists games in each of the following categories: 'in the courtyard; on the street; in the meadow; in the field; football; girls; Lent and Easter; Advent and Christmas; sea'. Presented like this, the 'old' traditional games form a commemorative guide through communal heritage.

Besides games and sports, there are other organised events during the festivity such as art exhibitions, evenings of poetry, etc. On the last day of the festival (which is always a Saturday) a large-scale celebration is organised (over a thousand citizens of Split 'pass through' Radunica on that evening, and many families accommodate their relatives from the other parts of town) with offers of free fried pilchards and homemade wine. There is also a bingo, and a concert of pop music. The entertainment, comprising concerts of singers and traditional choirs and poetry readings, is usually organised according to a modern-day model using announcers and a raised stage. This segment uses the formula 'something old, something new' with traditional choir singing, children's choirs, modern pop-singers and brass bands, but also with the usual sound-background typical of modern bars and coffee shops. Thus, one of the principles of the festival stated on the front page of the 'Days of Radunica Bulletin 1996' reads: 'You have a democratic choice!' relates even to the selection of music. The local community are least concerned about the traditional in the music of the festival.

Regarding the dramatisation of the performance of the festival, there is a clear combining of traditional and modern elements. However, these elements, although appearing together do not penetrate all the segments of the dramatisation with the same intensity and magnitude.

## The Social Functions of the Festival

This multi-day street festival is rather heterogeneous regarding its social functions. Two stand out. The first relates to the mobilisation of the community and is suggested by numerous actions undertaken regarding the embellishment of the street in which the whole community partici-pates: asphalt replaced by limestone blocks, traditional lanterns put up so the street is restored to its traditional appearance, and competitions organised with prizes for the best-decorated house and balcony.[8] The second function is commercial and can be seen mostly through higher con-sumption and increased earnings in local restaurants, bars, coffee shops and stores during the days of festivity. Both functions also relate to what the town has to offer tourists.

The festival and its rituals perform a therapeutic function for the community (providing a 'break in everyday life') and is reflected in the numerous games and entertaining events that comprise the festivities. The organisers themselves, concluding on the effects of the festival point out the opportunity to 'gather round, sing, be merry . . . '

The integrative dimension of this ritual is also emphasised, especially through strengthening the feeling of togetherness amongst domicile residents and settlers by accentuating the *mystical qualities and powers* of Radunica in 'enforcing' the unique lifestyle and system of values to the settlers of different social backgrounds. In this sense, the *Days of Radunica Bulletin* (1996) notes an interesting discussion on the legitimacy of the President of the Organizational Committee who is by origin a *vlaj* (inhab-itant of the rural hinterland). His social position is emphasised through the following words:

> . . . he was a hinterlander for 20 days only; on the twenty-first he stepped with his delicate foot in Trunbučac (a small street connected to Radunica) and has learned ever since, all the improprieties known to life in Radunica . . . Today he's a fine piece of a man, sings like a

nightingale . . . he's diligent and kind to children ( . . . ). He works in the school, plays ball, plays cards really well . . .

This initiation of *vlaj* into a *fine piece of a man* results in the end with the acceptance of community identity as one's own identity. This process leaves out the strict and definite procedure found in the traditional (but also in modern) 'ritual of initiation'. Still, on a symbolic level this procedure is retained in the sense of accepting specific elements of tradition such as songs and games etc.

Restoration and confirmation of identity is accentuated as a dominant function. This concerns primarily the identity of a community defined by affiliation to: (1) a town street – actually a small town-quarter; (2) the town of Split – since this town-quarter clearly presents itself as its representative; (3) Christian culture; and finally (4) post-modern society. In this sense, the 'Days of Radunica' can be regarded as a ritual event that provides an opportunity to all members of the community (including – temporarily – tourists) to publicly participate in celebrations and therefore symbolically confirm an acceptance of the 'traditional' community and an affirmation of their identity. Nourishing this identity based on traditional heritage confirms itself through preservation of old practices, the reminding of significant figures from the past, accentuating the (Chakavian) dialect that linguistically differs one group from the others, selecting traditional garments, music, food and other elements of celebration.

Speaking of selective acceptance of the past, it is interesting to identify the things from the past are being preserved, nourished and regarded as important for a community, from the ones that are being disregarded. Why are certain symbolic locations given preference over others? Which festivities are remembered and carried over through time, taking an important place in collective mind of the citizens? Regarding the 'Days of Radunica', none of the elements of the celebration are imposed; rather they are a clear reflection of free choice of the local community. Similarly, certain locations have a privileged, symbolic value to particular communities. Both historians and sociologists try to understand and define the past, through these symbolic locations, using certain elements that constantly reoccur. It seems that among the traditional elements that appear as part of the 'Days of Radunica' there are no significant traces of the great empires of Rome, Venice or Austria. Instead, the elements that are being carried over from the past are the elements of national, folk heritage and figures of patron saints that provided constant and spiritual sanctuary for people living in this politically turbulent territory.

Such retraditionalisation is also interesting as a phenomenon bound to sociability. At the same time it indicates the references used by a certain society for the construction of its identity. New social identity that in the 1990s filled the gap that was created through the collapse of socialist values, and partially leaned on what the community regarded as its own significant past. Therefore, this celebration can also be observed to be a reflection of the meaning of history and tradition in modern society. 'Days of Radunica' is a result of a particular reading of history and tradition. We have seen how far from 'true' tradition they really are. The function of tradition in this celebration is to provide for an additional value, as a sign of endurance and existence. What was common and traditional has now become urban and cultural and therefore through this festival, the tradition of folk festivities is interpreted and presented as a heritage of the common and traditional classes of the old Split.

## Conclusion

The case of 'Days of Radunica' analysed here and most of the traditional elements used – though presented under the name of Radunica – are not the exclusive heritage of this locality. Without question Radunica belongs to the same (broader) cultural circle where traditional heritage provides inspiration, but the novelty here is that the lack of local tradition is being compensated for by the use of elements from neighbouring, kindred traditions. Identity is thereby confirmed not only through genuine traditional elements, but also through an 'original combination' of elements from other traditions.

The plurality of themes and motives in this case makes it difficult to distinguish if this is a cult figure celebration (the central motive as 'officially' stated in the *Days of Radunica Bulletin*) or a folk festivity, a modern 'situation' ritual aiming not at ensuring further protection of a saint, but rather providing a therapeutic break from everyday life. Hence, the touristic value of this street festival also lies in its openness that can offer every visitor 'therapeutic' relaxation as a possible escape from the pressures of a modernised and increasing globalising world. This ludic element, or the element of play, combined with the picturesque heritage of a Mediterranean town, presents the prospect of becoming a permanent part of the tourist offer of Split in which the local community presents itself in a particular and outstanding way.

This study shows that festivals are used as a way of defining one's own continuity in ever-changing circumstances, and as a way to confirm identities and legitimacies in the current process of transition and restructuring of Croatian society. The initiative in this does not come here from town officials or tourist agents who sometimes are given the task of contriving such programmes. The festival portrayed here originates spontaneously, as an authentic expression of a living local community possessing a special value and cogency. Without restraints or imposed models, the society reinvents certain repressed elements of its own social identity and reintegrates them in its contemporary history which, on the symbolic level, can first be noticed in its festivities. Although the retraditionalisation of social life in European cities can be said to date from the early 1970s and 1980s,[9] it can be said with almost complete certainty, that the process of retraditionalisation in Croatia was not possible until 1990 when the opportunity for the development of pluralistic society arose.

Besides explanations within specific and local circumstances, it is also necessary to understand the phenomenon of this street festival in the global context. Although 'Days of Radunica' is motivated by reasons of keeping tradition, this ritual appears to be more of a post-modernist social gesture. There are more reasons for that, but we believe that the most important one is the way in which tradition is used, resulting in a specific post-modernist social manifestation: a modern, urban ritual. The lack of confidence in the omnipotence of science, as well as the pluralisation of culture, and of ways of life and relations towards tradition in general, have 'prepared the ground' on which it has been possible to 'construct' modern urban rituals that combine traditional and modern elements without any strict rules. This basically means that certain elements are singled out from the traditional heritage as circumstances require. This possibility of choice goes further into dimensions of time and space. In the time dimension it means that the 'new-old' ritual, such as 'Days of Radunica', includes medieval games and 18th-century costumes, at the same time recalling festivities from the beginning of the 20th century. The use of tradition, or the process of retraditionalisation, as a post-modern manifestation does not restrict itself to only one specific event that is being 'faithfully' reconstructed – more often it is a new event built on elements from all different traditional layers. However, these restrictions are not set aside only on the basis of time or age. They are also annulled in terms of space, allowing the takeover of other, mostly close/kindred, neighbouring traditions.

Generally, street festivals clearly reflect the mentality and the spirit of a town and its citizens, because of their minimal formality and their extensive 'space' for witticism. They satisfy a great deal of needs for sociability in local communities. The street festival 'Days of Radunica' can be seen as a certain response by a local community in its search for its expression and identity in new social circumstances. By marking the 'Days of Radunica' festival as a 'new-old mood', the organisers themselves have somewhat defined the nature of this event as a completely new ritual with strong traditional references. Since it enables the encounter of tradition (permanence) and modernity (novelty), a sociological analysis of this modern-day phenomenon should be placed in its historical context as well. Through time festivities have often changed their causes and themes, organisers and sponsors, times and places of events. Time is an important dimension, because it gives us the opportunity to see continuity as well as novelty and the transformations of events. Here, history does not only give us a time perspective referring to what is new, but it also becomes a part of the present time of one society.

**Notes**
1. Popular valiant competition, a spectacle.
2. Chivalrous games, sometimes on horses; by the 19th century the only one that remained was the *alka* game.
3. This non-protocol communication emphasizes informality. For example, the *Days of Radunica Bulletin* reads: 'The Mayor is always in good temper when in our company, so he started a song . . . '
4. Ante Trumbić (1864–1938) was Croatian politician.
5. Miniature donuts with raisins.
6. Fried bow-shaped sweet pastry.
7. *Briškula* and *trešeta* are traditional card games typical for the Dalmatia region and also for Mediterranean region.
8. All issues of the *Days of Radunica Bulletin* report on those events.
9. For more detail see articles published in miscellany (Boissevain, (1992).

**References**
Boissevain, J. (ed.) (1992) *Revitalizing European Rituals*. London and New York: Routledge.
Božić-Bižančić, D. (1982) *Privatni i društveni život Splita u osamnaestom stoljeću*. Zagreb: Školska Knjiga.
Cifrić, I. (1995) Sociologija u novom socijalnom kontekstu. *Društvena istraživanja* 4, 2/3 (16/17), 241–64.
Hobsbawm, E. & Ranger, T. (ed.) (1983) *The Invention of Tradition*. Cambridge: Cambridge University Press.
Novak, G. (1978) *Povijest Splita* (Vols I and II) Split: Matica Hrvatska.
Rihtman-Auguštin, (1990) Metamorfoza socijalističkih praznika. *Narodna umjetnost* 27, 21–32.
Rihtman-Auguštin, D. (1992) O konstukciji tradicije u naše dane: ritualim simboli i konotacije vremena. *Narodna umjetnost*, 29, 25–43.

*Chapter 8*

# Enhancing Vitality or Compromising Integrity? Festivals, Tourism and the Complexities of Performing Culture

Melanie Smith and Kathryn Forest

## Introduction

The aim of this chapter is to discuss the complex inter-relationship between festivals and tourism. It has long been recognised that festivals and tourism have a history of mutual benefit (e.g. Adams, 1996; Hughes, 2000; Quinn, 1996; Rolfe, 1992; Zeppel & Hall, 1992). Kirschenblatt-Gimblett (1998) describes how festivals afford visitors the perfect opportunity to engage with a destination and to penetrate the quotidian. This may include a glimpse of the so-called 'backstage' (Goffman, 1959) rather than a commodified experience of 'staged authenticity', but the difference is not always that easy to define. Authenticity is clearly a complex and contested social construct, especially in the postmodern era of globalisation. Some authors have argued that the 'post-tourist' is largely uninterested in authentic experiences (e.g. Rojek, 1993; Urry, 1990), and others (such as Boorstin, 1964) suggest that tourists actually go out of their way to seek *inauthentic* experiences, such as staged or 'pseudo' events. However, other authors have maintained that many tourists (especially cultural tourists) are seeking meaningful contact with local and indigenous people (e.g. MacCannell, 1976; Smith, 2003; Wang, 2000). Their quest may be one of personal or existential authenticity, whereby authentic experiences help to activate an existential state of Being (Wang, 1999). As a consequence, their engagement with the locale and its people is an essential component of their subjective experience of travel. The role that festivals play within this experience can be significant.

Getz (1994) notes that authenticity takes on a different meaning in the

133

context of traditional as opposed to created events. However, the concept of 'emergent authenticity' reminds us that all events were once created, and that a hierarchy based on the degree of authenticity is highly questionable. Nevertheless, questions should be raised about the extent to which festivals and events are being compromised by other factors, including tourism development, especially those that are firmly rooted in local or indigenous traditions. How far is artistic integrity affected by the need to popularise programming or performance? Is cultural performance trivialised by the development of tourist audiences? At what point does entertainment become exploitation?

Carlson (1996) suggests that the development of new audiences for local, small-scale, traditional performances and events can help to raise the profile of minority groups and their culture. It has also been suggested that festivals can play an important role in urban regeneration, especially from a community perspective (e.g. Smith, 2002). This chapter will discuss these viewpoints and others, using examples to ascertain the extent to which tourism development can enhance, revitalise and celebrate culture, rather than eroding, trivialising or commodifying it. In terms of examples, the authors will draw on a series of in-depth interviews undertaken during 2002 with a number of festival directors, cultural officers, arts development officers, and regeneration officers across three London Boroughs.

## Cultural Spectacles in the Postmodern Era: The Significance of Authenticity for Performance

It could be argued that in the postmodern era, authenticity of experience is a redundant concept. Eco (1986) suggests that as we are now living in a world of simulations and 'hyper-reality', where the real and the imaginary worlds are practically indistinguishable, and it is impossible to differentiate between authentic and inauthentic experiences. Goffman (1959) argues that the reality of everyday life that we perceive is as staged as the cultural performances that we attend, implying that all 'authenticity' is effectively staged. Edensor (2001) also argues that most tourist spaces are 'stage-managed'. This is perhaps of little consequence to the postmodern tourist or 'post-tourist', who no longer seeks authenticity of experience through travel (Feifer, 1985; Rojek, 1993; Urry, 1990; Walsh, 1992).

Of course, authenticity is a subjective attribution and a relative concept. Cohen (1988) argues that it is a 'socially constructed concept' and that the meaning is negotiable, as stated by Moore (2002: 55): 'One person's absolute fake is another's meaningful experience.' Jamal and Hill (2002) suggest that there are different kinds of authenticity, including 'objective authenticity' (usually referring to traditional or historical sites or artefacts), and 'constructed authenticity' (which may refer to staged events or artifically created cultural attractions). They also emphasise the importance of 'personal authenticity', which refers to the individual's emotional and psychological experience of travel. This follows Wang's (1999) argument that most authenticities are symbolic, and that the concept of authenticity is largely projected or constructed by tourists, rather than being an absolute value. Some of the deeper existential aspects relating to personal meaning and identity would not be issues for the post-tourist, who treats the experience playfully and with ironic detachment (Rojek, 1993). However, it could be argued that there are many tourists who would not subscribe to this viewpoint, and for whom travel still represents a quest for meaning and personal, emotional, and spiritual development. Cultural tourists would usually fall into this category, as they are more likely to be on some kind of quest for authenticity, either in terms of self-improvement or in terms of the sites, communities and activities that they engage with or in. They will want to engage fully with the destinations that they visit and interact with local inhabitants. Tourism will not be taken lightly or treated ironically, and they will not want to witness forms of exploitation, commodification or 'authentic fakery' (AlSayyad, 2001). Getz (1994: 425) confirms this viewpoint, describing authenticity as 'a difficult concept open to many interpretations, but of great importance in the context of cultural tourism and particularly event tourism'.

Getz (1994) refers to three perspectives of event authenticity: the anthropological perspective of the inherent meanings of festivity and celebration; the planning perspective of community control and the mobilising of local resident support; and the visitor experience and perception. In terms of performance, it has to be accepted that tourists cannot always be sure whether a performance is entirely authentic or not, whereas performers should have a very clear idea. The problem arises when tourists feel deceived or disappointed or the performer feels exploited, stereotyped or compromised. Clearly, local cultural performances and events should not be adapted or altered in such a way that it offends local sensibilities or compromises artistic integrity. However, in some cases, moderation of cultural performance may be a welcome development for some tourists. Turner and Ash (1975) suggest that the majority of tourists have a fairly limited sensual and aesthetic sense, therefore indigenous culture sometimes needs to be presented to them in a simplified format. The implication here is that tourists are by and large not 'sophisticated' enough to appreciate complex indigenous art forms (Turner and Ash refer to the example of Balinese culture and art). This may compromise the art form, depending on how local performers feel about simplifying or abridging their performance. It is probably true to say that the majority of tourists just want a taste of local culture, rather than a lengthy performance of dancing, singing or music. For example, the South Indian Kathakali story-plays were traditionally performed all-night in temples for (arguably not always attentive) Hindu audiences. They are generally presented as hour-long, one-off pieces to tourists in theatres or cultural centres. Similarly, some Maori perform-ances and cultural shows are modified to suit the needs of clientele in hotels, differing greatly from how they would be performed in the *marae* (Tahana & Oppermann, 1998). This process does not necessarily need to compromise the artistic integrity of the performers, nor does it render the performance inauthentic. Tourists have limited time to spare, they are not always familiar with local traditions, and they frequently encounter language barriers, and therefore need interpretation or translations. However, festivals are arguably different in that they are generally more accessible to the average tourist.

Tourism can also be considered as an asset. Besculides *et al.* (2002) and Boissevain (1996) remind us of tourism's role in revitalising traditions and renewing pride and identity such as in the case of the Maltese Fiesta where a balance was achieved between cultural promotion and dilution. 'Staged authenticity' can even help to protect a community's 'back' regions (Boissevain, 1996; Buck, 1977 in Getz, 1994) allowing locals to stage insiders-only events without any interferences. Van der Berghe (1993 in Getz, 1994) refers to the principle of 'emergent authenticity' according to which old traditions and events survive in more modern forms while new, 'invented' ones become an integral part of the community's calendar. The conclusion here is that culture and authenticity are not static concepts, but evolve rapidly and tourism is only one of many factors within the broader process of modernisation.

The following part of this chapter will explore the inter-relationship between festivals and tourism, focusing on a range of examples, including festivals that are community-orientated, and those which have been re-orientated towards, revived or created for tourism purposes. It will be argued that the size, scale and objectives of festivals will determine the extent to which artistic integrity and quality or authenticity of the product are influenced. It is also recognised that an increasing number of festivals are threatened by lack of financial support, therefore cultural continuity is being adversely affected. It is also a worrying phenomenon that the arts and cultural events are increasingly being used as tools for economic and social development (e.g. regeneration, community welfare, tourism), rather than being an end in themselves. This is perhaps the biggest threat to artistic freedom, as funding is often dependent upon measureable outcomes rather than the quality or integrity of the art form.

## The Relationship Between Festivals and Tourism: Synergies and Mutual Benefits

The notion of combining festivals and tourism is not a new concept, but one which dates back well over a hundred years (Adams, 1986). Kirschenblatt-Gimblett (1998) describes how a diverse range of festivals have proliferated since the growth of mass tourism in the post-war period, many of which have had the explicit intention of encouraging tourism. Rolfe (1992) demonstrated that over 50% of arts festivals, which had originated during the 1980s in the UK, had been partly aimed at increasing tourism in many cities. She suggests that although a large number of festivals are still largely community-orientated, they nevertheless succeed in attracting tourists, and around 56% of all festivals are created with a tourist audience in mind. Zeppel and Hall (1992: 69) describe how: 'Festivals, carnivals and community fairs add vitality and enhance the tourist appeal of a destination . . . Visitors primarily participate in festivals because of a special interest in the product, event, heritage or tradition being celebrated'. Kirschenblatt-Gimblett (1998) writes extensively about performing culture, noting that the European tendency has been to parcel each art form separately, splitting up the senses, and ensuring that art is experienced with sustained attention and the minimum of distraction and noise. Festivals, however, offer a whole host of sensory experiences and the performance spaces are not hermetically sealed. It is a form of ethnographic, environmental performance. Festivals can represent the quintessence of a region and its people, and therefore allow tourists to engage with a destination and its people in an authentic, interactive and participatory setting.

Hughes (2000) cites Levin (1981) who suggests that tourists are particularly attracted to festivals because of the holiday atmosphere that is created. This is particularly true of carnivals, which allow people not only to engage in festivities, but also to lose their inhibitions. Bakhtin (1965) describes the 'Rabelaisian' nature of carnivals, whereby participants and spectators alike are invited to indulge in sensuous and hedonistic pleasure. Sampson (1986: 34) describes the typical Trinidadian carnival as being 'the Alpha and Omega of mass hysteria: unrestrained jollity; carefree carnality; and calculated (sometimes spontaneous) crazy behaviour'. No wonder then that the Rio de Janeiro and Notting Hill Carnivals are two of the most popular events in the world with tourists. However, this is not without its problems, as we shall see later in this paper.

Hughes (2000) describes how many festivals that did not set out to attract tourists have done so anyway. This may be by default (i.e. tourists attend what are essentially community-orientated events because they happen to be in the area), or financial necessity and the growing sponsorship crisis forces festivals to 'internationalise' and seek higher profile acts and audiences. Some festivals are created simply with the intention of attracting tourists to a destination. For example, Quinn (1996) describes how certain music festivals in Ireland (e.g. Temple Bar Blues Festival in Dublin and Clifden Country Blues Festival in Galway) have been established in order to attract visitors to the locations in which they take place.

The increase in the number and popularity of events is also due to the realisation that they can be more than just 'ephemeral', local celebrations (Bramwell, 1997; Myerscough, 1992; Waterman, 1998). Their potential for attracting tourists is increasingly being recognised, and we can now refer to a new niche form called 'Event Tourism' (Getz, 1999; MacDonnell *et al.*, 1999). The growth of cultural tourism and of the short-break market in recent years has further contributed to this phenomenon (Richards, 1996). Even small, community events can develop into major attractions of a city's landscape, as pointed out by Bailey (1998), with significant benefits in terms of employment, direct expenditure, multiplier effect and increased investment opportunities (Allen & Shaw, 2000). As long as the destination can cope with large numbers of visitors in a short time-frame, festivals have the advantage of being suitable for localities that have few other attractions without necessarily entailing long-term investments or the building of special facilities (Law, 1993).

It is the unique way in which they are seen to reveal the quintessence of a locality (Kirschenblatt-Gimblett, 1998) that turns festivals into 'must-see' events or 'once-in-a-lifetime experiences' providing the destination with a considerable competitive advantage (Atkinson & Laurier, 1998; Dale, 1995), such as in Edinburgh, clearly established as Europe's 'Festival City' (Law, 1993; Scottish Arts Council, 2002; Smith & Jenner, 1998). Moreover, festivals can be crucial tools in extending the life-cycle of a destination and the length of stay by tourists, as well as to tackle seasonality as seen in New Orleans with the Creole Festival (Chacko & Schaffer, 1993). Alongside tourism development, events, especially mega-events, can also play a crucial function within strategies of city marketing and image-enhancement, as they attract considerable media coverage as well as national and international exposure and prestige (Bailey, 1998; Williams *et al.*,1995). Therefore, there has been a general shift in the nature of festivals, and events in general, from the short-term cultural focus to longer-term economic and social benefits and they have been increasingly employed as catalysts for wider developments (Allen & Shaw, 2000; Getz, 1997). This may include regeneration.

In terms of social impact, Carlson (1996) suggests that performance of all kinds can help to raise the profile of traditionally marginalised groups (e.g. ethnic minorities, women and homosexuals), allowing them to express and explore issues relating to self and society, objectification, exclusion and identity. The development of new audiences can help to raise political awareness of such issues, as well as drawing attention to the history and heritage of marginalised groups. Carnivals are a good example of this, or jazz festivals. International festivals such as WOMAD (World of Music, Arts and Dance) also allow diverse artistic communities of the world to display their cultures. The festival has traditionally adopted an anti-racist stance, as expressed by its founder Peter Gabriel, who established the festival in 1982: 'The festivals have allowed many different audiences to gain an insight into cultures other than their own through the enjoyment of music. Music is a universal language, it draws people together and proves, as well as anything, the stupidity of racism' (WOMAD, 2002). Smaller-scale ethnic festivals can also make a valuable contribution to the process of urban regeneration in terms of increasing community cohesion, racial tolerance, and fostering pride in a sense of place, heritage and identity. A good example of this is the Bradford Mela in the UK, an Asian Arts festival, which has also helped to raise the profile of Bradford as a tourism destination. In addition, Gay Pride events or 'Mardi Gras' (as they are now more commonly known) are becoming increasingly popular amongst non-gay revellers and tourists.

However, feelings of disinheritance and loss of ownership are sometimes becoming prominent amongst the aforementioned minority communities, who feel that their culture and traditions are being compromised by the development of broader, international and tourist audiences. The following section will discuss some of these issues in more depth.

## The Relationship Between Festivals and Tourism: Antagonisms and Conflicts

Some authors have suggested that a satisfactory balance does not appear unachievable between tourists' and locals' interests, economic development and quality of life, artistic innovation and tourism development (Griffiths, 1995; Hall, 1998). However, it is often difficult to reconcile differing priorities, especially in the case of festivals that were initially developed as community events, but which have since become re-orientated towards tourism. Festivals arguably share quite a few of the criticisms directed at tourism, as they 'internalize many of the tensions common to cultural tourism development including the dialectic opposition between culture and economy . . . local and global cultures' (Richards, 1996: 31). With the growth of the importance of events, many community festivals have rapidly evolved, becoming visitor attractions and targeting tourist markets. This phenomenon appears particularly strong in the UK according to Evans (1996), despite the fact that at least 50% of festival audiences in this country come from the immediate area (Allen & Shaw, 2000).

There is a deeply rooted belief that tension will arise over who the festival is designed for, whose culture is being portrayed by whom, who 'owns' the city, and who benefits. Several authors suggest that there is a fundamental distinction between community-orientated and tourism-orientated events (Arnold, 2001; Evans, 1996; Hall, 1992), with doubts raised over the sustainability of the latter. This debate even incorporates 'successful' events such as Glasgow 1990, which has been under scrutiny for mainly catering to tourists and revitalising the city centre but forgetting those living in deprived housing estates (Bianchini, 1999). The growing popularity of 'mediatic' mega-events (Bowdin et al., 2001; Getz, 1994), and 'pseudo-events' and 'contrived spectacles' as discussed earlier in this CHAPTER is a point of concern, especially considering their opportunity cost. They often entail huge investments and high risks, but leave limited long-term legacies beyond derelict sites such as in Seville 1992's Expo (Evans, 1996). Political processes drive these kinds of events: they are often elite-led, do not engage the public beyond a token invitation and exacerbate inequalities within a community (Hall, 1992).

Accordingly, with the evolution of festivals into economic tools (Chacko & Schaffer, 1993; Joppe, 1996), the financial dimension can often take over social, cultural and educational objectives. Waterman (1998) cites the Salzburg Festival as an example of how events can no longer be divorced from the commercial interests of tourism and place promotion. Festival activities do not only lose their local roots but become repetitive and unchallenging under the pressure of sponsors and the mass visitor market (Arnold, 2001; Rolfe, 1992) with some concern even surrounding the Edinburgh Festival (The Economist, 1994). In Greenwood's (1977) often-cited account of the Alarde ritual in Spain, a centuries-old tradition loses its inherent meaning to local communities as a consequence of being presented for tourist consumption. Atkinson and Laurier (1998) cite Bristol's International Festival of the Sea staged in 1996, as it excluded elements of the population (e.g. a group of 'travellers') as well as certain histories (e.g. slave trade, imperialism) that did not fit in with the landscape created for what Urry (1990) calls the 'tourist gaze'. The Festival portrayed the city solely in terms of its maritime heritage, thereby creating a fantasy –identity that did not correspond to the city's multicultural reality, as often happens in the tourist industry (Getz, 1994). This example can also be associated with the idea of contested space (Hall, 1992), particularly as locals were charged to enter their own docklands. An Anti-Festival of the Sea was eventually staged in Bristol as a sign of protest (Atkinson & Laurier, 1998). Therefore, an 'inauthentic' or imposed festival solely geared towards sponsors and tourists will ultimately cause the alienation of the local community and the commoditisation of its culture. Alienation can arise even with the best intentions: Fremeaux's (2000) study of the Arts Worldwide Bangladesh Festivals in London describes the loss of ownership of Bangladeshi communities in seeing a major event showcasing their culture being organised by a white, middle class arts organisation. The fact that the festival had community and regeneration objectives did not prevent the emergence of considerable tension.

Interestingly, it is often carnivals that tend to suffer the most from becoming tourist-orientated events, perhaps because they are by nature participatory and inclusive. Kirschenblatt-Gimblett (1998: 7) suggests that tourism can sanitise the carnival experience by aestheticising it and treating it ahistorically: 'carnival represented is carnival tamed'. Many carnivals were, of course, traditionally borne out of oppressive colonial regimes and partially represented the celebration of freedom from slavery. There is therefore a certain irony in the fact that many carnivals have effectively been 'hijacked' by white European tourists. For example, there have been growing concerns about the Notting Hill Carnival in London, which has grown from a small, localised event celebrating African-Caribbean culture, to a large, unwieldy event attracting over two million tourists. Many local African-Caribbean residents feel disinherited because of the large numbers of white, middle-class, non-local participants, especially as it has been suggested that the carnival should be moved into central London, thus displacing its roots even further.

The Gay Pride or Mardi Gras event in London has also recently been criticised for being increasingly de-politicised, largely due to the attendance of the event by a large number of heterosexual revellers. Originally, such events were highly politicised, as the marches which preceed such events still tend to be. They were largely a forum for the gay community to present a united front, and to express and assert their identity and rights publicly. However, in most cases, the lively celebrations that follow the march are becoming more of an inclusive public party than anything else.

Even the more sedate Venice carnival is not without its problems, especially in terms of the sustainability of the destination. It was not revived until 1980 as a community and tourist festival, following over two centuries of abandonment. The motivation was partly tourism-orientated in order to address seasonality, and partially to revive a vibrant tradition. Roiter (1991:43) describes how:

> Carnival has rediscovered its ideal setting in Venice; the masks have returned to identity themselves with the fabric and the authentic spirit of the city; there has been an effective explosion of revelry, retaining the primitive features of the feast of transgression and responding to the popular need for a pause, a brief respite from the demands of everyday living.

However, questions have already been raised about the extent to which extensive tourism development has compromised the everyday life and traditions of Venice residents. Venice has arguably become something of a living museum, even if it is not (yet) akin to a human zoo. It is also questionable as to how far the revival of carnival affords an authentic experience to locals or visitors alike. As stated by Crowhurst Lennard and Lennard (1987: 76):

> As a recent tradition the rebirth of Carnival – especially it unanticipated success – has given rise to similar controversies in Venice as in other cities where festivals have either been revived or sometimes even newly invented, that is, questions about authenticity, commercialisation, and a balance between resident and tourist involvement and needs.

This is becoming an all-too-familiar phenomenon, and can be particularly damaging to the native and indigenous traditions of minority groups, as stated by Mathieson and Wall (1992: 175): 'the new appreciation of indigenous culture, the revival of ancient festivals and the restoration of cultural landmarks have emerged in ways which pose long-term threats to the existence of culture in its original form'. Getz (1994) points out that the authenticity of traditional as opposed to created events is something very different, and clearly, much more fragile. Kirschenblatt-Gimblett (1998: 73) suggests that traditional festivals and events are often compromised by commercial or tourism development: 'The more ethnographic festivals and museum exhibitions succeed in their visual appeal and spectacular effect, the more they re-classify what they present as art and risk appealing to prurient interest.'

The size, scale and profile of such events are arguably the determining factors in the extent to which they become tourism-orientated. It is notoriously difficult for the majority of festivals and carnivals to secure consistent and sufficient funding on an annual basis, therefore they may be forced to raise their profile by attracting a wider audience. Nevertheless, tourism affords festivals few direct financial benefits, therefore it is questionable as to how far this is an appropriate or necessary development. It could be argued that many festivals should remain community events with a loyal local audience, rather than aspiring to become tourist events. However, the long-term sustainability of small-scale, local events is questionable.

## Festivals and Tourism in Greenwich

A series of in-depth, face-to-face interviews were undertaken during 2002 with a range of festival directors, cultural, arts development, and regeneration officers across three London Boroughs. Although the chosen case studies were largely confined to one Borough (Greenwich), it was recognised that it is not easy to confine the impact of cultural policy or events to Borough boundaries, especially in large conurbations such as London. The main aims of the research were to analyse the socio-cultural impacts of the chosen festivals, to explore the relationship between festivals and tourism, and to evaluate the role of the festivals in regeneration.

The London Borough of Greenwich is multicultural and ethnically diverse. It is also one of the most deprived Boroughs in the country. It has a distinctive tourism product, largely in the shape of the World Heritage Site, which consists of composite heritage attractions. Place promotion is mainly based on its image as the 'Home of Time', as well as its maritime past, which is inextricably linked to the theme of time. However, Greenwich has more recently promoted other, often more contemporary and arts-based attractions and events, such as the Greenwich and Docklands International Festival (GDIF), Black History Month and the Greenwich Film Festival.

The chosen festival case studies for this paper were the GDIF, Carnival 365 and Eltham Lights Up, however other local festivals and events (e.g. the Plumstead Anti-Racist Festival, the Greenwich Film Festival, and Black History Month) were also included in the discussions. Carnival 365 and Eltham Lights Up are one-day, small, local events, whereas GDIF is of a longer duration (usually around 10 days). All three festivals are led or supported by the Council (either financially or in-kind) and receive Single Regeneration Budget funding, thus their remit is partly determined by these factors. They all aim to bring high-quality entertainment in a familiar environment to peoples' doorsteps, (often for free), as well as providing animation and revitalising public life. These are seen as something of a 'gift' to a local community that does not usually enjoy access to cultural performances such as those provided by GDIF. In all cases, a concerted effort is made to involve locals in these events and the success rate is deemed high by the interviewees. (However, the authors recognise the bias inherent in the nature of the research, which has focused thus far on the opinions and evaluations of so-called 'experts' rather than local residents.)

Two of the festivals – Carnival 365 and Eltham Lights Up – are currently purely community-orientated events. Both these festivals were created relatively recently (within the last few years) hence they are not as deeply embedded in local community traditions as some of the aforementioned festivals in this chapter. However, they do serve to celebrate the culture and heritage of displaced groups or diasporas, which are common to large cities, especially Carnival 365, which has the added dimension of celebrating ethnic diversity and helping to combat racism. One of the festivals' main objectives is to help local communities see their locality in a new and positive light and foster a sense of belonging and pride, while at the same time allowing for 'capacity building' and 'empowerment' through workshops and outreach programmes, for instance. This is particularly important for this part of the Borough (South Greenwich), which is a deprived area with a large number of poor housing estates. A similar philosophy was adopted for the Lansbury Festival in 2001, which took place on a deprived housing estate in Poplar, East London. However, despite the initial 'feel good factor' which ensued during and immediately after the event, the lack of continuity has resulted in a collective feeling of despondency and anti-climax. Lack of funding curtailed the continuation or repetition of this event, which appears to be the fate of many small, community events. For example, the Greenwich cultural officer fears for the future of the Anti-Racist Festival in Plumstead, which used to attract high-profile acts, claiming that it is now *too* community-orientated and small-scale to survive for long. Similarly, the future of the Greenwich Film Festival, which could potentially become the Borough's 'flagship' event according to a former councillor, now hangs in the balance due to lack of adequate funding.

Many of these festivals appear to focus on regeneration in that they aim to celebrate local culture, help to strengthen community cohesion, and foster an enhanced sense of place. They are also used partly as socio-political tools in order to create better integration between ethnic and religious groups. It is debatable as to how far a tourist audience could, or would want to gain access to the 'backstage' of community lives through such events, as they are relatively small-scale and low profile at present. In fragmented and diasporic communities, it is also difficult to ascertain how far the event is a true reflection of 'authentic' culture. More importantly, however, it may be unwise to compromise the core objectives of such events in favour of tourism development.

Maintaining a balance between a loyal, local audience and a short-term tourism one is arguably a difficult (and not always desirable) task and a recurrent dilemma for many festival directors. When researching the case studies, it became clear that the interviewees were largely realistic about the small-scale, community-orientated nature of the events. However, there was also some divergence on the subject, with some interviewees deeming tourism development as inappropriate or ineffective in regeneration areas, preferring instead to direct resources towards local communities. Overall, it seems that interviewees revealed a predomintantly practical attitude: concerns over authenticity, a major theme in the literature, were hardly voiced. They were much more interested in the idea of 'ownership', community participation and consultation.

It was found that unlike the other two festivals, the GDIF is something of an 'aspirant' event in that it attempts every year to raise its profile further, both in London and beyond, by attracting world-class acts and artists and by cultivating a tourist audience. GDIF's organiser shows a positive attitude towards tourism, especially in terms of the economic benefits and investment it brings to localities, especially to local businesses, an opinion shared by other interviewees. Despite its community dimensions, GDIF is an international arts festival and it tries to maximise its tourism impact by working with various tourism agencies (e.g. London Tourist Board, local tourist offices), especially in Greenwich where 'tourist are part of the dynamics of the place', according to the festival director. The potential of GDIF to raise the profile of East London was acknowledged as being a priority, hence many events took place in different locations within the area. Although Greenwich is already a popular tourism destination, its main attraction is its history and heritage, therefore the GDIF helps to introduce a more contemporary dimension to the cultural tourism offer. The only foreseeable problem with this approach is that as the festival grows in size and status, attracting international acts and audiences, it may become increasingly 'placeless', reflecting little of local culture and heritage. However, if this is complemented, within the Borough or within East London, by a diversity of community-orientated events celebrating local culture, this may be of little consequence.

Although in the literature tourists' and locals' interests are often seen as almost mutually exclusive (Arnold, 2001; Evans, 1996; Hall, 1992), interviewees preferred to classify festival audiences into locals, visitors (e.g. Greater London) and tourists. While this categorisation might be particularly relevant in the case of London, it also shows that the issues are more complex than initially believed thereby bringing new perspectives on what tourism development might mean (e.g. cross-Borough movements). Furthermore, in the interviews, the commercialisation and commoditisation of local culture and the drift from socio-cultural objectives towards economic imperatives were not considered as inevitable consequences of tourism development. The question of authenticity was only mentioned once and, indeed, the fact that recently established festivals such as Eltham Lights Up are now part of the local calendar links with Van den Berghe's (1994) notion of 'emergent authenticity'.

Finally, it was considered that festivals are under pressure to meet the needs and expectations of a wide variety of stakeholders whatever their size and objectives. Exclusion can thus occur even with small, community-run events. Some interviewees mentioned the fact that just because an event is 'free' does not mean that the local community will not feel alienated whatever its content or quality. Although the community might feel more cheated if they had paid, equally negative feelings can occur in the case of free events of low quality. This is especially true if doubts are raised relating to opportunity costs, particularly if large sums have been invested (Allen & Shaw, 2000). The use of local artistic performers was also raised as an issue, the consensus being that they needed to offer a professional and high-quality artistic experience if they were to be involved.

Interestingly, it was suggested that tourism's impacts are often comparable to more general socio-cultural costs. The fact that none of the festivals studied is a major or mega-event perhaps contributed to this re-dimensioning of tourism's impacts. An alternative or complementary explanation is that tourism is very much part of the wider landscape in London. However, it also emerged that a properly run festival with an effective visitor management strategy can find a satisfactory balance between tourism and community development. Tourism revenue or extra funding can actually provide opportunities to enhance artistic content and expand community engagement (e.g. workshops, community programmes, evaluation and monitoring of impacts) and it is important that residents are aware of these benefits. One interviewee pointed out that there is actually scope for more festivals in East London, especially a 'flagship' event of international significance, which would help to raise the profile of the area, enhance its image, and provide a catalyst for further regeneration and tourism development. Of course, this kind of initiative should reflect the local area, try to engage with local communities and follow appropriate consultation procedures. Local ownership of a festival can indeed be developed even for tourist events as shown by Boissevain (1996) and Quinn (2000). A commercial festival could gain local suppport if the goals or themes were compatible with the hosts' ones and/or if the community feels it has been involved in some kind of consultation process. The management struture of the festival is very important and community participation crucial (Bowdin *et al.*, 2001). As suggested by Hall (1992), the issue of who controls the process often seems more important than the process itself.

## Conclusion

The aim of this paper has been to explore the relationship between festivals and tourism in a range of contexts, distinguishing between local and community-led events, and those festivals that have become re-orientated towards, or have been developed specifically with a tourist audience in mind. Although debates relating to authenticity and artistic integrity continue apace in the academic literature, it is clear from the latter part of this paper that the socio-cultural impacts of festivals and their role in regeneration might currently be the most significant issues for those directing or participating in festivals and festival management. The UK government's current determination to focus on regeneration, community involvement and empowerment, might paradoxically have an adverse impact on the arts, especially if they are incessantly used as a tool for something else rather than being an end in themselves. The question should also be raised as to how far these concepts are 'buzzwords' or tokenisms, and how far they reflect a genuine effort to meet the needs of local populations. As stated by Fremeaux (2000: 66):

> Crudely speaking, if at the moment money is in regeneration, attributed to projects facilitating capacity-building in communities, organisations are going to conceive their projects along these lines. Whether it reveals a genuine interest in these sorts of schemes, a true concern and true attempt to benefit the community or a startegy to get the money where it is, is currently an embarrassing question for most arts organisations.

It is a subject of ongoing debate as to how far the needs of local and tourist audiences can be reconciled within one event. It is equally difficult to measure the extent to which tourism development compromises the authenticity of events. As discussed in the earlier part of this paper, such terms are arguably becoming increasingly nebulous and, in some cases, meaningless. Culture, tourism and communities are all dynamic phenomena, thus any attempt to generalise about their transformation is somewhat tenuous. Contrary to the academic literature, which suggested that festivals are increasingly under threat from commercialisation, lack of funding or the pressure to function as tools or catalysts for wider economic development, the research implied that the interviewees were largely optimistic about festivals and the fact that they are no longer economic or 'ephemeral' tools. However, one must be wary of such results without triangulation from other sources. Indeed, it would be interesting to address similar issues from the perspective of local residents and festival audiences.

Overall, it is clear that one festival cannot be expected to fulfil numerous, sometimes conflicting objectives. Instead, complementarity needs to be achieved across the more general festival 'landscape' within a given geographical location allowing each event to have a more focused and targeted approach. Although festivals are increasingly being used for wider economic and social developments, including tourism, this does not need to compromise their core function. Instead, festivals can be seen as vibrant events that enhance the spirit of place for all those who reside in, visit or perform in their vicinity.

## References

Adams, R. (1986) *A Book of British Music Festivals*. London: Robert Royce Ltd.
Allen, K. and Shaw, P. (2000) Festivals mean business: The shape of arts festivals in the UK. *British Arts Festivals Association Report*, London: British Arts Festivals Association.
AlSayyad, N. (2001) Global norms and urban forms in the age of tourism: manufacturing heritage, consuming tradition. In N. AlSayyad (ed.) *Consuming Tradition, Manufacturing Heritage: Global Norms and Urban Forms in the Age of Tourism* (pp. 1–33). London: Routledge.
Arnold, N. (2001) Festival tourism: Recognising the challenges, linking multiple pathways between global villages of the new century. In B. Faulkener *et al.* (eds) *Tourism in the 21st Century: Reflections on Experience* (pp. 130–57). London: Continuum.
Atkinson, D. and Laurier, E. (1998) A sanitised city? Social exclusion at Bristol's 1996 International Festival of the Sea. *Geoforum* 29 (2,) 199–206.
Bailey, H. (1998) Local heroes. *The Leisure Manager* 16 (10), 24–7.
Bakhtin, M. (1965) *Rabelais and his World*. Cambridge: MIT Press.
Besculides, A., Lee, M. and McCormick, P. (2002) Residents' perceptions of the cultural benefits of tourism. *Annals of Tourism Research* 29 (2), 303–19.
Bianchini, F. (1999) Cultural planning for urban sustainability. In L. Nystrom (ed.) *City and Culture: Cultural Processes and Urban Sustainability* (pp. 34–51). Kalmar: The Swedish Urban Environment Council.

Boissevain, J. (1996) Ritual, tourism and cultural commoditization in Malta: Culture by the Pound? In T. Selwyn (ed.) *The Tourists Image: Myths and Myth making in Tourism* (pp. 105–19). Chichester: John Wiley & Sons.

Boorstin, D. (1964), *The Image: a Guide to Pseudo-Events in America*. New York: Harper and Row.

Bowdin, G. *et al.* (2001) *Events Management*. Oxford: Butterworth-Heinemann.

Bramwell, B. (1997) Strategic planning before and after a mega-event. *Tourism Management* 18 (3), 167–76.

Carlson, M. (1996) *Performance: A Critical Introduction*. London: Routledge.

Chacko, H.E. and Schaffer, J.D. (1993) The evolution of a festival – Creole Christmas in New Orleans. *Tourism Management* 14, 475–82.

Cohen, E. (1988) Authenticity and commoditization in tourism. *Annals of Tourism Research* 15, 371–86.

Crowhurst Lennard, S.H. and Lennard, H.L. (1987) *Livable Cities*. Southampton: Gondolier Press.

Dale, M. (1995) Events as image. In D. Leslie (ed.) *Tourism and Leisure: towards the Millennium* (Volume 2 – Perspectives on Provision). Eastbourne: Leisure Studies Association.

Eco, U. (1986) *Travels in Hyper-Reality*. London: Picador.

*The Economist* (1994) A lost Scottish accent. 27 August.

Edensor, T. (2001) Performing tourism, staging tourism: (Re)producing tourist space and practice. *Tourist Studies* 1 (1), 59–81.

Evans, G. (1996) The Millennium Festival and urban regeneration – planning, politics and the party. In M. Robinson *et al.* (eds) *Managing Cultural Resources for the Tourist* (pp. 79–98). Sunderland: Business Education Publishers Ltd.

Feifer, M. (1985) *Going Places: The Ways of the Tourist from Imperial Rome to the Present Day*. London: Macmillan.

Fremeaux, I. (2000) The Arts Worldwide Bangladesh Festival, Rising East. *Journal of East London Studies* 3 (3), 46–68.

Getz, D. (1994) Event tourism and the authenticity dilemma. In W.F. Theobald (ed.) *Global Tourism* (pp. 409–27). Oxford: Butterworth-Heinemann.

Getz, D. (1997) *Event Management and Event Tourism*. New York: Cognizant Communication Corp.

Goffman, E. (1959) *The Presentation of Self in Everyday Life*. New York: Doubleday.

Greenwood, D.J. (1977) Culture by the Pound: An anthropological perspective on tourism as cultural commoditization. In V.L. Smith (ed.) *Hosts and Guests – The Anthropology of Tourism* (pp. 129–38). Oxford: Blackwell.

Griffiths, R. (1995) Cultural strategies and new modes of urban intervention. *Cities* 12 (4), 253–65.

Hall, C.M. (1992) *Hallmark Tourist Events: Impacts, Management, Planning*, London: Belhaven Press.

Hall, V. (1998) UK focus – From the inside looking out. *In Focus* magazine (Tourism and the Millennium Edition), Spring, 12–15.

Hughes, H. (2000) *Arts, Entertainment and Tourism*. Oxford: Butterworth-Heinemann.

Jamal, T. and Hill, S. (2002) The home and the world: (Post)touristic spaces of (In)authenticity. In G.M.S. Dann (ed.) *The Tourist as a Metaphor of the Social World* (pp. 77–108). CABI, Wallingford.

Joppe, M. (1996) Current issues: Sustainable community tourism development revisited. *Tourism Management* 17 (7), 475–79.

Kirschenblatt-Gimblett, B. (1998) *Destination Culture: Tourism, Museums and Heritage.* California: University of California Press.

Law, C. (1993) *Urban Tourism: Attracting Visitors to Large Cities.* London: Mansell.

MacCannell, D. (1976) *The Tourist: A New Theory of the Leisure Class.* New York: Schocken.

McDonnell, I., Allen, J. and O'Toole, W. (1999) *Festival and Special Event Management.* Chichester: John Wiley & Sons.

Mathieson, A. and Wall, G. (1992) *Tourism: Economic, Physical and Social Impacts.* Harlow: Longman.

Moore, K. (2002) The discursive tourist. In G.M.S. Dann (ed.) *The Tourist as a Metaphor of the Social World* (pp. 41–60). Wallingford: CABI.

Myerscough, J. (1992) Measuring the impact of the arts: The Glasgow 1990 Experience. *Journal of the Market Research Society* 34 (4), 323–34.

Quinn, B. (1996) The sounds of tourism: Exploring music as a tourist resource with particular reference to music festivals. In M. Robinson *et al.* (eds) *Culture as the Tourist Product* (pp. 383–96). Newcastle: Centre for Travel and Tourism, University of Northumbria, Business Education Publishers Ltd.

Quinn, B. (2000) Whose festival? Whose place? An insight into the production of cultural meanings in arts festivals turned visitor attractions. In M. Robinson *et al.* (eds) *Reflection on International Tourism – Expression of Culture, Identity and Meaning in Tourism* (pp. 262–73). Sunderland: Business Education Publishers Ltd.

Richards, G. (1996) (ed.) *Cultural Tourism in Europe.* Wallingford, CAB International.

Rolfe, H. (1992) *Arts Festivals in the UK.* London: Policy Studies Institute.

Roiter, F. (1991) *Venetian Carnival.* Venezia, Zerella.

Rojek, C. (1993) *Ways of Escape: Modern Transformations in Leisure and Travel.* London: Macmillan Press Ltd.

Sampson, M. (1986) The origins of the Trinidad Carnival. In Arts Council of Great Britain, *Masquerading: The Art of the Notting Hill Carnival* (pp. 30–4). London: ACGB.

Scottish Arts Council (2002) What we do – arts at the heart of a nation (online). On WWW at http://www.sac.gov.uk/whatwedo.heart. (Accessed 20 March 2002).

Smith, C. and Jenner, P. (1998) The impact of festivals and special events on tourism. *Travel & Tourism Intelligence* 4, 73–91.

Smith, M.K. (2002) Celebrating cultural diversity in the inner city: the role of ethnic festivals in urban regeneration. In IFEA (eds M. Robinson and P. Long) *IFEA Conference Proceedings*, Bonn, February.

Smith, M.K. (2003) *Issues in Cultural Tourism Studies.* London: Routledge.

Tahana, N. and Oppermann, M. (1998) Maori cultural performances and tourism. *Tourism Recreation Research* 23 (1), 23–30.

Turner, L. and Ash, J. (1975) *The Golden Hordes: International Tourism and the Pleasure Periphery,* London: Constable.

Urry, J. (1990) *The Tourist Gaze: Leisure and Travel in Contemporary Societies.* London: Sage.

Van den Berghe, P.L. (1994) *The Quest of the Other: Ethnic Tourism in San Cristo'bal, Mexico.* Seattle: University of Washington Press.

Walsh, K. (1992) *The Representation of the Past: Museums and Heritage in the Post-Modern World.* London: Routledge.

Wang, N. (1999) Rethinking authenticity in tourism experience. *Annals of Tourism Research* 26 (2), 349–70.
Wang, N. (2000) *Tourism and Modernity: A Sociological Analysis.* Oxford: Pergamon Press.
Waterman, S. (1998) Carnivals for elites? The cultural politics of arts festivals. *Progress in Human Geography* 22 (1), 54–74.
Williams, P., Dossa, K. and Tompkins, L. (1995) Volunteerism and special event management: A case study of Whistler's Men's World Cup of Skiing. *Festival Management and Event Tourism* 3, 83–95.
WOMAD (2002) (online). On WWW at http://www.womad.org. Accessed 15 June 2002).
Zeppel, H. and Hall, C.M. (1992) Arts and heritage tourism. In B. Weiler and C.M. Hall (eds) *Special Interest Tourism* (pp. 47–65). London: Belhaven Press.

*Chapter 9*

# Creating the 'Rainbow Nation': The National Women's Art Festival in Durban, South Africa

Sabine Marschall

## Introduction

Since South Africa has rejoined the international community of nations, the country has become a popular tourist destination. Tourism currently counts as one of the largest growth industries and is generally perceived as a panacea for all ills. In this context, a number of new festivals have emerged and existing festivals are increasingly marketed as tourist attractions. While many of those festivals, including arts festivals, are primarily about popular entertainment and consumption, the National Women's Arts Festival is first and foremost about something else: women's empowerment and societal transformation. The festival was established at the Playhouse in Durban in 1995 in celebration of Women's Day (9 August), a new public holiday in post-apartheid South Africa.[1] It soon developed into a major event, filling five days and drawing increasingly large audiences. The festival aims to present performances of excellence in the entire spectrum of the visual, performing and literary arts; celebrate female creativity by providing a platform for showcasing women's talent; foster awareness of women's issues; and contribute to the empowerment and economic benefit of the artists.

For a number of reasons, the event was never marketed to tourists and the festival moved to Johannesburg in 2002, following a sad pattern within the dynamics of the South African art scene and depleting the city of Durban of an important cultural attraction. If this move turns out to be a permanent one, it will furthermore represent a lost opportunity in terms of local tourism development. This chapter will first discuss the uniqueness of the National Women's Art Festival and its contribution to gender-based empowerment and transformation in the current post-apartheid context. It will then suggest how the festival could be developed as a major cultural tourist attraction with important spin-offs for the city of Durban. This would not only result in economic benefits through sales (as is the case with most festivals), but it would also lead to empowerment of local communities in a much broader and more sustainable sense, while presenting the tourist with a unique experience that transcends superficial cultural exposure and consumption. Some of these practical and creative strategies can also be implemented in Johannesburg, although it is really Durban that needs an injection of cultural tourism most.

## Context

The time of the first General Elections in 1994, which formally marked the end of apartheid, sparked a lively debate around issues of national identity and a search for appropriate new national symbols that would represent the country's new value systems and capture the spirit of the 'new' South Africa (e.g. Wessels, 1994; Wakashe, 1994). With the coining of the term 'rainbow nation', which signified the post-apartheid effort at amalgamating diverse population groups without creating a 'melting pot', the celebration of the country's cultural diversity began to assume a position of central importance. Not surprisingly though, the reality of grinding poverty and underdevelopment soon pitched arts and culture against development priorities and economic empowerment of previously marginalised communities. In this context, cultural tourism can be a catalyst in the process of nation building by successfully combining celebration of culture with economic development.

## Tourism and Festivals

The city of Durban has a long tradition as one of the country's foremost tourist destinations due to its warm climate, Indian Ocean beaches and relative proximity to the Drakensberg holiday resorts and game reserves. Cultural tourism, however, is only just emerging with an emphasis on township tours and visits to the recently reconstructed Gandhi settlement on the outskirts of the city, which forms part of the Inanda Heritage Route (Kearney, 2001). The city can also boast a number of festivals, two of which are enjoying a national and to a certain degree international reputation: the family-oriented annual Vodacom Beach Africa (previously called Gunston 500), an international surf competition during the month of July, is much in line with Durban's established image as a beach destination.

The more recently established Awesome Africa (formerly called Living Treasures), an open-air music event at Shongweni Dam Nature Reserve just outside of the Durban metro area, attracts musicians from about 20 different countries with a focus on the African continent. [2]

During the past few years, South Africa has experienced a considerable proliferation of cultural festivals throughout the country (including some in very remote areas); many of these events have increased dramatically in size and scope, attracting ever greater numbers of visitors (Kakaza, 2000). Like the existing festivals in Durban, many of these events are specialised in nature, devoted to, for instance jazz, dance or choral music. South Africa's largest and most renowned festival still remains the National Arts Festival in Grahamstown (traditionally sponsored by Standard Bank), which features a broad range of visual and performing arts over a period of two weeks in July each year. Of the country's three metropolitan centres, Johannesburg is clearly leading the field with several specialised festivals and the broad based annual Arts Alive Festival. Cape Town appears to have only recently realised the potential advantages of hosting a large-scale cultural festival with its introduction of the Cape Town One City Festival in 1999, aimed at celebrating the city's many cultures. Durban currently has no equivalent – a void that could have been filled by the National Women's Arts Festival.

One of the motivating factors for this proliferation of cultural festivals is the fact that festivals have the potential of generating considerable revenue for the hosting city and its inhabitants, as well as employment, economic benefits and other opportunities for people further a field.[3] The Edinburgh Festival, the world's foremost art festival, generates 122 million pounds annually for the economy of Edinburgh, while sustaining over 4000 jobs nationwide (Anonymous, 2001).[4] Its closest relative in South Africa is the abovementioned National Arts Festival in Grahamstown. As opposed to these two festivals, which can look back on a fairly long history,[5] the National Women's Arts Festival in Durban and a host of other cultural festivals that have recently emerged in South Africa, are still in their infancy.

## Objectives of the Women's Arts Festival

Initiated by Gita Pather,[6] who then worked in the Playhouse Education and Development department, the Women's Arts Festival was held for the first time in October 1995 (Chorn, personal communication, 2001). The link with Women's Day celebrations was only established the following year, when the festival was shifted into the month of August. Since then the festival has steadily increased in duration, scope and visitor numbers. From a three-day event in 1995, the festival spanned five days in 2001, attracting about 10,000 visitors.[7] From being initially focused on dance, drama and music, the festival soon featured the complete range of artistic expressions including dance, drama, music, poetry, photography, fine art, crafts, story-telling and puppetry.

Apart from celebrating Women's Day as it happens throughout the country on or around 9 August each year, the objectives of the National Women's Arts Festival include activism, empowerment and equity. South Africa's new constitution is among the most progressive in the world with regard to women's rights, yet in reality many women are suffering – from poverty, lack of proper health care and basic services, domestic violence, rape and HIV/Aids. The festival uses creative means of expression to foster awareness of the women's plight. The equity objective applies to both people (performers and audience) and artistic genres. Due to South Africa's past ideology of racial and cultural superiority, many creative forms were frequently dismissed for not being western enough: this includes Indian dance, African theatre, crafts, poetry and story-telling (Khan 2000). The extraordinarily broad spectrum of creative genres featured at the National Women's Arts Festival is intended to validate and represent these diverse cultural expressions and thereby attract diverse audiences. This is further-more achieved by offering a range of different events – a mini-conference, theatre and dance performances, poetry readings in different languages, a gala concert – which invariably tend to attract somewhat different audiences in terms of race, class, gender and educational background. Many events, but most especially the gala concert, are successful in drawing highly diverse, multiracial crowds.[8]

The festival's empowerment objective refers on the one hand to women's personal growth. While the festival organisers are concerned about performances of excellence and high national or even international standard, there is also a strong commitment to fostering emerging talent and providing women from marginalised communities with an opportu-nity to showcase their creative abilities. Chorn (personal communication, 2001) recalls extraordinary success stories, such as the case of Caroline Duck and Sarahleigh Castelyn, whose play 'No Sir, I'm not on the menu' was first performed at the Women's Art Festival (in 1999), where it was highly acclaimed. It was later produced as a film and won the M-Net 2000 Editing Award for best team and best writer. Another example is Xoliswa Dlamini, former Technikon student, who performed at the late-night jazz events of the Women's Arts Festival in 1999, as well as being part of the cabaret 'Me and my voice'. The following year, she won the Old Mutual

Best Singer Jazz Award in 2000. Empowerment in this sense is especially important for black women, who – caught in the matrix of race, gender and traditional social structures – are often triply disadvantaged.

An important aspect of the festival in this context is the dance and drama workshops, offered for the first time in 2001. Facilitated by festival choreographers and directors, these workshops are targeted at various entry-level groups and artists and aimed at empowerment through capacity building (Anonymous, 2001d: 10). Such workshops ensure that the festival has a lasting impact and multiplier effect, especially in previously disadvantaged communities.

On the other hand, empowerment refers to economic empowerment for artists, many of whom are increasingly coming under pressure to survive in a context of a market-driven, science- and technology-oriented society. While initially an uncertain funding situation marked by ever changing sponsors[9] resulted in great difficulties in planning and marketing the event, until Transnet emerged as a highly supportive corporate sponsor. The fact that the parastatal almost doubled its sponsorship for the year 2001 (Chorn, personal communication, 2001) reflects firm commitment and confidence in the festival. This increase in funding has permitted the festival organisers for the first time to pay each performer a decent honorarium apart from covering expenses. The economic empowerment of performers and other participants of the festival, as well as the focus on women in the arts as entrepreneurs (this was the theme of the 2001 festival's mini-conference) have increasingly been pushed into the foreground as significant objectives of the National Women's Arts Festival. Recently, the festival organisers have established an association with the Lubombo Spatial Development Initiative (LSDI, undated):[10] In 2001, for the first time, the crafters of the LSDI's Greater St Lucia Wetland Craft Programme were invited to present their products at the Women's Arts Festival – not displayed for sale, but consciously exhibited as 'art' on par with the 'fine art' photographic exhibition mounted in the same gallery. While the craft women may in this case not have benefited financially in a direct manner, the extraordinary quality of the crafts generated much attention and created awareness of these products, which are sold at an elevated market level.[11] The National Women's Arts Festival is thus ideally positioned to forge a firm link between the arts, tourism and regional economic development. In the current situation in South Africa, where the arts have increasingly come under pressure, this triangular relationship may prove to be a highly successful strategy to demonstrate the relevance of the performing and visual arts and ensure their survival.

## Tourism Potential

In the emerging competition of festivals throughout the country and especially among the three main metropolitan areas, each festival needs to demonstrate its uniqueness to facilitate its marketing at a national or even international level. The National Women's Arts Festival is not only unique in South Africa, but probably in the world, due to the specific intersection of a focus on women (women artists, women's issues) and a vast diversity of artistic genres with an emphasis on inclusiveness and representiveness (performers hail from all parts of the country, representing different racial groups and a variety of local artistic traditions). There are many art festivals representing a wide diversity of genres – in South Africa alone, the Grahamstown Art Festival (including its fringe) or the Cultural Calabash in Taung (mentioned below) for instance are two prominent examples – but without a focus on women artists. On the other hand, various events are being held in celebration of Women's Day throughout South Africa, but none comes close to the scope and inclusiveness of the National Women's Arts Festival in Durban. Likewise women's events in other parts of the world tend to be focused on one creative genre or a small range. Examples include the National Women's Music Festival (NWMF) at Ball State University in Munice, Indiana (Anonymous, 2001b) or the Women's Voices Festival (WVF), a three-day outdoor festival in Canada, which (as opposed to the Durban event) is created entirely by women for women (Anonymous, 2001c).

The National Women's Arts Festival is in a sense a reflection of the values enshrined in the constitution of post-apartheid South Africa, as well as the Government's White Paper on Arts Culture and Heritage (1996), which defines expression of one's culture as a basic human right. It is a condensed embodiment of the cultural spirit and multiple creative identities of the new South Africa. It is part of the country's living heritage. This could be attractive for both 'serious' art interested cultural tourists, including international visitors, seeking an authentic, possibly educative, cultural experience, and for the average popular tourist interested in sampling a few local art events primarily for entertainment purposes. The tourism potential of the Women's Arts Festival lies in the convenient opportunity of supplementing recreational beach holidays or nature experiences with artistic experiences truly expressive of South African culture(s). It must be considered, as Bywater's (1993) research has shown, that only 5% of the tourism market is covered by 'genuine cultural tourists', who actually choose a holiday because of its cultural opportunities. Up to two-thirds of all tourists ('culturally attracted' tourists) would like some cultural attractions at destinations they choose for other reasons (Bywater, 1993 in Craik, 1997: 120).

There certainly are other places in South Africa that can boast attractive cultural festivals, many of which have also grown tremendously over the past years. Perhaps most comparable in terms of diversity of art forms represented is the North West Cultural Calabash in the remote village of Taung in North West Province. This art festival, incidentally also sponsored by Transnet, has grown from a one-day occurrence when it was first initiated in 1994, to a four-day event, attracting visitors from North West Province, Gauteng and even abroad (Kakaza, 2000). Unlike Taung and other places like it, the city of Durban already has an established reputation as a prime tourism destination and an infrastructure designed to cope with large volumes of visitors. This infrastructure (especially the hospitality sector) has furthermore been considerably improved and expanded since the International Convention Centre (ICC) was opened in Durban a few years ago.

## Vision

In order to market the festival effectively at a national and international level, more local and national co-ordination is needed in assuring the uniqueness and national character of the event. Being a national holiday, Women's Day is celebrated not only throughout the country, but also by various organisations and institutions within the same city, thus dissipating, to a certain degree, the impact of the festival in Durban. This present variety of separate initiatives throughout the Durban metro area[12] could be co-ordinated and consolidated under the umbrella of the National Women's Arts Festival, so that each and every activity relating to Women's Day celebration becomes part of the Festival and is listed in its official programme. Following the concept of the Grahamstown Art Festival and many other decentralised festivals, different events and activities targeted at different audiences would thus be spread over a number of venues throughout the entire city, including suitable venues (e.g. community centres) in townships and other previously marginalised areas (e.g. Cato Manor). Such expansion would encourage a greater level of active collaboration with existing women's organisations and other constituencies; it would ensure the representation of all local stakeholders; create synergy; and further increase the diversity of performances and audiences.

More importantly, in terms of the event's tourism potential, the expansion of the festival and its spatial spread of activities would facilitate the incorporation of a wide variety of fringe events (including outdoor events) and supplementary tourism products. Local communities and informal vendors could greatly benefit from the sale of food, drink, craft items, souvenirs and other merchandise. Minibus taxis could be contracted to transport visitors safely and reliably in between venues, and a host of other services could be provided at and around the respective venues and sites. Apart from immediate economic benefits, it can be presumed that considerable employment opportunities would be generated and a variety of spin-offs could be expected further a field.

Craik (1997) distinguishes between 'true' cultural tourists and 'casual' cultural tourists and points to an interesting relationship between the two. 'True' cultural tourists tend to be better educated, earn more, and possess more cultural capital. They seek out new forms of cultural tourism experiences and hence spearhead new forms of tourist development. Specialist forms of cultural tourism (such as the Women's Art Festival) can benefit from other ventures that package modified cultural experiences in forms that are more attractive to larger, accidental (or 'casual') cultural tourists. Merchandising (through posters, caps or T-shirts) is an especially effective way to create synergies between 'elite' cultural tourism and 'casual' cultural tourism' (Craik, 1997: 126).

As the enormous variety of creative genres is one of the festival's unique features, it is important to build on this strength and further expand the diversity. The greatest scope for development lies within the visual arts sector. It must be pointed out that the term 'art festival' often implies a focus on the major genres of the performing arts (theatre, classical music and dance): the Edinburgh Festival, for instance, has traditionally not featured the visual arts and in Durban, too, the emphasis of the National Women's Arts Festival was initially mostly on dance, theatre and music, mostly due to the disciplinary background of its initiators. The entire sector of the visual arts (fine art, community art, craft and photography) has only recently received more attention, but there are countless opportunities for expansion.

Following the current principles of the festival, the visual arts would be expected to reflect the many different expressive genres currently practised in South Africa (to emphasise the national character of the event) and those dominating in Durban or the KwaZulu-Natal region (to emphasise the uniqueness of the province and city). This could include anything from avant-gardist installations to graffiti. On some occasions, the visual art component of the festival could have a much more lasting impact. For instance, community artists could be invited to paint murals thematising the National Women's Arts Festival, Women's Day or generally women's issues, following the example of the Arts Alive murals around Johannesburg, painted from 1992 to 1995 (Marschall 2002). Apart from providing local artists with temporary employment, these murals would provide a celebratory context and backdrop for the festival within the city; constitute a lasting testimony to the festival; advertise the event to tourists throughout the year; and raise awareness of women's issues among local communities.

Displays of locally produced art, craft or other creative products of visual expression could assist in transforming nondescript venues into a festive ambience for dance or music performances. At the same time, these works could be offered for sale, thus providing tourists with an opportunity to purchase original art and artists to generate income. Art displays can encourage the visitor to linger a bit longer before or after the show s/he has come to see. In fact, the entire trip to the respective venue, especially when located in the townships or marginalised areas, can be structured to become a cultural experience for the visitor, involving multiple options such as eating in an informal restaurant, visiting a local shebeen or going on a brief tour to visit a local school or witness how people live.

## Integration of Communities

It is thus evident that an expansion of the festival into the townships can provide multiple opportunities for ordinary people and communities to be involved and derive economic benefits. However, in terms of the uniqueness of the festival and its true essence (as a celebration of Women's Day), it is imminent to ascertain at all times that authentic community events (whether dance, music or theatre) are not turned into artificially staged performances for tourists. All events organised under the umbrella of the National Women's Arts Festival should either be already in existence or be initiated by community-based groups such as schools, churches, women's organisations, etc. To a certain degree one may consider modifying an event to cater to visitors from outside the community, but it is important to ensure that the event first and foremost remains meaningful for the community, reflecting its specific concerns (be it domestic abuse, poverty of women or issues around child care) and its chosen mode of celebration. Incorporating these events under the umbrella of the Women's Arts Festival and giving them more exposure should first and foremost be seen as an encouragement for cultural expression.

'Self-expression is a prerequisite for self-empowerment' (Cohen-Cruz, 1995: 121). This is the basic philosophical underpinning of the American Festival Project (AFP), which can provide a valuable model for the organisation of an umbrella structure for the Women's Arts Festival. Conceived in 1982 by John O'Neal, the AFP is a network of culturally and racially diverse independent theatre companies with strong social empowerment objectives, an interest in cultural diversity and emphasis on centring art in the concerns of the community (Cohen-Cruz, 1995). This implies an acknowledgement of diverse definitions of 'art' and possibly widely differing standards of performances. In keeping with the group's empowerment goals, AFPs are initiated by community-based groups and carried out with a maximum of local participation. As Cohen-Cruz (1995: 124) suggests: 'Rather than a formal conception of art in a static relationship to a community, the AFP embodies art functioning dynamically in the ongoing contexts of people's lives, thus engaging them actively as subjects/doers, not objects/consumers'.

The challenge in any South African context is the enormous socio-economic and cultural gap between different sectors of the population. The very concept of an art festival may be foreign and perhaps of little interest to communities who have never had the opportunity to be exposed to art and who struggle to see its relevance. Bringing together members of such diverse social backgrounds, who may speak different languages, who have vastly differing priorities in their lives, who may adhere to different concepts of 'art', and who may subscribe to different ideas as to how Women's Day should be celebrated, is not an easy task. Following the example of the AFP, it is important that the diversity of performances or events should also be reflected in the governing body of the umbrella structure, being composed of representatives of various different constituencies. In other words, the goal should be true integration, rather than a patronising add-on situation, which so often appears to be the case in South Africa.

'If residents are actively involved in defining and presenting the distinctive aspects of an area, tourism should cultivate more pride and feeling of "ownership" in the industry', suggested Tabata in his discussion of cultural tourism development in Hawaii (Tabata, 1989: 71). It would also foster, one might add, a better comprehension of the tourism industry, an understanding of its possible impacts and realistic expectations of its economic benefits. The lack of such understanding is currently one of the persisting problems in implementing cultural tourism projects in South African communities. Enthusiasm for tourism development is quite overwhelming, as in many people's minds tourism equates with making fast and easy money. However, there is little understanding of what constitutes a suitable tourism product, how it must be marketed and managed, what tourists expect, what benefits communities can realistically anticipate and what the negative impacts of tourism could be. Especially with respect to the relatively new and strongly expanding sector of cultural tourism, many poorly trained entrepreneurial individuals are trying to exploit the new trend, but provide a poor service, thereby jeopardising the potential of the industry as a whole.

The key for a successful transformation of the tourism sector in South Africa is capacity building. Once again, the National Women's Arts festival could provide opportunities in this regard, for instance through the training and accreditation of guides. They could be employed for a fee to accompany visitors, making them feel safe, interpret for them where necessary, explain the significance of cultural performances and various experiences encountered along the way, be able to answer questions and thus enhance the tourist's understanding of contemporary urban culture. This concept is common and appears to work very effectively in other tourist destinations in Africa (e.g. Mombasa) and elsewhere. If a broad-based vision is adopted for the festival, the opportunities for involving ordinary people are almost limitless. However, in order to safeguard the unique character of the festival, the emphasis should always be on creativity rather than pure commercialism.

The possibilities of marketing through creative participation are virtually limitless, but I want to present one example to illustrate the point. It involves the various informal hair salons (*siyagunda lapha*), which are found throughout the city centre in Durban and other urban centres in South Africa. They have become a moderate tourist attraction in their own right and their painted signboards, featuring different hairstyles, have become collector's items. All the informal hairdressers in the city could be approached to participate in a competition for developing the most creative, fantastic Women's Day haircut, which would then be advertised on their signboards and rewarded in some way during the festival period. This would add a fun component in line with the city's established tourist reputation as a 'fun and sun' city, as well as spreading awareness of the event among sectors of the population that may otherwise be difficult to target.

## Active Involvement of Visitors

While it is important to involve local communities, it is equally significant to offer visitors the chance for hands-on experiences. In recent years, especially since the 1980s, when the heritage began to flourish all over the western world (and to a certain degree in the developing world), prompting Hewison (1987) to coin the term 'heritage industry', there has been a marked shift to enhance the educational experience of such sites with entertainment features ('edutainment') and the opportunity for hands-on experiences. This shift from attention to the exhibit to attention to the visitor or audience (see e.g. Uzzell 1989), and from an understanding of the visitor as passive recipient to active participant, has also affected the tourism industry. Expanding the National Women's Arts Festival along the lines of the vision outlined above would present countless opportunities for active visitor involvement. Short courses could be offered where visitors can learn certain dance movements, sing in a community choir, participate in playing the drums, acquire some basic communication skills in isizulu, participate in painting a community mural, learn to make craft items or watch a demonstration of their production. It is self-evident that such activities would provide economic benefit mostly for members from previously marginalised communities.

## Quality Assurance

For all these activities, however, it is imminent to establish structures that can assure the provision of high-quality service. Mallam (1989: 48) rightly emphasizes that

> the management and marketing performance of the project must be up to scratch in terms of the standards and quality of the overall visitor experience and service. The difficult but fascinating challenge of heritage-based leisure projects is the need to perform across the board. A fault in one area quickly lets down success in others. It is now, therefore, often necessary to make considerable further capital investments in more mundane and less glamorous facilities such as lavatories, facilities that are unlikely to attract direct charitable contributions easily.

There is no need to elaborate on the challenges that lie ahead with respect to getting services and venues up to scratch in these terms, especially when involving facilities in the townships or previously neglected areas. Guides would need to have excellent communication skills in English and ideally in other European languages; drivers of minibus taxis must adopt a safe driving style and provide reliable service; all food sale outlets must comply with health standards, etc. It must be acknowledged, as Craik (1997: 115) has observed, that 'although tourists think that they want authenticity, most want some degree of negotiated experiences which provide a tourist "bubble" (a safe, controlled environment) out of which they can selectively step to "sample" predictable forms of experiences'.

Such challenges can obviously only be met in stages or phases whereby each year only a carefully selected choice of suitable venues and services are incorporated into the programme and advertised as part of the official tourist route. The needed investment (both in terms of capacity building and facilities management) may appear daunting at present, but would greatly benefit local communities on a long-term basis. 'The ultimate integration of tourism into the local community occurs when the local people discover the convenience and desirability of using facilities designed originally for tourists', suggested MacCannell (1976: 169) in the mid-1970s, when tourism began to boom in Europe.

## Striving Towards Self-sustainability

The National Women's Arts Festival is invariably affected by the larger transformation processes of the local and national performing arts sector, as well as by pressure on government-funded arts and culture ventures. These pressures have indeed most recently resulted in the closure of the Playhouse Company. The National Women's Arts Festival could theoretically become an independent entity, preferably a section 21 company, or what Marc Mallam (1989) calls a 'heritage charity'. Even if sponsorship for the National Women's Arts Festival from the public sector (e.g. National Arts Council) could consistently be procured in future, the long-term aim should be an increasing degree of self-sustainability. Given the limitations of resources, the way forward lies in strategic partnerships and a pooling of resources.

Since the event has undeniably great potential for marketing the city of Durban and facilitating economic development, the Durban Events Corporation could be approached to fund and market the National Women's Arts Festival. Launched in 2000 by the Durban Metropolitan Council and managed by the Cape Town-based company, Octagon, the Durban Events Corporation is the sister company of Durban Africa, the organisation responsible for promoting tourism in the city (Baloyi, 2001 and Swart, personal communication, 2001). The Events Corporation invites proposals for festivals and events from the public, which are then evaluated and recommended to the Durban Corporation.[13]

Former marketing manager of Durban Africa, Lungile Dichaba (personal communication 2001), perceives the timing of the festival in early August as a disadvantage, because it falls outside the tourism peak season. Durban Africa currently consolidates its efforts around peak seasons determined by domestic school holidays in July, around Easter, in September and December. However, Durban Events Corporation account director, Kamilla Swart (personal communication, 2001), does not agree, pointing out that one could budget for the event if there was a commitment and conviction of its benefits. In terms of long-term tourism development in the city and the region, it will in any case be necessary to build up efforts between the established peaks of the year. During the year 2000, for instance, Durban Events Corporation had specifically called for proposals around Easter and long weekends in an attempt to facilitate this building up between peaks. Since the festival falls on a long weekend, it could, according to Swart, be marketed as the last event concluding the July season.

It is evident that current peak seasons are defined with the domestic tourist in mind, but it could be argued that the National Women's Art Festival provides a strong potential to attract international visitors, especially as the month of August falls into the peak holiday season in Europe and the United States. Although currently international tourist arrivals in Durban are not overly impressive, a growing number of charter flights is beginning to service the city. It is anticipated that Durban will become a major holiday destination for package tourists arriving in charter flights, especially from Hungaria, the Czech Republic and Germany (Cole, 2001). Such flights would facilitate offering special packages that specifically target cultural tourists.

From a tourism development point of view, cultural tourists, or what Tabata (1989) calls 'special interest travellers', are desirable to attract. These tourists tend to be open for and appreciative of new and possibly unconventional experiences, which allow them to learn about or share in the local culture. They thus help diversify the market and 'hedge' against fluctuation in the world tourism market. Cultural tourists tend to be higher educated, have higher 'cultural capital' and are more affluent than the average recreational tourist (Tabata, 1989: 72; see also Craik, 1997). Another important point observed by Craik (1997: 127) is that 'culture holds a greater appeal to women and young people than to men and older people, something that is curiously understated in the literature'. While traditionally tourism tends to appeal to the male gaze, more recently, and especially with the flourishing of cultural tourism, a marked 'feminization of the tourist gaze' has taken place. This is a result of the fact that cultural facilities and events attract more female visitors and that women are the primary tastemakers in choosing holiday destinations and activities (1997: 132–3).

Given the devaluated rand, admission tickets are likely to be perceived as extremely cheap for overseas tourists. A two-tier system for admission, which is frequently found and widely accepted in other tourist destinations with vast discrepancies between local income levels and tourist spending power, could be introduced in order to increase revenues generated from ticket sales. Another potential target group could be international conference organisers. A precedent was already set in this regard in August 2000 with the International Association of the History of Religion Congress, which attracted over 2000 delegates from all over the world. In this case, it appears that the dates of the conference (5–12 August) happened to coincide with the National Women's Arts Festival, a fact which the conference organiser, Rosalind Hackett (personal communication, 1999), was thrilled about, as she was keen to utilise the festival as a festive backdrop to the academic proceedings and an opportunity for delegates to enjoy a unique cultural experience and entertainment. Again, a strategic partnership between the marketing of the ICC and the National Women's Arts Festival, could ascertain that in future the festival is used as a draw-card to attract certain types of conferences and, vice versa, conference tourism is utilised to provide audiences for the festival.

Broadhurst (1989) in his article on 'The search for new funds' explores a variety of ways in which heritage and conservation projects can generate funds. Some of the options he outlines could easily be adopted for the National Women's Art Festival, such as the 'Friends' concept, i.e. founding a 'Friends of the Women's Arts Festival' organisation with annual membership fees (and call for donations) in exchange for concessions on ticket prices and other benefits. The 'Adopting Sites' concept involves identifying companies or organisations who are willing to adopt a particular site or venue used by the National Women's Arts Festival and commit themselves to providing funds and services towards the maintenance, preparation, management and possibly even upgrading, of this venue or site for the purposes of the festival. Private sponsors could also be identified who fund individual aspects of the project, for instance the training of guides or the purchase of paint.

## Media

For any event to become a tourist attraction, the media play a seminal role. Women's Day celebrations will and should obviously continue throughout the country, but some media co-ordination on a national level would be helpful to ensure that the many concurrent events are not receiving equal media coverage, especially not on national TV news broadcasts, thereby competing with the Durban event, dissipating its impact, and diluting the sense of its uniqueness. The press coverage of the National Women's Arts Festival has been very extensive, especially in the past two years, but mostly limited to local newspapers (with an occasional article in the national *Mail & Guardian*) and mostly confined to pre-production, publicity articles. It is notable that the festival currently does not feature on the arts diary website, the Guide to South African Arts, Culture and Heritage.

Just as important as the publicity and marketing aspect of media coverage is the publication of critical reviews, which assist in shoring up the festival's national profile, credibility and status within the national annual arts and festival calendar. It is here where the greatest need for attention lies. The current scarcity or complete lack of critical reviews of individual events, performers or the festival as a whole conveys the impression that the productions of the National Women's Arts Festival are not significant enough to warrant serious critical attention.[14] This is despite the fact that a number of news reporters and reviewers were specifically invited and funded to come from Johannesburg and other parts of the country to cover the event (Chorn, personal communication, 2001). One of the reasons may be the scarcity of specialised critics certainly on a local, but also on a national level. Perhaps one must in future consider inviting professionals from outside the newspapers to write reviews. As another possible reason for the lack of critical attention, one can only speculate that being a women's festival (which incidentally does not mean that all performers or visitors are female), the festival suffers from the same kind of largely unacknowledged but widely persisting, biased disregard that other women's events, ranging from art exhibitions to women's sports, are habitually subjected to in South Africa and other parts of the world. While it would be desirable that these biases could be changed globally, the more immediate lesson for the marketing/publicity coverage would be to highlight the focus on female creative expression as part of the uniqueness of the event, while at the same time carefully avoiding the impressing of an exclusive, feminist or sectarian event.

As the cultural tourism industry has only recently begun to flourish in South Africa and other developing countries, important lessons can be learned from the experience made in European countries. I would like to end this section with the apt words of Marc Mallam, which sum up the challenges and the opportunities that lie ahead for the National Women's Arts Festival:

If heritage projects are to succeed through the harnessing of the potential of the tourist and leisure industries, without unlimited public subsidy, then any heritage charities involved in such a project must learn that they are now becoming part of a very competitive and commercial industry. They will accordingly have to learn the necessary skills of that industry in order to compete successfully within it. However, they must at the same time remember to respect their inherent heritage characteristics and qualities and never compromise these to such an extent that the project loses its unique flavour or special ethos, which in the long run will always remain the foundations of any of the project's future 'commercial' success. (Mallam, 1989: 49)

## Conclusion

Given time and resources, any event could theoretically be built up to become a major tourist attraction and some people may perhaps not see why such resources should be allocated to an arts event. However, as has been shown above, as much as the National Women's Arts Festival itself deserves support for its contribution to women's empowerment and societal transformation, turning it into a tourist attraction carries the potential for significant and sustainable economic benefits for the broader local community. For the city of Durban, in competition with Johannesburg and Cape Town, chances are for a reversal of the city's traditional reputation as a cultural backwater, which regularly experiences scores of local talent from all genres of the visual and performing arts leaving to escape a persistent lack of opportunities.

As indicated in the introduction, the National Women's Arts Festival has fallen victim to the same pattern. When Gita Pather moved from the Durban Playhouse to the Market Theatre in Johannesburg, the festival sponsor, Transnet, wanted her to stay on as an Advisor to the National Women's Arts Festival (Pather, personal communication, 2003). However, as this was not a viable option for her, Transnet and the Johannesburg Development Agency (JDA) eventually approached her to recreate the festival for Johannesburg in 2002. Meanwhile in Durban, the Playhouse tried to pick up the pieces by organising some kind of fill-in-the-gap type of celebration – with deeply disappointing results. There are many ways in which one can celebrate Women's Day, but there is only one National Women's Art Festival in South Africa. It remains to be hoped that the festival will one day return to Durban to provide the city with a much-needed cultural injection, the people with economic empowerment and the tourists with a unique cultural experience.

## Notes
1. The day marks the anniversary of the 9 August 1956 march by thousands of

women to the Union Buildings in Pretoria to protest against the pass laws that restricted their movement (Anonymous, 1998d).
2. This festival, organised by Dan Chiorboli and Pitika Ntuli and sponsored by Standard Bank, emerged in 1997 from the Grahamstown National Arts Festival in Grahamstown.
3. The importance of festivals for tourism worldwide has motivated the Centre for Tourism and Cultural Change at Sheffield Hallam University in association with the International Festivals and Events Association Europe to hold a conference on 'Journeys of Expression: Cultural Festivals/Events & Tourism' in Bonn, Germany in February 2002. The present chapter was inspired by (but not presented at) this conference.
4. The Festival has 20 permanent members of staff and 200 temporary employees during the festival period (Anonymous, 2001).
5. The National Arts Festival in Grahamstown, for instance, was started by the Grahamstown Foundation in 1974 with 60-odd items. According to the official festival website (Anonymous 2001a), the festival now features about 600 events on the main and fringe programmes and close to 1800 performances. The number of visitors is estimated at around 100 000.
6. Directorship of the National Women's Arts Festival: 1995–8 Gita Pather; 1999–2000 Linda Bukhosini; 2001 Anriette Chorn.
7. No statistics about visitor numbers were kept in the early years of the festival. The figure for 2001 is based on ticket sales and estimates (Chorn, personal communication, 2002).
8. The gala concert, which each year appears to easily fill the Playhouse's large opera auditorium, is probably most successful in drawing considerable numbers of people, most of whom are Africans (both male and female). Depending on the respective performer, there is often an amazing level of engagement with the audience. This type of show contributes to transforming the historic legacy of the Playhouse as an elitist place for educated whites to a venue for the enjoyment of all people.
9. In 1996 the festival received sponsorship from Southern Life. But the company then went through a transformation and restructuring process and was thus unable to renew its commitment the following year. As a result, the festival had to be cancelled in 1997. In 1998 the National Arts Council (NAC) provided funding. Transnet came in as a sponsor in 1999 (Chorn, personal communication, 2001).
10. 'The Lubombo Spatial Development Initiative (SDI) is a concerted programme by the governments of Swaziland, Moçambique and South Africa to ensure that new investment occurs rapidly in the area. At its heart, it is a strategy to convert the mix of human and natural resources of the wider Lubombo territory into an internationally competitive zone of economic activity and growth' (LSDI, undated: 1).
11. According to Chorn (personal communication, 2001) the craft works attracted much attention and many people were disappointed that they couldn't buy any of the wares. Bronwen James (personal communication, 2001), who is in charge of the craft project, explains that each product is a unique, one-off object and the crafters did not have enough stock at that stage to offer the products for sale. The Greater St Lucia Wetlands Craft Programme is meant to empower rural craft women by improving the quality of their products (through product

development workshops) and introduce them to new national and overseas markets (e.g. African Art Centre in Durban, conference organisers, craft buyers in Johannesburg and Cape Town, etc.). Although currently the women benefit most from working to fill orders, the sale of these items at festivals and other such occasions could be facilitated in future, if enough time for preparation is allowed and crucial cash-flow problems for the purchase of materials are addressed.

12. The local press coverage of Women's Day activities convey an impression of the different activities and events staged by different communities in celebration of the day. In 1998 for instance, various organisations in Chatsworth organised a peaceful march and a packed programme of events at Gandhi Park in Chatsworth (Anonymous, 1998); in Mobeni Heights the local Women's Group celebrated Women's Day at the local Doorgha Hall (Anonymous, 1998a); at the Stella Sports Club in Glenwood was an exhibition of crafts made by women as well as several food stalls (Singh, 1998); an open day on economic opportunities for women took place at the Jubilee Hall of the Durban City Hall (Anonymous, 1998b); at the Square Space Theatre on the University of Natal campus a Women's Arts Festival was held, featuring various plays (Anonymous, 1998c).

13. Incidentally, the Durban Events Corporation has recently come under fire due to issues around transparency and accountability (Baloyi, 2001).

14. There are a few notable exceptions (e.g. Lakhani, 2000). Even if the criticism is negative, it nevertheless helps in establishing a critical reputation for the festival.

## References

Anonymous (1998) Commemorating Women's Day. *Mercury* 4 August.
Anonymous (1998a) Events planned to celebrate Women's Day. *Post* 5 August.
Anonymous (1998b) Women's Day celebration. *Mercury* 11 August.
Anonymous (1998c) Women's arts festival. *Mercury* 30 September.
Anonymous (1998d) 'Women power' has come a long way. *Daily News* 10 August.
Anonymous (2001) Edinburgh International Festival website, hosted by Company Net. On WWW at http://www.eif.co.uk/.
Anonymous (2001a) Standard Bank National Arts Festival, Grahamstown. On WWW at http://www.places.co.za/html/grahamsfest.html.
Anonymous (2001b) National Women's Music Festival (NWMF). Ball State University, Munice, Indiana. On WWW at http:// www.wiaonline.org/nwmf/.
Anonymous (2001c) Women's Voices Festival site. On WWW at http:// www.womensvoices.on.ca/.
Anonymous (2001d) The South African Women's Arts Festival 2001. Programme brochure.
Baloyi, M. (2001) Events body under fire. *Independent on Saturday*. 17 November.
Broadhurst, R. (1989) The search for new funds. In D.L. Uzzell (ed.) *Heritage Interpretation* (Vol.2. The Visitor Experience) (pp. 29–43). London and New York: Belhaven Press.
Bywater, M. (1993) The market for cultural tourism in Europe. *EIU Travel and Tourism Analyst* 7, 30–46.

Cohen-Cruz, J. (1995) The American Festival Project: Performing difference, discovering common ground. In N. Felshin (ed.) *But is it Art? The Spirit of Art as Activism* (pp. 117–40). Seattle: Bay Press.

Cole, B. (2001) More tourists to hit Durban shores. *Daily News* 29 October.

Craik, J. (1997, reprinted 2000) The culture of tourism In C. Rojek and J. Urry (eds) *Touring Cultures. Transformations of Travel and Theory* (pp. 113–36). London and New York: Routledge.

Hewison, R. (1987) *The Heritage Industry. Britain in a Climate of Decline.* London: Methuen.

Kakaza, L. (2000) A feast of festivals. *Guide to South African Arts, Culture and Heritage.* On WWW at http://www.artsdiary.org.za.

Kearney, L. (2001) New tourism project launched. *Natal Mercury* 24 September.

Khan, F. (2000) Sisters ready to shake up the city. *Daily News* 8 August.

Lakhani, K. (2000) Women's Arts Festival meets audience head on. *Daily News* 16 August.

LSDI (undated) Official report. Published by the LSDI Project Manager (no place of publication indicated).

MacCannell, D. (1976) *The Tourist.* London and New York: Macmillan.

Mallam, M. (1989) Can heritage charities be profitable? In D.L. Uzzell (ed.) *Heritage Interpretation (Vol. 2. The Visitor Experience)* (pp. 44–50). London and New York: Belhaven Press.

Marschall, S. (2002) *Community Mural Art in South Africa.* Pretoria: Unisa Press.

Singh, K. (1998) Women entrepreneurs to feature at arts and crafts exhibition. *Post* 5 August.

Tabata, R. (1989) Implications of special interest tourism for interpretation and resource conservation In D.L. Uzzell (ed.) *Heritage Interpretation (Vol. 2. The Visitor Experience)* (pp. 68–77). London and New York: Belhaven Press.

Uzzell, D.L. (ed.) (1989) *Heritage Interpretation (Vol. 2. The Visitor Experience).* London and New York: Belhaven Press.

Wakashe, T. (1994) South Africa's heritage needs to be democratized. *Restorica* 28, 35–6.

Wessels, A. (1994) In search of acceptable national symbols for South Africa. *Journal for Contemporary History* 19 (2), 262–87.

White Paper on Arts Culture and Heritage (1996) Department of Arts, Culture, Science and Technology, Pretoria.

**Personal communications**

Chorn, Anriette (2001 and 2002) Playhouse Company. Several personal and telephonic communications.

Dichaba, Lungile (2001) Durban Africa. Personal communication. Durban.

Hackett, Roselind (see 1999) Several personal conversations. Durban.

James, Bronwen (2001) Personal interview. Durban, 11 December.

Pather, Gita (2003) Market Theatre. E-mail communication. Johannesburg, April.

Swart, Kamilla (2001) Durban Events Corporation. Personal interview. Durban, 6 December.

*Chapter 10*

# Kyrgyzstan's Manas Epos Millennium Celebrations: Post-Colonial Resurgence of Turkic Culture and the Marketing of Cultural Tourism

Karen Thompson, Peter Schofield, Nicola Palmer and
Gulnara Bakieva[1]

## Introduction

At the beginning of the 21st century the global cultural tourism market is characterised by unprecedented access to major heritage sites. Consequently, emerging nations that are in the process of developing tourism require strong and differentiated brands to improve their imageability and position themselves effectively in the mind of prospective consumers. In the Central Asian republic of Kyrgyzstan, there has been a resolute attempt to employ the pre-eminent national heritage icon, Manas, in this respect. Batyr-khan Manas is the principal hero of the Manas epos, an acclaimed collection of epic tales that tell of the formation, life, struggles and triumphs of the Kyrgyz people and represent the highpoint of a widespread Central Asian oral culture. The significance of this heroic epos, some 553,000 lines in total, was highlighted in 1995 when the Kyrgyz government spent an estimated US$8 million on a series of festive celebrations for the Manas epos millennium event and UNESCO declared 1995 the 'International Year of Manas' in recognition of its importance in human history.

Given the current renaissance of Turkic culture in the region and attempts by many nation states, including Kyrgyzstan, to preserve its integrity, it is not surprising that Manas has come to symbolise the embodiment of the Kyrgyz self-image, spiritual unity and independence. Against this backcloth of both nationalistic and Turkic cultural resurgence and the rapid development of tourism in the region, this chapter is broadly concerned with the political, cultural and potential economic significance of Manas and the millennium festival. The chapter addresses the symbolic nature of the Manas epos and its influence on both the unification of Kyrgyzstan and the enhancement of the country's national and Turkic identity. The case of the Manas epos millennium celebrations event is then used to illustrate the relationship between the uses of the Manas 'legend' in the construction of a national identity and in the positioning of the cultural tourism product. This chapter subsequently assesses the potential usefulness of the Manas epos in the creation of a destination image for Kyrgyzstan and in the positioning of Kyrgyzstan in the global tourism marketplace.

## Tourism, Culture, Heritage and Identity

The commoditisation of 'culture' and the rise of 'cultural tourism' are ultimately dependent upon emphasising those features and characteristics that define a place and its people as unique and on generating interest and translating this into tourist demand. Britton (1991: 464) defines cultural tourism as occurring 'where cultural sites, events, attractions and/or experiences are marketed as primary tourist experiences'. Other authors claim that the concept of cultural tourism may be linked to historical events, sites and attractions, and that heritage tourism itself may form part of a cultural tourism category (BBC News, 2001). At the beginning of the 21st century, the global cultural tourism market is characterised by unprecedented access to major heritage sites. In the International Scientific Committee on Cultural Tourism (ICOMOS) Charter on Cultural Tourism (1976: 2) 'cultural tourism' is described as a form of tourism where the discovery of monuments and sites is a key aspiration of the tourist. Craik (1997: 121) elaborates further upon this suggesting that cultural tourists not only seek to discover but seek to learn about ' . . . people's lifestyle, heritage and arts in an informed way that genuinely represents those cultures and their historical contexts'.

However, tourism's employment of culture as a selling tool involves selectivity and 'competing constructions' rather than absolute truths (Seaton, 1998). The very idea of 'genuine' representations of culture and historical events is notoriously problematic. Places, peoples and pasts are part of a symbolic economy that trades on cultural identities and markers of histories, and as such they are contested and negotiated by those who produce and consume them.

The extent to which competing constructions exist within a destination, in particular with respect to the representation of culture, has been questioned (see for example, Mellinger, 1994; Morgan & Pritchard, 1998). To what extent can a shared sense of national heritage and culture amongst indigenous populations ever be attained? Witoszek (2001), examining the relationship between collective memory and national identity in Sweden, Germany and Italy, argues that, in accordance with ideas belonging to the Tartu School of Semiotics,[2] culture exists as a non-hereditary memory of a society expressed in a system of symbols and norms. However, despite culture, as a symbolic object, being open to redefinition over time, the idea of shared cultural symbols is not refuted by Witoszek (2001: 1) and 'memes', 'imaginative units of social memory which preserve and mediate communal identity or communal crisis over time', are proposed to exist. The importance of 'cultural identities' in the light of increased transnationalism and globalisation and the potential demise of the nation state has also been noted (Clark University, 2001).

In post-communist nations, previously imposed national consciousness and collective culture appear to encourage the creation of revised cultural identities linked to pre-communist ethnic heritage (Rorlich, 1999). Bichel (1997: 3) discusses how, with respect to countries in Central Asia, newly elected national identities are expressed with a heavy emphasis upon ethnicity and 'have at least as much to do with self-expression and self-assertion as they do with historical evidence, precedent or cultural revival'. In short, national identity building in these countries is perceived to be a direct response to avoiding being re-conquered. Fairbanks (2001: 52) notes how 'leaders such as Askar Akayev of Kyrgyzstan have defied long odds to save their countries from dissolution or re-absorption into a new Russian empire'. These attempts to sustain independence result in national identities being created that resemble 'ethnic nationalism' whereby patriotic feeling is based on ' . . . the perception of cultural or historical links where only members of this ethnic group are nationals of the state' (Oxford Young European Society, 1999: 1).

The uncertainty and turbulence of the new global economic order, and in particular the dissolution of the USSR, have had profound effects on Central Asian countries such as Kyrgyzstan. The resurgence of this republic has been driven by post-industrial activities associated with the increasingly sophisticated cultures of consumption, rather than traditional targets of growth promotion strategies: industrial and manufacturing production and employment (apart from the mining of rare metals such as gold).[2] Within this context, there has been a growing recognition of the role of culture in framing and shaping the country's economy and society resulting in attempts to develop a cultural strategy for regeneration.

The cultural or historical links selected as the basis for the creation of a post-communist identity pre-date Soviet rule and can only be understood within the context of the history of the ethnic Kyrgyz population.

## The Historical Context of Kyrgyz Culture and Identity

The culture of each region within Central Asia, as with regions of Europe, is eclectic: a product of thousands of years of spatially constrained historical events. Although archaeological evidence of settlements in Kyrgyzstan may be traced back 300,000 years, it was not until the 16th century that the Kyrgyz people migrated to the land today called Kyrgyzstan. The history of the land and its people is complex, but key periods within Kyrgyz history are highlighted in Table 10.1, in order to provide a brief insight into factors shaping the traditional cultural heritage of the indigenous Kyrgyz people (Bashiri, 1999a; KSATS, 1999).

**Table 10.1** Key periods within Kyrgyz history

| |
|---|
| 200 BC – The Kyrgyz were ancient Turkic tribal people, inhabiting land around the region of the Yenisei River in southern Siberia. |
| AD 1000 – Under the leadership of a heroic leader (Manas) the Kyrgyz had overthrown the Uyghur Empire (in the geographical area now known as Mongolia) and established a Kyrgyz Khanate in its place, extending from Lake Baikal to the Irtish River and from the present Krasnoyarsk City to the great Chinese Wall. |
| AD 1207 – Following the Mongol onslaught, led by the troops of Ghenghis Khan, the Kyrgyz settled as mountain-dwelling pastoral nomads in the grasslands of the Tien Shan and the process of Islamisation occurred. |
| AD 1876 – The Kyrgyz were incorporated into the Russian Empire. Kyrgyz grazing lands were confiscated by Russian peasants. |
| AD 1916 – Tsar Nicholas II drafted Kyrgyz youth into the Russian army. |
| AD 1920–30 – During the command of Stalin and collectivisation, the Kyrgyz were forced to abandon nomadic practices and made to settle in makeshift towns and villages. |
| AD 1930–40 – All manifestations of the Kyrgyz past were diluted or dissolved in efforts towards Soviet collectivisation and industrialisation. Russian became the official state language, legal codes, death rituals, pilgrimages, circumcisions and Islamic marriages (all adopted as Kyrgyz practices) were forbidden. |
| AD 1991 – Independence was gained from the USSR, the Kyrgyz Republic was formed. Today, it is led by Central Asia's only non-communist president, Askar Akayev, and has a democratic government and a free market economy. |

## Epic poetry in Central Asian culture

Epic poems (also known as 'epos' or 'dastan') have been identified as a historically and culturally significant feature of the intangible heritage of Turkic nations by; *inter alia*, Reichl (1992: 15): ' . . . it is important to realise, when discussing Turkic oral poetry, that it is intimately connected to the complex and diverse historical development of the Turkic tribes and nations.' Such poetry is significant, not merely for reasons of artistic merit, but rather for its role as an ornate oral history, passing value systems from one generation to another. It is argued that all Altaian epic poems are the reworking of a 'mother epos', fragments from which have been preserved and embellished by new experiences (Inan, 1968, Togan, 1972). In Siberia, the Altaians and Yakuts have incorporated the shamanistic rituals of their ancient belief systems into their poetry, whilst Arabic literature has left its mark on the epos of the Ottoman Turks and Uzbeks. More poignant, however, are the common Turkic traditions which are in evidence throughout the epic poetry of Central Asia: 'Every aspect of the life of the heroes . . . bears vestiges common to Turkic culture' (Yologlu, 1995: 38).

At a time when access to the Soviet Union was still restricted and the preservation and publication of nationalistic epos little encouraged, Paksoy (1989) accounted for at least 50 mainstream epos in Central Asia. The actual figure may be higher. The core of Turkic epic poetry has been created by the nomads of the Steppes, in particular the modern Kazakh and Kyrgyz peoples (Reichl, 1992). Of the 50 Turkic epics to be published by the Turkish Language Institution as part of a preservation project, 34 are from Kyrgyzstan. Kyrgyz epic poetry is an elaborate and exceptionally detailed oral history of the most important triumphs and set backs of the Steppe tribes and can be related to various periods of their history.

## Kyrgyz Epos and Manas

As a result of their nomadic and war-like existence, constant intermingling with other tribes, and later the oppression of Tsarist Russia, it was not until the October Revolution of 1917 that the Kyrgyz acquired a written language.[4] The prolonged absence of a written language and the subsequent reliance on the oral method of passing on information has led to a series of epic poems that is argued to be exceptionally rich in historical fact and tradition:

> Everything the people had learned, created, experienced for many
> centuries was preserved in an oral artistic form. Folklore became the
> memory of the people, the keeper of all its achievements, ideals and

conceptions, knowledge and reminiscence – all the facts about its historical development. (Musayev, 1994: 95)

Among the 34 Kyrgyz epos identified by the Turkish Language Institution, by far the longest, best known and most enduring is the Manas epos. This epos can be divided into three volumes which tell of the life and death respectively of Manas, the leader of the Kyrgyz tribes during the most successful period of their history, his son Semetei and grandson Sejtek.

Whilst there is no agreement among experts regarding the origins of the Manas epos, it is believed that the first volume refers mainly to the time of the Kyrgyz Great Power in the 9th and 10th centuries (Auezov, 1961; 1999) and that the main events portray the conquering of Chinese Turkestan from the Uyghurs. Most scholars believe that Manas was the military figure who led this conquest and who died in AD 847 (Auezov, 1999). Historical documents from as early as the 15th century make mention of the Manas epos, however the second and third volumes of the epos (Semetei and Sejtek) are thought to represent the struggles of the Kyrgyz against the Kalmaks in the 16th and 17th centuries (Jhirmunski, 1999). This chronological confusion supports the view that the events portrayed in Manas are layered as a result of its protracted composition (Musayev, 1994), representing historical events over an extended period of the history of the Kyrgyz nation. Thus, one can identify in the different layers historic events and mythological plots alongside ancient beliefs and everyday activities.

The outline of the plot adheres to the pattern of the epos genre in Central Asia, whereby the exploits of a hero (*Alp* or *Batyr*) on behalf of his people are related by special bards (*akyn*). However, unusually for the genre, the narrators of the Manas epos (*manaschi*), are not normally accompanied by any musical instruments. The skill of the narrator is judged not only by his knowledge of events and details, but also by his creative talents in being able to compose his own variant, said to be inspired by prophetic dreams. Thus, deviations exist in the plot of the epos across different variants, caused by the creative will of the *manaschi* and the school with which he is connected (Musayev, 1994). There are currently 65 versions of the epos maintained in manuscript form by the Kyrgyz National Academy of Sciences, all recorded in Kyrgyzstan.

## Promotion and Suppression of Manas in Recent History

Recording of the Manas epos began towards the end of the 19th century with the first fragments ('Manas' Childhood', 'Marriage of

Manas' and 'Funeral Feast for Kokotoy') being written down and translated into Russian by a Kazakh traveller and ethnographer, Chokan Valikhanov in 1857. Valikhanov is recognised as having discovered the Manas epos and his description of it as the 'Iliad of the Steppes' is still widely cited. The period immediately following the October Revolution saw the recording and transcription of the two longest and best-known versions of the Manas epos. The first was recorded between 1922 and 1926 from the *manaschi* Sagynbay Orozbakov in the old Arabic script and comprises more than 180,000 lines. The second version, recorded from Sayakbay Karalaev is the longest ever recorded (over half a million lines), incorporating all three volumes of the epos. It was written down between 1935 and 1937 in Latin script. Orozbakov's version, whilst shorter, is thought to be the most authentic, as the Soviets are believed to have enforced politically motivated omissions and amendments on Karalaev's version.

The 1930s was a period of great scientific interest in the Manas epos, however many attempts to record, study and preserve the epos were suppressed by the Soviets. At first, those involved in the research and publication of Manas were persecuted.[5] Later, attempts were made to prevent performances or recitals of the epos.[6] The recording of Karalaev's version of the Manas had taken place as a prelude to a 1000 year jubilee of the epos which was planned initially for 1937, then rescheduled twice for 1940 and 1947 (Bayjiev, 1999a). In the event, this jubilee did not take place until 1995. Publications that had been produced for the jubilee were burnt and the authors arrested. Many of those responsible for research into the Manas epos were imprisoned, disappeared or were shot, including the scientists who had made the famous recordings from Karalaev and Orazbakov. The reasons for the suppression of the Manas epos were perceived pan-Turkic and pan-Islamic undercurrents which were damaging to the common, supranational culture that the Soviets were promoting (Paksoy, 1989). It was asserted by the Kyrgyz Communist Party that 'bourgeois nationalists' had encouraged the *manaschi* to introduce anti-Soviet sentiments.

In the 1950s the discussion was reopened and a five-day conference was held on the Manas epos in June 1952 for scholars from all over the Soviet Union. This conference went some way to educating Soviet leaders on the historic and cultural significance of the Manas epos, concluding 'that the national epos Manas was a national work, expressing thoughts and expectations of working classes and that a summary variant should be created, having completely taken 'anti-popular' features out of it' (Bayjiev, 1999b: 239). However, at that time very little of the Manas epos had been translated into Russian and those fragments which were published in Russian between 1945 and 1949 related a great Kyrgyz victory over the Chinese. Out of context these fragments had a certain nationalistic fervour and ultimately hindered the staging of the long-awaited jubilee. In the late 1970s there were again calls for permission for the staging of a 1000 year jubilee, however it was not until after the dissolution of the Soviet Union and the declaration of the new Kyrgyz Republic that the 1000 anniversary celebrations of the Manas epos were finally hosted.

## Manas as a Cultural Icon

Manas may be identified as an iconic figure, upon which the Kyrgyz cultural identity is based. The use of an iconic figure in national identity building is not unusual in itself (Alexander Nevsky for Russia, William Wallace for Scotland and St George for England, for example).

Witoszek (2001) remarks upon the way in which narratives, rites, characters and icons often function as referents of national identity. Speaking of the Manas expert Mukhtar Auezov, Bashiri (1999b) reports how Manas has been argued to transcend temporal and spatial boundaries as an iconic figure belonging to all Turkic people regardless of socio-economic, political and geographical affiliation.

This assertion obscures our (Western) comprehension of the adoption of Manas as a cultural icon in comparison with our understanding of tourism employment of other iconic figures, particularly celebrated UK icons such as Robin Hood, King Arthur, William Wallace and Owain Glyndŵr. In particular, it is interesting to explore the extent to which the legend of Manas is accepted as a shared form of national heritage and culture not only within a single nation, Kyrgyzstan, but also across the whole region of Central Asia.

The naming of Manas in other Turkic epics (Musayev, 1994) suggests that belief in Manas is shared to some extent across other nations in Central Asia. However, Manas is solely utilised in the national identity promoted by the Kyrgyz people. Hence, for marketing purposes, he offers the potential for Kyrgyzstan to differentiate itself from other Central Asian nations. It has been envisaged that, in future, the Manas epos may be used to promote self- and collective consciousness of the Kyrgyz nation (Okeeva, 2001). However, the possibility also exists for Manas to become an integral element of the heritage tourism product of the Kyrgyz Republic. In order to achieve this, there is a need to increase the level of awareness of the Kyrgyz epic outside of Kyrgyzstan.

## Promoting Manas: The 1995 Manas Epos Millennium Celebrations

Hallmark events both influence, and are products of, the society, economy and the environment in which they are located and, as a result, are 'explicit and implicit political occasions' (Hall, 1992: 84). The 'imagineering' or image building associated with such events creates a situation in which both personal and institutional interests receive a high degree of visibility although, it is the macro-political level we are concerned with here, together with the power of events to advance particular political objectives by effectively using the high media profile to strengthen ideologies and to highlight certain features, themes and values in order to change the perceived meaning and structure of place.

Amidst the chaotic political geography of Central Asia, emerging nations such as Kyrgyzstan are attempting to reposition themselves for a global audience by creating a distinctive image in the interests of differentiating the country from competitors, attracting investment and enhancing touristic appeal. Increasingly, special events are being viewed as an integral part of tourism development and marketing plans; they are the image builders of modern tourism and are the primary means by which tourist destinations are placed or kept on the map (Hall, 1992). Festivals and events at national, regional and destination levels have been used to develop a favourable image in the international marketplace (Ashworth & Goodall, 1988). In marketing destinations, marketers select and illustrate certain aspects of society and culture that reflect and reinforce preferred interpretations from the overall stock of cultural knowledge and information (Morgan & Pritchard, 1998). Kyrgyzstan's Manas epos millennium celebration in 1995 is a useful example of a hallmark event at national level focusing on a particular, preferred, facet of culture. However, the aim of enhancing the external image of Kyrgyzstan as a culturally rich destination may be argued to have been secondary to the key objective of rebuilding and reinforcing a shared national identify for the newly independent state.

On 26 June 1992, less than a year after Kyrgyzstan became an independent state, President Akayev declared plans for the celebration of the 1000th anniversary of the Manas epos. Given the lack of clarity over the exact period of origin of the epos, the date of the celebration can be said to be largely extraneous. The Kyrgyz government gained the support of the United Nations Educational, Scientific and Cultural Organisation (UNESCO), which agreed to undertake the role of disseminating information about Manas on an international level and declared 1995 'International

Year of Manas' as part of its international calendar of events, reflecting UNESCO's interest in masterpieces of the oral and intangible heritage of humanity (UNESCO, 2001). The Manas millennium celebrations took place throughout the whole of 1995, but culminated in a four-day event at the end of August. The total cost of the four-day event alone is reported to have totalled more than 8 million euros (Mayhew *et al.*, 2000), an enormous sum for a country whose GNP in the same year was estimated to be approximately 700 euros per head of population (World Bank, 2000). The majority of the financial burden was borne by the Kyrgyz government; however UNESCO also provided some funds as part of their program for the preservation of world heritage.

## Nature of the Event, its Objectives and Legacy

The substantial cost of the event to the Kyrgyz government bears witness to its strategic importance, which can be examined in terms of three key objectives, outlined in Akayev's decree (see Asankanov & Omurbekov, 1995): the promotion of national identity in the wake of independence and following a period of cultural repression, the raising of awareness of the cultural and historical significance of Manas among the people of Kyrgyzstan and the promotion of the Manas epos and its traditions on an international scale. The Manas epos is described as the encyclopaedia of the Kyrgyz nation. It has been described as the single most important source of historical, socio-cultural and geographical information about the Kyrgyz people (Galieva, 1995). Additionally, the Manas epos has acted as a major influence on all art forms among the Kyrgyz people (Asankanov & Bekmukhamedova, 1999), having been described as the 'tuning fork' of Kyrgyz art (Lusanova, 1995: 99). Its appeal, not just for its artistic and literary merits, but also as a living epos containing the entire folklore of the nation, makes the Manas epos a logical tool for the promotion of national identity. Furthermore, the epos embodies the idea of unification of all Kyrgyz tribes under an exemplary leader and defender in an epoch when the Kyrgyz nation was at its most powerful. The society depicted in the epos shows many of the characteristics of a modern democracy, including equal rights, free elections and a council of elders (Galieva, 1995), characteristics that a fledgling democracy might aspire to.

A three-day conference entitled '"Manas" Epos and the World's Epic Heritage' took place during the August celebrations. This conference examined various aspects of the epos: its role as a historical-ethnographic source, the reflection of ethno-cultural links in the epic works of Central Asia, the study of the variants of the Manas texts, socio-political aspects of the Manas epos and the role of Manas in the arts (Askarov *et al.*, 1995). During this conference the evidence for the existence of Manas as a real historical figure was discussed. Connections between the epos and ancient monuments and historic sites in Kyrgyzstan were observed.

As part of the Manas 1000 celebrations, operas and plays composed mainly in the 1930s, which had been based on Manas but were rarely staged during Soviet times, were reinterpreted and performed. All of the theatre that took place during the event was performed by amateurs. The involvement of children was achieved through an open exhibition of children's art entitled 'Manas Through the Eyes of Children'. In the Talas region, at the *Manas Ordo*, where Manas is said to have lived and died, there was a re-enactment of fragments of the epos, filmed by the distin-guished director Tolomish Okeev which involved over 3000 people from the local area. The costumes and set were elaborate and expensive, but amateur actors and actresses played all the roles, which encouraged the learning not only of the lyrics of the epos, but also of traditional music, cuisine and games. Contests, in the form of recitals of parts of the Manas epos, had taken place throughout the first half of the year and the prize-winners were assembled in Bishkek and Talas for the August event. Also present were those few *manaschi* still alive. A primary objective was to identify potential future *manaschi* among the prize-winners, in order to maintain the oral tradition.

The goal of promoting Manas abroad was equally emphasised in the orchestration of the event. For a small and relatively insignificant country such as Kyrgyzstan, ownership of the world's longest epos presents the opportunity for creating a competitive advantage, particularly where that epos is so strongly associated with the history, culture and folklore of the country. An event of this scale (and expense) was seen as a vehicle for the international recognition of Kyrgyzstan as an independent state with an educated population and a rich cultural heritage. It was further felt by those familiar with the Manas epos, that such a key literary and scientific work should be accorded greater significance worldwide.

Fifteen countries were represented at the millennium event, including the presidents of Turkey, Uzbekistan, Azerbaijan and Kazakhstan. The United Nations Director General, Federico Mayor, was also present. The Manas epos was translated and published in 14 languages for the event, a remarkable achievement given its length and complexity. These transla-tions were partly funded by UNESCO, which also financed the publication of some of the promotional and educational literature for the event and funded the filming of a video for international distribution, capturing the culture and customs of the Kyrgyz people and exhibiting the dramatic landscape of the country. Two institutions were set up with the aim of publicising the existence of the Manas epos and its rich content nationally and internationally: the State Directorate for the Promotion of the Manas Epos and the Manas Heritage Organisation.

As part of the attempt to widen the destination product portfolio and promote a new destination image, the event was the catalyst for the construction of several visitor attractions on the Manas theme. A visitor complex was established at the *Manas Ordo* in the Talas region. This incorporated a visitor centre, Manas museum, a theatre and an arena for playing the national game *ulak-tartysh*. A Manas Heritage Village (*Manas Aiyly*) was built on the outskirts of Bishkek. This heritage village is a representation of the *Manas Ordo*, the village where Manas and his people lived, constructed out of modern materials but inspired by images from the Manas epos (weaponry, costume, etc.) In the centre of Bishkek, at the front of the Philharmonic Hall, an elaborate monument was constructed to the *manaschi* who kept the epos alive. Opening ceremonies for these visitor attractions took place during the four-day event in August.

The legacy of the event can be judged in terms of its success in promoting Manas and its traditions nationally and internationally. Within Kyrgyzstan itself, views have been expressed that there were few long-term outcomes of the 1995 Manas epos event (Okeeva, 2001). Certainly, in financial terms the event was not a success; heavy expenditure on domestic promotion of the event hampered generation of profits. However, examining the event from an external perspective and discounting any short-term economic motives, several positive outcomes may be noted. In particular, after years of Soviet oppression, the event enabled the Kyrgyz people to publicly celebrate and disseminate national pride and cultural identity without fear of retribution.

On a national level, Manas has become a potent symbol of the new state of Kyrgyzstan. Meanwhile, the publicity created by the event has hastened the drive to preserve the oral tradition and the Manas epos itself. In 1997 the United Nations Development Programme allotted US$150,000 for a project untitled 'Support for Manaschis and Akyns'. UNESCO also continues to partially fund the two organisations set up at the time of the event, although these have been reduced in size and importance due to lack of government funding. A recent achievement has been the transferral of all 65 of the epos to CD-Rom. On an international level, however, the degree of success in enhancing external awareness of the cultural legacy of the Manas epos is arguably more difficult to measure. The perceived importance of Manas in creating a destination image for Kyrgyzstan can, however, be partially gauged by examining current destination marketing practices and themes.

## Creating an Appropriate Destination Image for Kyrgyzstan

In strategic management terms, the use of the Manas epos event to attract publicity and tourists should not be separated from the broader context of tourism development and destination marketing including the creation of an appropriate image and identity, which is an important element in the process of positioning a place product. Currently, both the Kyrgyz tourism product and the Republic itself could be described as under-positioned because awareness of the destination in the world's major tourist generating areas is poor; market exposure to either actual experience of the Republic or media images has been limited. As a result, Kyrgyzstan remains undifferentiated from its neighbouring Central Asian states, with the exception of the more discerning end of the market. The country's 'official' tourism marketing continues to be dominated by images of mountains and lakes and is reflected in the promotional strap line: 'land of sky high mountains' (KSATS, 2001). This is understandable given the Republic's comparative advantage in natural resources, but given that most countries highlight their physical beauty and that Kyrgyzstan has hitherto positioned itself as 'Asia's Switzerland' (Haberstroh, 2000), there is a risk of product substitutability.

The Manas legend has an important role to play in positioning the Republic because it represents the country's 'core values' (Morgan & Pritchard, 2002). Manas symbolises the Kyrgyz self image in terms of the way in which they prescriptively see themselves as historically constructed and culturally re-constructed and thereby captures the spirit of the country and in that way differentiates it from other Central Asian countries. Whilst a belief and interest in the Manas legend is shared to some extent across other nations in Central Asia because it features in other Turkic epics (Musayev, 1994), it is associated with only the Kyrgyz national identity. The use of Manas in promoting Kyrgyzstan through events and official tourism literature therefore represents an effective means of developing a more romantic image of, and a spiritual attachment to, the country. Reference to this pre-eminent national icon also serves to highlight the post-Soviet resurgence of Kyrgyz culture and the need to identify a unifying force to address the country's marked religious, cultural and political divisions. Additionally, it underlines a shift in emphasis away from the traditional over-dependence on the nation's natural resource-based tourism towards a more balanced product based on a broader cultural formula. However, using Manas to market the country more effectively through the development of a personality for the place brand, although evident, is as yet underdeveloped.

## Marketing Manas: 'Official' Images of Kyrgyzstan

Images of tourist destinations are created, filtered and mediated through cultural and ideological structures (Morgan & Pritchard, 1998). Therefore, brochure material often draws on indigenous markers and cultural symbols to represent the product and reinforce particular ways of seeing and interpreting the destination. The overall portrayal of Manas in the official promotional literature is generally consistent with the legend understood by the Kyrgyz people and is not misrepresented in the way that Transylvanian tourism marketers have distorted the factual history of their national hero, Prince Vlad, by promoting the fiction of Dracula. Moreover, there appears to be little danger that the commercialisation of the Manas epos in the millennium celebrations and subsequent promotions will degenerate into a commodified spectacle that could obscure the country's real history, present a packaged landscape for tourist consumption and ultimately achieve little more than a triumph of image over substance.

An indication of the way in which Manas has been characterised in order to market cultural tourism products in the post-millennium period and a measure of the government tourism agency's respect for the legend can be gained by examining the official tourism marketing literature. Current government agency and tour operator brochures, whilst clearly making reference to cultural tourism and the Manas epos, continue to feature prominently the tourism products based on the country's abundant mountains and lakes. A statement in the Kyrgyz State Agency of Tourism and Sports 'Kyrgyzstan: Land of Sky-High Mountains' brochure underlines this point, 'nature is the main wealth and resource of our country' (KSATS, 2001: 4), as does the title of the brochure. This emphasis is not surprising given that 94% of Kyrgyzstan is mountainous and that the Republic is still struggling to find its political and cultural identity having been one of the most Russified of the former Soviet states, particularly in the north of the country.

The aforementioned brochure does include a special feature entitled, 'In the Land of Legendary Manas', which outlines the significance of the epos, provides a brief summary of its content and highlights areas of the country that are directly connected to the legend. An example of the latter is the 'Promised Land' of the Talas valley where numerous natural and man-made monuments bear the Manas name. The brochure claims that in the Talas valley it is possible to 'obtain a strong insight into and appreciation for the immortal epic of Manas' (KSATS, 2001: 24). It goes on to inform the prospective visitor that 20 kilometres from the town of Talas, near the village of Tash-Aryk, lies an ancient cemetery where the 14th century Gumbez (burial tomb) of Manas is located. This tangible relic arguably reinforces the Kyrgyz ownership of the Manas legend, particularly given the intangibility of the epos' oral tradition in Central Asia. The historical evidence would therefore seem to suggest that this iconic figure represents more than mere Kyrgyz folklore and self-expression. Moreover, Manas' recognition throughout the region suggests that a significant latent inbound cultural tourism market exists which, in turn, could reinforce the association between Manas and the Kyrgyz national identity.

It is interesting to note that the two-page Manas feature in the 'Kyrgyzstan: Land of Sky-High Mountains' brochure is one of four; the other three relate to the country's natural environment and are longer than the Manas feature, which appears after the others at the end of the 26 page brochure. The Central Asian Tourism Corporation's (2001: 6) 'Great Silk Road Tours' brochure features Manas and the epos under an ethnography section at the start of the brochure but does not mention the legend elsewhere, even when featuring sites which are connected with Manas. The World Tourism Organisation (2001: 15) 'Silk Road' brochure also lists the 'Tomb of Manas' as an attraction, but no other details relating to Manas are given. Similarly, the Glavtour (2001: 14) 'Kyrgyzstan' brochure mentions the Manas Aiyly heritage village in Bishkek but there are no other references to Manas in the 72-page document. Overall, the low-key promotion is perhaps surprising given the importance of Manas to the national psyche and the cultural bias of many of the brochures, but it serves to illustrate the somewhat cautious approach that is being taken to marketing Manas.

The low-key brochure images also reflect the relatively slow development of Kyrgyzstan's cultural tourism product. Whilst, the Ministry of Tourism acknowledges that historic sites throughout the country associated with Manas are important places of pilgrimage for domestic tourism and international visitors from other Central Asian countries (Akmatova, 2001), their development, including that of a 'Manas Trail', is hampered by several factors. The State Agency for Tourism and Sport has few funds, and priority is given to the development of international tourism because the domestic tourism market is in decline due to the low income levels of the majority of the population. The Talas region, which is most closely associated with Manas, is difficult to reach from Bishkek and best approached from Dzhambul in Kazakhstan. This can lead to visa problems for international visitors. Additionally, the Talas region appears to have little to offer the overseas visitor and the interpretation of the *Manas Ordo* site is principally directed towards domestic visitors as a place of pilgrimage. In the short term, these difficulties represent constraints on the development of cultural heritage tourism in Kyrgyzstan. In the longer term, there is perhaps an opportunity to ensure that a more authentic cultural heritage tourism experience of place is developed and sensitively marketed for tourist consumption.

## Conclusion

It is clear that Manas represents a powerful symbol of resurgence and unity in a country with marked political, economic and cultural divisions. What is less clear is whether or not Manas, within the context of the tourism masterplan and cultural development strategy, has the potential to contribute to long-term stability and prosperity by attracting, rather than repelling (as in ancient times), the raging hordes, or whether the spectacle of the Manas epos is a short-lived phenomenon and represents a fleeting moment in the country's turbulent reformation. Given the literary and historic significance of the epos and its strong association with Kyrgyz history, culture and folklore, however, its political and cultural influence is likely to be significant.

It is likely that Kyrgyzstan's abundant natural resources, particularly its mountains, will continue to dominate both images of prospective visitors and their subsequent experience of the country. In tourism terms, the promotion of Manas generally, and the Manas epos event specifically, has nevertheless helped to address the imbalance by highlighting authentic cultural heritage as both a key component of the tourism product and an element with significant potential for future development. The emergence of a distinctive identity from the country's mixed blessing of heritage has also improved the Republic's imageability and strengthened its position in the tourism marketplace. Politically, in addition to Manas' current role in differentiating Kyrgyzstan from its Central Asian neighbours, the legendary spiritual and military leader of the nation is once again playing an important part in unifying the Kyrgyz tribes, strengthening Kyrgyzstan's national identity and spearheading the development of the Republic's cultural strategy for regeneration. The Manas epos is a significant cultural heritage that is shared throughout Kyrgyzstan and as such, it is a strategic common denominator with which people on both sides of the Republic's political divide can identify. However, given the aftermath of 11 September and the fact that Islam strongly influences the south of the country, it is difficult to determine whether a poem, even an epic such as the Manas epos with its powerful symbolism, can help to achieve all of the government's development objectives.

## Notes

1. Before publication of this book, Gulnara Abduvasitovna Bakieva sadly passed away at the age of 45. Her death is a tragic loss to the fledgling tourism research community in Kyrgyzstan.
2. According to the Tartu school of semiotics, Moscow, 'culture' is defined as a collective semiotic mechanism for the production, circulation, processing and storage of information. It is both a collective memory and a programme for the generation of new messages. It regulates human behaviour and how humans project structuredness upon the world.
3. In 1995, industry (including mining, manufacturing, power, construction, logging and fishing) contributed an estimated 24.3% of GDP and provided 19.3% of employment. The services sector contributed an estimated 32.1% of GDP and provided 38.7% of employment (World Bank, 2000).
4. It is generally agreed that the Kyrgyz people used a written Turkic language called orkhono-yenisei in circa 7th century, however this language was not preserved. For more information see Malov (1952) and Paksoy (1995).
5. Torekul Aitmatov, father of the famous modern-day author Chingiz Aitmatov, was one of the first Manas researchers to disappear. His remains were found in 1991 in a mine near Bishkek, with 127 other men.
6. In 1938 the playwright Kasym Tynystanov, creater of the modern Kyrgyz alphabet, was shot for including an episode from Manas in one of his plays.

## References

Akmatova, L. (2001) Personal communication with Ludmilla Akmatova, Kyrgyz State Agency for Tourism and Sports, Bishkek, 21st November.

Asankanov, A.A. and Bekmukhamedova, N. (1999) *Akyns and Manaschis: Creators and Keepers of the Kyrgyz People Spiritual Culture*. Bishkek: United Nations Development Programme.

Asankanov, A.A. and Omurbekov, T.N. (1995) *The Epos Manas is the Unique Masterpiece of the World Cultural Treasury*. Bishkek: National Organising Committee for Preparation and Celebration of the 1000th Anniversary of the Epos 'Manas'.

Ashworth, G. and Goodall, B. (1988) *Marketing in the Tourism Industry: The Promotion of Destination Regions*. London: Croom Helm.

Askarov, T., Asankanov, A., Omurbekov, T., Abetekov, A. and Bekmukhamedova, N. (Eds) (1995) *'Manas' Epos and the Worlds Epic Heritage*. Bishkek: Kyrgyz Republic National Academy of Sciences.

Auezov, M.A. (1961) *The Kirghiz Heroic Epos 'Manas'*. Frunze: National Academy of Sciences.

Auezov, M.A. (1999) Time of the epos 'Manas' origin. In M.T. Bayjiev (ed.) *The Great Kyrgyz Epos 'Manas', Book 1, Manas* (pp. 213–261). Bishkek: State Directorate for the Promotion of Manas.

Bashiri, I. (1999a) Kyrgyzstan: An overview. On WWW at http://www.iles.umn. edu/faculty/bashiri/courses/Kyrgyz.htm.

Bashiri, I. (1999b) Manas: the Kyrgyz epic. On WWW at http://www.iles.umn. edu/faculty/bashiri/manas/manas.htm.

Bayjiev, M.T. (1999a) A word of the author. In M.T. Bayjiev (ed.) *The Great Kyrgyz Epos 'Manas', Book 1, Manas* (pp. 159–77). Bishkek: State Directorate for the Promotion of Manas.

Bayjiev, M.T. (1999b) My heartache 'Manas'. In M.T. Bayjiev (ed.) *The Great Kyrgyz Epos 'Manas', Book 3, Sejtek* (pp. 212–75). Bishkek: State Directorate for the Promotion of Manas.

BBC News (2001) On WWW at http://news.bbc.co.uk/1/hi/england/1718397. stm.

Bichel, A.R. (1997) *Identity/Difference in Central Asia.* New York: ICARP Publications.

Britton, S. (1991) Tourism, capital, and place: Towards a critical geography of tourism. *Environment and Planning D: Society and Space* 9, 451–78.

Central Asian Tourism Corporation (2001) *Great Silk Road Tours.* Bishkek: Central Asian Tourism (Kyrgyzstan) Corporation.

Clark University (2001) Cultural identities and global processes. On WWW at http://www.clarku.edu/departments/culturalid/.

Craik, J. (1997) The culture of tourism. In C. Rojek and J. Urry (eds) *Touring Cultures. Transformations of travel and theory* (pp. 113–36). London: Routledge.

Fairbanks, C.H. (2001) Disillusionment in the Caucasus and Central Asia. *Journal of Democracy* 12 (4), 49–56.

Galieva, Z. (1995) The 'Manas' epos as a historical source. In T. Askarov, A. Asankanov, T. Omurbekov, A. Abetekov and N. Bekmukhamedova (eds) *'Manas' Epos and the World's Epic Heritage* (pp. 3–4). Bishkek: Kyrgyz Republic National Academy of Sciences.

Glavtour (2001) *Kyrgyzstan.* Bishkek: Glavtour.

Haberstroh, M. (2000) Kyrgyzstan – Asia's future Switzerland. On WWW at http://cdf.gov.kg/en/country/travelarticles.htm.

Hall, C.M. (1992) *Hallmark Tourism Events: Impacts, Management and Planning.* London: Belhaven.

ICOMOS (1976) *Charter on Cultural Tourism.* Brussels: ICOMOS.

Inan, A. (1968) *Makaleler ve Incelemeler.* Ankara: University of Ankara.

Jhirmunski, B.M. (1999) Introduction in learning of epos Manas. In M.T. Bayjiev (ed.) *The Great Kyrgyz Epos 'Manas', Book 2, Semetei* (pp. 245–318). Bishkek: State Directorate for the Promotion of Manas.

KSATS (1999) Briefly about Kyrgyzstan. On WWW at http://homepage.kg/~olga/ briefly.html.

KSATS (2001) *Kyrgyzstan: Land of Sky-High Mountains.* Bishkek: Kyrgyz State Agency for Tourism and Sports.

Lusanova, E.S. (1995) The philosophical and aesthetic 'tuning fork' of Kyrgyz art. In T. Askarov, A. Asankanov, T. Omurbekov, A. Abetekov and N. Bekmukhamedova (eds) *'Manas' Epos and the Worlds Epic Heritage* (pp. 99–100). Bishkek: Kyrgyz Republic National Academy of Sciences.

Malov, S.E. (1952) *Yenisei Written Language of the Turks.* Moscow: Academy of Sciences of the USSR.

Mayhew, G., Plunkett, R. and Richmond, S. (2000) *Central Asia*. London: Lonely Planet Publications.

Mellinger, W.M. (1994) Towards a critical analysis of tourism representations. *Annals of Tourism Research* 21, 756–79.

Morgan, N. and Pritchard, A. (1998) *Tourism Promotion and Power: Creating Images, Creating Identities*. Chichester: Wiley.

Morgan, N. and Pritchard, A. (2002) Contextualising destination branding. In N. Morgan, A. Pritchard and R. Pride (eds) *Destination Branding: Creating the Unique Destination Proposition* (pp. 11–41). Oxford: Butterworth-Heinemann.

Musayev, S. (1994) *The Epos 'Manas'*. Bishkek: Kyrgyz Polygraph Kombinat.

Okeeva, A. (2001) Personal communication with Aziza Okeeva, National Commission for UNESCO, Bishkek, 22nd November.

Oxford Young European Society (1999), Nationalism – what has it achieved? On WWW at http://members.tripod.co.uk/oyes/discuss/natlism.html.

Paksoy, H.B. (1989) *Alpamaysh: Central Asian Identity under Russian Rule* Connecticut: Association for the Advancement of Central Asian Research.

Paksoy, H.B. (1995) Nationality or religion. *Association for the Advancement of Central Asian Research (AACAR) Bulletin* VIII (2), 13–25.

Reichl, K. (1992) *Turkic Oral Epic Poetry: Traditions, Forms, Poetic Structure*. New York: Garland Publishing Inc.

Rorlich, A. (1999) History, Collective memory and identity: The Tatars of sovereign Tatarstan. *Communist and Post-Communist Studies* 32, 379–96.

Seaton, A.V. (1998) The ethics of tourist destination promotion. On WWW at http://www.mcb.co.uk/services/conferen/jan98/eit/2_seaton.htm.

Togan, Z.V. (1972) *Oguz Destani*. Istanbul: No publisher.

UNESCO (2001) Masterpieces of the oral and intangible heritage of humanity. On WWW at http://www.unesco.org/culture/heritage/intangible/index.shtml.

Witoszek, N. (2001) Collective memory and national identity: the case of Sweden, Germany and Italy. On WWW at http://www.iue.it/RSC/Concom/mem.html.

World Bank (2000) *Statistical Handbook: States of the Former USSR*. New York: World Bank.

World Tourism Organisation (2001) *Silk Road*. Madrid: WTO/UNESCO.

Yologlu, G. (1995) Traces of common Turkic culture in the heroic Epics of the Yenesei Kyrgyz. In T. Askarov, A. Asankanov, T. Omurbekov A. Abetekov and N. Bekmukhamedova (eds) *'Manas' Epos and the Worlds Epic Heritage* (pp. 38–9). Bishkek: Kyrgyz Republic National Academy of Sciences.

*Chapter 11*

# The Camp Oven Festival and Australian Identity

Shirley Chappel and Gregory Loades

## Introduction

Festivals celebrate the things people value. Lavenda describes festivals 'as stories told by members of a culture about themselves' (Lavenda, 1991 cited in Getz, 1995: 314). Greenwood's case study (1989) of the festival in Fuenterrabia in Spain's Basque country is an example of the festival as story-teller. In recalling the victory of the townspeople of Fuenterrabia over the French in the siege of 1638, Greenwood shows how the festival provided an historical text. Because its preparation and staging involved almost all the population of the town regardless of status, occupation or customary hostility towards one another, it reproduced the solidarity of the community at the time of the siege. Through their focus on what is commonly defined as 'heritage', festivals can also increase a community's knowledge, awareness and appreciation of earlier lifestyles and highlight the importance of ordinary things. According to Malouf, it is the work of heritage 'to pay as much attention to what is ordinary and specific as to what is exemplary and rare' (Malouf, 2000: 10). Malouf asserts that ordinary and specific objects 'give identity to the group, help to define it, give it cultural and social cohesion' (2000: 2). The Australian context approached in this chapter, although being inhabited by Aboriginal people for thousands of years, is still young as a place of European settlement. It is therefore still in the early stages of constructing and interpreting its European past and in identifying objects that will give Australians a shared sense of identity (Malouf, 2000: 3).

The Camp Oven Festival at Millmerran in southern Queensland, Australia, has an 'ordinary thing', a camp oven, as its centrepiece. In the early days of European settlement in Australia, shepherds cooked their food in an oven in the ground. Early settlers used a form of camp oven when they camped out on their properties away from the homestead or while they were on the road droving. The modern camp oven, the successor to this early cooking utensil, is a round, cast iron cooking vessel made to stand on legs that enable it to settle evenly in hot ashes. Since the mid-19th century the vessel has been manufactured by Furphy's Foundry, another part of Australia's heritage, and a sponsor of the Camp Oven Festival. To those skilled in its use, a camp oven is by no means ordinary. As a cooking utensil it has proven itself to be a versatile part of Australia's culinary history. It is a symbol of Australia's much prized outdoor living.

Through its contribution to heritage preservation, the Camp Oven Festival asserts a particular image of 'Australianness' that developed in rural Anglo-Celtic Australia in the 19th century. This chapter argues that the festival is an attempt to defend the primacy of this image at a time when notions of Australian identity are vigorously contested as a consequence of rapid social, economic and demographic change. Through reference to the history of European settlement on the Darling Downs, a region of which Millmerran is a part, the chapter shows how the Anglo-Celtic settlers adapted to a new environment and became 'Australian'. It makes reference to 'the bush', the name used in Australia to describe country areas anywhere away from the city. In Australia in the 19th century, 'bush' replaced the English words 'woods' and 'forests'. This, in itself, is a statement about an emerging Australian identity (Baker, 1966: 76).

## Context

The rolling plains of the Darling Downs comprise some of the most fertile agricultural land in Australia and have been identified as part of Australia's 'fertile crescent' (Waterson, 1968: 1). For one seeking to visit Millmerran for the first time, the town is difficult to locate on a map, a fact well understood by the Camp Oven Festival chairperson, Valentine Harris, who noted in her 2002 media release that, in the past, the perennial question had been: 'Where exactly is Millmerran?' (Harris, 2002). According to Harris, the 'stunningly successful' 2002 Camp Oven Festival indicated that Millmerran is now 'well and truly' on the map. Access to Millmerran is greatly assisted by its location on a major highway that links the town with Australia's eastern capital cities (Brisbane, Sydney and Melbourne), used by heavy vehicle traffic, interstate buses and tourists who came to the 2002 festival in mobile homes, caravans, four-wheel drives 'and even the odd horse drawn vehicle' (Harris, 2002).

An overview of the history of European settlement on the Darling Downs shows the emergence of characteristics that contribute to the 19th-century image of 'Australianness' that the Camp Oven Festival celebrates. The early European settlers (known as Pure Merinos) were 'transplanted Britishers' who aimed to make money from grazing sheep for wool and to re-create a society modelled on a dying 18th-century rural society in England that 'existed largely in [their] imagination' (Waterson, 1968: 11–12).

In their dealings with their employees, the Pure Merinos tried to maintain a master-servant relationship but the attempt was aborted by the rapidly emerging egalitarian spirit that became a feature of 'Australianness'. Despite their preference for the class-based status formalities of Britain, they had to accept that in Australia Jack was 'a damn sight better than his master' (Waterson, 1968: 20) and that they should not expect displays of deference from their workers. The Pure Merinos, however, were in the minority. Other pastoralists were people of humbler origin who, because of the nature of sheep-farming, could not escape working closely with their workers. Characteristics of 'Australianness' were forged in a harsh environment marked by unfamiliar physical conditions, loneliness and violence. Competition for land and water and sheep-stealing by the Aborigines resulted in violent clashes between white settlers and Aborigines. Although some kind of accommodation was reached when the settlers employed Aborigines as stockmen, the displacement of the indigenous people from their control of the land left an issue that became part of Australia's debate about identity in the 20th century.

The emergence of an Australian identity on the Darling Downs did not mean total rejection of the British connection. People in Millmerran Shire had a 'fresh and strong' sense of belonging to the British Empire, clearly shown at the time of the First World War, which 'fired the imagination' (Rogers & Macqueen, 1981: 103). Many soldiers of the Shire were killed in action fighting for Britain during the Great War, their memory now honoured by the Returned Services League, which has worked tirelessly to keep the 'spirit of Australian Nationalism' alive and well in Millmerran (Rogers & Macqueen, 1981: 110).

## Economic Development in Millmerran

Millmerran's rural economy had its starting point in the activities of the sheep farmers on the Darling Downs in the 19th century. By the 1880s, the Millmerran district was famous for its fine quality wool and was being carried 'on the sheep's back' with most people employed on sheep stations

(Curtis, 1981: 43). Land legislation in the 1860s and 1870s resulted in closer settlement and the establishment of agriculture on family farms for which family members provided the labour. The fertility of the black soil was an advantage for growing a variety of crops but the farmers faced many difficulties including floods, drought, rust, price fluctuations, economic depressions and indebtedness (Waterson, 1968: Chapter 7). When the commodity prices were high, as in the period following the Second World War, the people enjoyed considerable prosperity. Subsequently, however, there were threats to this prosperity. Synthetics challenged wool. Meat exports were threatened by Britain's entry to the European Common Market necessitating the search for new markets (that fortunately were found). Deregulation of the banking system led to unwise borrowing from foreign banks and to increases in overseas debt (White, 1992: 35). When this debt exceeded $100 billion, it was dealt with by increased interest rates to slow down imports and therefore the foreign debt (Manne, 1992: 52). For the rural sector in Australia this sometimes meant farm bankruptcies. In this period of change and uncertainty, political leaders told Australians that they should no longer rely on their traditional economic activities but should seek greater economic diversity. In the 1980s tourism, as an economic activity, was given serious attention.

## Tourism in Millmerran

Millmerran Shire's promotional material shows that it is well set up for tourism, particularly heritage tourism. Arguably, the Camp Oven Festival is the crown jewel of its tourism product. In 2002 Millmerran won a Tidy Town award, an indication of local pride. Its principal brochure welcomes tourists to the 'friendliest shire on the Downs' and invites them to 'enjoy a relaxed drive through some of the most productive landscapes in Australia which also offer a significant sampling of early Queensland history' (Millmerran Shire Council: *Where the East Finishes and the West Begins*). Its attractions include a historical museum, the site of one of the earliest settlements in the Shire, and the Shire's 'black spot', an historic cemetery where the victim of the first person hanged for murder in nearby Toowoomba is buried. Murals on the outside walls of buildings also capture the historical theme. The walls of the Old Millmerran Butter Factory, for example, show the development of the local dairying industry. On the walls of the swimming pool building, artists have depicted swim fashions through the years as well as the kind of waterhole in which Millmerran residents swam before the swimming pool was built in 1966, Guests are also invited to camp for a spot of fishing on the banks of the Condamine River. For the 2002 Camp Oven Festival special attention was given to providing amenities for motor-home and campervan owners.

## The Camp Oven Festival 2002

In 2002, the two-day Camp Oven Festival programme sought to celebrate, promote and preserve 'the skills and traditions of a wonderful period in Australian history' in a 'laid back, easy paced, friendly country atmosphere' (Harris, 2002). Visitors came from across the nation, defying the pessimism caused by the rural downturn and drought.

The camp oven cooking competitions, demonstrations and judging were important items on the two-day program. The food prepared was a reminder of the Australian diet before migration to Australia after 1947 exposed Australians to the tastes of the Mediterranean and Asia that have now become commonplace. A sign in the 2002 programme described the food on offer as 'Fair Dinkum Aussie Camp Oven Tucker', the Australian idiom for genuine Australian food (Australian Camp Oven Festival, 2002). Contestants in the cooking competition prepared stew, curry, roast beef, corned beef, gravy and 'vegies', the standard fare of Anglo-Australians of earlier times. Some festival participants demonstrated their skills in damper[1] throwing. In 2002, damper throwers were competing for cash prizes and a record of achievement in the Guinness Book of Records.

Another 'ordinary object' associated with traditional Australian outdoor living is the billy, a metal container used for boiling tea, 'a symbol of refreshment, of hospitality and . . . a people often on the move' (Blainey, 2003:358). According to Australian tradition, the most refreshing tea was 'that which was made in a blackened billy' (Blainey, 2003: 358). The 2002 festival gave participants the chance to display their skills in billy boiling speed tests. In 19th century Australia, 'bushmen fought one another for the title of the best maker of billy tea' (Blainey, 2003: 358). Wood-splitting, sheep-shearing, fence-painting and black-smithing were other competitions on the programme, all reminders of the skills people on the Darling Downs needed to master in order to live in the bush in the 19th century.

Festival attendees had the opportunity to enjoy the bush poets and yarn-spinners telling their stories of Australian bush characters. Country music reflected the country theme although the open-air dance featured contemporary forms of social dancing. Music for dancing, however, was provided by the Ridgee Didge Bush Band whose name is pure Australian slang. (Ridgee Didge means 'original' or 'genuine'.) At the merchandise stall, attendees could buy camp ovens, camp oven cookbooks and aprons as souvenirs of the festival. Through its various activities, the Camp Oven

Festival celebrated that period in history when the 'typical Australian' image was born.

## The Australian Legend

The image of 'Australianness' that had its genesis in the Australian bush in the 19th century is very much associated with Russel Ward's book *The Australian Legend* (1966, which was first published in 1958). Ward painted a word picture of the so-called 'typical Australian', the romantic figure who became Australia's 'national culture hero' in the 20th century (Ward, 1992: 190). The original 'typical Australians' were pastoral labourers and other bush workers who endured the hardships of the Australian inland in order to open up the country for economic development. These men were convicts and ex-convicts from the British Isles and Anglo-Celtic Australians who had been born in Australia (the so-called 'native born').

To cope with 'the rough and makeshift conditions of frontier life' (Ward, 1966: 73), they developed qualities that came to be regarded as 'typically Australian' (Ward, 1966: 106). The loneliness of life in the bush necessitated that 'every man had habitually to treat every other man as a brother' (Ward, 1966: 83). The isolation of the bush-dwellers also highlighted the importance of showing hospitality to strangers. The need to survive in the bush required 'rough and ready improvisation' (Ward, 1966: 87). The 'typical Australian' was 'rough and ready', 'quick to decry any appearance of affectation', 'taciturn rather than talkative', 'a knocker [critic] of eminent people', 'fiercely independent', anti-authoritarian, egalitarian and 'very hospitable' (Ward, 1992: 179–80).

Arguably, 'collectivist mateship' (Ward, 1966: 83) was the core value developed at that time. The true Australian must be loyal to his mates 'through thick and thin' (Ward, 1992: 180). In the late 19th century, the collectivist mateship of the bushmen was exemplified by the development of the trade union movement. In 1886 when wool prices fell, pastoralists tried to reduce payments to shearers, thus providing the reason for the shearers to unite against the employers. 'Once the idea of trade union combination was put before them, it seemed to most bushmen merely a natural extension of the non-political, but cherished and familiar, sentiments associated with the concept of mateship' (Ward, 1966: 214). From these beginnings grew the Australian Labor Party, the party of 'the mates'. By the end of the 19th century, the bushmen's image of 'Australianness' had become established as the way in which Australians would distinguish themselves from their British ancestors. 'This is not to say that thenceforward all Australians believed and thought like pastoral workers, but rather that thenceforward most people liked to believe that they tended *naturally* to do so' (Ward, 1966:208). In the 20th century, the values and qualities of the bushmen became associated with Australian soldiers in various theatres of war in Turkey, France, North Africa and New Guinea.

In the 19th century, the emergence of an Australian identity found expression in the pages of the *Sydney Bulletin*, the so-called 'Bushman's Bible' that recorded the attitudes of the bush-workers. In 1893 it formulated a set of aims based on these attitudes. The aims included democracy, republicanism, secular education, abolition of titles of nobility, socialist economics, a united Australia protected against the world, and a 'white' Australia from which '[t]he cheap Chinaman, the cheap nigger and the cheap European pauper' would be 'absolutely excluded' (in Ward, 1966: 224–5).

The *Bulletin* recorded the stories of the bush in folk songs and other literary pieces. Vance Palmer (1963: 169) refers to the 'special type' of Australian who emerged from 'sketches of countless occasional writers of the [eighteen] eighties and nineties'. He describes this type as 'a laconic but sociable fellow with his own idiom'. In particular, he draws attention to this 'typical' Australian's 'humour of a dry sardonic kind' (1963: 169). The bush balladeers provided stark pictures of the hardships bushmen faced and described the simple pleasures that made life endurable.

## Change and Contested Identities

Tourism in its various forms reflects the age in which it occurs. In the European Middle Ages, for example, the pilgrimage mirrored the religiosity of the times. At the time of the Industrial Revolution, Thomas Cook's standardised travel packages reflected the principles of mass production. Similarly, the Camp Oven Festival reflects the resurgence of an image of 'Australianness' that developed in the 19th century, the creation of the people who, through the pastoral industry, opened up the Australian bush to European-style economic activity. Although this image (in the form of movie actor Paul Hogan and his alter ego, Crocodile Dundee), has served Australia well in attracting overseas tourists, it has been somewhat challenged since the Second World War by a range of other images.

At the time of the federation of the Australian colonies in 1901, the Australian Parliament enacted legislation (popularly known as the White Australia Policy) that, in practice, excluded non-Caucasians from Australia. Although exceptions were made to the initial legislation in ensuing years, the overall result was the creation of an Anglo-Celtic nation. Following the Second World War, inspired by the slogan 'Populate or Perish', Anglo-

Celtic Australia brought large numbers of non-English speaking migrants from continental Europe. Political leaders reassured Australians that the newcomers would be assimilated. ('They'll be just like us'.) In fact, there was a cultural exchange. For example, the arrival in Australia of Italians and other continental Europeans resulted, among other things, in the establishment of European-style restaurants in which the serving of table wines was commonplace. Influenced by this example and with the discretionary income made available by the prosperity of the 'lucky country' (Horne, 1964), Australians began to experiment with 'lifestyle' (Beeston, 1995: 192) and to take wine with their meals. Pasta and other continental European dishes destroyed the monopoly of 'meat and three veg' in the Australian diet. To complete the cultural exchange, the children of the migrants adopted the easy-going, casual Australian style while retaining aspects of their ethnic identity.

In the 1960s, Australians began the process of abandoning their discriminatory *White Australia Policy* by permitting the admission of Asian migrants. The trickle became a flood after 1975 with the arrival of large numbers of refugees from Indochina. Consequently, Australia now had an extremely diverse population so that there was no longer a single, obvious Australian identity. At the level of the national government it seemed that assimilation would be replaced by multiculturalism as 'the official definition of national direction' (Kelly, 1994: 4).

According to the multicultural policy developed at that time, all Australians should be able to maintain their own culture 'without prejudice or disadvantage' and should be encouraged 'to understand and embrace other cultures' (Galbally Report in Jupp, 2002: 87). Although diversity was encouraged, it was to exist within the basic structures and principles of Australian society and English was to be the national language (Saunders, 1991: 137). Public money was made available for the creation of institutions and services that would help implement the multicultural agenda. Critics saw multiculturalism as divisive and expensive and a challenge to the dominance of Anglo-Celtic values (Manne, 2001: 3). Dixson (1999: 43) argues that while Australian intellectuals and officials 'wisely and humanely affirmed newer ethnicities in grieving for the homes they have lost', they failed to realise that Anglo-Celtic Australians also were entitled to mourn the loss of the old Australian identity.

The changes that eclipsed the Australian image associated with the Legend were not confined to matters of ethnicity. They also involved a decline in the dominance of the rural image although rural Australia continued to play a key role in the Australian economy. In the period following the Second World War, the words 'Australian Way of Life' were used to describe Australian identity (White, 1981: 158). The content of this description showed a move away from the rural ideal of the Australian Legend. The ideal Australian Way of Life was now located in the cities and suburbs rather than in the bush. Influenced by the American alliance and American culture, the ideal was anti-communist, affluent, bourgeois and consumerist. The new ideal was underpinned by the prosperity of an industrialising post-war Australia. In keeping, however, with the Legend, there was no place for cultural difference. Non-Anglo Australians were expected to assimilate.

In the 1960s, however, the revolutionary fervour of the anti-Vietnam war movement provided the context for expressions of dissatisfaction with the Australian Way of Life. In the 1970s, social critics condemned not only the Australian Way of Life but also the content of the Australian Legend. In 1970, Humphrey McQueen argued that the Australian character had never been 'egalitarian or collectivist' but 'petty bourgeois, and . . . forged, not by a worthy nationalism, but by a jingoistic and vicious racism' (in White, 1981: 168). In the 1960s and 1970s, public policy in Australia moved away from the racially exclusive, intolerant and assimilationist policies of the Australian Legend and the Australian Way of Life (White, 1981:168). The abandonment of these policies peaked in the 1990s.

## The Identity Debate of the 1990s

For those who feared its eclipse, 'Australianness' seemed to face its greatest threat in the early 1990s during the administration of Prime Minister Paul Keating. By the end of the 1990s, however, there were clear signs of its resurgence. Keating's view of an inclusive Australia was based on celebration of cultural difference and acknowledgement of different historical experiences among Australian citizens – Anglo-Celtic, Aboriginal and post-1945 migrants.

The contest among competing identities in the Keating years was fuelled by the debate concerning native title to land. In 1992 the High Court of Australia rejected the long-held doctrine of *terra nullius* according to which Australia, at the time of European settlement in 1788, belonged to nobody. In the same year Prime Minister Keating, in a speech to Indigenous Australians, acknowledged the European settlers' responsibility for dispossession of the Indigenous people and stated that the failure of non-Indigenous Australians to empathise with the dispossessed had 'degraded all of us' (Keating, 1992 in Watson, 2002: 289). The Native Title Act of 1993, the Australian Parliament's response to the High Court decision, indicated the existence of native title where Indigenous people had maintained their connection with a particular area of land and 'where their title has not been extinguished by acts of Imperial, Colonial, State, Territory or Commonwealth governments' (Attorney-General's Department, 1994: C7).

In the negotiation of the Act, Indigenous people, once regarded as an insignificant dying race, occupied centre stage with white politicians, miners and farmers, all of whom had a vested interest in the outcome. This situation was an affront to those people anxious to protect the dominant culture. For them 'the very fact of a visible proud indigenous identity represents an attack on the legitimacy and universality of self-understanding' (Leach, 2000: 49).

The Keating administration's support for an Australian republic, combined with its vigorous pursuit of links with Asia, also contributed to the identity debate in Australia. Keating denounced Australia's 'cultural cringe' to Britain and noted that 'a great number of Australians, especially of non-Anglo descent, felt no particular association [with the British monarchy]' (Watson, 2002, 418–19). Republicans sought 'symbolic independence from Britain' and 'completion of the decolonisation process' (Manne, 2001: 47–8) one hundred years after the birth of the Australian nation. Opponents of Keating's support for a republic were alarmed by this threat to Australia's British heritage even though Keating argued that the relationship between an Australian republic and Britain 'would be the stronger for being more mature' (Watson, 2002: 417).

Keating's promotion of the Australia-Asia connection also caused alarm within sections of the Australian population. The rapid emergence of Asian economies at that time, combined with Australia's geographical position, caused the Keating government to strengthen its engagement with Asia. This involved, among other strategies, funding the education system to make Australians Asia-literate. Some Australians were asking the question 'Is Australia an Asian country?' (Fitzgerald, 1996) and engaging in debates concerning Asian values. While confirming Australia's commitment to Western values, Keating noted that Australians share many values with Asians relating to 'family, work, education, order and accountability' (Keating in Watson, 2002: 680).

By the mid-1990s, the old certainties based on Anglo-supremacy were therefore being challenged in Australia by a combination of native title, multiculturalism, republicanism and the Asia push. While this was happening, there was also a growing division between urban elites (who lauded the changes) and rural Australia, the territory of the 'real Australians'. This occurred against a backdrop of rural discontent caused by decline in the prosperity of the family farm and farm revenues, with no commensurate reduction in production costs (Manne, 2001: 165).

The coming to power of the socially conservative Prime Minister John Howard in 1996 constituted a turning point in the debate about identity and heralded a revival of the rhetoric of the Australian Legend. Although the major parties in Australia had given support to a non-discriminatory immigration policy and multiculturalism, in 1988 Howard, then Leader of the Opposition, had expressed concern at the pace at which the Australian population was diversifying. In policy formulation at that time he canvassed 'assimilationist nationalism' (Brett, 2003: 185) and linked it with equality of opportunity. While in opposition in the 1980s, he and his followers had argued that, by dividing society into special interest groups, multiculturalism kept communities 'separate from Australian society' and therefore denied them equality of opportunity within the Australian community (in Brett, 2003: 186). On the eve of gaining office in 1996, he committed his government to 'ending the increasing divisiveness in [Australian] society and to defending the mainstream against special interest groups' (Howard, 1995 in Kalantzis & Cope, 2001: 60). Kalantzis and Cope define 'mainstream' as 'middle Australia, settled rather than recently immigrant Australia' (2001: 59–60). They assert that the essence of the mainstream is 'quintessentially to be found in the mateship of the bush' (2001: 61); that is, in the idea of 'Australianness' that emerged in the 19th century. In a conference address in 1996, Howard described the Australian ideal as 'the sense of community and mateship and looking after each other in adversity, which you find in rural Australia' (in Kalantzis and Cope, 2001: 61). Howard's idea of a cohesive nation was based on adherence to the 19th-century ideal of 'Australianness'. That ideal in Australia's past co-existed with a discriminatory immigration policy and an Indigenous policy that excluded Aborigines from mainstream society (Kalantzis & Cope, 2001: 62).

Howard, however, did accept Indigenous people as part of the mainstream Australian population but, while willing to acknowledge their socioeconomic disadvantage and to support practical solutions to correct this disadvantage, he did not otherwise accept the idea of their entitlement to special consideration. On the matter of a treaty with Indigenous Australia, for example, he considered it 'an absurd proposition that a nation should make a treaty with its own citizens' (in Brett, 2003: 200). Native title also accorded to the Aborigines special rights not available to other Australians. Accordingly, the Howard government used its law-making power to roll back some of the native title gains made by the Indigenous people at the time of the Keating administration.

As a constitutional monarchist, Howard saw no need to change Australia's constitutional arrangements even though his opponents contended that a multicultural nation with the Queen of England as Head of State was an anachronism. To Howard, the British legacy is 'part of being Australian' (Horne, 2001: 61), a position Vietnamese-Australians and Italian-Australians may find difficult to understand. Nevertheless, true to his pre-election promise, he called together a constitutional convention to debate a model for a republican constitution to be put to the Australian people at a referendum. Despite the fact that opinion polls showed that most Australians favoured a republic, the 1999 referendum failed to support the establishment of a republic because of disagreement among the republicans concerning the manner in which the Head of State would be chosen. Following the failure to achieve support for the republic in the referendum, interest in the republic faded. The Prime Minister saw no need to revive it and the British connection remained intact.

While not totally abandoning the Asian connection, Howard's government emphasised historical, cultural and military links with Britain and the United States, seen most obviously in Australia's involvement in the Coalition of the Willing in the 2003 invasion of Iraq opposed by Australia's Islamic regional neighbours. Howard summed up his position on the Asian connection in a statement to the Australian press in 1999: 'We are a European, Western civilisation with strong links to North America but here we are in Asia' (in Broinowski, 2003: 228). In Howard's language Asia was '*that* region', not '*our* region' (in Broinowski, 2003: 220). On coming to power in 1996, his government's slogan was: 'Asia first but not Asia only'. As time progressed, however, its actions suggested the primacy of United States foreign policy in Australia's international relations. While continuing to see Asia as a major source of its economic well-being, its close adherence to defence and foreign policy from Washington ensured unwillingness among Asian leaders to accept Australia as an equal partner in the region.

The 1996 national election also resulted in the entry to the Australian Parliament of populist Independent politician, Pauline Hanson, from Queensland. In her maiden speech, she poured out 'the grievances of the old White Australia against the economic and social changes of the past thirty years' (Brett, 2003: 192), thus voicing the concerns of country voters and citizens of the outer suburban areas who gave her electoral support. Neo-liberal economic reforms had attacked protection of Australian industry, denied non-viable services such as banking, health and education to rural and regional areas, encroached on public ownership of utilities, and plunged the country into the uncertain world of global economic competition. Socially, like Howard, Hanson espoused the idea of a unitary nation, later reflected in the name of the party she founded, the One Nation Party. Throwing so-called political correctness to the wind, she attacked multiculturalism, Indigenous land rights, Asian immigration, closer ties with Asia, and the so-called 'elites' who sponsored the special interest groups that she claimed fostered disunity and division (Leach, 2000: 43) Although the electoral successes of Pauline Hanson and the One Nation Party were short-lived, they indicated 'that the tolerance of diversity in Australian politics and society was not as strong as widely assumed' (Ward *et al.*, 2000: 12). They also indicated the survival of racism and xenophobia, the dark side of the Australian Legend.

## The Resurgence of the Australian Legend

Although the 19th-century ideal of 'Australianness' did not die during the period of its vulnerability, various movements appeared to threaten its existence. Its resurgence began in the 1980s when it received a new lease of life in popular culture (Brett, 2003: 203). Brett attributes this to the impact of globalisation and the growth in international and domestic tourism that motivated Australians to focus their attention 'on the uniqueness of the country's natural environment and on the people who lived outside the cities' (2003: 203.). Australians showed their interest in the Legend's image of 'Australianness' at that time in a variety of ways. Films with a bush theme were popular and Australian country music had a large following. Rural work clothes such as Akubra hats[2] and riding boots became fashion items.

Tapping into this revival, in the political arena in the 1990s Hanson and Howard promoted the Australia Legend as the source of Australia's core values. In 1998 Hanson's One Nation Party made its position clear in the following statement:

> The survival of any national culture relies on a common national memory of events, history and traditions. It is such a common national memory that binds people together into a nation. But the policy of multiculturalism attempts to discredit and destroy our shared story and impose upon us a different story. (In Leach, 2000: 47).

The 'shared story' is the story of Anglo-Australia. To evoke the Legend that is at the heart of Anglo-Australia, Hanson used such words as 'egalitarianism' and 'a fair go' (One Nation Party, in Leach, 2000: 48). According to Hansonites, in order for Australians to be equal, they must be all the same (Leach, 2000: 51). A 'fair go' means that people 'are given unhindered opportunity to act as they wish to act so long as they do so without resort to underhand methods and aid from others' (Baker, 1966: 126). There is no place for special deals for special interest groups.

Historically, the Australian Legend was linked with workers and the Australian Labor Party. While retaining the support of the trade union movement, in the 1970s the Labor Party began to move away from its working-class image and its association with the content of the Legend. While it continued to support republicanism, it eliminated the White Australia Policy. By the 1990s it no longer resembled the kind of workers' party it had once been. Its move away from socialism to economic ration-alism in the 1980s 'loosened its grip on the egalitarian imagery of the Australian legend' (Brett, 2003: 203). This gave Howard the chance to adopt, selectively, the imagery of the Legend to suit his purposes although his emphasis on the importance of the individual and small government was worlds apart from the collectivism and socialism of the Legend. (His opposition to republicanism has already been noted.) He now spoke the Legend's symbolic language. In 1998, for example, he proclaimed: 'Being Australian means doing the decent thing in a pragmatic and respectable society which lives up to its creed of practical mateship . . . Australians are a down-to-earth people . . . Rooted deep in our psyche is a sense of fair play and a strong egalitarian streak' (in Brett, 2003: 204). On another occasion he explained his interpretation of 'egalitarianism' in the following words: 'One of the greatest things about living in Australia is that we're essentially the same. We have a great egalitarian innocence' (in Rundle, 2001: 26).

According to Brett (2003: 205–6), the Australian Legend gave Howard

> a flexible language of social cohesion that is distinctively Austral-ian and which enables him to generate a convincing contemporary rhetoric. It enables him to talk to rural Australia, where aspects of the legend still inform people's daily lives, as well as to families in the suburbs where it connects with a deeply held commitment to ordinariness.

While Howard's use of the language of the Legend has a certain appeal to 'ordinary Australians', it is not entirely congruent with the ideals of the Legend. Egalitarianism may still mean that socially Jack is at least as good as his master but economically Jack is now considerably poorer than his master. In the 1870s, according to the *Sydney Morning Herald*, Australia's workers were 'the most fortunate, the best paid and the most prosperous in the world' (in Thompson, 2001: 74). Since the 1980s, however, 'Australia in wealth and income terms is one of the least egalitarian of the first world democracies' (Thompson, 2001: 74). According to Thompson, Australia has 'moved away from a fairly benevolent aspiration that sought to ensure that everyone had a reasonable standard of living to a confused set of aspirations largely centred on the idea of survival of the fittest' (2001: 73). Already awash with American popular culture, since the 1980s, Australia has moved towards American individualism and away from the collectivism extolled by the Legend (Watson, 2001: 42).

Howard's attempt to seek Australia's core cultural values in the Australian Legend is problematical. The cultural values of the Australian Legend are not the cultural heritage of a significant part of Australia's highly urbanised plural society in the 21st century. For Indigenous Australians, the era of the Legend represents the time of dispossession, the bushmen's callous brutality towards them (Ward, 1966: 82), and the decimation of the Aboriginal population through venereal disease (Ward, 1966: 97). For Asian-Australians, the period of the Legend saw the birth of the White Australia Policy. Elements of assimilationism, the White Australia Policy and fear of Asia 'still linger in the political psyche of the nation' (Jayasuriya, 2003: 197). Fear of 'the other' has been used with considerable electoral success in the treatment of Middle Eastern and Central Asian asylum-seekers and in the border protection legislation of 2001 which has overtones of the White Australia Policy of 1901. In its 21st century xenophobia, Australia recalls the xenophobia of the creators of the Legend.

## Conclusion

In a variety of ways at the beginning of the 21st century, many Australians are nostalgically recapturing the spirit of the Australian Legend. In times of change there is no doubt comfort in reminders of the past. In the Camp Oven Festival, the politically conservative citizens of Millmerran present an image of life associated with those earlier times. That Millmerran through its Camp Oven Festival is able to do this successfully is not surprising. Like other rural Australians, they are closer to the Legend than any other part of Australia. They are familiar with the landscapes that the 19th-century bushmen knew. They share the same disasters. They are less ethnically diverse than urban Australians and therefore more closely in touch with relatively unadulterated traditions. In the manner of the balladeers of the Legend, the bush poets who perform at the Camp Oven

Festival tell the story, as they see it, of the 'real Aussie', albeit in somewhat altered circumstances brought about by the passage of time. There are stories of drought and other hardships to which life in the bush is prone but there are also stories now of mortgage foreclosures for farmers who have fallen upon hard times.

Over the years, Australians have devised many festivals to celebrate their cultural diversity. The Camp Oven Festival takes its place among these many celebrations as a representative of the time when non-Indigenous Australians adapted to the conditions in a strange land and developed a style that distinguished them from their ancestors.

## Notes
1.  Plain damper is a loaf made from flour and water. With the addition of treacle, syrup, mixed fruit, currants, butter and dripping to this basic mixture, camp oven cooks can create other forms of damper known as Brownies, Puftaloons and Johnny Cakes.
2.  The wide-brimmed Akubra is an important statement of rural 'Australianness'.

## References
Attorney-General's Department (1994) *Native Title: Legislation with Commentary by the Attorney-General's Legal Practice*. Canberra. Australian Government Publishing Service.

Australian Camp Oven Festival (2002) *Welcome to Camp Oven Country!* Millmerran, Queensland. (Festival programme.)

Baker, S. (1966) *The Australian Language* (2nd edn). Sydney: Currawong Publishing Company.

Beeston, J. (1995) *A Concise History of Australian Wine* (2nd edn). St Leonards, New South Wales: Allen & Unwin.

Blainey, G. (2003) *Black Kettle and Full Moon: Daily Life in a Vanished Australia*. Camberwell, Victoria: Viking.

Brett, J. (2003) *Australian Liberals and the Moral Middle Class: From Alfred Deakin to John Howard*. Cambridge: Cambridge University Press.

Broinowski, A. (2003) *About Face: Asian Accounts of Australia*. Carlton North, Victoria: Scribe Publications.

Curtis, D. (1981) Wool and Millmerran. In N. Macqueen (ed.) *Back Creek and Beyond: Millmerran's Story of Change 1881–1981* (pp. 42–8). Toowoomba, Queensland: Darling Downs Institute Press.

Dixson, M. (1999) *The Imaginary Australian: Anglo-Celts and Identity – 1788 to the Present*. Sydney: University of New South Wales Press.

Fitzgerald, S. (1996) *Is Australia an Asian Country?* St Leonards, New South Wales: Allen & Unwin.

Getz, D. (1995) Event tourism and the authenticity dilemma. In W. Theobald (ed.) *Global Tourism: The Next Decade, Butterworth Heinemann* (pp. 313–29). Jordan Hill, Oxford.

Greenwood, D.J. (1989) Culture by the pound: An anthropological perspective on tourism as cultural commoditization. In V.L Smith (ed.) *Hosts and Guests:*

*The Anthropology of Tourism* (2nd edn) (pp. 171–85). Philadelphia: University of Pennsylvania Press.

Harris, V. (2002) *Media Release: Australian Camp Oven Festival*, Millmerran.

Horne, D. (1964) *The Lucky Country: Australia in the Sixties* (2nd revised edn). Harmondsworth: Penguin.

Horne, D. (2001) *Looking for Leadership: Australia in the Howard Years*. Ringwood, Victoria: Viking,

Jayasuriya, L. (2003) *Fin de siècle* musings. In *Legacies of White Australia* (pp. 190–8). Crawley, Western Australia: University of Western Australia Press.

Jupp, J. (2002) *From White Australia to Woomera: The Story of Australian Immigration*. Cambridge: Cambridge University Press.

Kalantzis, M and Cope, B. (2001) An opportunity to change the culture. In P. Adams (ed.) *The Retreat from Tolerance* (pp. 57–85). ABC Books, Sydney.

Kelly, P. (1994) *The End of Certainty: Power, Politics and Business in Australia* (revised edition). St Leonards, New South Wales: Allen & Unwin.

Leach, M. (2000) Hansonism, political discourse and Australian identity. In M. Leach, G. Stokes and I. Ward (eds) *The Rise and Fall of One Nation* (pp. 42–56). St Lucia, Queensland: University of Queensland Press.

Malouf, D. (2000) *National Trust Heritage Lecture*. On WWW at http://www.nsw.nationaltrust.org.au/dmalouftalk.html. Accessed 15 February 2001.

Manne, R. (1992) The rift in conservative politics. In J. Carroll and R. Manne (eds) *Shutdown* (pp. 49–63). The Text Publishing Company, Melbourne.

Manne, R. (2001) *The Barren Years: John Howard and Australian Political Culture*. Melbourne: Text Publishing.

Millmerran Shire Council (no date) *Millmerran Shire: Where the East Finishes and the West Begins.* (Brochure.)

Palmer, V. (1963) *The Legend of the Nineties*. Melbourne: Melbourne University Press. (First published in 1954.)

Rogers, J. and Macqueen, N. (1981) Pride and Patriotism. In N. Macqueen (ed.) *Back Creek and Beyond: Millmerran's Story of Change 1881–1981* (pp. 42–48). Toowoomba, Queensland: Darling Downs Institute Press.

Rundle, G. (2001) The opportunist: John Howard and the triumph of reaction. *Quarterly Essay* 3. Melbourne: Black Inc.

Saunders, C. (1991) In search of a system of migration review. In D. Goodman, D.J. O'Hearn and C. Wallace-Crabbe (eds) *Multicultural Australia: The Challenge of Change* (pp. 134–48). Newham, Victoria: Scribe Publications.

Thompson, E. (2001) Challenges to egalitarianism: Diversity or sameness? In H. Irving (ed.) *Unity and Diversity: A National Conversation, The Barton Lectures* (pp.69–87). Sydney: ABC Books.

Ward, I., Leach, M. and Stokes, G. (2000) Introduction: The rise and fall of one nation. In *The Rise and Fall of One Nation* (pp. 1–19). St Lucia, Queensland: University of Queensland Press.

Ward, R. (1966) *The Australian Legend* (paperback edn). London: Oxford University Press. (First published in 1958.)

Ward, R. (1992) The Australian Legend. In G. Whitlock & D. Carter (eds) *Images of Australia* (pp. 179–88). St Lucia: University of Queensland.

Waterson, D.B. (1968) *Squatter, Selector and Storekeeper: A History of the Darling Downs, 1859–1893*. Sydney: Sydney University Press.

Watson, D. (2001) Rabbit syndrome: Australia and America. *Quarterly Essay* 4. Melbourne: Black Inc.

Watson, D. (2002) *Recollections of a Bleeding Heart: A Portrait of Paul Keating P.M.* Milsons Point, New South Wales: Knopf.

White, C. (1992) Mastering risk: The story of Australian success. In J. Carroll and R. Manne (eds) *Shutdown* (pp. 27–37). Melbourne: The Text Publishing Company.

White, R. (1981) *Inventing Australia: Image and Identity, 1688–1980.* North Sydney: Allen & Unwin.

*Chapter 12*

# Christmas Markets in the Tyrolean Alps: Representing Regional Traditions in a Newly Created World of Christmas

Oliver Haid

## Introduction

The cultural area of the German language can be attributed a certain competence in the celebration of Christmas festivity. Not only was the famous Christmas Carol 'Silent Night', penned in Austria in 1816, but also the Christmas tree and Christmas themed markets also draw their origins from the German speaking countries (Vossen, 1985). The imagery surrounding Christmas festivity has, to a significant extent, acquired the quality of a 'national characteristic', especially in the border areas of the German speaking countries.

The case of Christmas markets in the South and North Tyrol illustrates a tension between internal and external perceptions associated with the recent phenomenon of Christmas themed tourism as these two adjacent provinces belong to two different European states. South Tyrol was, despite its mainly German speaking population, one of the areas of the Austro-Hungarian Empire that the Kingdom of Italy gained in the peace treaty of Saint Germain in 1919. After a process of compulsory Italianisation in the era of fascism and continued ethnic tensions after the Second World War, the province has today achieved the status of autonomous rule. From a linguistic and ethnic point of view the population of South Tyrol can today be divided between Italian citizens with German as their mother tongue (approximately two thirds), Italian citizens with Italian as their mother tongue (approximately one third) and a small group of

Italian citizens with Ladin as mother tongue; a Rhaeto-Roman language, who live in two secluded valleys (Baur *et al.*, 1998).

North Tyrol, together with the district of Eastern Tyrol, form the province of Tyrol within the Federal Republic of Austria and represents a linguistically homogeneous area of German speakers, but with an increasing number of immigrants from Eastern European and Islamic countries.

The development of tourism linked to the festivities of Christmas highlights a very sensitive dimension of local and regional identity. Here, the representation and re-invention of rural Advent customs of the German speaking population are offered for tourists (mainly from other Italian provinces) but within towns with mixed ethnic populations. Christmas markets in various South Tyrolean towns as well as those in North and Eastern Tyrol developed throughout the 1990s and have succeeded in attracting tourists from the southern areas in steadily increasing numbers. Italian tourists at Christmas have turned the normally deserted civic centres in late November and early December into crowded places with themes decorations and a festive atmosphere. Problems with transport and hygiene logistics have accompanied this development. Nevertheless, the Christmas markets and the cultural offers they provide appear to be, at least in the South Tyrolean context, one of the best examples of public festivity where the deeper structures of cultural identity and ethnicity are evident.

## The Concept of Christmas

Christmas markets have a very long tradition (in some cases stretching back to the medieval period), and generally represent unchallenged continuity in important urban centres. Early accounts state that for Kölln, one of the settlements that later grew into the city of Berlin, the offer of candles and honey cakes occurred in two very populated places during the Christmas period in the mid-15th century (Lorenz, 1986). However, these occasions of exchange or the general markets taking place during Advent can be legitimately mentioned among the ancestors of today's Christmas markets. The latter are 'themed' markets for the preparation of the year's most important family festival and not merely markets arranged on a special day.

Due to the fundamental importance of its relations to the contemporary concept of Christmas, a closer view needs to be taken regarding the historical evolution of this festival. The history of success of Christmas is viewed today by German cultural historians and folklorists as a by-product of the evolution of the 19th-century family model with its drift towards the 'educationalisation' of family relations and feasts. An opinion, expressed by Ariès (1984), amongst others, posits that that the civil family concept underwent processes of 'emotionalisation' and 'intimisation'. More recently authors have tended to describe the development as the change from a system of purpose defined family relations (reciprocity) to a principle of selfless care (Habermas, 2000). Christmas acquired more the character of a family than a religious feast. Special substitution figures for parents and other relatives as present bringers were discovered or re-invented, and among these were St Nicholas as Santa Claus or Father Christmas, and the Christ Child. (Weber-Kellermann, 1978). Weber-Kellermann (1976) realised that this new relationship between children and custom figures had to be of a very different character than that between family members simply because Santa Claus and the Christ Child could not be rewarded for their presents. She also observed the increase of meanings for presents within bourgeois society. Therefore the 19th-century boom in toy production can rather be explained by the contexts of social history and folk custom than by the processes of industrialisation. Besides the emergence of a very productive home industry and toy catalogue business, Christmas markets also developed in this epoch as the most important places for toy sales. The markets acquired, from the late 18th century onwards, more the character of special toy trade fairs (Weber-Kellermann, 1978).

The first and foremost Christmas market was the one in Berlin, where a glamorous evening and night-life had developed by the 18th century. The market, illuminated by candlelight, attracted numerous middle-class and bourgeois families as well as industrial workers who populated the market square often until three in the morning (Lorenz, 1986). The Prussian kings and other members of the royal family visited these markets and contributed in this way to their success as social events. As a result the Christmas markets had to be mentioned in late 18th-century tourist guides of the Prussian capital (Lorenz, 1986). With more than 300 stands in 1805 (Lorenz: 1986) the Berlin Christmas market became the guiding star for markets in other German cities, Protestant as well as Catholic. Dresden, Frankfurt and Nuremberg soon staged their own Christmas markets with their own regional toy and sweet specialties and became themselves symbols for the German way to celebrate the Christmas festival. Their primary function as a source for children's presents was gradually lost during the 20th century with the introduction of department stores and shopping malls (Weber-Kellermann, 1978); however, their importance in city marketing and their function as tourist events have come to the fore instead. The following remarks on the Tyrolean and Alpine context should help to illustrate these changes better.

## The Development of Christmas Markets in the Tyrol

The first boom of Christmas markets in Germany reached the Tyrolean area. An account of 1856 shows the presence of a Nicolas market in Innsbruck, the provincial capital of the Tyrol. At various stands sweet-meats, toys, books and liquors were offered to old and young customers (*Innsbrucker Nachrichten*, 1856: 1949–50). It was, however, a market staged in the days before the 6th of December; still the dominant donation festival of that time. Soon after, Christmas acquired its modern function as family festival and the Nicolas market lost its importance (Forcher, 1991).

For more than a century, the radiation of the German Christmas market tradition did not gain a foothold in the Tyrolean Alps. Innsbruck took its chance to adopt the German formula in the 1970s, in the era between the Olympic winter games of 1964 and 1976. Besides the resumed Nicolas market on the 5 and 6 December, and the 'first real Christmas market of Innsbruck' (*Tiroler Tageszeitung*, 1927: 21) launched in a shopping centre in the year 1970, an annual Christmas market was started in 1975 in the medieval old town of Innsbruck (*Tiroler Tageszeitung*, 1975). With the famous 'golden roof' in the background the market could count on a very topical and appealing aesthetic and it soon became an institution in the town's calendar of events. The Christmas market in Innsbruck today is located on two different squares of the historic centre, and remains a very successful enterprise. It was the first and it is the biggest market of its kind in the Tyrolean Alps.

The history of success in Tyrolean Christmas markets can, however, not be understood without noting the special geographic location of the tradition it partakes in and celebrates. When in the year 1991 Christmas markets were established also in South Tyrol (the mainly German speaking province of Italy), the marketing concept included the Italian tourist market. The idea was to utilise the images of German culture and the German – yet not always Tyrolean – traditions in relation to the sphere of Christmas to create winter events for Italian tourists. So the South Tyrolean markets were advertised in wide areas of Northern Italy, where December is a very quiet season. After a low-key starting phase of a few years the concept worked out more than successfully. Italians came in hundreds of thousands, by train, in their cars, in buses and in mobile homes and they populated the markets of all bigger Tyrolean and South Tyrolean towns. After Bolzano/Bozen[1] (1991), Merano/Meran (1991), and

Bressanone/Brixen (1991), the towns of Vipiteno/Sterzing and Brunico/ Bruneck (1998) opened their Christmas markets followed by Hall (2003), Imst (2001) and Lienz (1997) in the Austrian Tyrol (*Echo*, 2003). The trend soon left the linguistic boundary behind. The city of Trento set up its own Christmas market in the late 1990s, enticing many Italian tourists on their way north, to the Tyrolean or German markets. Markets in Arco, Levico, Udine and Trieste followed. In Garda (a province of Trento) a Christmas market was organised in 2002 in collaboration with the city of Innsbruck in order to arouse the tourist's curiosity for this more Alpine setting.

This mushrooming of Christmas markets needs also to be seen in the context of the growth and success of 'gastronomic tourism' that has been witnessed in recent years. The town of Meran, for example was overrun by 25,000 mostly Italian tourists on the 8 December 2001. More than 500 buses and 300 mobile homes caused traffic gridlock (*Dolomiten*, 2001c). In the city of Bozen, more than 1400 mobile homes were counted on that same day (*Dolomiten*, 2001c). Strains were also experienced in 2003, when Bozen counted 260,000 visitors, 500 buses and 4000 mobile homes on the weekend between 6 and 8 of December (*Dolomiten*, 2003a). When traffic in the city area, as well as on the Brenner motorway, was blocked, a public outcry echoed through the media and reproaches to the organisers could not be discounted easily. In the course of the first agitation a majority of the city council, especially the environmentalists and ultra-conservatives,[2] pleaded for dropping the market in the following year (*Dolomiten*, 2003b). In order to ease the rush to the markets, publicity campaigns seeking to stop the market did not seem to be sufficient. Cancelling the event, and leaving the profits to other towns, seemed to be more efficient. In August 2004, half a year later, the same city council decided to have a market every year. Christoph Engl, the head of the Südtirol Marketing Gesellschaft (South Tyrolean Marketing), which had invested millions of Euros in high profile promotional campaigns for the markets, blamed the commercial interests of stand-holders for the arrangements appealing to mass consumers. In a press interview he complained about the dominant concentration on the offer of products instead on the atmosphere, the programme and the unique character of the region (Rohrer, 2003).

Also in letters to the editors of regional newspapers a certain cultural disassociation of members of the local population from the Christmas markets can be noted: ' . . . an insult to the Bozen native people's cultural perception' (*Dolomiten*, 2001b: 45). Public criticism focused especially on the dominance and 'kitschy' character of items and decorations of Far-Eastern and Italian production. Already in 1997 a member of the provincial assembly criticised the offer of weather stations, dog food and 'porchetta' (Italian for baked suckling pig) as well as the playing of jazz and rock music at the Bozen Christmas market (*Dolomiten*, 1997a). All of the items mentioned did not seem to coincide with the concept of German Christmas markets, and more with the usual offers at fun fairs. The impression that arose in the course of the expansion of Christmas markets was that Italian tastes had come to dominate the markets and that Italian traders outnumbered local ones. This impression can only be sustained partially. A glance at the list of the 66 stands rented in 2001 at the Christmas market in Meran, a town located 30 kilometres northwest from Bozen, shows that the overwhelming majority of stand owners, namely 29 of them, were run by firms from the same town. Another 23 stands had been rented by firms from other South Tyrolean towns or villages. A third group, consisting of 10 stands, could be considered as 'Italian' since the respective firms had their base in different Italian cities and provinces: Venice, Milan, Urbino, Bologna, Trieste, Reggio Emilia. Their share in the market is indeed relatively small, however, their product offers could, be perceived as disturbing, especially if the groups are compared with the extremely low presence of German firms (2 stands), Austrian firms (1 stand) and Czech firms (1 stand), according to Thomas Sigmund, from the 'Kaufleute Aktiv' association. Around 40 applications for stands had to be turned down because they were not considered fitting to the image of the market (*Live – Blick im Advent*, 2000).

The organisers and the others responsible for the markets prefer to adhere to the model of German Christmas markets. Dieter Steger (*WIKU*, 2003: 9), Director of the South Tyrolean Union of traders and service industries, puts it like this:

> The concept of Christ Child markets intends that these markets should be less keen on commercial advantages than on the coherence and originality of South Tyrolean Christmas. If the Christ Child markets continue to decay to the character of mass festivals this would imply a danger for their success on a long-term basis. So this is why the Christ Child markets count on authenticity as well in assortment as in communication.

And Christoph Engl from SMG adds: 'The more we set up tents of the type of popular festivals the more we will attract the masses and then we will destroy that atmosphere that forms the Christmas market' (Rohrer, 2003: 41).

In characterizing the strategies adopted by the rural Tyrolean population to psychologically master the effects of modernity since the 1960s, Manfred Steinlechner has written about the 're-mythologizing' Tyrolean society (Steinlechner, 1985: 3746). Steinlechner draws his examples from the context of local architecture, traditional oriented associations, and local festival and custom organising committees. Many of his conclusions apply to the rural, mainly German speaking areas of South Tyrol. The psychological consequences in the construction of an illusory world of intact rural traditions, he suggests, are, among others, insulation against real experience of the world and hostilities against persons representing cultural variation in order to prevent a cynical attitude towards oneself. Any variation in the fields preserved by cultural conservativism is to be viewed in the eyes of Steinlechner as a deviance from their myth of origin (Eliade, 1963).

This model, as significant it might be for South Tyrolean rural culture, is partly but not completely applicable to Christmas markets, because the same local traditions that have materialised and are performed are included in public functions. The very recent shift of regional rural traditions into the town centres during the markets has detached them from their local contexts. For those adhering to constructions of identity based on the ideology of rural cultural preservation, these traditions might be in danger of being watered-down by the various economic and cultural influences of their new context. In this case, only 'authentic' customs and traditions are able to transmit the vaguely perceived character and consecration of the rural past.

But, what is this 'special' atmosphere and what does the 'originality of South Tyrolean Christmas' mean if we hold that Christmas markets were introduced in this area only in 1991? And, why does this polemic not exist in the North Tyrolean context?

## Regional Customs and the Polysemics of Performance

Organisers of Christmas markets in the North, as well as the South Tyrol, tend to bring in regional or local customs to fill the time frame of the market as a festive event. This provides a cultural historic deepness, a certain rural aesthetic and a strongly needed diversion in the context of competition between the eastern Alpine towns. When markets are being created, special events in the time limited programme and representations of regional traditions are important for the locations. Local visitors and Italian tourists often do not visit only the Christmas market when there are so many possibilities of choice in the area. Several travel brochures examined by the author show that coach tourists venture to different markets over a weekend or during a week: to markets in Munich, Nuremberg, Salzburg, Innsbruck and South Tyrol. Austrian and German markets count on the regular, weekend 'Italo-Invasion' (*Tiroler Krone*, 1997: 12). However, in Innsbruck and at other Austrian market sites stands are not rented by Italians and consequently Italian products are not on offer here. Local polemics about these markets do therefore not take the character of any identity crisis.

Controversies regarding 'taste' have also dominated the discourse surrounding the Christmas markets. In Innsbruck for example, the custom of the parade of the Christ Child with carriages, hundreds of angels and shepherds on every fourth Sunday during Advent (and begun in 1934), has generated vigorous discussion regarding 'taste' (Forcher, 1991; Kapfhammer, 1977). In 1972, for instance, the golden shimmering costumes were considered too kitschy for contemporary spectators (*Tiroler Tageszeitung*, 1972). For many years the custom was integrated into the event calendar of the Christmas market. During the 1990s the organisers were no longer willing to carry the costs for this parade, and so after several years without the custom, in 2003 the mayor of Innsbruck announced the reintroduction of the Christ Child parade and promised generous public funding for this purpose (*Tiroler Tageszeitung*, 2004).

Organising committees do not always return to urban, bourgeois customs such as Nicholas processions and Christ Child parades. Rather, they make more use of the forms and figures of the wide range of Alpine winter or Christmas customs or create completely new customs. The terms of historisation and folklorism (Bausinger, 1966 Moser, 1962) have been used to grasp the phenomena around the contemporary processes of adaptation and exploitation in tourism. Even if we take for granted that customs follow economic interests and the rules of showmanship already in traditional societies, there still lies a deep dislocation between traditional customs and their contemporary contexts. As Köstlin explains: 'Totally clear is that with them [the customs] something traditional, something relating and belonging to a different society, is reaching into our present' (Köstlin, 1999: 11).

In some cases the presence of tourists has altered the form of the festivity, particularly in the urban context. Performing, for example, traditional 'noise and catch' customs in the middle of the tourist masses is not permitted and the behaviour of those who carry the masks of the devilish figures *Krampus* or *Percht*[3] accompanying St Nicholas in parades has been adapted to a more calmer and restrained performance than is carried out in rural areas.

At the Innsbruck Christmas market a roofed wagon has served as stage for custom performers since the year 2000. This not only allows more people to watch the performances, it also allows the possibility of interviewing the performers and providing the public with more background information (*Saison Tirol,* 2000). The speeches are broadcast on the regional station of the federal radio network. Less restrictive to performers are newly arranged and invented customs that make extensive use of traditional practices. For the town of Meran, a 'new' pagan ritual was invented in 1996 that included a procession of *Krampusses,* witches and conjurers on the 21st of December, winter solstice. At every street corner the group of approximately 40 'pagans' wearing masks, animal skins, and feathers stopped and performed the ritual of extinction and resuscitation of light. The spectacle was invented by a local artist and photographer, Oswald Pertramer, who tried to humorously re-enact these rituals. For the 'pagans' some actors from the town's theatre were engaged, as well as traditional *Krampus* and *Klaubauf* performers from Vinschgau Valley who also contributed to the outfits of the group (*Dolomiten,* 1997b).

The performers in the devil's mask of *Krampus,* the companions of St Nicolas on 5 and 6 December, come from the surrounding villages and valleys. They are engaged by the organising committees of the Christmas markets to bring in local colour and they attend the market square according to the timetable of the event programme. So for instance, on the afternoon of 6 December 2001 at the Meran market, three devils and one St Nicolas in white clothes planted themselves in the centre of the promenade, where the market's stands were located. Their behaviour was rather shy; they stood in a circle and only moved when schoolchildren or other young persons tried to tease them. Then they would react and run behind the assailant, but only for a few metres because of the danger of alarming visitors. However, this was not exactly the reaction that would have protected them from being teased again. The situation worsened when other young people arrived at the market having followed the traditional St Nicolas carriage procession with sweets and nuts being thrown to children and passers-by that had been going on in the old town at the same time (programme announced in *Dolomiten,* 2001a: 24). Shortly after the markets, St Nicolas and his masked followers retreated into a pub in the old town, leaving their pursuers, a group of 50 children and teenagers, at the doorstep. Nevertheless, the small crowd was still not willing to give up. For a while they were shouting 'come out, come out'. The performers left the pub only an hour later, when the situation had calmed down. They were in a hurry by then, as they were already awaited in the nearby village of Lana where they would act as real frighteners for children and teenagers (interview with Hannes Friedl, 'Krampus performer', Meran, 6 December 2001).

The above illustrates some of the issues that can arise from the powerful co-existence of different contexts and spheres of meaning when regional customs are applied in tourism. There are no problems when the interests of the customary context are excluded or largely repressed, as for instance in the exploitation of 'Nicolas-folklore for secular interests', as Mezger (1993: 257) has denominated the enormous boom of Nicolas and Santa figures in the iconography of consumption (Miller, 1993) during the last decades.

As a further attraction for the Meran Christmas market in the year 2001 a further appearance from St Nicolas and his *Krampuses* was included in the programme. On 7 December they literally landed on a meadow near the town's hospital. A group of 30 parachutists, dressed as devils, angels and Nicolases started that afternoon on a high-mountain site near to the town (*Dolomiten*, 2001a). One Nicolas even parachuted in on a wooden sleigh and landed without injuries. There were several hundred spectators at the landing place, especially families with children. However, none of the men personifying *Krampuses* acted as in the customary context. It was not really expected from the members of the Flying Club 'Adlerhorst' to act as demonic figures as the entire situation was so different from the usual environment in which the customs are practised.

## Conclusion

Local customs have always been exposed to a relative degree of influence from different interest groups. Changes in society have always resulted in changing the social, religious and apprehensive sphere of the customs practised. Even if these new orientations did not appear on the surface, through performed and consequently visualised rites, they were still perceptible by the local population. Tyrolean customs and religious practices during the weeks of Advent, as far as they survived the ever more perceptible process of secularisation during the 20th century, have in recent years been discovered as tourist attractions by the organisers of Christmas markets. In bringing performers of local customs to the markets in the city and town centres, new public spaces for these customs have been created. Here, traditional and new contexts could overlap, posing to performers the problem of acting within the regulations of each of them. But is it 'authentic' enough to satisfy tourists, organisers and the resident population? Christoph Engl, the South Tyrolean Marketer-in-Chief stressed that one of the main tasks in organising these markets is to ensure 'that we are not going too far away from the authentic background' (Rohrer, 2003: 41). In fact, the newest strategy by the organisers of the Bozen Christmas market is to bring visitors to villages where the customs are 'at home'.

Since 2002 the custom of *Klöckeln*, in former times a social custom that included the collection of food and money by the young and the poor, has been advertised as being a typical Christmas custom of the area in the programme of the Christmas market and in other information materials for tourists (Azienda di Soggiorno e Turismo Bolzano, 2002; BM, 2002). The fact that the custom can only be seen in a village situated in a surrounding valley (Sarntal) may be interpreted as a strategy to disseminate the masses visiting the market in the old town. But the custom is performed only on Thursdays when the tourists were not too numerous. Their number is, of course, still high enough to exert a strong influence on the organisation of the custom, under the direction of the valley's Board of Tourism. Here the traditional contexts are affected more directly by Christmas market tourism because other 'non-tourist' occasions at which the customs could be practised, do not exist.

So, the rudiments of local Advent customs that have survived until the present would seem to have been discovered by market organisers in almost an 'ethnological' way and serve as 'authentic' Tyrolean Christmas traditions to which the various markets would like to belong. But they do not. Rather, they are the result of a recent trend in Italian and Central European tourism and also perhaps a reflex of an idealisation of the family holiday called Christmas within societies that have loosened family relations and bonds. As Weber-Kellermann (1976) and Cox and Matter (1978) suggest, such events can make their participants forget the dropping of social contacts in everyday life, and may also help to overcome the psychic burdens that are especially felt in the season preceding the Christmas holiday.

## Notes

1. Italian administration soon introduced Italian place and field names, mostly invented or deduced from medieval Latin versions. Today, in the autonomous province of Bolzano/Bozen the double names are the official and politically correct denominations. In order to keep reading efforts low the place names are later mentioned only in their German form.
2. The neo-fascists as well as the pro-Austrian right-wing parties of the German community.
3. Popular figures in Austrian customs of the winter time. Both are clad in fur and carry masks with horns.

## References

Ariès, Ph. (1984) *Geschichte der Kindheit*. München: Deutscher Taschenbuch Verlag. (First published as (1960) *L'enfant et la vie familiale sous l'ancien régime*. Paris: Plon.)

Azienda di Soggiorno e Turismo Bolzano (ed.) (2002) *I Mercatini Originali dell'Alto Adige. Bolzano 29/11 – 23/12/2002*. Bolzano: ASTB.

Baur, S., Guggenberg, I. von and Larcher D. (1998) *Zwischen Herkunft und Zukunft. Südtirol im Spannungsfeld zwischen ethnischer und postnationaler Gesellschaftsstruktur. Ein Forschungsbericht.* Merano/Meran: Alpha&Beta.

Bausinger, H. (1966) Zur Kritik der Folklorismuskritik. In H. Bausinger (ed.) *Populus revisus. Beiträge zur Erforschung der Gegenwart* (pp. 61–74). Tübingen: Tübinger Vereinigung f. Volkskunde e.V. (Volksleben 14.)

*BM. Bolzano Bozen Magazine* (2002) (3).

Cox, H.L. and Matter, M. (1978) Das Weihnachtsfest als Indikator für soziale Veränderungen in der gegenwärtigen Gesellschaft. Eine Pilotstudie zur Erfassung der Einstellung Bonner Volkskundestudenten zum Weihnachtsfest 1976. *Rheinisch-westfälische Zeitschrift für Volkskunde* 24, 96–115.

*Dolomiten* (1997a) 115 (286) 12 December.

*Dolomiten* (1997b) 115 (292) 19 December.

*Dolomiten* (2001a) 119 (280) 5 December.

*Dolomiten* (2001b) 119 (281) 6 December.

*Dolomiten* (2001c) 119 (283) 10 December.

*Dolomiten* (2003a) 121 (282) 9 December.

*Dolomiten* (2003b) 121 (292) 20/21 December.

*Echo* (2003) (12) December.

Eliade, M. (1963) *Aspects du Mythe*. Paris: Gallimard.

Forcher, M. (1991) Als das Christkind den hl. Nikolaus verdrängte. *Tipp. Innsbrucker Zeitung* 16 (25) (17 December), 1–3.

Habermas, R. (2000) *Frauen und Männer des Bürgertums. Eine Familiengeschichte (1750–1850).* Göttingen: Vandenhoeck & Ruprecht.

*Innsbrucker Nachrichten* (1856) 3 (281) 5 December.

Kapfhammer, G. (1977) *Brauchtum in den Alpenländern. Ein lexikalischer Führer durch den Jahreslauf.* München: Calwey.

Köstlin, K. (1999) Brauchtum als Erfindung der Gesellschaft'. *Historicum. Zeitschrift für Geschichte* (4), 9–14.

*Live – Blick im Advent* (2000) (1) 20 December.

Lorenz, Ch. (1986) *Berliner Weihnachtsmarkt. Bilder und Geschichten aus 5 Jahrhunderten.* Berlin: Berlin Information.

Mezger, W. (1993) *Sankt Nikolaus zwischen Kult und Klamauk. Zur Entstehung, Entwicklung und Verdrängung der Brauchformen um einen populären Heiligen.* Ostfildern: Schwabenverlag.

Miller, D. (ed.) (1993) *Unwrapping Christmas*. Oxford: Clarendon.

Moser, H. (1962) Vom Folklorismus in unserer Zeit. *Zeitschrift für Volkskunde* 58, 177–91.

Rohrer, J. (2003) Das Christkind und die Kaiserjäger. *FF. Südtiroler Wochenmagazin* (51/2) (18 December), 40–2.

*Saison Tirol* (2000) (5).

Steinlechner, M. (1985) Tirol in der Moderne. *Das Fenster* 19, 3744–9.

*Tiroler Krone* (1997) 9 December.

*Tiroler Tageszeitung* (1927) 26 (275) 28 November.

*Tiroler Tageszeitung* (1972) 28 (286) 12 December.

*Tiroler Tageszeitung* (1975) 31 (288) 13 December.

*Tiroler Tageszeitung* (2004) 60 (165) 19 July.

Vossen, R. (1985) *Weihnachtsbräuche in aller Welt. Weihnachtszeit – Wendezeit Martini bis Lichtmeß*. Hamburg: Hamburgisches Museum für Völkerkunde.
Weber-Kellermann, I. (1976) *Die Familie. Geschichte, Geschichten und Bilder*. Frankfurt a.M.: Insel.
Weber-Kellermann, I. (1978) Das *Weihnachtsfest. Eine Kultur- und Sozialgeschichte der Weihnachtszeit*. Luzern – Frankfurt a.M.: Bucher.
*WIKU Wirtschaftskurier*. Supplement to *Dolomiten* (2003) 121 (289) 17 December.

*Chapter 13*

# The Placeless Festival: Identity and Place in the Post-Modern Festival

Nicola E. MacLeod

## Introduction

A new era of widespread social, political, technological and economic change, described by Jameson (1984) as 'late capitalism' and by Lash (1990) as 'postmodernism', has been characterised by a dislocation of socially embedded notions such as 'place' and 'history' (Harvey, 1990). In this vein, previous realities of 'authentic existence' expressed through meta-narratives and the authority of respected institutions, have been supplanted by *simulacra* and notions of a 'hyper-reality' (Eco, 1986; Urry, 2002). This discursive framework and the particular time scheme it involves (the idea that we might be living in 'new times'), is by no means a new one (Smart, 1993: 15). However, it does appear that processes set in motion by modernity have considerably intensified in recent decades and the increasing globalisation of capital, industrial, tourism and information flows have caused effects to be experienced within increasingly wider social, economic and political contexts.

Modernist anxiety over the 'lack of authenticity' and 'authentic experiences' in contemporary society has been discussed since the 1970s through debates within the fields of tourism sociology and anthropology (Cohen, 1988; MacCannell, 1976). The idea that life is somehow 'less real' or 'genuine' than that experienced by our predecessors has been regarded as a form of nostalgia proper to the industrial and postindustrial societies. As individuals we may regret a loss of community, of an idealised, often rural existence and the 'depth' of place-knowledge experienced by our ancestors. At the same time, we positively feel our lives, relationships, culture and tourism experiences to be 'real'. In this sense, the virtual, highly mediated and staged image becomes part of our lived experience and part of our contemporary authenticity. And here precisely lies the dilemma of the academic debate on authenticity, which is oscillating between the quest for a positive concept and an analytical approach of social discourse.

Linked to the notion of authenticity (and to the academic dilemma related to its approach) are the notions of 'place' and 'community'. The argument that postmodernism has brought about a rupture between people and their association with places has its basis in the physical and social mobility of individuals and the concomitant movement away from the places and communities they were brought up in. In addition, the demographic recomposition of many places has been said to challenge the very link between place and community. Through the development of new types of transport, hospitality, leisure and commercial infrastructures in most urban and rural spaces, new types of places are being developed. Arguably, the disarticulation between communities and these new types of highly standardised and thus exchangeable places makes them largely meaningless 'non-places' (Augé, 1995). In touristic terms, it has been suggested that these are 'in-authentic' commodified stages or 'empty meeting grounds' (MacCannell, 1992).

However convincing such arguments may be, the notion of 'real places' providing individuals and communities with a shared sense of identity appears to be just another aspect of nostalgia. The idea of 'place' has always been contested, holding different meanings simultaneously and over time. Places where tourists gather have always been more than just arenas of purely commercial exchange and commodification. Tourists take part in social life and may also enjoy the playful and artificial pastiche of contemporary culture (Urry, 2002) or find a sense of community with fellow travellers in these new forms of place (Wang, 1999). In this sense, the opposition between 'authentic place' and 'non-place', expressed through the feeling of 'loss of place' or 'placelessness' (Relph, 1976), needs to be considered within the context of a discursively constructed symbolic continuum rather than a positive scientific quest for truth.

This chapter aims to examine the complex processes related to the discursive notions of 'authenticity', 'place' and 'community' in the contemporary era of postmodernism as they operate through the particular focus of festivals that provide a pertinent time and space frame. Tourism has often been seen as transforming (other people's) festivals in a negative way leading to a commodification and consequent social meaninglessness of cultural performances and productions (Greenwood, 1977). In this sense, the festival, reformulated by 'external' normative frameworks and aesthetic models, risks becoming what Augé (1995) has labelled as a 'non-place'. In view of this, the touristic commodification and production of the 'local' further contributes to the contemporary processes of social alienation and feelings of 'placelessness'. Besides investigating this pessimistic view on change, the chapter also explores the potential for the 'postmodern' festival to provide a new context for cultural sharing and transcendence in which tourists may play a role as catalysts for the innovation of new hybrid cultural forms and the revival of a sense of 'local pride' in host communities.

## Place and 'Placelessness'

Relph's work *Place and Placelessness* (1976) explores the very strong link between people and places that imbues places with meaning and identity. According to the author, individuals have strong associations with the places of their childhood and the settings of significant life experiences. Furthermore, he stresses that our sense of place is very much determined by our experience of 'insideness' and 'outsideness', which arise from our feeling of belonging and influences our perspective on place (Relph, 1976: 49).

Relph elaborates four sub-divisions of 'insideness' and 'outsideness' to specify different levels of experience. An 'existential insider' feels 'completely at one' with a place and understands symbols and significations of place that are often difficult to access as strangers. This first type of insider is opposed to 'empathetic' and 'vicarious' insiders who experience a place through previously known forms of literature and texts (including television, film and the internet). According to Relph, the experience of 'outsiders' can be either 'existential' or 'objective', the first being alienated from the world and its meaning, and the second experiencing a place with a geographer's eye. Finally, an 'incidental' outsider experiences a place 'as little more than the background or setting for activities,' the place being subordinate to the activity (1976: 52).

Based on this categorisation system, Relph stresses that an authentic 'sense of place' comes from lived experience, an understanding of the intangible essence of place, the experience of being an insider, and a holistic production of place that is in keeping with human need and scale. According to this kind of discourse, the pre-industrial village with living, working, socialising, worshipping and festive spaces creating a holistic human environment is typically put forward as a prime example of such an 'authentic' place. This 'authenticity' emanates from a deep knowledge of one's surroundings and an awareness of places as settings for meaningful human activity where action and place are inextricably linked. In the contemporary context, individuals may feel nostalgia for such imagined and idealised places that they see as the 'lost authentic places of their past'; a nostalgia that is being exploited by the heritage industry (Walsh, 1992: 148).

This objective and historically specific view of authenticity has been contested. Cohen (1988) suggests that authenticity is not an absolute attribute of objects or places but instead is a socially constructed phenomenon. Consequently, authenticity emerges over time; it is an ever-changing system of representation rather than a fixed setting of objects or ideas. Cultural geographers have also questioned the notion of authenticity of place, suggesting that this denotes that places are static and timeless where in fact 'the identities of place are always unfixed, contested and multiple' (Massey, 1994: 5). Eco has suggested that within American culture, the search for increasingly 'real' places and experiences has led to the creation of what he calls 'hyper-reality', where the absolute fake becomes the ultimate goal (Eco, 1986). There can be no authentic sense of place as there are no longer any 'real' places, just simulations. The simulation thus becomes a form of the 'real'.

At the same time, the feeling of having 'lost' an authentic relationship with a place is significant for many individuals. According to Relph (1976), such a feeling is a result of 'mass communications, mass culture, big business, powerful central authority and the economic system which embraces all these' (Relph, 1976: 90). Since the 1970s, these processes have intensified and more recently authors have reflected on the effects of global communication networks on people's sense of place. In this context, the loosening of the link between place and identity is seen as one of the key distinguishing characteristics of the postmodern era (Lash, 1990; Walsh, 1992). Harvey (1990), for instance, attempts to explain how new modes of production, consumption and communication have affected our experience of space and time, suggesting a dual process of an acceleration of perceived time on one hand and the perceived 'shrinking' of distances on the other. For Bertens (1995), these 'compression signals' are two related effects of capitalism; the pace of life is being speeded up and spatial barriers are being overcome in a way giving the impression that the world implodes. At the same time, technological advances in communication and transport allow more of the world to become known, either at first hand or through the media. As Harvey (1990: 293) argues: 'The whole world can watch the Olympic Games, the World Cup, the fall of a dictator, a political summit, a deadly tragedy . . . while mass tourism, films made in spectacular locations make a wide range of simulated or vicarious experiences of what the world contains available to many people.'

## Tourism and 'Placelessness'

If postmodern society is characterised by the dislocation of people from their temporal and spatial identities, then it may be argued that the postmodern condition is that of 'placelessness'. Commentators describe a consequent rootless and ephemeral quality to contemporary life, which is lived at a speed never before experienced (Harvey, 1990). This dislocation has in turn created an emphasis on consumption and the need to create lifestyles, through the act of consuming, as a backlash to loss of identity.

Wider choice in consumer goods and services and their accumulation may be seen to create meaning through identification with a desired way of life or community. Tourism consumption has played a particularly influential role in lifestyle creation and is an important means by which people can recreate themselves both literally and symbolically. The growing presence of the media, the greater ease of travel and the attendant popularising of 'culture' and 'heritage' products are components of new middle-class lifestyle patterns and indicators of a need to situate oneself in a knowable world amidst a mass of other possible worlds (Harvey, 1990). Each of these processes emphasises a relationship with place that is increasingly based on consumption rather than on 'knowing'. Consequently, tourists increasingly inhabit landscapes populated not by 'real' communities but by temporary collectives of similar tourists and hosts. However, rather than being an alienating and artificial phenomenon, this may actually be a source of comfort to tourists. As Relph (1976: 33) suggests, 'in present-day Western society people feel at home whenever they are with people of similar interests, regardless of the particular place they are in'. Wang (1999), following Turner (1969) describes the feeling of what he calls 'inter-personal authenticity' experienced by groups of tourists as *'touristic communitas'*. In this sense, the quasi-pilgrimage of contemporary tourism can engender similar senses of 'shared authenticity' than those experienced by pilgrims. The accoutrements of tourism can hence provide a sense of home and security whilst on the move.

The global expansion and standardisation of tourism creates an often predictable approach to the provision of tourism facilities and experiences, to the extent that vernacular identity becomes irrelevant in the face of an international norm (Ritzer & Liska, 1997). The city and its different subspaces are the principal hosts for these largely anonymous and geographically disconnected 'spaces of flows' (Castells, 1996 cited in Bonink

& Hitters, 2001). Airport lounges, hotels and exclusive restaurants are further examples of these standardised places which cater to the mobile and privileged, but are often said to be disconnected from the culture and lives of surrounding communities (Augé, 1995; Bonink & Hitters, 2001). However, such 'non-places' do not necessarily provoke a predictable reaction by travellers, neither are they meaningless for the communities who service these areas and feel some sense of genuine engagement with their place of work.

The processes of standardisation related to globalisation are not restricted to tourism and its spaces, but also transform the everyday lives and spaces of 'host communities' (Featherstone, 1991). Transformation is being linked here in particular to processes of 'aestheticisation', which provide a helpful approach to explore the growing role of festivals in urban settings. In this sense, the creation and consumption of culture becomes the key function of postmodern cities competing in a global market. Tourism destinations are no longer simply regions favoured for their natural beauty (for example, the traditional resorts such as the Alps, the French Riviera and the Lake District) but are places marketed in terms of their connections with events, people and contemporary themes (Herbert, 1995).

In this context, cities are no longer primarily functional centres of industrial productivity, but are rather spaces where culture is displayed and consumed in an increasingly intensified manner. Ironically, in British and North American cities, motifs of their earlier industrial identity are employed to create 'cultural tourism' products (Walsh, 1992). However, the 'culture' offered in these new visitor destinations is an aestheticised and often highly standardised commodity that bears little relation to its social context. As Featherstone (1991: 99) puts it: 'the postmodern city marks a return to culture, style and decoration but within the confines of a 'no-place space' in which traditional senses of culture are decontextualised, simulated, reduplicated and continually renewed and restyled'.

Urban planning has contributed to this process by creating public spaces for the presentation of cultural events. These public spaces often shift from places to communicate civic pride and symbols of power to exclusive arenas for leisure consumption (Aitchison *et al.*, 2000). Emergent playful public spaces using theme-park elements challenge connections with the local history and geography (Cybriwsky, 1999). Tourists visiting these urban settings encounter a growing standardisation in terms of the possibilities of experience and the environments in which these are created. Capital cities across the world increasingly have more in common with each other than with the towns and villages of their own countries. In addition, these cities compete with one another to host events that are believed to be a requirement for an international cultural tourism industry.

In this context, cultural festivals and mega-events have become part of a more generalised city archetype; the organisation of such events has been applied as a repetitive formula to facilitate destination promotion, cultural regeneration schemes and the reviving of unpopular venues (Evans, 2001). As Waterman (1998: 60) suggests:

[T]he cultural facets of festivals cannot be divorced from the commercial interests of tourism, regional and local economy and place promotion. Selling the place to the wider world or selling the festival as an inseparable part of the place rapidly becomes a significant facet of most festivals.

Cities thus become stages for events and festivals that merge the cultural and the everyday life of urban areas until the entire city is in festival mode for most of the time (Richards, 2001). In Edinburgh, Scotland, the 'cultural calendar' includes festivals taking place across at least six months in every year (Prentice and Andersen, 2003) so a chance visitor to the city is very likely to find it *en fête*. Consequently, as festival provision and global tourism grow, festive strategies increasingly use common (and often interchangeable) themes and elements of spectacle to appeal to an increasingly international audience.

## Festivals, Place and Identity

Transformations of place and sense of place have inevitably generated significant implications for the concept of the festival. Festivals are often thought of as celebrations of the specificities of social groups and communities. From a geographical perspective, they have been defined as 'one of the many practices that humans evolve in the process of connecting with their places, making homes for themselves and carving out landscapes in their own likeness' (Quinn, 2000: 263). In this context, the 'local' represents the particular way to define such social identities in relation to a place (De Bres & Davis, 2001), whereas the 'ethnic' often delivers criteria to define communities by social-cultural or kinship parameters.

Although many contemporary festivals in Europe are associated with the religious calendar, their form and meanings often pre-date those of the Christian pantheon and the symbolic. While vestiges of ancient rituals remain in communal celebrations, the postmodern and locally decontextualised concept of the festival, which has flourished worldwide in the last 30 years, no longer focuses upon local production and consumption of meaning. Rolfe (1992: 7) notes that the largest proportion of arts festivals ever organised in the UK were founded from the mid-1970s onwards with a central feature being 'the celebration or reaffirmation of community or culture'. The potential for festivals to construct and express the cultural identities of place and community means that cultural tourists in search of an authentic engagement with the locals can expect to find this within a festival. The increase in cultural tourism, and the emphasis on city marketing practice has led to festivals becoming a prime tool for tourism development and destination promotion (Hughes, 1999). Events have drawn increasingly international audiences and different event typologies have been devised in the newly created field of event and festival management (Getz, 1997).

So, what has happened to the idea of an authentic sense of place central to most festivals? The discussion above has outlined the processes leading to a sense of placelessness – a dislocation of place and identity. It has been suggested that placelessness, although not a universal phenomenon, may have an impact on the ways that people experience and react to place and the creation of new places, particularly those specialised places of tourism consumption. Clearly these processes have had an effect on the festival as a communal mediator of place and identity. The next sections of the chapter will analyse some perceived trends within postmodern festival development.

It has been seen that the issue of authenticity in terms of place has been overcome and that meaning and authenticity of experience is something that may be constructed within the individual celebrant themselves rather than consumed in 'genuine' settings. The global traveller neither expects nor seeks authentic festivals. Building on this argument, it is suggested that a consequent trend towards spectacle and the carnivalesque has become observable, creating festivals that are global in appeal, ungrounded in local identity and demonstrate the characteristics of placelessness proposed by Relph (1976). Such 'global parties' (Ravenscroft & Matteucci, 2003) place their emphasis on international norms of conviviality rather than on indigenous forms of celebration and meaning, and as such may demonstrate the alienation of people and place. However it is also suggested that these gatherings may also play an important role in providing opportunities for transcendent communal experiences otherwise absent from everyday life.

## Visitors, Communities and a Sense of Place

The festival as an event hosted by a resident population for their own consumption and enjoyment has increasingly been offered as an entertainment for visitors, particularly in urban areas, and this, it is suggested, will change the nature of the festival and its link with local place and culture. As Getz (1994: 313) notes: 'When festivals and other special events are consciously developed and promoted as tourist attractions, there is a risk that commercialization will detract from celebration; that entertainment or spectacle will replace the inherent meanings of the celebrations.' The question here is not whether a festival that is consumed by visitors will ever be truly authentic, but rather what effect the presence of visitors will have on the festival itself and how visitors and local communities experience it.

It has been suggested that postmodern tourists are not in search of the real and genuine but instead take delight in pastiches of the real (Rojek, 1993; Urry, 2002), akin to MacCannell's (1976) idea of 'staged authenticity'. It has already been noted that authenticity may reside in the experience of individuals, particularly when they are participating in an event (Wang, 1999), rather than in an externally validated concept of what is real. In their research of the San Fermin Fiesta in Pamplona, Ravenscroft and Matteucci (2003: 13) note that neither residents nor visitors to the fiesta 'are naive enough to believe that authenticity resides in representation or even cultural (re)production. Rather [ ... ] authenticity resides with the intensity of emotion experienced by the individual'. Getz (1994) believes that the lack of sincerity inherent in tourist-orientated events may be offset for the host community by the very real benefits that accrue from the promotion of such events (such as revived traditions, the fostering of community spirit and revenue). However, he does suggest that an authentic sense of locality is crucial to heritage events 'which celebrate a nation's or community's traditions, values and sense of place' (1994: 321).

The increasing number of visitors attending festivals suggests that 'incidental outsidedness' may be the most prevalent condition amongst festival goers and, consequently, place-identity is negligible in the consumption process. In this sense, the contemporary festival visitor who simply enjoys the spectacle with no desire to understand the specificities of the host environment becomes an 'incidental outsider' within a community. This would seem to be born out in the case of the Edinburgh Festival, where Prentice and Anderson (2002: 5) note that the importance of sociability may override any search for an authentic sense of place:

The recurrent importance of gregariousness may imply that the festival itself becomes a destination, rather than simply an attraction of place-based destinations. The experience of gregariousness may ultimately be independent of any specific place, and what makes festivals special has been found to center around uniqueness and quality, as well as atmosphere.

The Pleasance Fringe Festival venue in Edinburgh provides a good example for this shift of meaning. This popular temporary venue has been set up each year since 1984 in 'The Pleasance', Edinburgh University's historic Student Union building. The cobbled courtyard, winding stairs and informal bars and restaurant areas characterise the Edinburgh venue but the ambiance of the temporary space has been translated into a North London context with the opening of a permanent venue of the same name by the company that promotes and runs the temporary Edinburgh venue. A site with a similar cobbled yard and adjacent restaurant was found for The Pleasance, London enabling a London audience to experience the August Edinburgh Festival Fringe throughout the year in a former timber store.

These observations indicate that the specificities of place are of less importance to postmodern festival visitors who increasingly experience a continuum of place and placelessness in their travels. It has already been noted that contemporary visitors 'carry their world with them' and will feel at home when in the company of similar people and apparently familiar places, no matter where the visitor may find themselves (Relph, 1976). Frequent travellers may hence increasingly experience a sense of familiarity rather than disorientation on their travels. Indeed the festival may attract a particular type of visitor who is actively seeking the company of like-minded people, rather than that of local communities. Waterman (1998) suggests that 'high-brow' arts festivals in particular try to maintain an elite group identity that may deliberately exclude local people. Festival publicity materials may reach 'only those who are already tuned to the right wavelength' and pricing mechanisms can ensure that 'a desirable audience forms the bulk of those attending' (1998: 67).

The visitors themselves may become part of the temporary place-identity of a festival as is the case in the Wexford Festival held in the south-east of Ireland (Quinn, 2000). This festival, launched in 1951 by a small group of local middle-class opera devotees, was deliberately elitist in its aspirations and its policy of attracting outsiders rather than the local population, although local people were extensively involved behind the scenes. Wealthy international visitors, carrying the trappings of their own lifestyle with them, consequently became a spectacle for the local towns-people who came out to 'indulge in the glamorous and exotic atmosphere created by the foreign singers, producers, directors and visiting dignitaries attending the festival' (Quinn, 2000: 268).

However, it would be wrong to assume that a host community's sense of its own authentic culture and identity is inevitably being denied by these developments in the creation and promotion of festivals. The definition of community and community culture is problematic in an increasingly multi-cultural and displaced society, and it is simplistic to conclude that host cultures are somehow being despoiled by the increase in tourism-orientated events and the wider processes of globalisation. Those living in host destinations consume the same products of global culture as much as the international traveller. The development and consumption of 'authentic indigenous cultural products' may not be an immediate concern for local communities, as De Bres and Davis (2001) discovered in their analysis of a festival in the Kansas River Valley that was aimed at both visitors and residents. The authors note that although 'tourist commodifications' of local culture were clearly in evidence (for example the celebration of an overly-simplified 'pioneer culture'), the festival was still appreciated by the host community as it promoted a positive sense of pride, kinship and community.

Therefore the festival visitor as an 'incidental outsider' may not primarily be seeking an authentic experience with local place and identity, but instead may be in search of convivial experiences with similar people converging in the 'no-place' spaces of festival destinations (Feather-stone, 1991). Consequently a range of placeless global festivals have appeared in the last decade to meet demand of the international festival visitor, address destination-marketing strategies, and satisfy income generation targets. Festivals such as Edinburgh's Hogmanay have been specially created for these purposes and some have evolved from small, local community events to become international gatherings such as the Noting Hill Carnival. However, the overriding theme of these festivals is the notion of the 'global party', with an emphasis on conviviality and consumption.

## Global Parties and the Placeless Festival?

The festival as a locus for international visitors and a tool for place marketing increasingly employs standardised elements of the spectacle to appeal to a large-scale audience. The presence of outsiders 'shifts the construct of the festival from celebration to spectacle, from production to consumption' (Ravenscroft & Matteucci, 2003: 4) and the centrality of tourism in the development of festivals has resulted in the replication of elements of such spectacle across the globe. The notion of celebration denotes shared thanksgiving or commemoration and is usually found within closely knit groups such as families. Spectacle, conversely, suggests a distancing between the viewer and that which is being visually consumed. While a host community will present a spectacle for an audience to witness, sharing and understanding the roots of the event are less important.

It is accepted that very diverse populations can come together to celebrate global events but in these situations, elements of spectacle are used to provide a more objectified focus for communal consumption. This has can be witnessed in London where firework displays are increasingly used to mark important events or dates within the cultural calendar. No longer restricted to the traditional Guy Fawkes commemoration of 5 November, fireworks are seen at Christmas, New Year, weddings, to mark the end of outdoor concerts, events and festivals. Spectacles may utilise local cultural signifiers to provide differentiating motifs but essentially the product is a standard one.

In their analysis of the San Fermin Fiesta in Pamplona in Spain, Ravenscroft and Matteucci (2003: 12) demonstrate how this event has ceased to be commercialised as part of the local cultural heritage and instead been placed on the 'global party map'. The festival originally honoured the martyred Saint Fermin, but its fame was secured as the setting for Ernest Hemingway's novel *The Sun Also Rises* (1926). Today, the famed bull-running (which tests the bravado of participants and over the years has resulted in death and injury as they place themselves in the path of a charging bull) and the week-long street party make the festival particularly popular with younger visitors. Some 300,000 visitors attend yearly and 60% of these come from outside Spain. The event is televised, which further contributes to its popularity. Although in essence still a unique and indigenous event, the local communities of Pamplona are becoming distanced from the fiesta, taking on roles as service providers or as agents of 'local colour' for international visitors rather than as participants in a meaningful yearly celebration (Ravenscroft & Matteucci, 2003).

It may also be argued that the recently created Edinburgh Hogmanay Festival is another event placed firmly on a world map of global parties appealing to an international audience. The traditions of Hogmanay (New Year's Eve) in Scotland historically revolve around the home, the houses of friends and family and a number of rituals such as 'first-footing' (visiting friends after midnight) where visitors offer a piece of coal to ensure heat and light in the coming year. Such practices are still widely observed. However, the success of the summer festivals programme in Edinburgh, in combination with a desire to increase tourism in the low-season prompted the City to launch a three-day Hogmanay Festival in 1993. The festival incorporated largely decontextualised spectacles such as torch-light processions, fun fairs and a huge open-air street party featuring live music on the eve of 31 December (Hughes, 1999). Since then, the festival has continuously expanded and the 2002–3 Festival was seven days long. Controversy and safety issues arose in 1996–7 when 350,000 people converged in Princes Street, the main party area, creating a potentially lethal crush of bodies. The Accident and Emergency Department of Edinburgh's Royal Infirmary reported that the number of patients treated during the festivities exceeded those presented at most of the UK's major disasters (O'Donnell *et al.*, 1998). In 1997–8, the free party became a ticket-only event. Although the event is estimated to generate £36.5 million (54.3 million Euros) for the City and is televised across the world (Black, 2003), it is regularly criticised for its high public cost and relatively low attendance figures from the local population. In 2001, World-Party.com, an online festivals guide, voted it the fourth 'best festival' in the world (Edinburgh's Hogmanay, 2002).

The 2003–4 Hogmanay Festival featured an eclectic mix of visual culture in the production of the spectacle. The torch-light procession, now increasingly attracting local residents as participants, included the burning of a Viking long ship and a representation of the Taj Mahal in fireworks. The mingling of the ancient and modern appears as a typical expression of postmodern pastiche. The fire motifs have their roots in the ancient fire-festivals still practised along the east coast of Scotland and the Indian references acknowledge both the local resident Indian communities and the contemporary interest in Scottish locations from the producers of 'Bollywood' films. The event is thus a very typical expression of playful postmodernism. The communal multi-cultural spectacle has perhaps not replaced the home-based supposedly mono-cultural celebration that still takes place in homes across Scotland and beyond, but has borrowed the name and the spirit of the event – celebrating the threshold between the past and the present.

The presence of tens of thousands of overseas visitors and the global media are a source of considerable pride for the event organisers and provide a context for cultural innovation. Such events may therefore be regarded as important sites for cultural integration and the celebration of communality in a globalised society that offers few other opportunities for communal experiences. International celebrants and local communities can engage in conviviality that transcends borders and cultural differences. The presence of visitors may indeed act as a catalyst for new cultural forms and social spaces. Such global parties have become a form of special interest tourism in their own right and a new cultural 'season' of popular events has emerged as evidenced in the aforementioned online festival guide and recently published guidebook *World Party* (Dakota, 2002), which provides a guide to 40 festivals that will appeal to those seeking a collective cultural experience. The guide covers an eclectic mix of the religious and the hedonistic and includes Munich's 'Oktoberfest', India's Kumbh Mela and the Burning Man Festival in Nevada, USA. The only unifying features of these festivals are that they must be at least five years old and be able to attract a minimum of 5000 (mainly international) visitors.

The contemporary holiday calendar recalls traditional feasts and celebrations, however, the ritual and mystical significance has often been removed and, in the words of Hughes, 1999: 129) 'all we are left with today are the visual signifiers and decorative artifacts of earlier ritualistic practice such as feasting and drinking at Christmas and the practice of exchanging greeting cards and presents'. Such traditional motifs are used to provide atmosphere and colour but the events themselves are increasingly distanced from local identity and participation, and turn instead to new forms of transnational festivity, spectacle and consumption.

## Conclusion

The processes that have contributed to a disarticulation between ideas of identity and place have produced an approach to festival development and promotion that increasingly depends for its appeal on a new type of transnationalised festivity rather than local meanings, traditions and social practice. These processes can be approached through the globalisation of communications network and the expanding international tourism market. In this context, communities and community festivals are no longer considered as unique and interesting emanations of local culture but as opportunities for convivial consumption in an international 'placeless' atmosphere. In analogy to the culture of the airport lounge or the hotel cocktail bar, festival formats may now be replicated in a series of international venues throughout the world.

In many cases, festivals which ostensibly offer a unique and place-based experience, such as, for example, the bull-running of Pamplona and the Hogmanay rituals of Edinburgh, are being transformed to tourist commodities where historic patterns are being replaced by an emphasis on the spectacular as the preferred experience of the visitor. However, it may also be argued that the local communities actively engage with the cultural products of a globalised society and may use these events to negotiate social change and enact new formulations of the 'local'. The future for such festivals therefore seems uncertain as they continue to expand and attract larger numbers of international visitors. Featuring in 'league tables' of the year's 'best festivals' can only be a short-term objective, as is the introduction of increasingly spectacular experiences. As visitor-oriented festivals inevitably become more footloose and less grounded in local place and society, it is as yet unclear whether they will become nodal points of cultural transcendence for hosts and visitors alike or simply another global brand in the international tourism market.

## References

Aitchison, C., MacLeod, N.E. and Shaw, S.J. (2000) *Leisure and Tourism Landscapes: Social and Cultural Geographies.* London: Routledge.

Augé, M. (1995) *Non-Places: Introduction to an Anthropology of Supermodernity.* London: Verso.

Bertens, H. (1995) *The Idea of the Postmodern.* London: Routledge.

Black, E. (2003) Call to scrap Hogmanay party blasted. *The Scotsman* 15 February.

Bonink, C. and Hitters E. (2001) Creative industries as milieux of innovation: The Westergasfabriek, Amsterdam. In G. Richards (ed.) *Cultural Attractions and European Tourism* (pp. 227–40). Wallingford: CABI.

Cohen, E. (1988) Authenticity and commoditization in tourism. *Annals of Tourism Research* 15, 371–86.

Cybriwsky, R. (1999) Changing patterns of urban public space: Observations and assessments from the Tokyo and New York Metropolitan Areas. *Cities* 16 (4), 223–31.

Dakota, D. (2002) *World Party.* London: Big Cat Press.

De Bres, K. and Davis, J. (2001) Celebrating Group and place identity: A case study of a new regional festival. *Tourism Geographies* 3 (3), 326–37.

Eco, U. (1986) *Travels in Hyper-reality.* London: Picador.

Edinburgh's Hogmanay (2002) Edinburgh's Hogmanay joined world elite festivals league. On WWW at http://www.edinburghshogmanay.org/press_specific.cfm?id+9. Accessed: 20 March 2003.

Evans, G. (2001) *Cultural Planning: An Urban Renaissance?* London: Routledge.

Featherstone, M. (1991) *Consumer Culture and Postmodernism.* London: Sage.

Getz, D. (1994) Event tourism and the authenticity dilemma. In W. Theobald (ed.) *Global Tourism: The Next Decade* (pp. 313–29). Oxford: Butterworth-Heinemann.

Getz, D. (1997) *Event Management and Event Tourism.* New York: Cognizant Communications Corporation.

Greenwood, D.J. (1977) Culture by the Pound. An anthropological perspective on tourism as a cultural commodization. In V.L. Smith (ed.) *Hosts and Guests – The Anthropology of Tourism* (pp. 129–38). Oxford: Blackwell.

Harvey, D. (1990) *The Condition of Postmodernity.* Oxford: Blackwell.

Herbert, D.T. (1995) Heritage as literary place. In D.T. Herbert (ed.) *Heritage, Tourism and Society* (pp. 32–48). London: Mansell.

Hughes, G. (1999) Urban revitalization: The use of festive time strategies. *Leisure Studies* 18, 119–35.

Jameson, F. (1984) Postmodernism or the cultural logic of late capitalism. *New Left Review* 146, 52–92.

Lash, S. (1990) *The Sociology of Postmodernism.* London: Routledge.

MacCannell, D. (1976) *The Tourist: A New Theory of the Leisure Class.* New York: Shocken.

MacCannell, D. (1992) *Empty Meeting Grounds: The Tourist Papers.* London: Routledge.

Massey, D. (1994) *Space, Place and Gender.* Cambridge: Polity

O'Donnell, J., Gleeson, A.P. and Smith, H. (1998) Edinburgh's Hogmanay celebrations: Beyond a major disaster. *Journal of Accident and Emergency Medicine* 15 (4), 272–3.

Prentice, R. and Andersen V. (2002) Festivals as a creative destination. *Annals of Tourism Research* 30 (1), 7–30.

Quinn, B. (2000) Whose festival? Whose place? An insight into the production of cultural meanings in arts festivals as visitor attractions. In M. Robinson *et al.* (eds) *Expressions of Culture, Identity and Meaning in Tourism* (pp. 263–73). Sunderland. Business Education Publishers Ltd.

Ravenscroft, N. and Mattueucci, X. (2003) The festival as carnivalesque: social governance and control at Pamplona's San Fermin Fiesta, *Tourism, Culture and Communication* 4, 1–15.

Relph, E. (1976) *Place and Placelessness.* London: Pion.

Richards, G. (2001) The experience industry and the creation of attractions. In G. Richards (ed.) *Cultural Attractions and European Tourism* (pp.55–69). Wallingford: CABI.

Ritzer, G. and Liska, A. (1997) McDisneyization and 'post-tourism'. In C. Rojek and J. Urry (eds) *Touring Cultures: Transformations of Travel and Theory* (pp. 96–109). London: Routledge.

Rojek, C. (1993) Ways of escape: Modern transformations in leisure and travel. London: Macmillan.

Rolfe, H. (1992) *Arts Festivals in the UK.* London: PSI Publishing.

Smart, B. (1993) *Postmodernity.* London: Routledge.

Turner, V. (1969) *The Ritual Process: Structure and Anti-structure.* Chicago: Aldine.

Urry, J. (2002) *The Tourist Gaze.* London: Sage.

Walsh, K. (1992) *The Representation of the Past: Museums and Heritage in the Postmodern World.* London: Routledge.

Wang, N. (1999) Rethinking authenticity in tourism experience. *Annals of Tourism Research* 26 (2), 349–70.

Waterman, S. (1998) Carnivals for elites? The cultural politics of arts festivals. *Progress in Human Geography* 22 (1), 54–74.

*Chapter 14*

# Gay and Lesbian Festivals: Tourism in the Change from Politics to Party

Howard L. Hughes

## Introduction

Many gay and lesbian festivals originated as protest marches for gay[1] rights but now appear to have lost this political focus and have become more celebratory and commercialised and significant tourist attractions. With respect to the UK experience, in particular, such festivals have also, more recently, been characterised by conflict over purpose, organisational upheaval and financial difficulty. The aim, in this chapter, is to examine the development of such festivals with particular consideration of the tourism dimension. The Manchester Lesbian, Gay, Bisexual and Transgender (LGBT) festival will be used as a case-study.

Most of the material for this chapter was derived from secondary sources, especially papers in academic journals and articles in the gay press. Academic papers were important for the framework of the chapter whereas press articles were sources for detail and opinion relating to LGBT festivals. There is, at this stage, a lack of research relating to the tourism-festival relationship and especially relating to the reaction of the Manchester LGBT community. Despite obvious reservations about the press as a reliable source, it is, until primary research is undertaken, one of the few readily available sources. It may well, in fact, accurately represent opinion and be an accurate record; in addition, its significance as source material lies in its role as a source of opinion and influencer of public perceptions.

Despite this reliance on secondary sources, the development of ideas and propositions has been informed by personal experience and informal conversations with friends and acquaintances as well as with people who use Manchester's Gay Village for leisure purposes. Many matters of detail and some further insights have been provided by conversations with a number of key players in the LGBT community including business people in the Village and people who are, or have been, actively involved with the organisation of the festivals. These 'primary' sources are not meant to be representative of opinion and are not the main source for the content of the chapter or conclusions reached though they have often given credence to the secondary material used.

## Gay Identity and Gay Space

Homosexuality has been regarded as deviant in many societies and discriminatory proscriptive legislation often exists in the case of males, in particular. In addition to the legislative issues, homosexuality (especially male) continues to be problematic for many in respect of societal disapproval which may manifest itself in physical and verbal abuse and discrimination (Beyond Barriers 2002; Mason and Palmer 1996; Stonewall 2001; Webb 2002; www.beyondbarriers.org.uk).

As a consequence, gays and lesbians adopt avoidance strategies that will reduce the possibility of conflict whether overt or covert, physical or verbal. Many will, at least in some situations, seek to conceal their sexuality and will live false lives. Given the 'outsider' position of gays, the adoption and acceptance of a homosexual identity is one that has to be 'signed up' for in a way that heterosexuality does not. That possibility has been largely confined to social space such as bars (Haslop *et al.*, 1998). The formation of a gay identity and gay community is associated with 'gay space', which is 'a physical manifestation of gay community' (Hindle, 1994: 11) usually a spatially discrete concentration of bars and clubs but also cafes, shops, residences and public space. It permits gay identity to be validated by relationships with others, provides social space and support networks and serves as an expression of sexual and cultural identity (Castells & Murphy, 1982). It offers 'havens' for self-expression (Binnie, 1995) and symbolises empowerment and the ability to bring about social change (Duncan, 1996). Control of space is an important element of identity given that most public space is heterosexualised (Valentine 1996).

Gay space is also associated with activity as well as with buildings. In 'imaginary geographies' (Shields, 1990), places become coded as 'gay places' and one of the key components of this construction is a calendar of gay events along with visible gay life and gay amenities (Duyves, 1995). Given this, parades and festivals can be empowering; they act as a symbol in creating group identity (Davis, 1995) but also in reinforcing 'difference'

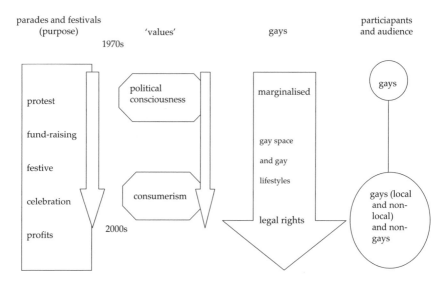

**Figure 14.1** Summary of developments over time

(Graham, 2002). A parade or festival 'asserts a sense of self by locating the queer body within a particular social environment – namely the street' – as heterosexual space (Polchin, 1997: 386). Events such as festivals and parades are vehicles for the expression of commonality, for celebration and are symbols of presence, visibility and self-esteem (Heckert, 2000). They act as common points of reference. Parades and festivals are a further step in coming out as a more public display of sexuality. They may also serve to alter attitudes by creating understanding and tolerance. The 'straight' community may, though, feel threatened or may see gays as merely objects of curiosity or entertainment.

Despite societal marginalisation, the association of gay life and gay identity with a particular lifestyle characterised by events, festivals, bars, clubs and publications means that it has become increasingly possible to identify as gay in a positive self-esteem sense. Being gay has shifted from a negative criterion of being marginalised to a more positive assertion (see Figure 14.1).

Essentially, however, this gay life and identity is determined by patterns of consumption (including body perfection, clothes and leisure activities) being used as markers of difference (Featherstone, 1987). There have also been concurrent advances in achieving equal rights for gays and in social acceptance though inequalities remain (Yates, 2002; Anon., 2003a). There is increased acceptance of gays, there are a number of high-profile public figures (in politics and entertainment) who have been prepared to be open about their homosexuality and gay space and gay lifestyles have become more open and accepted. Not surprisingly, these advances in acceptance and the development of gay space and of distinctive gay lifestyles 'have had a powerful effect on the political thinking of some gay men and lesbians' (Gluckman & Reed, 1997: xv) so that there seems to be less need for 'protest'. The enhanced opportunity to consume has encouraged an interest in 'self' rather than fostered a 'political community' and is seen as being, in part, responsible for the lessening of political interest generally as well as specifically amongst gays.

Nonetheless, 'the rapid growth of gay culture – even of a gay capitalism to cater for it – whilst it made life better for gay men . . . did not achieve the breakthrough of overcoming capitalist society's homophobia' (Workers Power 1991: 27). The acceptance of a gay lifestyle as a means of liberation has pre-dated many of the legal advances and has been an implicit acquiescence in material advancement regardless of social approval. The ability to buy into a gay lifestyle may, though, detract from more fundamental issues relating to sexual liberation (Field, 1995; Whittle, 1994). Consumerism may well be an opportunity to assert economic power but spending may be an expression of freedom that is illusory (Binnie 1995) and that is fostered by the business community itself 'to undermine potential threat to its power' (Knopp 1995: 158).

Almost as a confirmation of this liberation through lifestyle, gay men are alleged to have a high travel propensity and high travel spend (MAPS, 1998; Mintel, 2000; Wood, 1999). This is not necessarily the case, however, and it is clear that the 'typical' gay or lesbian does not have an above-average disposable income (Badgett, 2001). Travel and holiday decisions may, nonetheless, be influenced by the existence of gay space (Hughes 2002).

## Gay Parades, Festivals and Tourism

LGBT parades and festivals are undoubtedly elements of gay tourism: 'the innumerable Gay Pride events which now take place all over the world provide their own impetus for international gay travel' (Russell, 2001: 51). (LGBT events encompassing marches, parades and festivals are often referred to generically as Pride events.) Contemporary gay parades are commonly regarded as owing their origin to the Stonewall incident (variously referred to 'riot' or 'rebellion') in New York in June 1969. Police harassment of patrons of a gay bar in Greenwich Village (New York) led to public disturbances over three nights. The 'riots' took on iconic status and were commemorated in a gay march through New York and in other US cities on the first anniversary in 1970.

Many of the earliest Pride marches and festivals were to commemorate Stonewall and to demand equal rights for gays and lesbians. Protest parades have, however, become more festive and carnivalesque and, in the process, have generated a wider audience than as purely political events (see Figure 14.1). There are a large number of Pride events worldwide; in 2001, events were planned by over 150 organisations in 23 countries. Some, such as those in New York, Toronto and San Francisco were 'mega-events' whereas others were on a much smaller scale (www.interpride.org). Most have become accompanied by festivals and now expect to attract tourists. The annual Europride is the largest gay festival in Europe; the Europride in Cologne in 2002 is believed to have attracted 1.3 million visitors (Zarra & Ward, 2003). Worldwide, Pride events are believed to have drawn a combined attendance of 15–20 million in 2000 (www.interpride.org).

Sydney Mardi Gras has been one of the more successful as a tourist event but has always been characterised by concern over its direction (Ryan & Hall, 2001). Its origins lie in a 1978 protest march to commemorate Stonewall and to demonstrate for equality of human rights. The name Mardi Gras was adopted in 1979 and the event moved to summer (February) in 1981. (The term Mardi Gras has been adopted by some LGBT festivals, including Manchester's, as a generic term for festival and carnival. This is despite the original application of the term to pre-Lenten, non-gay-related celebrations.) Pre- and post-parade parties and arts programmes were a feature of Sydney's festival within four years. It has become a month-long festival covering a range of cultural events culminating in the Parade and Mardi Gras Party. The 1998 festival was estimated to have had an impact of A$99 million (approx. EUR 60 million) on the city (www.mardigras.org.au). The festival features prominently in the programmes of tour operators targeting the gay market: the UK operator, Man Around labels it 'the greatest show on earth'.

The bankruptcy of the Sydney Mardi Gras organising company in August 2002 led to criticisms such as: 'it's grown too big and too commercialised . . . the event has lost its political edge' (Marks, 2002: 17). The new organisers, New Mardi Gras Ltd (NMGL) have sought to re-examine the purpose of the event. They claim that Mardi Gras has always been political but 'every year there are demands that the Parade be more political . . . and in the same year, complaints that it is too political and should be more glamorous' (NMGL, 2002: 1). It is claimed that the fun and celebration have contributed to the breakdown of barriers and to acceptance. The fundamental objects, it is suggested, should remain (amongst others) the pursuit of equal rights, increased visibility, education of the public and to 'affirm identity of GLBT people and enhance self-esteem' (NMGL, 2003). Nonetheless, a commentator on the 2003 Mardi Gras claimed that it is 'firmly in bed with corporate sponsors' (Fickling, 2003: 23).

London's Pride events have had a chequered history especially recently with different organisations competing to organise the festival element. Public protests were organised by the Gay Liberation Front (GLF) in London in 1970 and 1971, leading to the first London 'Gay Pride' in July 1972 (www.sbu.ac.uk/stafflag). GLF arose in New York immediately after the Stonewall riots and was a 'fighting organisation born in the streets and spent most of its time fighting in the streets' (Halifax, 1988: 28). It was established in Britain in 1970 but 'GLF horrified the established gay reform groups of the time . . . [The] Campaign for Homosexual Equality viewed GLF's street campaigns and denunciations of the system as the sort of activity that gave gays and lesbians a bad name' (Halifax, 1988: 31). The Gay Pride in the following year (1972) was organised by the Campaign for Homosexual Equality (formed in 1969) and was still predominantly a 'political' event.

The London Pride has gone through several transformations since, in respect of organisation, focus and name: the term 'Pride' was dropped for the 1999 event, following a change of organiser, to be replaced by 'London Mardi Gras'. Unlike many other events such as that in Sydney, it is a one-day event of march and festival. There has been ongoing debate about the commercialisation of the festival (Field, 1995) and of the principle of a free festival. Organisers, who have included consortia of London gay businesses, have been criticised 'for turning a free community event into a depoliticised and over-commercialised festival' (Smith, 2002a: 41). Nonetheless, the organisers of the 2002 Mardi Gras had a reported deficit of £450,000 (approx EUR 630,000) following low ticket sales; sales were reported as 28–35,000 compared with projections of 50–60,000 (Branigan, 2002). Following an agreement with creditors, London Mardi Gras continues. The 2003 event will revert to its old name of Pride and the festival will be held in Hyde Park with an entry fee of £20 (approx. EUR 30). The fact that it is being held in this park is widely interpreted as a sign of its 'respectability'. In addition, the organisers intend that the 2003 Pride Parade should have a political focus and community involvement in this is being actively encouraged (Anon., 2003b).

Notwithstanding the festival character of Pride events, there is still a strong belief that these are primarily human rights events. Interpride, the international co-ordinating body of individual Prides, claims that 'together they represent the strength and commitment of people . . . who are determined to achieve, maintain and expand the rights of GLBT people' (www.interpride.org). For as long as there is a view that LGBT people are denied equality of human rights, Pride marches and festivals will undoubtedly continue. The first WorldPride was held in Rome in 2000 as a particular gesture against the Vatican's millennium celebrations as well as discrimination against the Italian LGBT community (Graham 2002; www.interpride.org). Given their festive qualities, it seems unlikely that Pride events would disappear even should equality be achieved. In addition, equality under the law will not necessarily remove societal disapproval or the desire to celebrate or to accentuate difference. The fact that Interpride registered events in only 23 countries suggests that there may be more Prides yet to emerge. Human rights continue to be denied to LGBT people in many countries (Amnesty International UK, 1997).

## Manchester's LGBT Festivals

Gay activism in Manchester, although it has long existed, has not manifested itself in the form of Pride marches, largely because of the existence of the London Pride march. The emergence of a Manchester LGBT festival, held over four days at the August Bank Holiday weekend, coincided with the development of the Gay Village during the 1990s. Manchester has significant gay space which is commonly referred to as 'the Gay Village', a part of the city where a number of gay businesses, especially bars and clubs, are located. It is an area that is fundamentally city centre but which was, until recently a run-down warehouse district fronting the Rochdale Canal. A current description is: 'ever-throbbing, never-sleeping' and 'the birthplace of Manchester's brilliant outdoor cafe-bar scene' (www. lonelyplanet.com). It is characterised by an appropriation of space recognised by, for instance, the pedestrianisation of Canal Street (the principal Village street) to accommodate street socialisation and display. There is also a high concentration of gay households in the immediately surrounding area (Hindle, 2000). The existence of the Gay Village has stimulated a campaign by Marketing Manchester (MM) in conjunction with the British Tourist Authority to promote Manchester as a 'gay tourist destination' (Hughes 2003).

During the LGBT festival, the appropriation of space by gays spills over from the Village into the centre of the city in the form of the annual festival parade. This, since at least 1992, has taken a course outside the Village so that the central retail streets of Manchester are closed to traffic for an afternoon. Space appropriation continues within the Village for the festival itself with the closure of several streets to traffic (in addition to Canal Street) and the use of streets, a park and public car parks for street markets, entertainment (usually pop and rock concerts), a funfair, exhibitions, food sales and, until recently, on-street bars. Village bars and clubs usually have extended hours for the sale of alcohol and clubs for music and dancing. There are, invariably, a number of special events in bars and clubs including special club nights at larger 'straight' venues.

The origins of the festival lie not in politics in the form usually associated with Pride but more in a concern with HIV issues. The emergence of HIV/Aids has given rise to a number of 'political' organisations and movements, which have included pressing for action about the pandemic (such as the US-based direct action organisation ACT UP) or working to assist the welfare of those with the virus (such as the Terence Higgins Trust). The Manchester LGBT festival arose out of a fairly limited local concern which was the desire to raise funds for a local hospital ward that cared for people with HIV. This fund-raising was organised by Village business people (from the Rembrandt hotel and Clone Zone shop) and initially (1989) was a few stalls on Canal Street selling 'bric-a-brac'. This fund-raising function remains the primary stated purpose of the festival. Most of the funds in 2002 (£65,000; approx. EUR 97,500) were distributed to two local HIV/Aids charities, to a local body with a remit for both HIV prevention and programmes for the general health of LGBT people and to a number of smaller LGBT groups and charities. The HIV focus is reinforced by the HIV and Aids Remembrance Vigil that has characterised every festival since 1991.

Arrangements became more formal with the setting up of 'the Village Charity' organisation not only to run the festivals (from 1991 onwards) but also to raise funds throughout the year. This body ran the festival under a number of different titles but settled on the term 'Mardi Gras' for the 1995 festival. The closure of the Village Charity after the 1997 festival was coupled with financial difficulties and (unsubstantiated) allegations of misuse of funds. The 1998 and 1999 festivals occurred largely because of initiatives from Manchester City Council. They were run by Mardi Gras 1998 Ltd, a not-for-profit organisation that included a local councillor as chair of the board of directors. As in earlier years, there was no financial assistance from the City Council but financial matters were dealt with by the Council's Treasurer's Department. The 1998 festival raised £131,000 (approx. EUR 183,400) for HIV charities but no funds were raised for charities by the 1999 festival; this was followed by the demise of Mardi Gras 1998 Ltd largely as a reaction to public opinion. Nearly £500,000 (approx EUR 700,000) had been raised (mostly from entry tickets) but most was accounted for by expenditure, especially on safety measures.

For the following two years (2000 and 2001), the festival was master-minded by a person with a number of businesses in the Village; it was renamed 'Gayfest'. This was generally more successful in terms of fund-raising (£100,000 in 2000; approx. EUR 140,000) though there was a further change of organisation for the 2002 festival following the abrupt departure of the key individual in Gayfest.

Organisation for 2002 was taken on board by the Village Business Asso-ciation (VBA) set up in the aftermath of the Gayfest misfortune; the name 'Mardi Gras' was restored. VBA is an area-organisation that is an alliance of most bars and clubs in the Village (gay and straight) and others such as local housing associations. It was established as a pressure group with a concern for all matters affecting the Village and not just to organise the LGBT festivals. It has no full-time organisation or staff. The fact that the 2002 event was run by an organisation dominated by local businesses could be interpreted as giving the festival a priority other than fund-raising for charity, let alone political statement. The chair of the VBA stated 'this event will be purely commercial' (Anon., 2002a: 4) and fund-raising was, for the first time, undertaken directly by the charities (in 'Operation Fundraiser') rather than by the festival organisers. The festival has always, apart from the two entry ticket years, been a free festival. The 2002 Mardi Gras was, however, noticeable for the surfacing of political activism. Cancellation of the festival was announced during the week it was due to be held. This was attributed to disagreement between the organisers on the one hand and the police and the city council on the other about an 'alcohol tolerance zone' (ATZ) – a zone where outdoor drinking would be allowed. At a public meeting, attended by between 200 and 400 people, it was agreed to hold a protest march to the Town Hall on the day that the Parade would have occurred and the weekend would be a 'weekend of gay pride'. These intentions were hailed by the local Lesbian and Gay Foundation as 'one of the most important in the history of the LGBT community in Manches-ter. Not since the famous clause 28 rally of nearly ten years ago did the city witness such a mass mobilisation of our communities' (Anon., 2002b: 4–5). There were allegations of police homophobia and, more subtly, a VBA press release stated that other events would be monitored to 'ensure that the gay community is not being unfairly treated' (21 August 2003). On the Thursday before the weekend, Mardi Gras was reinstated, following a compromise about the ATZ and apologies about alleged homophobia. Attention switched back from protest to 'the UK's biggest, most spectacu-lar, most outrageous free gay party' (Anon., 2002c: 1).

Manchester's LGBT festivals have clearly never had the political element that characterised Pride marches and events. The perceived commercialisation of Pride events, however, is matched by a similar view of Manchester's festivals. The more obvious involvement of business people in the organisation and operation since 2000 has generated cynicism about motivation and a view that vested interests are being pursued. Criticisms have included comments about excessive generation of profits by bars and clubs and also about how it has become an extended party weekend without particular significance or community relevance or involvement (see Cooper, 2002). The 2003 Mardi Gras will include ticket-only entrance (£10; approx. EUR 15) to the Village for the first time since the 1999 entry ticket position. There is an assurance that all of this entrance fee, collected by 'Operation Fundraiser' (see above), will be devoted to the usual gay and lesbian charities.

In 2003, Manchester will host Europride 2003 (15–25 August) as well as hold Mardi Gras, as usual, during the latter part of that period (22–25 August). Europride, an annual event similar in content to most national Pride events, has been held in a number of significant centres of gay life including Cologne in 2002, Rome in 2000 (WorldPride), Paris in 1997 and Amsterdam in 1994. There are evident 'political' elements in the 2003 event including a day conference organised by the City Council on an 'agenda for equality' in the public sector for lesbians and gay men. An underlying aspiration of Europride 2003 (as with all) is 'to make Europe a place where lesbian, gay, bisexual and transgendered lives enjoy the same rights as everyone else' (Pollock 2003).

## Manchester's LGBT Festivals and Tourism

Manchester's LGBT festivals are widely regarded as attracting non-locals to watch the parade and to participate in festival events (Pritchard *et al.*, 1998). The numbers of 'tourists' are not known though various figures have been quoted. They are quoted in different forms and it is not always clear whether they refer to only, all, or some combination of, the parade observers, parade participants and people in the Village over the weekend. Additionally, there is no clear indication of how many of those numbers are non-locals, day-visitors or staying visitors. The basis for any of these estimates is unknown.

One estimate is that the Manchester festival has attracted 60,000–80,000 person visits (quoted in Pritchard *et al.*, 1998: 278). Another suggestion was that 'up to half a million people watch the grand parade through the city centre' (Moreton, 1999: 1) and the 1999 parade was believed to have had 600,000 spectators (Mardi Gras 98 Ltd 1999). Further guesstimates include 385,000 participants and spectators for the 2001 parade (Harper, 2002b) and between 100,000 and 250,000 people 'visiting' the 2002 Mardi Gras (Cooper, 2002; Smith, 2002b; Zarra & Ward, 2003). The support of the local newspaper for the 2002 festival was, in part, justified by the view that 'Mardi Gras brings thousands of visitors into the city each year' (Harper, 2002a: 4). The only near-reliable figure is that of people in the Village in 1998 and 1999. For these festivals, entry tickets (in the form of wristbands purchased in advance in order to gain access to bars in the Village) numbered 51,000 in 1998 and 45,000 in 1999 (Mardi Gras 98 Ltd, 1999). Even this figure needs to be treated with caution given the acknowledged possibility of multi-use and of failure to purchase.

There has never been a conscious policy to attract tourists, as such, though there was some UK-wide promotion for the 1998 and 1999 festivals. Increased press (especially, but not only, gay) attention over the years and word-of-mouth have undoubtedly been significant factors in widening its supposed geographical appeal. The festivals feature in promotional material of MM and of the City Council. It is referred to in MM's Manchester travel guide aimed at the general market as 'a bacchanalian blow-out beyond all reasonable proportion, as revellers revel and party-goers party as at no other time in the calendar' (MM, 2001: 37). MM's specifically gay guide to the city refers to it as 'the gayest weekend of the year . . . Gay boys and girls the world over come to Manchester to party' (MM, 2002: 8). Tourist guides such as Lonely Planet, which are aimed at the general tourist market, also feature the festival as a particular highlight: 'visit at the end of August and you can join the 500,000 revellers kicking up their heels in Manchester's Gayfest parade' (www.lonelyplanet.com). The city is referred to, in one report, as 'one of the world's gay capitals which hosts the Mardi Gras and Queer up North festivals' (Braham, 1999: 39).

Europride 2003 is undoubtedly regarded as having a tourism dimension. It is likely that the desire to rescue the 2002 Manchester festival was related very much to the need to ensure Europride took place, given its perceived importance (Anon., 2002a: 4). As well as the concern for equality it is regarded as an opportunity to generate tourism and project an image of 'a modern forward thinking city that celebrates the range and diversity of its people' (Martin-Smith, 2003: 3). It is significant that MM took a key role in Manchester's Europride bid and that the VBA, Manchester City Council and MM are contributing to the organisation of Europride. The North West Development Agency is offering financial support to Europride for promotion and raising the city's profile in Europe. It is expected to attract 300,000 people, overseas visitors are estimated at 15,000 (from Germany, the Netherlands and France in particular) and visitor spending at £22 million (approx. EUR 31 million) (www.europridemanchester.com). The tourism aspect is emphasised further by the identification of Europride 2003 as a component of the Four Seasons programme to be implemented by the city council during 2003 and 2004. This is a programme of sporting events and cultural festivals that will, hopefully, attract 300,000 extra visitors (MCC press release, 23 January 2003). The intention is to build on the experience of the Commonwealth Games 2002 and 'be the basis for an international cultural event comparable with the Edinburgh Festival or Sydney Festival' (Manchester City Council press release, 23 January 2003: 2).

## Consequences and Conclusions

Has tourism been the cause or effect of the shift from politics to party for LGBT festivals (see Figure 14.2)? The promotion (however indirect) of gay festivals as tourist attractions has been a key factor in the development of some, and as such may be considered to have been beneficial. It has also, however, strengthened the perception of festivals as being concerned with 'party' and contributed to the de-politicisation of many. Tourism has, from this perspective, been the 'cause'. An alternative view is that the shift towards 'party' and de-politicisation has been occurring anyway (related to consumerism and reduced interest in politics) and this shift, through more emphasis on carnival and festival, has created tourism. Tourism, from this perspective, has been the 'effect'. The situation is evidently not clear-cut and the two are intertwined: non-locals cause 'more party' and 'more party' attracts non-locals.

The Manchester LGBT festivals have never been political and have always been 'party' though with a philanthropic, fund-raising objective. There has been little obvious promotion or development of the festivals as a tourist attraction but they have received widespread publicity, there is general agreement that non-locals are attracted and they are utilised in the city's tourist promotional material. There is a definite tourism element to them that has occurred more by default than by design. Tourism may have been the outcome of Manchester's initiative in having these festivals (effect) but, more recently, those festivals have been regarded as opportunities to develop tourism (cause). As they have not been 'political', tourism cannot, in this instance, be held responsible for a de-politicisation of the Manchester LGBT festivals. It is arguable though that the festivals are indicative of, and have been contributory to, a wider de-politicisation. Nonetheless, whatever the political aspect or the (festival-tourism) casual

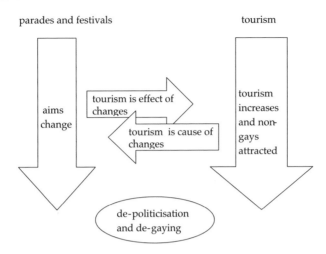

**Figure 14.2** Tourism-festival connection

sequence, it is probable that the festivals have contributed to the separate, but related, development of the de-gaying of Manchester's gay space.

Whatever de-gaying effect the LGBT festivals have had on Manchester's gay space and life is difficult to isolate from that of increased awareness of the Gay Village generally. This has arisen from continuous 'word-of-mouth', the current MM campaign and influences such as that of the television series 'Bob and Rose' (2001) and 'Queer as Folk', which were both set and filmed in Manchester and the Village in particular. 'Queer as Folk', a six-part Channel 4 television series (screened in 1999), centred on the lives of two gay men living, working and playing in Manchester. In the USA it was seen in unauthorised 'pirate' versions and subsequently in video and a US cable television network has produced an American version.

The composition and atmosphere of the Village has undoubtedly altered since the late 1980s. Its 'success' has led to continuing debate about whether its 'gayness' has been diluted through the influx of straight patrons and whether such a dilution is desirable or not. The Gay Village has been contested space between gays and straights and, for some who are unsympathetic to homosexuality, it is an unacceptable space. There have also been reservations within the 'gay community' itself about who in the 'gay community' it targets and who, as a consequence is excluded (see Aitkenhead, 2000; Manning, 1996; Whittle, 1994; Wilson, 2001). Its success and acceptance has led to an influx of non-gay customers; this is a sign of 'acceptance' but also a source of tension (Skeggs, 1999). The presence of non-gays throughout the year has attracted criticism arising from a fear of antipathetic and homophobic intrusion (and abuse and violence) arising from the concentration and identification of a specific gay space.

The LGBT festival is considered to have added to these tensions for, as the *Guardian* newspaper commented, 'straights pour into the village for the event' (Anon., 1999: 13). The LGBT festival has, until recently, been the only significant event in the city over the August public holiday period and has attracted many to the Village who would otherwise not have come, some to gaze but others to de-stabilise. In the process 'gay sexuality is being exploited as an urban spectacle' (Quilley, 1997: 291) and this may add to already-existing tensions: between gays and straights and between locals and visitors (Hughes 2003). Gay space is diluted as a centre of empowerment and cultural strength and gay people no longer feel 'ownership'. Gay space is being 'touristified' and, whilst it is a sign of heterosexual acceptance, it also establishes heterosexual control (Pritchard *et al.*, 1998). Manchester's gay space continues, therefore, to be contested space. The de-gaying and contestation may be lessening, however, following the closure of some businesses in the Village (probably due to over-expansion) and a coincidental increase in the number of 'straight' bars in other parts of the city.

For the future, it may be more appropriate for Manchester's LGBT festival to avoid the large scale of some previous years and to make it a more manageable community-based event. This may avoid the undesirable incursion of non-gays that characterised those same years and return the festival to being more than its current perception as a 'drinking and clubbing weekend'. The implication may be that the VBA role in the festivals should diminish alongside a more conspicuous community input. The impetus of Europride 2003 with its more focused vision and objectives, experienced organisers and greater resources may serve to revitalise the more local event of Mardi Gras. It may encourage the involvement of the local LGBT community and stimulate it to further involvement in subsequent years. Striking a balance between these factors will not be easy and rejecting or reducing the tourism element may be a necessary strategy if festival and Village are to remain meaningful to the community.

## Note

1.  In order to demonstrate inclusiveness, festivals and organisations typically label themselves 'lesbian, gay, bi-sexual and transgender': LGBT, or with the addition of Q for 'queer' in the case of Sydney. In this paper the term 'gay' will normally be used to cover all of LGBT except where otherwise indicated.

## References

Aitkenhead, D. (2001) Village people. *Guardian* 24 October.

Amnesty International UK (1997) Breaking the silence: Human rights violations based on sexual orientation. London: Amnesty International UK.

Anon. (1999) Majorities unwelcome. *Guardian* 30 August, 13.

Anon. (2002a) The Village people. *OUT* (14), 4.

Anon. (2002b) Mardi Gras raises £64,850. *OUT* 17, 4–5.

Anon. (2002c) The official statement from MCC, GMP and VBA. *DAILY OUT* (22 August), 1.

Anon. (2003a) Sex laws face major change. *Gay Times* January, 56.

Anon. (2003b) Pride parade gets political. *Gay Times* May, 60.

Badgett, L. (2001) Money, myths and change: The economic lives of lesbians and gay men. Chicago: University of Chicago Press.

Beyond Barriers (2002) *Survey of Lesbian, Gay, Bisexual and Transgender People in Scotland*. Glasgow: Beyond Barriers.

Binnie, J. (1995) Trading places, consumption, sexuality and the production of queer space. In D Bell and G Valentine (eds) *Mapping Desire: Geographies of Sexualities* (pp. 182–99). London: Routledge.

Braham, P. (1999) Manchester. *Travel and Tourism Intelligence City Reports* 3, 39–51.

Branigan, T. (2002) Gay festival £400,000 in the red. *Guardian* 3 August, 7.

Castells, M. and Murphy, K. (1982) Cultural identity and urban structure: The spatial organisation of San Francisco's gay community. In N. Fainstein and S. Fainstein (eds) *Urban Policy under Capitalism* (pp. 237–59). London: Sage.

Cooper, T. (2002) Via Fossa manager responds to MardiGras criticism. *OUT* 18, 10.

Davis, T. (1995) The diversity of queer politics and the redefinition of sexual identity and community in urban spaces. In D. Bell and G. Valentine (eds) *Mapping Desire: Geographies of Sexualities* (pp. 284–303). London: Routledge.

Duncan, N. (1996) Renegotiating gender and sexuality in public and private spaces. In N. Duncan (ed.) *BodySpace: Destabilising Geographies of Gender and Sexuality* (pp. 127–45). London: Routledge.

Duyves, M. (1995) Framing preferences, framing differences: Inventing Amsterdam as gay capital. In R. Parker and J. Gagnon (eds) *Conceiving Sexuality: Approaches to Sex Research in a Post-Modern World* (pp. 51–66). London: Routledge.

Featherstone, M. (1987) Lifestyle and consumer culture. *Theory, Culture and Society* 4, 55–70.

Fickling, D. (2003) Lycra and lucre at Mardi Gras. *Observer* 2 March, 23.

Field, N. (1995) *Over the Rainbow: Money, Class and Homophobia*. London: Pluto Press.

Gluckman, A. and Reed, B. (1997) Introduction. In A. Gluckman and B. Reed (eds) *Homo Economics: Capitalism, Community and Lesbian and Gay Life* (pp. xi–xxxi). London: Routledge.

Graham, M. (2002) Challenges from the margins: Gay tourism as cultural critique. In S. Clift, M. Luongo and C. Callister (eds) *Gay Tourism: Culture, Identity and Sex* (pp. 17–41). London: Continuum.

Halifax, N. (1988) *Out, Proud and Fighting: Gay Liberation and the Struggle for Socialism*. London: Socialist Workers Party.

Harper, S. (2002a) Bid to save Mardi Gras. *Manchester Evening News* 21 August, 4.

Gay and Lesbian Festivals	253

Harper, S. (2002b) Gays' demo over Mardi fiasco. *Manchester Evening News* 20 August, 1.

Haslop, C., Hill, H. and Schmidt, R. (1998) The gay lifestyle: Spaces for a subculture of consumption. *Marketing Intelligence and Planning* 16 (5), 318–26.

Heckert, J. (2000) Beyond identity? Questioning the politics of pride. MSc dissertation, School of Social and Political Studies, University of Edinburgh.

Hindle, P. (1994) Gay communities and gay space in the city. In S. Whittle (ed.) *The Margins of the City: Gay Men's Urban Lives* (pp. 7–25). Aldershot: Arena.

Hindle, P. (2000) The influence of the Gay Village on migration to central Manchester. *The North West Geographer* 3, 21–8.

Hughes, H. (2002) Gay men's holiday destination choice: A case of risk and avoidance. *International Journal of Tourism Research* 4 (4), 299–312.

Hughes, H. (2003) Marketing gay tourism in Manchester: New market for urban tourism or destruction of gay space? *Journal of Vacation Marketing* 9 (2), 152–63.

Knopp, L. (1995) Sexuality and urban space: A framework for analysis. In D. Bell and G. Valentine (eds) *Mapping Desire: Geographies of Sexualities* (pp. 149–61) London: Routledge.

Manning, T. (1996) Going straight? *City Life* 306, 16; Happy but not gay? *City Life* 310, 14; Milking the pink pound. *City Life* 311, 14–5.

MAPS (1998) *The Pink Pound 1998: Strategic Market Report*. London: Market Assessment Publications Ltd.

Mardi Gras 98 Ltd (1999) *Lesbian and Gay Mardi Gras Community Report* (November). Manchester: Mardi Gras 98 Ltd.

Marks, K. (2002) Anger as Sydney's Mardi Gras goes bust. *Independent on Sunday* 11 August, 17.

Martin-Smith, N. (2003) (EuroPride Manchester board member quoted) On WWW at www.europridemanchester.com/press (p3). Accessed 9 March 2003.

Mason, A. and Palmer, A. (1996) *Queer Bashing: A National Survey of Hate Crimes against Lesbians and Gay Men*. London: Stonewall.

Mintel (2000) *The Gay Holiday Market*. London: Mintel International Group.

MM (2001) *Manchester: An Event in Itself 2001–02*. Manchester: MM.

MM (2002) *Manchester UK: The Lesbian and Gay Guide to Manchester 2002*. Manchester: MM.

Moreton, C. (1999) Time gentlemen please. *Independent* 29 August (features section), 1.

NMGL (2002) *Mardi Gras: Dodo or Phoenix?: Background Paper. November 2002*. Sydney: New Mardi Gras Ltd.

NMGL (2003) *New Mardi Gras Constitutional Committee: Objects Discussion Paper. February 2003*. Sydney: New Mardi Gras Ltd.

Polchin, J. (1997) Having something to wear: The landscape of identity on Christopher Street. In B. Ingram, A. Bouthillette and Y. Retter (eds) *Queers in Space: Communities, Public Places, Sites of Resistance* (pp. 381–90). Seattle: Bay Press.

Pollock, J. (2003) (UK EuroPride co-ordinator quoted) On WWW at www.europridemanchester.com/press (p. 3). Accessed 9 March 2003.

Pritchard, A., Morgan, N., Sedgley, D. and Jenkins, A. (1998) Reaching out to the gay market: opportunities and threats in an emerging market segment. *Tourism Management* 19 (3), 273–82.

Quilley, S. (1997) Constructing Manchester's new urban village: Gay space in the entrepreneurial city. In B. Ingram, A. Bouthillette and Y. Retter (eds) *Queers in*

*Space: Communities, Public Places, Sites of Resistance* (pp. 275–92). Seattle: Bay Press.

Russell, P. (2001) The world gay travel market. *Travel and Tourism Analyst* 2, 37–58.

Ryan, C. and Hall, M. (2001) *Sex Tourism: Marginal People and Liminalities*. London: Routledge.

Shields, R. (1990) The system of pleasure: Liminality and the carnivalesque at Brighton. *Theory, Culture and Society* 7, 39–72.

Skeggs, B. (1999) Matter out of place: Visibility and sexualities in leisure spaces. *Leisure Studies* 18, 213–32.

Smith, R. (2002a) Is this the end for Mardi Gras? *Gay Times* September, 41.

Smith, R. (2002b) Manchester saves its Mardi Gras. *Gay Times* October, 40.

Stonewall (2001) *Profiles of Prejudice: A Survey by MORI for Citizenship 21 Project*. London: Stonewall.

Valentine, G. (1996) Re-negotiating the heterosexual street: Lesbian production of space. In N. Duncan (ed.) *BodySpace: Destabilising Geographies of Gender and Sexuality* (pp. 146–55). London: Routledge.

Webb, J. (2002) A date with hate. In R. Yates (ed.) Sex uncovered. *Observer* supplement 27 October, 49–53.

Whittle, S. (ed.) (1994) *The Margins of the City: Gay Men's Urban Lives*. Aldershot: Arena.

Wilson, N. (2001) Gaychester RIP. *Attitude* 84 (May), 65–7.

Wood, L. (1999) Think pink! Attracting the pink pound. *Insights* January, A107–110.

Workers Power (1991) *Lesbian and Gay Liberation: A Trotskyist Strategy*. London: Workers Power (Britain).

Yates, R. (ed.) (2002) Sex uncovered. *Observer* supplement 27 October.

Zarra, E. and Ward, D. (2003) Europe's biggest gay festival to be held in UK. *Guardian* 11 February, 12.

## Websites

On WWW at www.beyondbarriers.org.uk. Accessed 8 April 2003.

On WWW at www.europridemanchester.com. Accessed 9 March 2003.

On WWW at www.interpride.org. Accessed 16 February 2003.

On WWW at www.lonelyplanet.com/destinations/europe/manchester. Accessed 12 February 2003.

On WWW at www.mardigras.org.au. Accessed 6 February 2003.

On WWW at www.sbu.ac.uk/stafflag. Accessed 6 February 2003.

## Chapter 15

# Mobility, Diaspora and the Hybridisation of Festivity: The Case of the Edinburgh Mela

Elizabeth Carnegie and Melanie Smith

## Introduction

Along with the contemporary idea of globalisation as a liberating process, characterised by increasingly mobile flows of people, the term also tends to subsume the more historically rooted notion of diaspora: ethnic populations that have become dispersed due to variety of 'push' and 'pull' factors. The ideas of both globalisation and diaspora hence problematise traditional notions and boundaries of state and nationality. Indeed mobile populations usually function outside of the containers of the nation-state thus constantly struggling with the opportunities and challenges of dislocation, identity and the meanings of being at 'home' but also away from home. Not surprisingly, the relationships between diasporic communities and their adopted nation-states are complex and emerging and are heavily weighted around the idea of 'culture', which becomes an arena to explore and test such relationships. Old cultural reference points battle against new ones as diasporic communities search for internal and external definition, recognition and their identities as something that is both part of something past, and something future.

Over a number of years, in the UK and in many other so-called developed nations, we can observe a growing number of festivals and events that have mobilised and recomposed, to varying extents, aspects of culture of diasporic populations. Thus, occasions such as the Notting Hill Carnival are scripted as highly visible expressions of the culture and history of Trinidad designed to celebrate the Trinidadian and wider Caribbean culture and community identity. But diasporic festivals increasingly have audiences that extend beyond their immediate cultural constituency, acting as, if not literally being, tourists. The presence of these 'other' audiences largely reading such festivals outside of the contexts in which they were originally composed raises a range of issues relating to both their production and consumption, and generates a set of dynamics that reaches into tourism practice, social and cultural policy, and wider themes of shifting social identities and hybridity.

In this chapter we explore such issues through the particular case of the 'Mela'; a festival traditionally serving to celebrate ethnic community and folk cultures and identities in India but increasingly becoming a showcase for global and hybridised cultural forms referred to Indianness. The term 'Mela' is derived from a Sanskrit word meaning 'gathering', and is used in a generic sense to describe a range of community events in the South Asian sub-continent. The cultural activities included in Mela are many and varied, incorporating (amongst others) music, dance, fashion, food, and more recently, film. In recent years, Mela has become an increasingly prominent feature within the cultural calendar of many Western European countries, particularly in the United Kingdom, and has gradually developed from small-scale community-based events to become a focal point for 'national' celebrations of diasporic cultures. As with Caribbean Carnivals, Melas have come to symbolise all that is 'colourful' about diaspora, transforming ethnicity into a cultural showcase for growing numbers of non-Indian participants and tourist audiences. Whilst this is perhaps an ineluctable consequence of globalisation, transnational mobility and the creation of hybridised social spaces, it does raise questions about the appropriation of such cultural forms by emigrant communities, non-Indian audiences and public cultural policy in the UK, and the power relationships inherent within their development. British government agendas for instance, claim to promote cultural diversity. But what does this mean in terms of discourse and action? Can it be seen as a 'genuine' attempt to further social integration? Cultural purists might well balk at the apparent hybridisation of cultural and artistic expression and performance within the context of Mela. The preservation of artistic integrity is arguably paramount in the conceptualisation of Mela, but how far is the changing composition and demands of audiences, together with the integration of Mela festivals in wider tourism development agendas, dictate the nature of programming and performance? Is the melange of cultural forms that constitute Mela representative of the multifarious nature of diasporic cultures and identities? This chapter explores such questions and draws upon the case study of Mela in the City of Edinburgh in Scotland.

## Globalisation and Bollywood Dreams

That Indian culture, or rather 'Asian' culture, should be represented in Britain in various forms is, of course, not surprising, given the relationship between the two nations in both the historical colonial sense and in post-colonial times. Though the growth of the Indian diaspora in the UK over the years is both complex and varied, it is expressed through an assortment of points of popular cultural connection experienced and negotiated by the population as a whole in everyday ways. Indian cuisine, in both 'pure' and hybridised forms, has, over the past 40 years or so evolved to become a highly successful and influential feature of the British 'national' menu.

Further significant South Asian influences within contemporary British culture relate to the performing and visual arts. In the 1960s, Indian music began to feed into the popular music scene when the Beatles worked with classical sitar player Ravi Shankar. More recently the folk music of rural India has pervaded mainstream popular music in a form known as Bhangra. Indeed, Bhangra music appears to have become the cultural form that many young South Asians have adopted to express a sense of roots and identity (Baumann, 1996). For older generations, however, the hybridisation that Bhangra is represents the dilution of a traditional art form (Chaudhary, 2003). In the realm of the popular visual arts, the Indian cinema has reached out from its own highly successful, Mumbai-based, 'Bollywood' film industry, to infuse British life whether it be in the form of local Bollywood dance classes or theatre and television productions. Cinema has also allowed the exploration of the attractions and complexities of the Indian diaspora challenging both British attitudes and those of modern-day or second-generation Indians.

Ferguson (1998) notes how the globalisation of the media has led to the fragmentation of cultural representation, which is then reconstituted and usually referred to as cultural hybridity. The UK report of the 'Commission on the Future of multi-ethnic Britain' (known as the Parekh Report) published in 2000 suggested that 'the process of mixing and hybridisation will increasingly be the norm where rapid change and globalisation have made all identities potentially unstable' (Parekh Report, 2000: 27). But, as Flusty (2004: 112) argues, 'all cultures are hybrids of other cultures' influences and always have been. Thus hybridity is neither new nor distinct, but an omnipresent underpinning of cultural formation.'

The Parekh Report (2000) highlights the difficulties of referring to Asians as a single homogeneous group in counterpoint to the realities of clear distinctions along the lines of nation, race, religion, caste, language, culture, etc. While not always recognised, there is obvious variation between Bangladeshis, Gujaratis, Pakistanis and Punjabis; as well as between South Asians, East African Asians and Chinese; and between Hindus, Muslims and Sikhs, etc. The Parekh Report (2000) also notes the tensions within South Asian communities between generations, with parents and children often in disagreement about the processes and outcomes of integration with regard to loss of tradition and identity. Baumann (1996) describes how cultural distinctiveness within Asian communities is often defined by parents in terms of their own pre-emigration traditions and heritages. Within this context, the Parekh Report (2000) suggests that there is too much emphasis on separating 'ethnic' traditions from the 'Western' canon, and on conserving the past rather than promoting new creativity in the present.

Such debates between generations are normal within the context of the processes and problems of adjusting to diasporic living where questions of identity and belonging come to the fore. In the ferment of change, the loss of cultural reference points, and the social, economic and political challenges that diasporic communities face, new reference points are born. As Weeks (2000: 240) points out, threatened communities 'construct out of this a community of identity which provides a strong sense of resistance and empowerment'.

Brah (1996: 181) suggests that it is no longer appropriate to discuss diaspora in Britain along a 'majority/minority' axis, rather: 'Diaspora space as a conceptual category is 'inhabited' not only by those who have migrated and their descendants but equally by those who are constructed and represented as indigenous.' Thus the children of first-generation immigrants have become indigenised, and are often searching for a new 'identity' within the context of multi-cultural Britain. Bauman (2001) questions whether individuals, and in particular those deemed weak and powerless within wider society, have the freedom to change their identity or at least the spatial, political and economic reference points that feed notions of identity. Arguably, in a vacuum of social integration, economic equity and political access, diasporic populations have reached for cultural symbols that can have a cohesive affect, whether they are 'new' or involve the re-working of tradition, akin to the way that the African Caribbean population have drawn on reggae music both as a progressive musical form and as symbolic of a 'roots' feeling. Baumann (1996) suggests that many Asian teenagers wish to see the emergence of an 'Asian culture' in symbolic terms, which can transcend differences of religion, caste and regional affiliation.

It is against this wider canvas of emergent popular cultural expressions and practices that challenge the idea of 'tradition' amongst diasporic and host communities, and which generate new hybridised cultural forms (traditions), that we need to consider the festival format of Mela. The original concept of Mela was based predominantly on 'traditional' and folk cultures, rather than any sense of the 'popular'. However, as an 'imported' model of festivity, questions are raised with regard to the Mela's re-configuration relating to its new social role and cultural standing, its form and its audiences.

## Melas and the Showcasing of Ethnic 'Cultures'

Outside of its original 'home', the Mela effectively acts as a means of profiling one or more 'cultures' to 'other' cultures. The constituencies of Mela audiences become de facto, wider, and this shapes their form and social, economic and political role. Festivals certainly have the power to challenge political and social norms and create important economic opportunities for marginal communities utilising, as they do, various artistic forms. Morley (2000), for instance, suggests that World Music Festivals have helped to undermine the cultural hegemony of white 'Britpop' and allowed commercial marketing opportunities for non-white, non-Western music.

Khan's (1976) work on ethnic minority arts suggested that ethnic contributions enhanced the UK's cultural provision considerably. By showcasing and performing elements they associate with 'their' culture, minority groups were able to assert their identity. Carlson (1996) has similarly suggested that cultural performance can allow traditionally marginalised groups to explore relationships between self and society, as well as issues relating to objectification, exclusion and identity. Likewise, Candida-Smith's (2002) work also sees performance as a memory trigger, which is linked to memories of traditional ways of life. This is an important point to note in the case of diasporic cultures, where there is often a strong sense of both 'over here' and 'over there' (i.e. 'back home') (Kaur & Hutnyk, 1998). Jermyn and Desai (2000) optimistically state that barriers to ethnic participation in the arts are gradually being removed. However, Mowitt (2001: 8) is more cynical, suggesting that there is a great deal of tokenism in Government support for ethnic minorities: 'In a global white world, a little local colour goes a long way.' In the same vein Lippard (1990) outlines the key problem with discourse in ethnic art, in that it tends to be *about* the 'other', rather than *by* the 'other'. Appropriation of ethnic cultural forms is not uncommon in the programming, interpretation and representation of art. In addition, audience development for ethnic and minority events can be contentious, with claims, for instance, that Caribbean Carnivals and similar events are becoming 'whitewashed' or over-promoted for tourist audience (Errol, 1986).

In our work we noted that many directors interviewed were keen to drop the term 'Asian' from Mela in order to suggest that it is an inclusive celebration. In some instances, the programme of Melas are designed to emphasise this point such as the case of the Rochdale Mega-Mela held in the North West of England where African drumming is included as one of the activities. In comparison to African Caribbean Carnivals, it could be argued that Melas are less overtly political in their origins. Whereas Carnivals were generally born out of the oppressive context of imperialism, colonisation and slavery (Alleyne-Dettmers, 1996), Melas appear to be predominantly celebrations of community cultures. However, it would be naive in the extreme to suggest that Melas are de-politicised events. There are concerns about appropriation, especially in areas where local authorities have been keen to commandeer Melas in order to add local colour to their tourist promotional efforts. Moreover, in some areas of the UK where racial tensions run high, Melas become highly political events and some Mela directors fear for the future of their festival. Other pointers of apparent appropriation that we found during the course of our work included that the majority of Mela directors were white rather than Asian; however, from discussions with these directors, it is clear that they were often invited to take the position, especially in cases where there were internal political tensions.

Audience development is a problematic issue for Melas with many directors struggling to attract young Asians to their events as they are perceived to be overly traditional. The desire appears to be to retain an Asian focus, but within a world context, therefore hybridisation that reflects national and global influences predominates. The Mela of the future will no doubt celebrate the rich traditions of Asia whilst reflecting the dynamic nature of British Asian culture. There are clearly some concerns about non-target audiences (i.e. white tourists). At present, white people constitute approximately 50% of audiences. However, the general consensus of directors is that Melas should be more widely promoted. This clearly makes more commercial sense; however, care must be taken not to alienate core Asian audiences in the process.

## The Edinburgh Mela

The Edinburgh Mela celebrated its 10th year in 2004. In 2003 it extended to three days (Friday, Saturday and Sunday), and received a record 40,000 visitors. This was an increase of 10,000 on 2002 figures. Professionally staffed and funded from the onset, it has a full time chief executive and half-post administration manger, a part time marketing manager and a number of short-term staff including production manager, administration and site staff. It also hosts creative residencies. Professionalism is recognised as being the key to developing the reputation of the Edinburgh Mela, and crucial in attracting necessary sponsorship. In 2003 Edinburgh Mela was sponsored by a leading mobile telephone company and supported by the European Mela Network, and organisation that helps to raise the profile of Melas in general.

The Board of the Edinburgh Mela comprises 12 people comprising the Lord Provost of Edinburgh and a senior academic of a local University College. Nine members are from South Asia representing local communities and businesses. The chief executive, was described as being 'heavily persuaded' by some of the leaders of the community to chair the Board from the onset as they had witnessed other potential ventures fail as a consequence of internal politics. Additionally, there are three consultative forums held throughout the year with invited audiences from 120 local organisations resulting in some 28 representatives from other communities within the City.

According to Tweedie (2004), the Edinburgh version of the Mela has 'rejected the concept of multi-culturalisation in favour of inter-culturalisation', in a bid to create a genuinely and generally inclusive event intended to become an established part of Edinburgh's festival portfolio. Positioned within the summer festival season, and over the last weekend of the International Festival, the Mela inevitably draws a mixed audience of locals and tourists. The decision to cite the Mela within the festival season was taken for a number of reasons. First, the Edinburgh Mela was modelled on the longstanding successful Mela held in Bradford in Yorkshire which itself was part a wider festival and was viewed by the organising committee in Edinburgh to be a model that worked well in attracting audiences. Second, from the onset the Edinburgh Mela has received local government funding, but it was argued that the later in the year an event is held, the more chance it has of obtaining money from other grant award bodies. Third, in a UK context, a key concern to an event that traditionally happens out of doors, is the weather. Tracking of the weather favoured that particular weekend minimising the risk of cancellation. Fourth, it was also suggested by Tweedie (2004) that as the tourist season is coming to a close towards the end of August, people who are tied up with working in the hospitality industries are able to free up time to participate in the Mela. It also seems likely that weather and funding considerations apart, the decision to position it during the main Edinburgh Festival would both ensure an audience for events and give some sense of parity of esteem to the Mela as it would happen in tandem with prestigious festival activities. It would also benefit from the Edinburgh Festival's publicity machine.

## Aims of the Edinburgh Mela

The decision to create a Mela in Edinburgh, which has now grown to Scotland's largest Mela, outpacing the Glasgow equivalent, grew from the organisers belief that despite there being 15 key festivals in Edinburgh, with 40 smaller ones throughout the year, little was being done within the City to celebrate and reflect the arts and culture of the world. Tweedie (2004) argues that Edinburgh's cultural activities, and in particular those of the official International Festival are ' . . . heavily dependent on the much more developed world, especially Europe and North America . . . at that time what was termed the third world was largely excluded because of the vision of the people that controlled the International festival'. Although international groups visit the city to participate in festival events, these are not necessarily attended by local audiences and rarely create a forum for multi-ethnic groups throughout the year. Accusations of elitism about the cultural product that is the Edinburgh International Festival are not new and similar arguments reflect class issues within the City (Halfpenny, 2002).

The Edinburgh Mela sought to redress this imbalance through producing a programme of events that has the following aims (Edinburgh Mela Artistic Policy Document, 2003). First, that the Mela would seek to enhance the self-respect of all people in minority communities and especially young people. This recognised the potential for Melas as creating a time and space for allowing all generations to celebrate together. It also pointed to the fact the within an increasingly culturally diverse Scotland, new approaches were required to bring about recognition and celebration of that diversity. Second, the aim was for the Mela to be recognised as a major festival in its own right and to become a significant player at local, regional, national and international level. Third, the aim was to construct a method of organisation and operation that stressed networking, partnership and collaboration, and that built in opportunities for members of the community to achieve both group and individual development.

These aims span the realms of both aspiration and generality but point to the fact that the Mela, outside of its 'original' space and cultural context, is far more of a sensitive event socially and politically. As a festival that has, in effect, 'travelled', the aims of Mela are driven to an extent by wider agendas of social inclusion and the involvement of the associated diasporic communities. A large percentage of the visitors to the Edinburgh Mela are white, although Tweedie (2004) argues that some international audiences, for example Brazilians, would have more in common with the Mela than some local Muslim audiences, as Brazil has a long tradition of carnival and local Muslims may not come from such a culture of openness in terms of display. He acknowledges twin concerns about audiences and indeed Mela participants and sums up the dilemma of this form of trans- posed festivity: 'If the majority of attendees are white then it is no longer a Mela, . . . [yet] a Mela which represents some monoculture wouldn't be a Mela' (Tweedie, 2004).

### Scotland in the Mela, or the Mela in Scotland?

The Edinburgh Mela is held within the cultural landscape of Pilrig Park, an inner city green space in a working-class suburb of Edinburgh. Partly recalling Mowitt's (2001) observation that a little local colour goes a long way, the area is 'dressed' for the event to add colour and to create a sense of the (relative) exoticism of Mela. Indian Melas, as Tweedie (2004) notes, ' . . . don't need to concern themselves with production, as there is so much wealth around them. But here if we want to have a creative envi- ronment which involves cultural diasporas we have to be creative about how we do it.'

The decision to hold the Mela in a fixed venue, geographically close to where many of Edinburgh's South Asian population work and live was deemed to be an important part to create a sense of ownership of the space, and continuity from one year to the next. This is by no means a belief held uniformly by the Board and a small minority would like the Mela to move away from its community roots and to develop a more popular approach that reflects the growing interest in popular and hybridised culture. It is worth noting that when a similar suggestion was made to move the Notting Hill Carnival in London to Hyde Park instead, it created something of a furore from local residents. The connections to a geographical sense of place, heritage, identity and ownership were clearly overwhelmingly strong. In the case of the Edinburgh Mela, this has created a split in the Board between those who believe that the Mela should remain a showcase for traditional culture rather than popular culture and those who wish to use the Mela as a forum for renewing interest in, or indeed gaining the interest of, second-generation South Asians and in this way ensuring tra- ditions are not lost as a consequence of a different way of life.

Recent programmes of the Edinburgh Mela have generally reflected a balance between traditional and folk performances and more recent artists designed to attract the younger festival goers. The 2005 event included performers 'Legacy' fronted by Tariq Khan one of the most successful singers in the British Asian music industry, 'Alaap', pioneers of the Bhangra music scene since 1977, as well as more traditional musical acts playing Classical and popular songs in Bengali, Hindi, Tamil, Punjabi and other South Asian languages. There was also a Mela multi-cultural fashion show. Recent sponsors of the event also reflect a span between tradition and the contemporary. Apart from support from Edinburgh City Council, sponsors of recent events have included Cobra Beer, the Scottish Arts Council, the Government of Maharashtra, and the Royal Bank of Scotland. There are signs of a trend away from tradition towards a more populist programme and 'feel' to the Mela, though ideas of this being a festival that celebrates tradition foremost would still appear to dominate.

Interestingly, the Edinburgh Mela is also concerned with Scottish traditional culture and music and Mela 2002 featured major fusion events involving upwards of 50 musicians and singers from Scotland, China and Pakistan providing a tribute to poet Hamish Henderson with his poem 'Roses Come to Bloom' and also incorporating a fusion version of 'Freedom Cam A'Ye'. This concert was funded by a UK trade union, the Performing Rights Foundation and the Arts Council. This raises several points worthy of consideration. Is the inclusion of Scottish traditional music in Mela part of the process of acculturation, a reflection that Scottishness is part of the dual identity of Scotland's Asian diaspora? Or, does it in fact highlight the minority nature of such music within Scotland, where popular culture or high cultural art forms as exemplified by the International Festivals, hold sway? Is this fusing of Scottish and traditional Asian music a way of fusing identities or is it in fact keeping Scottish traditions (or a version of what are deemed to be Scottish traditions) alive in an increasingly changing society? If so, this would reprise the point made earlier about identities becoming increasingly unstable in a fast changing society.

Bauman's (2001: 100) view that ' ... recasting quite real individual frailties and infirmities into the (imagined) potency of community, results in conservative ideology and exclusive pragmatics', may well be relevant to the emphasis still placed within the Edinburgh Mela on 'traditional' South Asian *and* Scottish cultures, with the added desire to create continuity, if not actively resist changing patterns of cultural and leisure activities. However dual (or multiple) identities can create the potential for a deeper understanding of self (Said in Moustafa & Andrew, 2001) rather as Daiches (1957) understood his relationship of being Scottish and Jewish, both identities forged within or between two worlds allowing for a subjective and changing reappraisal of self that is prompted by the signifiers of each. In his words: 'I found the sound of the bagpipes extremely moving. It awakened my sense of Scottish history with its violence and its pageantry and its fatal predilection for the lost cause . . . Scotland came for me more an emotion than a country.' (1957: 59)

This perception of Scotland as a country that is both colonised and coloniser, creates an interesting tension, sometimes quoted as a form of 'melancholy' (Watson, 2003), or a culture of inferiority (Beveridge & Turnbull, 1989). Such terms are often positioned against the ruling neighbour, England, and indeed Scotland has created an 'imagined community' (Anderson, 1992). It is in this spirit of Daiches' definition of Scotland as an 'emotion more than a country' that the Edinburgh Mela has developed Scottish flavoured events that represent hybrid cultures of both worlds, drawing on the symbols of a largely imagined Scotland or a definition of Scottishness to create a way for Scotland and its various communities to be defined and self-define creatively. It can be argued that Scottish Asians become acculturated into Scottish cultures and their dual identity develops as a Scottish Asian consciousness rather than Asian/British (Mann, 1992). The Edinburgh Mela is actively seeking to develop relationships within the diaspora to ensure that Scottish Asians retain contact with the cultural expressions of South Asia and that Mela events represent these relationships through the creation of new performance pieces. As a consequence of these partnerships, Edinburgh Mela trained personnel are, at the time of writing, going to Bangladesh to develop artworks with traditional artists and musicians which they will then bring back to appear at the Edinburgh and other Melas within the UK.

## Future of the Edinburgh Mela

In common with other Melas, the Edinburgh Mela is concerned with ensuring that it continues to celebrate the Asian diaspora inclusively, and with integrity and with what it terms 'magic' (Edinburgh Mela Artistic Policy Document, 2003). But also it aims to promote the Scottish connection and to grow and develop creative links and participation within the diaspora that will benefit both communities. Participation in the organisation and programming of the Mela festival by both the Asian communities and the Scots is an integral part of mobilising the event to deal with the overlaying and re-working of identity issues with their inherent tensions between the traditional and the popular and between the generations. Asians who participate in the festival often do so to please their parents rather than from any belief that the Mela is expressing ideas about their own current or future sense of identity and values. Indeed, television coverage ahead of the 2003 event concentrated on the role of the Mela in teaching young girls how to wear the sari and to experience the cultural and musical traditions of their mother's generation.

The Edinburgh Mela Youth Forum, working through the Edinburgh Festivals Youth Development Fund, holds events throughout the year to establish community involvement and to widen participation. It would seem that key tensions remain linked to generational differences as much as anything else. As Tweedie (2004) pointed out: 'We've been told in the Youth Forum by one young guy aged 18 or 19 . . . "These folk would nae been seen fuckin' de'd at a Mela", because they think it is nothing to do with them. They are modern Scots'. So called 'modern' Scots might well display similar attitudes toward 'traditional' Scottish activities.

In terms of audiences for the Mela, it would seem clear that the fusion between an Asian programme, with its balance between traditional and popular performances, and 'traditional' Scottish inputs, will continue to generate an equally mixed and by and large, a 'balanced' audience profile between Asians and non-Asians. However, through the normative processes of social and generational change, it would seem that there is an increasing drive to popularise the programme to build and maintain audiences. Indeed, Mela directors interviewed suggested that many young people would not attend Mela if it simply reflected 'traditional' cultures. This may mean continuing concerns (social, moral and aesthetic concerns) amongst the older generations of Asians, but such concerns are part of the wider and on-going negotiations of identity and belonging that face diasporic communities in the UK.

From a tourism perspective, the prospect of showcasing Asian culture and 'Scottishness' within one programme would seem to be an attractive one. As with many festivals within an increasingly transnational context, the Mela provides an opportunity in time and space for direct cross-cultural encounters. Asian culture, or rather selected expressions of it, becomes, albeit temporarily, part of the wider tourist landscape with a capacity (not always fully realised) to attract the attention of domestic (and to a lesser extent) international tourists. The attraction of the Edinburgh Mela in touristic terms would seem to link directly with its hybrid nature, both in terms of its attempts to position South Asian cultures within the Scottish/Scots context and in terms of the mixture of old and modern South Asian traditions built into the programme.

## Conclusion

The Edinburgh Mela, despite differences of opinion on the Board, appears to be determinedly avoiding the potential pitfalls of adopting a purely popular culture approach, which would move the Mela from the community grounds it currently occupies into a mainstream space. It is now an established part of the wider Edinburgh summer festivals programme, and organisers remain aspirational in their desire to see it grow in numbers and reputation. The Mela, effectively a festival that has itself travelled and that provides a particular model for social gathering and festivity, reflects hybrid cultures, and to some extent creates a forum to explore ideas about Scottish cultural identity (both to and by Scots) and, within the South Asian diaspora, ideas about being South Asian in Scotland. Tweedie acknowledges that is easier to grow tourist audiences, and this inevitably means grow a white middle-class audience, than it is to sustain and develop links with certain local audiences including South Asian Scots and local Scots who live within the geographical area where the Mela is currently sited, and crucially with young audiences. There is some irony that the more established and professional the Edinburgh Mela becomes, the more tourists it attracts, the less likely it is to remain at the community level. This is already apparent in recent activities, which whilst they genuinely reflect they reflect the wider Asian diaspora, they are in many cases ticketed events rather than free to all visitors. The future of the Mela in this form is only ensured if the organisers succeed in developing year-round activities, which can reinforce the sense of community ownership of, and participation in, the festival across the generations.

## References

Alleyne-Dettmers, P.T. (1996) *Carnival: The Historical Legacy*. London: Arts Council of England.
Anderson, B. (1992) *Imagined Communities: Reflections on the Origins and Spread of Nationalism*. London: Verso.
Bauman, Z. (2001) *Community: Seeking Safety in an Insecure World*. London: Polity.
Baumann, G. (1996) *Contesting Culture: Discourses of identity in multi-ethnic London*. Cambridge: Cambridge University Press.
Beveridge, C. and Turnbull, R. (1989) *The Eclipse of Scottish Culture: Inferiorism and the Intellectuals*. Edinburgh: Edinburgh University Press.
Brah, A. (1996) *Cartographies of Diasporas: Contesting Identities*. London: Routledge.
Candida-Smith, R. (ed.) (2002) *Art and the Performance of Memory: Sounds and Gestures of Recollection*. London: Routledge.
Carlson, M. (1996) *Performance: A Critical Introduction*. London: Routledge.
Chaudhary, V. (2003) The big bhangra. *The Guardian* 15 August.
Daiches, D. (1957) *Two Worlds*. Edinburgh: Canongate Classics.
Edinburgh Mela Artistic Policy Document (2003).
Errol, J. (1986) Mama look a Mas. In *Masquerading: The Art of the Notting Hill Carnival* (pp. 7–19). Arts Council of London: Great Britain.
Ferguson, R. (1998) *Representing 'Race': Ideology, Identity and the Media*. London: Arnold.

Flusty, S. (2004) *De-Coca-Colonization: Making the Globe from the Inside Out*. London: Routledge.

Halfpenny, L. (2002) *Edinburgh Mela*. Personal communication, 10 October.

Jermyn, H. and Desai, P. (2000) *Arts – What's in a Word?: Ethnic Minorities and the Arts*. London: Arts Council of England.

Kaur, R. and Hutnyk, J. (1998) *Travel Worlds: Journeys in Contemporary Cultural Politics*. London: Zed Books.

Khan, N. (1976) *The Arts Britain Ignores: The Arts of Ethnic Minorities in Britain*. London: Commission for Racial Equality.

Lippard, L. (1990) *Mixed Blessings: New Art in a Multicultural America*. New York: Pantheon Books.

Mann, B. (1992) *The New Scots*. London: John Donald.

Morley, D. (2000) *Home Territories: Media, Mobility and Identity*. London: Routledge.

Moustafa, B. and Andrew, R. (2001) *The Said Reader*. London: Granta.

Mowitt, J. (2001) In the wake of Eurocentrism: An introduction. *Cultural Critique* 47 (Winter): 3–15.

Parekh Report (2000) *The Future of Multi-Ethnic Britain*. London: Profile Books.

Tweedie, A. (2004) Personal communication with the chief executive of Edinburgh Mela, 21 April.

Watson, M. (2003) *Being English in Scotland*. Edinburgh: Edinburgh University Press.

Weeks, J. (2000) *Making Sexual History*. London: Polity.

*Chapter 16*

# Taking Québec City: Protest, Carnival and Tourism at the Summit of the Americas

Kirsty Robertson

## Introduction

By 2001, journalist and activist Naomi Klein was warning that the 'anti-globalisation' movement was in danger of becoming a fan culture, with activists flocking to cities around the world, following the G8 and World Trade Organisation (WTO) leaders 'as if they were the Grateful Dead' (Klein, 2002: 24).[1] Klein's touristic analogy was taken up by not only conservative reporters criticizing the movement, but also by activists seeking to both strengthen and broaden protests against neo-liberal/capitalist agendas. Tugging at the semantic threads involved in the metaphoric use of discourses of tourism by all sides, this chapter seeks to complicate the debate, analysing how tourism is used both to spread a fear of dissent through wider society, but also to provide an accessible framework for Northern-hemisphere protesters. The use and subversion of tourism by protesters, I argue, provides a metaphor that can be used to attract participants from a wide range of backgrounds, falling into the situation noted by Klein only when the experience of tourism and spectacle overtakes the experience of protest.

Data on the global justice or 'anti-globalisation' movement is, in a certain sense, difficult to collect. The myriad reasons people might have had for going to Québec City, the numerous tactics used by the loose coalition of direct action groups, unions and individual protesters, and the unwillingness of those in the movement to be pinned down through definition, make empirical research difficult at best. Further, this chapter is one that deals with the protest movement from the perspective of visual culture, offering suggestions rather than concrete answers, and using a variety of sources to analyse but one element of the unwieldy nature of the global justice movement. Through the examination of first-person accounts, documentaries, newspaper and television news reports, editorials, internet activity and police reports, I have tried to open up an under-analysed aspect of the movement, suggesting that the problematic position for those who live in the North Atlantic neo-liberal environments that have created the conditions for the protest itself, is often answered through contradictory means, combining the subversive with the familiar, the protest with the festival and the transnational with the national.

## 'We'll Protest and Blah Blah Blah'

In Québec City, from 20 April to 22 April 2001, the heads of state of 34 countries gathered at the Summit of the Americas in order to negotiate the implementation of the Free Trade Area of the Americas (FTAA), an agreement that would extend the 1994 North American Free Trade Agreement (NAFTA) across the Western hemisphere. While the Canadian (and other) government(s) highlighted the supposed benefits of expanding capitalism and investment to poorer countries, activists noted the widening inequality between and within nations, and the potentially harmful effects of the agreement on the environment, human rights, health, education, and labour (CSIS, 2000; Editorial Collective, 2001; FTAA, 2001).[2] As the April weekend drew closer, newspapers in Canada ran numerous stories focusing on previous large-scale protests (namely the 'Battle For Seattle' at the WTO meeting in Seattle in 1999), predicting violence, mass arrests, and general chaos (Baxter, 2001: A3; Bronskill, 2001a: A8; Bronskill, 20001b:A3; Jaimet, 2001: A5).

Playing on this fear of violence, the Canadian government invested $100,000,000 (CDN) (approx. 70,000,000 EUR) in security, building a four-kilometre long, concrete-reinforced chain-link fence around the Old Town of Québec City where the negotiations were to take place.[3] Six thousand police personnel (with the army on alert) protected the 13.5 kilometre square area, armed with tear gas, pepper spray, water canons, riot gear, rubber bullets, and in some cases with 'lethal force' (although no one was killed during the weekend). Predicting mass arrests, the prisons around Québec City were emptied, access through Canadian borders strictly controlled, and the area around the centre of the city shut down except to a small number of accredited journalists and those negotiating or serving the negotiators (Editorial Collective, 2001; Lapointe, Wong & Ménard, 2001). In the end, an estimated 60,000 protesters arrived and for three days turned the new part of Québec City, the suburban and university areas outside of the core, into a zone of protest. Activists carrying gas masks, posters, giant puppets, swimming goggles and bandanas met up with labour marchers, protesters on stilts, students acting out political skits, drummers, radical cheerleaders, members of the Anarchist Black Bloc, bands and a huge range of affinity groups from all over the world. Three hundred arrests, 5,148 cans of tear gas, and 903 rubber bullets causing numerous burns, broken bones, at least one lost finger and one near fatal injury (a protester who was hit in the throat with a rubber bullet was saved through an emergency tracheotomy) created an even more violent spectacle for the media than had been predicted (Camille, 2002: 60–1).

The impressive Québec City, set on a cliff above the St Lawrence River, one of Canada's prime tourist locations, and a protected UNESCO world heritage site, had taken on a new image. In the build up and aftermath of the protests in Québec City, reporters in the national newspapers often dismissed activists, referring to them as 'parasites', 'SUV activists', '$100,000 a year union officials', 'ideologically irritating party animals', 'waddling corporate union bosses' 'stoned rioters', 'yuppies looking for a 60s fix' and more generally, kids 'mumbling on their tongue studs' and 'looking for a place to party' (Doelen, 2001: A6; Canadian Press, 2001c: A2; Canadian Press, 2001b: 10). However, it was the following statement, issued just before the summit by Canadian Prime Minister Jean Chrétien, that quickly became both a means to criticise and to support activists. 'They say to themselves', he told an interviewer, 'let's go spend the weekend in Québec City, we'll have fun, we'll protest and blah blah blah' (Canadian Press, 2001b: 10).

The dismissal of protesters as comfortable middle-class kids out for a weekend of fun became a point of contention for many activists. From the Blah Blah Blah film collective, organised by actress Sarah Polley and well-known artist John Greyson, to posters reading 'I'm here to take down the system and blah blah blah,' Chrétien's words quickly took on a life of their own, where, in an example of a classic *détournement*, they were reclaimed and used against the original sentiment. The statement was also picked up by Clayton Ruby, a well-known Canadian constitutional lawyer, who told a *Globe and Mail* reporter, 'if it's really a weekend of fun in Québec City, we can do without the fence. A few more tourists shouldn't bother [Chrétien]' (Canadian Press, 2001b: 10). In Ruby's statement, the contested terrains of tourism and protest collide, while his challenge to the Prime Minister reveals the double language aimed at protesters characterised as both threatening and dismissible.

In spite of the growing fear in the newspapers, the Mayor of Québec

City did welcome the activists, opening community halls, universities and colleges to provide places to sleep, defining participants in terms of visitors and possible tourists. Though later admitting that providing places to sleep was in part a way of diffusing tension, Mayor Jean-Paul L'Allier insisted in late March 2001: 'I do not want the Summit of the Americas cancelled . . . The summit, in itself, is an extremely positive event both because of what will be discussed and because of the visibility it will give Québec as a tourist destination and welcoming city' (McKenzie, 2001).

Though L'Allier retracted his comments after viewing the violence in the streets, the travel to the destination of the protest, the festival-like atmosphere of the action(s), the mapping out of routes through the city, the use of national/tourist monuments as specific locations of protest activity, and most importantly, the near obsessive need to capture the experience of protest in the two-dimensional realm of photography, do reflect a tourist experience. But to what extent does this experience mimic the often exploitative nature of middle-class international tourism?

## Tourist Gazes/Tear Gas Hazes

According to Kevin Meethan, all tourism, including travel to protests, in some way replicates 'a global process of commodification and consumption involving flows of people, capital, images and cultures' (Meethan, 2001: 4). Travelling to, and participating in, protest hence comes dangerously close to replicating the systems of global capital it seeks to challenge.[4] This discrepancy between goal (overcoming neo-liberal economic policy) and method is acknowledged by activists, but one might argue is also used to provide a certain sense of familiarity that might attract other interested groups. Philosopher Brian Massumi (2003), for example, argues that in spite of primarily negative news coverage of the anti-WTO protests in Seattle in 1999, word spread through other methods (for example the internet and word of mouth) prompting additional activists to travel, in spite of the apparent dangers, to protests such as that in Québec City. Further, the widely held belief among activists that the global justice movement can effect change, suggests that the easy dismissal of protesters as tourists does not account for all of the ways tourism is used as a strategy by participants.

Thus, while accepting that there is a central flaw within the anti-capitalist movement in the Northern hemisphere, I would like to complicate Klein's statement, quoted at the opening of this paper, by engaging with debates over tourism and spectacle within frameworks of protest, globalisation and the international spread of capitalism. Klein argues that it is not that protests have become ineffective, but that they are in danger of being cut off from the issues at hand. She writes, 'something is gravely wrong when the protests still seem deracinated, cut off from urgent daily concerns. It means that the spectacle of displaying a movement is getting confused with the less glamorous business of building one' (Klein, 2002: 159).

What Klein is challenging is not the protests themselves, but their spectacularisation, both in the media and in the minds of protesters. Without community support, protest threatens to become little more than weekend theatre, playing directly into what the Situationist Guy Debord, writing in the late 1960s, termed the 'society of spectacle' (Debord, 1967, 1994). A society in which spectacle rules is one in which the brightly coloured images of protesters, or violent images of protesters versus police become the reality that erases the issues behind the protest itself, effectively turning dissent into something to be consumed – a tourist experience emptied of significance. Activist Philippe de Grosbois worries that this has already happened, writing:

> These summits make for strange situations. There is the 'spectacle' of revolution, not the revolution itself. The spectacle makes a whirlwind tour from city to city, from Seattle, to Washington, to Prague and Québec. Everybody tastes their own 'piece of the spectacle,' but the real uprising remains to be seen. (Grosbois, 2001: 43)

The issues noted by Grosbois and Klein – a lack of continuity between actions, and the way that each is remembered as a specific event, rather than part of an ongoing struggle – are problematic. However, I would nuance this argument, suggesting that it is not the action of the protest, but the way that each protest is remembered as a primarily *visual* event that first allows meaning to be easily manipulated, and second allows for the construction of protest as something to do – an isolated tourist event. Once rendered two dimensional, and reconfigured in terms of the visual, the gaze of the protester becomes what John Urry called the tourist gaze – a socially organised and systematised gaze that in many ways echoes the tenets of a consumer society (Urry, 1990).[5]

Numerous scholars have outlined the dominance of the visual sense in Western culture (Crary, 1990, 1999; Jay, 1992, 1993; Levin, 1993; Rodaway, 1994; Rorty, 1980). Others have linked the gaze and visuality to the spread of capitalism, noting in particular the visual technologies for the reproduction of popular and commodity culture and the focus of the consumer upon the product (Baudrillard, 1998; Crary, 1999; Jameson, 1991; Virilio, 1994). Urry brings these two together in his analysis of the tourist gaze, demonstrating the role of the visual sense in the consumption of tourism, and the different consequences for those looking, and those being looked at (Ioannides & Debbage, 1998; Urry, 1999, 1995). Urry also marks a distinction between what he calls the romantic and collective tourist gaze. He writes: 'In the romantic form of the tourist gaze the emphasis is upon solitude and spirituality; in the collective form a place becomes the object of the gaze precisely because of the presence of other people who provide an aura of excitement' (Urry, 1999: 284).

I would like to adapt Urry's definition to the space of the protest, suggesting that the collective tourist gaze is complicated through scopic regimes that have protesters participating in the intensely visual elements of protest (costumes, posters and parades for example), while at the same time being constantly under surveillance through police presence, photography and videotaping (Lapointe, Wong & Ménard, 2001; Toronto Video Activist Collective, 2001). This notion is further complicated when it is taken into account that in spite of the spectacular elements of the action, within the protest itself vision is subsumed into an overwhelming sensory experience – the sound of bongo drums and chants, of riot sticks beating on shields, of whistles and shouts, the acrid smell and taste of the tear gas, and the tactile press of thousands of bodies. In this haptic moment, with vision no longer predominant, protesters are forced to make sense of the situation in new ways, creating an unstable situation where protest in the Northern hemisphere balances precariously on an edge between incorporation (the reclamation of protest by visual regimes) and chaos (the protest spinning out of control).

This precarious balance continues in the memorialisation of the action. In the video *Tear Gas Holiday*, a documentary that follows Canadian student protesters to Québec City, groups of students are filmed discussing why they are going, offering detailed analyses of complex political issues, and dismissing the FTAA as an agreement that breeds inequality. Later in the video, one of the original conversants sits on the bus back to Ontario after the protest, obviously exhausted, dirty and suffering the after-effects of tear gas. She holds up a small piece of the chain link fence from the perimeter and says: 'I'm so glad I have it . . . it's my souvenir.'

The protester's seemingly contradictory analyses between participation and ownership fit nicely into the precarious balance of protest, but also into analyses of performance and festival as something that happens, but within specific parameters that allow for the reaffirmation of the status quo in the wake of the action. What is performance, asks anthropologist Richard Schechner, who answers that it is heightened behaviour, publically performed outside of everyday life, creating a space that has the purpose first of producing an often disruptive and dramatic rupture in everyday life, and second of instilling solidarity through collective action and an atmosphere of risk (1993: 9). Drawing on the Russian scholar Mikhail Bahktin, Schechner argues that the mere act of taking to the streets 'challenges official culture's claims to authority, stability, sobriety, immutability, and immorality' (1993: 46).

The carnival-like atmosphere of the protest, like metaphors of tourism, draw people to what appears to be a joyful and exuberant, but at the same time subversive, festival of dissent. The use of humour, the breaking the windows of McDonalds with blocks of Rocquefort cheese,[6] the 'pink bloc' who dress as fairies and use feather dusters to tickle the police, huge puppets that act as political messages, radical cheerleaders, and in Québec City the now infamous toy catapult, which used medieval siege technology to catapult teddy bears over the security fence, bridge boundaries between local and global, art and politics, violence and efficacy (Sheehan, 2003: 8). Such tactics specifically play into the notions of spectacle and visuality, and protesters use them hoping that they will draw attention (Opel, 2003: 53).[7] Though the toy catapult in Québec, made by a group in Winnipeg, was later used by police to justify the arrest of well-known Montreal activist Jaggi Singh, the launching of teddy bears over police lines became an important element connecting the protest to an historical lineage of the symbolic inversion of social relations in public carnival, and also an effort to show the generally erroneous characterisation of activists as violent (Leclair, 2003: 6–14; Toronto Video Activist Collective, 2001). However, though the use of parody in this case was successful in the mainstream media coverage, where reporters were forced to come to terms with criticising teddy bears, the catapult had no long-term effect.

For the moment of the protest, however, the protester becomes at once spectator and participator/actor in a carnival, in this case a carnival of dissent. Once the protest or carnival is over, Schechner argues 'the liminal period ends and individuals are inserted or reinserted into their (sometimes new, sometimes old but always defined) places in society' (1993: 47). Hence the young woman's reconfiguration into souvenir of what she earlier in the video defines as the symbolic violence of the fence as separator. In the aftermath of the protest, a sharp split between actor/participator, and spectator/viewer occurs, making it difficult even for those who participated in the protest to memorialise it as other than a space and place outside of daily life.

It is through photography, I suggest, that the metaphor of tourism plays out most completely. Photography has become an essential part of the experience of protest and an important part of its spectacularisation. Grosbois notes: 'I was a little nervous and brought along all my gear: raincoat, ski goggles, masks, camera . . . ' (2001: 42). 'I went armed with a camera and a microphone . . . ' writes David Widgington (2002: 26). For many at the protest, the camera became a talisman, a protective fetish that warded off the vast unfamiliarity of the scene, distancing the unknown by gazing through the comforting square of the camera lens (Marks, 2000).

I've argued above that in the sensory moment of the protest, the organised visual consumption of tourism, the careful packaging of sites/ sights is rendered null and void. But I suggest that it is also this moment where the pressure to reclaim traditional modes of viewership is strongest, and thus the moment that is most easily repackaged and reformatted into acceptable and digestible frames of reference. Once photographed, the protest has the potential of spreading through internet, independent publications and personal sharing, but also of being used against protesters in cases of arrest and mainstream media accounts. Cameras allow one to see at a time when vision is confused by the haze of tear gas. Configuring protest in this way, through the camera, turns protest into something to be watched, something to be looked at. The protest, to adopt Urry's terminology, threatens to become a sign of itself, a pseudo-event with explosive potential that can be quickly recycled into consumable imagery (Urry, 1990: 3). Here, the spectacle holds within it the threat of its own unraveling – the threat of making protest 'insouciant, but deliciously safe' (Sheehan, 2003: 143).

## Nationalising the Transnational

Travelling to protests on buses, in aeroplanes, in cars, on bicycles and by foot, protesters, consciously or not, regularly replicate patterns of tourism. Those stopped at borders, searched, and turned back, often work particularly hard to maintain the seemingly unthreatening role of tourist. 'I told them I was coming to a business meeting,' joked one protester in Québec City.[8] Taking Chrétien's remark that protesters had come to Québec to 'protest and blah blah blah', students made their way through the streets chanting 'we're here for a reason, and it's not tourist season!' (Toronto Video Activist Collective, 2001). The popularity of Québec as an already established tourist location (for both the Winter Carnival, and the UNESCO protected old city) served as a backdrop for the festival-like atmosphere while providing a powerful symbol for protesters to demonstrate the lack of accessibility to the public. Posters combined the *Bonhomme*, the mascot of the popular annual Winter Carnival, with anti-FTAA propaganda, while the theme of the gathering became the somewhat pedantic '*Carnivale*

*Contre La Capitalisme'* (Palladino & Widgington, 2002: 40). The irony of the so-called FTAA 'democracy clause' was highlighted through the fact that the enclave created at Québec City was created around one of Canada's most well-known tourist sites. For numerous protesters, the blocking off of the very public sites of the Chateau Laurier and the Plains of Abraham had the repercussion of highlighting the secrecy of the talks at the expense of public input (Lapointe, Wong & Ménard, 2001). This was rendered particularly clear through activist photos of the Plains of Abraham behind the fence, while the official photos featured the heads of state against the backdrop of the Chateau (Toronto Video Activist Collective, 2001).

However, the focus on the Plains of Abraham, and Québec City as a tourist site, also has the effect of highlighting the privilege of those able to travel to the location. Taking up this argument, some activists are beginning to complain that because of the use of spectacle, a primacy has been placed on protest in the Northern hemisphere (i.e. the 'Battle for Seattle') supporting the tenets of capitalist globalisation by refusing to acknowledge sustained protest movements in the Southern hemisphere.[9] Canadian journalists, for example, were quick to place a national slant on what many protesters saw as a transnational event. Part of the construction of protesters as tourists disguised a belief that they had come from somewhere else, that even if they were Canadian, the behaviour on the April weekend was somehow 'unCanadian.' One reporter wrote:

Within minutes, a 50-metre section of the infamous chain-link fence surrounding the conference centre was down and disturbing, unfamiliar photos of Canada were flashing around the globe . . . And in an ugly twist on the nation's favourite game, hockey pucks filled the air (Canadian Press, 2001).

For protesters, however, particularly Canadian ones, the lack of state protection of dissent, now replaced by a line of riot gear clad police, questioned the easy tenets of liberalism with which Canadians are so familiar.

The easiest dismissal came through constructing protesters as outsiders – either violent anarchists or in many cases, disgruntled separatists. A month before the summit, once it had become obvious that there would be dissent, Anglophone papers began to link tourism dollars brought to Québec City through the summit, with a concession on the part of the government to give the lucrative summit to the capital of Québec. Essentially, in 1999, the Canadian government passed a bill that came to be known as the Clarity Act, which severely restricted the Québec government's attempts to secure sovereignty for the province. The federal government attempted to placate the anger of the separatist provincial government by offering to Québec City the summit. This was agreed before the WTO protests in Seattle, when it was assumed that direct economic benefits would outweigh protest, bringing a minimum of $100 million (CDN) (approx. 70 million EUR) to the local economy (Travers, 2001: A6). Sovereignty debates played throughout the protests, in part because of the numerous Québec flags held by protesters, the blocking off of the politically symbolic Plains of Abraham, and the refusal of the Canadian government to allow Québec Premier Bernard Landry to address the summit as the head of a sovereign nation (Canadian Press, 2001b: 10).[10] Violence in the Québec streets could then easily be constructed as the work of those who were not interested in supporting a unified centre to the Canadian nation.

On both sides, Québec City came to be seen as a space outside of Canadian self-construction. For conservatives it was a place where partying rioters wrecked the image of Canada as a peaceful and demo-cratic nation. For protesters, the Canadian authorities responsible for the police presence had taken on a much more violent face of state policing, radically challenging Canadian beliefs in the right to dissent (Palladino & Widgington, 2002; Toronto Video Activist Collective, 2001). Realising this discrepancy, the Canadian government and mainstream media were carefully spinning rhetoric in order to differentiate between 'violent' and 'peaceful' protesters. Although all were targeted with tear gas, the spin allowed for the maintenance of an idealised separation from the violence outside the perimeter – only 'violent' protesters were targeted, and the police acted with restraint. Peaceful (and hence 'Canadian') protesters were allowed to voice their opinions, primarily at the People's Summit, and the labour march (which actually led people out of town, ending beside the highway) (CSIS, 2000; Sharpe, 2001: 17;).

Within discourses of nation/nationalism, tourism has increasingly come to be seen by activists as a visible and attackable aspect of global capital-ism. In 1998, Canadian protesters combined with American and European groups to bring an end to the seal hunt off Prince Edward Island by threat-ening to call a boycott to tourism in the area (Willis, 1998: A1).

In 1999, the Ontario Coalition Against Poverty (OCAP) specifically targeted business leaders, film productions and tourists in Toronto during the Toronto 2008 Olympic BID in order to draw attention to the growing homeless problem in Canada's largest city. As police began to act on the mayor's call not to allow the homeless to sleep in city parks, OCAP released an ultimatum to the press to 'guarantee that large numbers of tourists leave Toronto this summer with stark images of the homeless loudly interfering with their enjoyments of what the commercial tourist traps have to offer' (Benzie, 1999: A6). In 2001 The Neskonlith and Adams Lake Indian Bands, set up camp outside Sun Peaks, a tourist resort in the

British Columbia interior, in order to blockade Snow Job, a huge outdoor concert run by Much Music (Canada's equivalent of MTV) on land that was part of a unsettled land claim. Local newspapers worried that the protest might cost the area more than $1 million (CDN) (700,000 EUR) in tourist dollars (Canadian Press, 2001a: A6).

International summits continue to be constructed as spaces of tourism. In 2002, the G8 summit was held in the remote location of Kananaskis in the Canadian Rockies (themselves a prime tourist location). The 'picture-postcard' meeting place lies in the shadow of 'soaring Mount Kidd', with only one road in, facilitating police and army control of protests (Krauss, 2002: A8). Impressed by the stunning landscape and lack of protesters, trade leaders were given what Gordon Christie, executive Director of the Calgary and District Labour Council called 'a $400 million [280 million EU] . . . photo op in the mountains'. That photo opportunity, however, was welcomed by Tourism Calgary, arguing that the summit gave the region a $243 million (CDN) (170 million EUR) boost, while creating 1800 jobs in the tourism sector (although these jobs would last only one year) (Welner, 2002: A8).

Distanced by the wilderness terrain between the town of Kananaskis and the city, not to mention armed police and army personnel, helicopters and fighter jets, protesters were forced to stay in Calgary, some 60 kilometres away. Thousands of protesters gathered nonetheless, drawing together against a 'Wild West' party held for delegates in Calgary. The city, famous for the annual Calgary Stampede, one of the biggest tourist draws in Canada, organised a $300,000 (CDN) (210,000 EUR) party designed to echo the Stampede and to 'drum up tourism and business as a spin-off of the two day meeting' (Semmens, 2002: A9). The invitation-only party featured a Western barbeque, square dancing, an indoor rodeo and wild-west parade, with a fireworks finale at midnight. Several blocks away, determined to undermine the façade of Calgary as a 'lily-white, clean, wonderful city', and the construction of the summit as an economic opportunity, protesters hosted their own 'Hoot and Holler' party, an alternate location to voice concern over G8 policies (Semmens, 2002: A9).

In Québec City, all of these issues came together – tourism, nationality, creativity, globalization, visuality – in a heady mix that continues to affect activist practice and police training in Canada today. What I have argued is that protest cannot be easily dismissed as tourism, either by a Canadian status quo, or even from within the movement itself. Naomi Klein's statement quoted at the opening of this paper suggests that the anti-globalisation movement is moving away from a concerted effort to overthrow structures of power, into a spectacular weekend event that opens the movement to threats of mainstreaming, acceptability and dismissal as a form of extreme tourism. What I hope I have argued in this chapter is that these ideas are not so simple, but form a tangled web of use and resistance to accepted ideas of tourism, dissent and Canadian nationality. While it can be argued that in Canada, what remains of the Québec City protest are primarily visual reconfigurations – documentary films, artworks, posters, and so on – while global capitalism moves on, for a time 'anti-globalisation' was brought into the living rooms of most Canadians. The combination of humour, dissent, violence, spectacle, nationalism and globalisation worked within and against each other to produce a strangely touristic, yet unbounded experience, summarised perhaps in an email that I sent home from Québec City: ' . . . and the tear gas? It was breathtaking.'

## Notes

1. The term 'anti-globalisation' has been used here for convenience, although it should be noted that many activists do not use it, as it implies a dislike for all forms of globalisation. Most activists see themselves as pro fair-trade, and anti free-trade, working on behalf of transnational movements, and with supporters from a variety of backgrounds and nations.
2. The FTAA follows the directives of GATT (the General Agreement on Tariffs and Trade). In 1994, the GATT became WTO, which has as one of its aims the gradual phasing out of all barriers to international trade and competition. These barriers include things such as rules, policies, and practices of individual governments that protect culture, health care and social welfare, but might interfere with trade (Jones, 2002: 17). The most controversial element of the FTAA follows Chapter 11 of NAFTA, and gives corporations the right to sue governments for profits they stand to lose from laws that discriminate against their products – for example environmental or cultural protections (Jones, 2002: 18). Activists worry, pointing to numerous cases already in progress, that governments will be less willing to pass laws protecting health care, or the environment, for example, for fear of being sued.
3. Why a chain link fence? Aside from the speed with which it could be assembled, David Widgington argues that the permeability of the chain link, the ability to see through it, was a means to not be identified with totalitarian regimes (i.e. Communism) through any link that might be made to the Berlin Wall (2002: chapter 27).
4. For more information on the contested relationships between tourism globalisation and capitalism, see, for example, Holmes (2001), Iyer (2000) and Lippard (1999).
5. Though this essay will draw on some of the concepts of the carnival outlined by the Russian scholar Mikhail Bakhtin, I'm arguing against his notion that 'standing midway between life and culture, carnival is a concretely sensuous experience of the world that, while being inadequately conveyed in abstract concepts, is quite open to be translated into artistic images and thus into literature' (Brandist, 2002: 138).

6. Rocquefort cheese was used because it was a product chosen by the United States for retaliatory 100% surcharge when the European Union refused to import hormone treated beef (Sheehan, 2003: 10).

7. Greenpeace, for example, from the 1970s developed their strategy of launching 'mind bombs', image events that were picked up by the mainstream media, with the purpose of forcing viewers to transform the way they viewed the world (Opel, 2003: 53).

8. Comment overheard by the author in Québec City, 21 April, 2001.

9. Nor is this a new problem. In 1989, Tzvetan Todorov wrote in the introduction of his book *Nous et les Autres*, of his discomfort with the easy use of and belief in Marxist theory and language by those who had not experienced, as he had, the repression of the Stalinist state in Russia.

10. The Plains of Abraham in Québec City are the location of the 1759 defeat of the French forces at the hands of the British. The 1759 battle is often seen as the beginning of division between French and English Canada.

## References

Baudrillard, J. (1998) *The Consumer Society: Myths and Structures*. London and Thousand Oaks, CA: Sage.

Baxter, J. (2001) Trade experts say protest misdirected. *Calgary Herald* 19 April, A3.

Benzie, R. (1999) Anti-poverty activists vow sabotage. *Ottawa Citizen* (20August, A6.

Bronskill, J. (2001a) Radicals arm for Quebec: CSIS spies say summit of the Americas could see replay of Seattle-style violence. *Montreal Gazette* 13 February, A8.

Brandist, C. (2002) *The Bahhtin Circle: Philosophy, Culture and Politics*. Ann Arbor: University at Michigan Press.

Branskill, J. (2001b) CSIS warns gov't of anarchist violence at G8 summit: Radical elements have history of destructive protest. *Edmonton Journal* (27 April, A3.

Camille, (2002) Medic alert. In L. Palladino and D. Widgington (eds) *Counter Productive: Québec City Convergence Surrounding the Summit of the Americas* (pp. 57–62). Montreal, Canada: Cumulus Press.

Canadian Press (2001a) Protest may cost Kamloops big bucks.' *Nanaimo Daily News* 23 February, A6.

Canadian Press (2001b) Briefs: Crackdown hurts Canada's reputation, protesters say. *Halifax Daily News* 17 April, 10.

Canadian Press (2001c) Let chaos not hold democracy hostage. *Toronto Star* 21 April, A2.

Crary, J. (1990) *Techniques of the Observer: On Vision and Modernity in the Nineteenth Century*. Cambridge, MA: MIT Press.

Crary, J. (1999) *Suspensions of Perception: Attention, Spectacle and Modern Culture*. Cambridge, MA: MIT Press.

CSIS (Canadian Security Intelligence Service) (2000) *Anti-Globalization: A Spreading Phenomenon* (August). On WWW at http://www.csis-scrs.gc.ca/eng/miscdocs/200008_e.html. Accessed 15.02.2002.

Debord, G. (1967 [1994]) *Society of Spectacle* (D. Nicholson-Smith, trans.). New York: Zone Books.

Editorial Collective (2001) *RESIST!: A Grassroots Collection of Stories, Poetry, Photos and Analyses from the Québec City FTAA Protests and Beyond*. Halifax, Canada: Fernwood Publishing.

FTAA (2001) *Free Trade Area of the Americas Homepage*. On WWW at http://www.ftaa-alca.org/. Accessed 21.07.2003.

Grosbois, P. (2001) A Québec city diary. In Editorial Collective (ed.) *RESIST!: A Grassroots Collection of Stories, Poetry, Photos and Analyses from the Québec City FTAA Protests and Beyond* (pp. 40–6). Halifax (Canada): Fernwood Publishing.

Holmes, D. (ed.) (2001) *Virtual Globalization: Virtual Spaces/Tourist Spaces*. London and New York: Routledge.

Ioannides, D. and Debbage, K.G. (1998) *The Economic Geography of the Tourist Industry*. London and New York: Routledge.

Iyer, P. (2000) *The Global Soul: Jet Lag, Shopping Malls and the Search for Home*. New York: Random House.

Jaimet, K. (2001) Protesters push to meet heads of state: Government refuses demand for formal meeting outside fence. *Ottawa Citizen* 18 April, A5.

Jameson, F. (1991) *Postmodernism or, The Cultural Logic of Late Capitalism*. London: Verso.

Jay, M. (1992) Scopic regimes of modernity. In S. Lash and J. Friedman (eds) *Modernity and Identity* (pp. 3–28). Oxford: Blackwell.

Jay, M. (1993) *Downcast Eyes*. Berkeley: University of California Press.

Jones, M. (2002) Everything must go! In *Counter Productive: Québec City Convergence Surrounding the Summit of the Americas* (pp. 13–22). Montreal: Cumulus Press.

Krauss, C. (2002) Security tight for G8 talks at idyllic spot in Canada. *New York Times* 26 June: 2002), A8.

Klein, N. (2002) The vision thing: Were the DC and Seattle protests unfocused, or are critics missing the point? In *From ACT UP to the WTO: Urban Protest and Community Building in the Era of Globalization* (pp. 265–73). London and New York: Verso.

Klein, N. (2002) *No Logo: Taking Aim at the Brand Bullies*. Toronto: Vintage.

Lapointe, P., Wong, G., Ying Gee and Ménard, J. (2001) *A View from the Summit).* Video-recording. Ottawa: National Film Board of Canada.

Leclair, L. (2003) Carnivals against capital: Rooted in resistance. In *Representing Resistance: Media, Civil Disobedience and the Global Justice Movement* (pp. 3–15). Westport, CT: Praeger.

Levin, D. (1993) *Modernity and the Hegemony of Vision*. Berkeley: University of California Press.

Lippard, L. (1999) *On the Beaten Track: Tourism, Art and Place*. New York: The New Press.

McKenzie, R. (2001) Mayor offers lodging to summit protesters. *Toronto Star* 27 March.

Marks, L. (2000) *The Skin of the Film: Intercultural Cinema, Embodiment and the Senses*. Durham, NC: Duke University Press.

Massumi, B. (2003) Navigating moments: An interview with Brian Massumi. *21st Century Magazine*. Interview by Mary Zoutnazi. On WWW at http://www.21cmagazine.com/issue2/Massumi.html. Accessed 20.04.2004.

Meethan, K. (2001) *Tourism in Global Society: Place, Culture, Consumption*. New York: Palgrave.

Opel, A. (2003) Punishment before prosecution: Pepper spray as postmodern repression. In: *Representing Resistance: Media, Civil Disobedience and the Global Justice Movement* (pp. 44–60). Westport, CT: Praeger.

Palladino, L. and Widgington, D. (2002) *Counter Productive: Québec City Convergence Surrounding the Summit of the Americas.* Montreal: Cumulus Press.

Phipps, P. (1999) Tourists, terrorists, death and value. In: *Travel Worlds: Journeys in Contemporary Cultural Politics.* London and New York: Zed Books.

Rodaway, P. (1994) *Sensuous Geographies.* London: Routledge.

Rorty, R. (1980) *Philosophy and the Mirror of Nature.* Oxford: Blackwell.

Semmens, G. (2002) Activists plan protest for G8 party. *Calgary Herald* 25 June: A9.

Sharpe, E. (2001) Publisher's foreword. In Editorial Collective (ed.) *RESIST!: A Grassroots Collection of Stories, Poetry, Photos and Analyses from the Québec City FTAA Protests and Beyond* (pp. 16–17). Halifax, Canada: Fernwood Publishing.

Sheehan, S. (2003) *Anarchism.* London: Reaktion Books.

Todorov, Tzvetan (1989) *Nous et les autres: la réflexion française sur la diversité humaine.* Paris: Éditions du Seuil.

Toronto Video Activist Collective (2001) *Tear Gas Holiday: Quebec City Summit 2001* (video-recording). Toronto.

Travers, J. (2001) Québec summit won't help tourism. *Charlottetown Guardian* 15 March, A6.

Urry, J. (1990) *The Tourist Gaze: Leisure and Travel in Contemporary Societies.* London: Sage Publications.

Urry, J. (1995) *Consuming Places.* London: Routledge.

Urry, J. (1999). Sensing the city. In D.R. Judd and S. Fainstein (eds) *The Tourist City* (pp. 71–86). New Haven and London: Yale University Press.

Virilio, P. (1994) *Vision Machine* (J. Rose, trans.). London: BFI.

Welner, C. (2002) Summit costs could reach $500 million. *Toronto Star* 28 June: A8.

Widgington, D. (2002) Divestment portfolio. In L. Palladino and D. Widgington (eds) *Counter Productive: Québec City Convergence Surrounding the Summit of the Americas* (pp. 23–32). Montreal: Cumulus Press.

Willis, N. (1998) Seal hunt threat to P.E.I.: Nations threaten tourism boycott. *Charlottetown Guardian,* 28 March: A1.

# Index